For Bob and Marianne,

    You have brightened my life in many ways as I worked on this project. Thank you and please continue!

        Fondest wishes,
        Barbara

VOICES of the SILENT GENERATION

STRONG WOMEN TELL THEIR STORIES

BARBARA BAILLET MORAN

Barbara B Moran

AVISSON PRESS, INC.
GREENSBORO

Copyright © 2006 by Barbara Baillet Moran. All rights reserved. For information, contact Avisson Press Inc., P.O. Box 38816, Greensboro, North Carolina 27438 USA.

First Edition
Printed in the USA

Library of Congress Cataloging-in-Publication Data

Moran, Barbara Baillet, 1938-
  Voices of the silent generation : strong women tell their stories / by Barbara Baillet Moran. — 1st ed.
    p. cm.
  Includes bibliographical references.
  ISBN 1-888105-71-2 (cloth)
    1. Women— United States—Biography. 2. Women— Social conditions—20th century. 3. United States—History—1933-1945. 4. United States—History—1945- I. Title.

CT3260.M665 2005
920.72'0973'0904—dc22
[B]

2005048345

Frontispiece: Eleanor Gendron Baillet
1914-1995

for Bill Moran
and
Kathryn Moran Silberman
Kevin Moran
Colin Moran
Chris Moran
The Baillet family
The Silberman family

We have in us, for the time of this life, a marvelous mingling
 both of weal and woe.
      Julian of Norwich

Is it so small a thing
To have enjoyed the sun,
To have lived light in the spring,
To have loved, to have thought, to have done;
To have advanced true friends, and beat down baffling foes?
      Matthew Arnold

Children: "Mom, can we get a pygmy goat?"
Beleaguered mother: "What on earth would we do
with a pygmy goat?"
Children: "Mom! What a question! Love it, of course.
And get two more so she won't be alone."
      Family archive

Table of Contents

PREFACE *11*

PART I
THE FIFTIES AND ITS SILENT GENERATION

I. What is the Silent Generation? *21*

II. Growing Up with Plenty and Paradox *23*
    1. innovations affecting daily life
    2. social climate
    3. stabilizing forces
    4. learning wariness
    5. a climate of intimidation
    6. choosing art, not action
    7. "problems have been solved"
    8. student activism: present and absent

III. Inherited Virtues *41*
    1. stoicism, self-reliance and reserve
    2. religious belief
    3. frugality vs. consumerism
    4. trusting everyone over thirty…
    5. …or not
    6. sexual mores: inherited but changing

IV. Music for a New Era *53*
    1. rock and roll
    2. but not for all

V. Race, Ethnicity and Civil Rights *58*
    1. postwar ethnic issues
    2. black members of the silent generation: civil rights vanguard

VI. "We never knew we were a generation." *67*

VII. Women of the Silent Generation *69*
    1. women, work and World War II
    2. postwar years
    3. stirrings in the fifties
    4. welcome to the sixties
    5. seventeen strong women

PART II
ORAL HISTORIES

DORIS BETTS, Chapel Hill, NC. Revered professor of writing, her six novels received critical praise, as did collections of short stories. Leading North Carolina literary figure. Mother of three. *83*

SHELLY WEINER, Rovno, Ukraine, Atlanta, Greensboro, NC. As a child during World War II escaped with her mother from the Nazis. Immigrated to the United States in 1949 at age twelve. As an adult has worked to assist other persecuted people. Mother of three. *104*

VIRGINIA SEIPT, New York City, NY. A television pioneer, first woman to produce televised sports. Traveled the world with NBC Sports. Now a freelance television producer. *124*

SIDNEY CALLAHAN, Ardsley-on-Hudson, NY. Author of over a dozen books, sought as speaker and retreat leader. In her mid-sixties, after the death of her daughter-in-law, Sidney began raising her infant granddaughter. Mother of eight. *140*

SHIRLEY FRYE, Greensboro, NC. Civic leader, educator, television station public affairs director. With her husband has won numerous awards for their contributions to city and state. Mother of two. *154*

DR. MARILYN LOCKWOOD, Erie, PA, Washington, D.C. Planned births of her three daughters around medical school and residency schedules. Specialized in medicine for adolescents and women. Growing up on a farm in the forties, Marilyn always knew she wanted both family and career. *170*

Strong Women Tell Their Stories

GLORIA KITTO LEWIS, Ann Arbor, MI. Widowed at thirty-seven. Nine years thereafter lost one of three sons. A gifted violinist, Gloria also taught English and writing. Now remarried to a fellow musician. *188*

SATO HASHIZUME, San Francisco, CA. Registered nurse, home health care specialist. Spent years of childhood in World War II internment camps. In retirement has recovered her family's lost history. *203*

SR. MARY BARBARA PHILIPPART, Manazo, Peru and Cincinnati, OH. Missionary nun, spent over twenty years at a village in the High Andes of Peru. A well-trained community organizer, Sr. Barbara guided village development. Shining Path guerrillas killed villagers, tied up and robbed Barbara. Eventually, was the only missionary nun allowed to remain in Peru. *223*

MARIE MCKEEVER, Fremont, CA. Spent childhood with family in both Mexico and California. Two of Marie's three children have special needs. Founded parents' group that wrote new state legislation benefiting children and their families. A heroine for many California families. *235*

VIVIAN SHAPIRO, Princeton, NJ. A social work researcher and mother of four, became first lady of University of Michigan, then of Princeton University while husband Harold was president. Combined family and campus duties with graduate studies, earning a PhD in her mid-fifties. *251*

RUTH LOCKLEAR REVELS, Pembroke and Greensboro, NC. In hometown of Pembroke, activities of Lumbee Indians were severely restricted. With late husband Lonnie, Ruth has been a life-long advocate for native people; founded the Native American Center and a Native American Art Gallery. Mother of two. *266*

GLORIA VAN DUYNE, Flint, MI. Started a successful retail business while raising her children. City leader in politics, social services and the arts. Mother of six, grandmother of twenty-four. *284*

VELMA GIBSON WATTS, Winston-Salem, N.C. Raised by relatives while Jim Crow laws prevailed in the South. Ancestors were free-issue at the time of Emancipation; a tradition of education emerged that benefited all subsequent generations of Gibsons. Medical educator and Director of Minority Students at Bowman Gray Medical School. Mother of two. *299*

Voices of the Silent Generation

GAY CHENEY, Greensboro, NC and Southwestern U.S. Dancer, choreographer, and teacher. A childhood by the sea inspired her earliest art. Her reverence for landscape of the Southwest and Native American culture and religion form the core of Gay's mature work. *313*

DARYL HAFTER, Ann Arbor, MI. Earned PhD from Yale when children were very young. Put career on hold for eight years to raise her two children, then resumed academic career. After years of solo work in French archives, Daryl has earned an international reputation for her original contributions to the history of women and work. *328*

In tribute to a mentor, an essay on:
LOUISE AMES, New York City, NY, and Martha's Vineyard, MA. Skilled athlete, musician and natural leader. Among other community contributions, founded a family nature study center along the North Shore of Long Island. Mother of four. *343*

CONCLUSION *347*

APPENDIX *355*

ORAL HISTORY QUESTIONS *358*

ACKNOWLEDGEMENTS *361*

ENDNOTES *364*

RECOMMENDED READING LIST *377*

Preface

Dismissed as the silent generation, women who began their adult lives in the l950s were deemed politically voiceless, dependent on men for self-definition, lacking in professional ambition, content with house and hearth. In later years, younger feminists pitied the last wave of American women to be psychologically shackled by low expectations--society's, and their own.

But many women coming of age at the time did not fit this description. They conformed neither to the formulaic images of the time, nor to later feminist models. As a member of this birth cohort, I have long admired peers who, from youth on, seemed marked by a sure sense of direction. Virtually fearless in the face of struggle, tragedy, success and disappointment, these women possessed a sense of entitlement that once characterized men only.

As one who was not fearless, and who, along with many others, needed some aspects of feminism to unlock a sense of my own potential, I carefully observed those who were ahead of their time. In 1989, I began to collect and record life stories of strong women then between fifty and sixty years of age. At that time, little public attention had been paid to this age cohort, small in numbers as it was. Sandwiched between the war generation and the postwar population explosion, those born during the Depression were less than half as numerous as baby boomers.

Some years before modern feminism emerged, these women had already begun careers and/or families. The women's and civil rights movements were not yet available to help free their psyches and open the world to them. Many nonetheless drew upon a range of resources to create lives that included rewarding relationships and significant work.

Now in their own sixties and seventies, they have few regrets. How did this happen? During a time of unprecedented social turmoil, how did such women so successfully navigate narrow, unmarked paths?

Whence came their strength? That is the primary question that led to this book. I began by considering my own family. My mother was a strong woman. "In the next life I'm coming back as a man," she said many times during my childhood, often with a laugh, sometimes with a rueful smile. I

Voices of the Silent Generation

was an adult before I appreciated the complexity of my mother's personality and the full meaning of those words.

My mother's early life was unpromising. Eleanor Gendron's parents were able to offer neither opportunity nor encouragement to their bright, eager daughter. Early feminism was then a light too dim and distant to steer by. Somehow, her energy and spirit, mixed with some anger, prevailed. Marriage to Ted Baillet was fortuitous and they combined diligence and imagination, their major resources, as they set forth during the late nineteen-thirties.

Eleanor and Ted founded a solid family and soon earned places as respected community leaders in the burgeoning suburbs of New York City. Always industrious, Eleanor was ahead of her time in combining family, college courses and a full-time job during her three children's adolescent years. She could be feisty and stubborn, even combative, but was also resilient, loyal, enthusiastic and at the end, heroic. In a final twenty years of illness, repeated surgeries and inexorable physical diminishment, she was a brave and uncomplaining stoic, always maintaining keen interest in her twelve grandchildren, the world's follies and the exigencies of the Dow Jones.

With World War II and the Depression its central experiences, my parents' age group, the "greatest generation," passed down convictions, habits, social mores to the silent generation, who would in turn find those inherited values shifting like desert sand under their feet.

Who was I to begin this project? For much of my adult life my husband, Bill Moran and I lived with our four children on or near university campuses: University of Michigan at Flint, State University of New York at Stony Brook, and University of North Carolina at Greensboro. For twenty-three of those years Bill was chancellor or president. Serving as first lady of two campuses afforded opportunities to travel extensively and to meet distinguished people from government, the arts, science, sports and business. Living on campuses for so many years, we dealt with generation after generation of students and faculty. We entertained alumni, benefactors, patrons of the arts, legislators.

We had unexpected encounters: Two weeks before President Gerald Ford came for lunch at our campus home, a team of Secret Service men pored through every closet in the house. On a gray luncheon day, the same team, plus twenty more, ringed the house outside, taking turns with trips into our family room for a buffet and respite from the rain. "No one ever offers us a meal!" exclaimed several wet and bedraggled men, as they sipped hot coffee.

Strong Women Tell Their Stories

At a conference, President Jimmy Carter spoke to us eagerly and with a father's pride, of his daughter's social activism. Margaret Mead proffered advice on marriage to a man with a public career. On separate occasions, I asked the wrong questions of Aaron Copland and Itzhak Perlman and was accordingly rebuked by each.

Bill and I discussed amateur music-making with Rudolf Serkin and Arthur Fiedler. (Serkin, with a sly smile: "Amateur groups are fine. Just be sure fifty percent of your musicians are professionals.") At a dinner in Ann Arbor, Truman Capote entertained us with typically outrageous observations. Over tea in our North Carolina home, British actress Rosemary Harris revealed her innate shyness and abundant generosity. There were lively lunch and dinner discussions with journalists, and years of correspondence with South Africa's Anne and Alan Paton. On a weekend visit, novelist Chinua Achebe spoke movingly of his nation's plight, but also amused a small group with the wit for which Ibo people are admired. We took pleasure in Eudora Welty's musical cadences as she charmed a pride of literary lions. Cornel West displayed his prodigious verbal energy throughout lunch, dinner and a long evening. During lunch with a group of student teachers we listened attentively to Madeline L'Engle's recollections of her solitary childhood and budding imagination.

Our family was well acquainted with, and also entertained, groundskeepers, clinic staff, indoor maintenance people, secretaries, clerks, cafeteria workers--all those who keep a large university campus humming, and without whom it would grind to a halt. In my own career as storyteller, writer and lecturer, I also met members of theatrical and literary circles outside the university.

In seeking strong women for this project I was able to draw directly from a broad network for introductions to potential participants. Thus assisted, I sought out and interviewed vigorous women from various races, religions, social and economic backgrounds, and regions of the country. One woman went to bed hungry as a child, another was called to lunch by a butler. Their adult professional and personal lives also varied widely, though many started in education, one of the few fields then readily available to women. Virginia Seipt, network television's first female sports producer, traveled the world covering athletic events for NBC. Writer Doris Betts won an Academy Award. Sidney Callahan raised seven children and wrote over a dozen books. Mexican-American Marie McKeever battled the California legislature and won. Barbara Philippart founded a cooperative knitting business in a Peruvian village.

Voices of the Silent Generation

All would currently be described as middle or upper middle-class, though by no means did all begin their lives in comfort. They variously survived early loss of a parent, divorce, loss or incapacitation of a child, immigration, early widowhood, depression, and ethnic, racial, or religious discrimination. Sato Hashizume endured discrimination at its most severe, spending a portion of her childhood in an Idaho internment camp during World War II. Shelly Weiner, hidden with her mother for months in an underground pit while machine-gun battles raged above them, was one of the few members of her family to survive the Holocaust. Sato, Shelly and others who might have remained victims were able to transcend their circumstances and press ahead.

In sessions lasting four to fourteen hours, at homes or offices and in one case, the narrow back halls of NBC's New York studio, thirty women (seventeen of whom were selected as most representative) candidly discussed their lives with me. During hours of interviews, most revealed deep vulnerability as well as strength. We shared tears and laughter as they described events both humorous and poignant.

As is to be expected with any group of individuals, a given task can produce varied results. How much more so with their own life stories. We worked with a general format and a list of questions, but new issues often arose while others were passed over. It had not occurred to me to ask about love of animals, for instance, yet the collection would be much the poorer without Doris Betts' comments on the animals, domestic and wild, that so enrich her family's life.

Most discussed the questions in sequence, thus permitting use of topic headings such as mentors, children, work, social change. Others responded more fluidly, thus topic headings were omitted. Due to the nature of their work, for example, Virginia Seipt, Barbara Philippart and Ruth Revels literally gave their stories on the run, with this editor running along in their wakes. Readers may thus expect minor variations in presentation of the oral histories. After all, these are *strong* women.

Response to requests for photographs was also mixed. Some had ready access to their own history in images; others did not. Sidney Callahan replied, "I'm afraid to open that cupboard!" In complete sympathy, I settled for a photograph of Sidney taken on interview day.

All spoke of childhood in the forties and of the most influential people in their lives, mentors as well as parents. Some told of struggle and tragic loss--and what recovery required of them. I asked about sources of their resiliency, ability to meet challenges. Had religion been a significant force in their lives? Which virtues, talents did they possess? From those who had children I sought reflections on family life. They discussed the satisfactions of work, whether paid or voluntary. To what extent did its claims interfere with private life? What were their thoughts on growing older?

While containing universal elements, each story was unique. Civil-rights and community leaders Shirley Frye and Velma Watts grew up under Jim Crow laws in the segregated rural South. Native American Ruth Revels grew up under three-way segregation in a town where all jobs were prohibited to Indians. Dancer, choreographer and environmentalist Gay Cheney realized in her thirties that she was a lesbian. Writer Doris Betts, from a rural background and lacking a college degree, went on to become chairman of a university faculty. Social work scholar and former first lady of Princeton University, Vivian Shapiro overcame a childhood blighted by her family's difficult immigration experience and losses in the Holocaust.

The stories were taped and transcribed over several years while I was also occupied with family and university matters. The common themes did not emerge until all the stories were gathered. Reading them as a collection, I was struck by the similarities underlying so wide a variety of experiences and backgrounds. Despite their profound differences, the women I spoke with were alike in important ways.

As is typical of other birth cohorts, men and women born during the Depression hold a host of basic premises and convictions in common. A white woman from a comfortable Northeastern suburb shares a strong sense of propriety with a woman who faced discrimination for much of her life. Southerner Doris Betts, of Scots-Irish descent, shares a comic sense of the absurd with Marie McKeever who spent much of her childhood in Mexico.

Indeed, I discovered that the very values and experiences held in common were also those that helped them enter adult life with the strength and flexibility to forge successful lives. Widowed at thirty-seven, Gloria Lewis earned a Ph.D., then found that Michigan's suddenly devastated economy diminished teaching possibilities in her chosen field. She found and maintained a position teaching technical writing while continuing to perform as a violinist. Gloria's resiliency and perseverance guaranteed her employment throughout Michigan's toughest times.

With her six children on triple-split school sessions, coming and going throughout the day, Gloria Van Duyne started a stationery business in her home. Gloria now runs her own large stationery and gift store, and continues to volunteer for a variety of causes.

Voices of the Silent Generation

Each of these seventeen women understood very well, and at an early age, that struggle and possibly sacrifice would be required from her. Postponement of budding careers for family needs is a recurring theme in the stories. However, just as the times were different, so too were expectations, and most did not view such choices as unmanageable sacrifices. Some resumed careers in later years; others took a different turn.

All rose to meet challenges, and most of the women interviewed believe early adversity was partially responsible for their strength. A typically American, can-do spirit shines through. Though unusual for women in the early sixties, Marilyn Lockwood finished medical school, cobbling together assorted jobs and scholarships to earn her way. At the same time, Daryl Hafter pursued an advanced degree, an unlikely effort for a pregnant young mother in those years. The same persevering spirit led her to learn both French and Spanish in order to continue the research she and her husband had chosen. Ruth Revel's Lumbee Indian grandfather raised his family under the harshest of legal and social restrictions, but told them, "If you can't earn a dollar, earn fifty cents." His children and grandchildren all managed to forge successful lives.

Each woman tells her own story best, so rather than discuss here all of those common elements, I offer readers the same pleasing discoveries I had while gathering, then rereading, these chronicles.

In order to provide a historic context for the oral histories, I studied the post-World War II era and the fifties, the period when these women began their adult lives. The fundamental ideas and attitudes uniting the women became even clearer. Not surprisingly, they coincide with themes common to the larger picture of America in the forties and fifties. Characteristics shared by women were common to men as well. As I continue to listen to stories from the silent generation, I am no longer surprised that unseen bonds transcend differences of background and experience. Born during the Great Depression, a difficult decade in the nation's history, and connected across boundaries of space and culture, we share and were shaped by values and virtues of a long-ago time.

The oral histories were recorded during the 1990's, well before the September 11, 2001 World Trade Center attacks. While their stories preceded those overwhelming events, these women learned something of global catastrophe during their wartime childhoods. Their own Depression-era parents never promised perfect, comfortable lives: the human predicament was acknowledged, if not perfectly understood. People soldiered on, just as will those who face a radically altered twenty-first century world.

While collecting these tales I was moved, but also encouraged, by their content. Younger women grappling with hard choices may find relief here as they encounter choices made, suffering endured, imaginations employed. In hearing each other's stories, we find the strength to press on, to discover what we most need to know: something of what life may offer, something of what will be required. Living on a college campus through the years of collecting these oral histories, I had numerous opportunities to read excerpts to student, faculty and women's groups. On each occasion I was touched by the women students' demonstrated thirst for knowledge about other times, other decisions, but especially about lives that, by most measures, have turned out well.

My hope is that the reflections of mature women will help others to recognize timeless imperatives to greet their own lives boldly and generously.

Part I provides historical background for the collection of oral histories in Part II. What occurred in the fifties to create a period later called both quiescent and turbulent? Entering the world as young adults in the 1950s, the silent generation experienced a decade far less placid than popular myth would subsequently suggest. Its youth were restrained by tradition and custom but were by no means oblivious to the Cold War, early civil rights events, and new currents of thought and behavior eddying about them.

Were the majority of women simply victims and compliant consumers, as received wisdom has long insisted? Much evidence suggests that they functioned effectively in education, family and community life. While unwelcome in politics, law and business, many, nonetheless, led productive lives within the constraints imposed by society. Additionally, census figures indicate that women held positions in every known job category, though not in large numbers. The energy and ability women displayed, whether in limited arenas or not, were predictors of wider opportunities to come.

One of the many currents running through the postwar years and beyond was that of gradual change in women's expectations for themselves. Initially, rather than dismantle barriers, they sought ways to circumvent some of them. While these efforts were only partially successful at the time, they laid the groundwork for a later erasure of boundaries, toppling of walls.

In attempting to understand women of the period, it is useful to first consider the silent generation as a whole, framing it against events of the forties and fifties. In addition to incomplete views of women, many historians and commentators offer unsympathetic images of the entire decade, its young adults in particular. I have assessed criticism directed at the group, and sought reasons for it. What lies behind the term silent generation, and was it a fair label?

As history seems best told when newsworthy events are interwoven with human chronicles, I have tried to portray the silent generation with facts, stories and perceptions from a puzzling and seminal time in America's history.

Barbara Baillet Moran
2005

Part I

*The Fifties and
Its Silent Generation*

1. WHAT IS THE SILENT GENERATION?

A certain sporting sense is required to write about a given decade as a full, rounded story rather than as the siftings from a landfill of events, people and artifacts. Still, striving to order the past is a human instinct and packaging it into ten-year portions is for most of us a natural and comfortable way of managing our memories. The nineteen-fifties resist neat packaging; boundaries overlap and blur between the immediate postwar period, when these seventeen women were in school, and the decade of the fifties, when they emerged as young adults.

After the ravages of the Great Depression and World War II, recovery and renewal occupied America in the late forties. The fifties, with its flourishing economy, has long been characterized as a complacent, uninspiring time. One observer recently described "a decade still shadowed by misconceptions and stereotypes." [1] Indeed, the two decades shared common values; seeds sown in the war years germinated in the fifties, blossoming soon after into twin social revolutions--the civil rights movement and a reinvigorated feminism. Both movements eventually shook the country to its foundations.

Some historians depict a sterile, repressive era, preoccupied with material possessions. Others see the extension of postwar rebuilding into the fifties as an essential preliminary to social and economic reforms yet to come.[2] In fact, the period bristled with contradictions. Observers today agree that the many paradoxes signaled turbulence both under the surface and just ahead: startling new ideas in the midst of stability, artistic originality in the face of political repression, close-knit communities and increasing mobility, and stirrings for change among women and minorities despite calcified social codes.

Though it is unfamiliar to many today, the imprecise term "silent generation" was retained for this essay. As the only label ever attached to the group born in the Depression (in England, it is the Air Raid Generation, for what they endured as children), it is commonly used by historians of the period. Given a cascade of televised self-promotion and unseemly self-revelation as the new millennium opened, it is for some perhaps preferable to be identified with discretion and reserve.

Because the women I interviewed are part of the much-maligned silent generation, I searched for reasons underlying criticism of those who came of age in the fifties. Through the lens of that search, several reasons to defend the silent generation emerged.

Voices of the Silent Generation

Historians and demographers vary in describing its parameters, with some giving a span from 1925-1942, others offering 1930-1945 or 1929-1940. For my general purposes, the decade 1930-1940 suffices. The generation later called silent was one of the smallest birth cohorts the country has ever known, now comprising between ten and twelve percent of the nation's population. Those born in the United States during the 1930s arrived in the midst of the worst national economic failure in American history, the Great Depression. Following the stock market crash in 1929, unemployment rose to twenty-five percent of the working population. At the Depression's lowest point, nearly half of all white families lived in poverty, as did almost ninety percent of black families. As the economy plummeted, so did the birth rate, dropping in 1935 to 18.4 per thousand (compared to a high of 33 per thousand in 1900) and producing just under 27 million new Americans during the decade. The ranks were thin indeed.[3]

That smallest generation was immediately followed by the largest in the nation's history, a demographic anomaly called the baby boom. The birth rate, which had decreased gradually throughout the century, rose briefly in 1942 and 1943 ("furlough babies"), then accelerated sharply, to the surprise of no one, just nine months after V-J Day. Some 76.4 million new Americans were born between 1946 and 1964; they constitute forty percent of the nation's population today. Sheer numbers meant that baby boomers would influence every facet of the nation's life. Purchases for and by them shaped the marketplace, and boomer habits, tastes and mores largely determined the social texture of the rest of the century. A large, vociferous, exuberant, cultural juggernaut

The silent generation arrives, low birth rate notwithstanding, 1930s.

soon overwhelmed voices of the preceding generation.

The origin of the term "silent generation," remains murky. In 1951 *Time* Magazine lamented that the "most startling thing about the younger generation is its silence...it does not issue manifestos, make speeches or carry posters." Two years later *Newsweek's* editors reported on students in seven colleges. While praising them as hard-working, ambitious, and eager to start new families, *Newsweek* opined that they seemed more interested in their own lives than in a world in need of mending. Young people of the fifties were regularly assailed for indifference to society's problems during their college years. A critic of the critics later countered that the name was invented in the early sixties by a political left disappointed by students' lack of interest in the left's causes.[4]

This largely hostile view of the silent generation persisted and devolved into ragged myth. Despite their record of achievement and leadership since youth, Americans born in the 1930s are still dismissed condescendingly today by historians as having been a placid lot in youth, too preoccupied with their own goals to bother with social protest.

Painting with so broad a brush obscures significant details. Whatever the putative shortcomings of its youth, many remember the decade as a lost moment of sanity, stability and self-restraint. Recent research reports higher rates of social capital--community, social and civic connections and sense of mutuality--in the fifties than in any period since. Accordingly, virtues of trust, reciprocity and honesty were also more in evidence.[5]

Indeed, a close reading of the times reveals that a web of history, tradition and custom influenced young people of the fifties, making much of their behavior all but inevitable.

II. GROWING UP WITH PLENTY AND PARADOX

While the silent generation grew up in contradictory times they clearly enjoyed significant advantages, the first being childhood spent in a country celebrating the end of World War II.

The war's beginning brought a merciful end to a decade of economic stagnation, followed by wartime deprivation. The country rallied patriotically on behalf of the armed forces, who needed all the rubber, metal, chemicals, and food they could get. Rationing was introduced and coupons as well as cash were needed to buy limited amounts of sugar, meat, butter, coffee, cheese, oil, tires and shoes, among other items. Gas rationing limited most citizens to two gallons weekly. For Christmas in 1943, children were told not to expect bicycles, rubber boots, doll carriages or balls that bounced. Adults knew there would be no toasters, alarm clocks, radios or phonographs. Turkeys and cranberries were in short supply and whipped cream was out of the question. Even advertisements reversed gears and advised, "Use it up, wear it out, make do, or do without."

The war also introduced millions of Americans to new places, people and ways of life. Nineteen-year old boys from small towns came home weary, but worldly men. Military victory left most of the country invigorated, refreshed and hopeful; the Depression's fear and resignation were banished. The economy was intact and fast becoming the most productive the world had ever known.

Marine maneuvers, World War II

A strong new national confidence paralleled the extraordinary post-war prosperity. The requirements of war had jump-started the economy in 1940. Remembering the Depression, and with little to buy during the war years, Americans had purchased war bonds and saved their money at triple the normal rates. Christmas of 1943 was the first year people had money to spend but little available to buy. By the war's end, weary of scarcity and buoyant with hope for better days, the public was ready to spend.

War, deprivation and Depression had left the country's infrastructure in disrepair; roads, utilities, and schools needed rebuilding. New housing was urgently needed. Businesses that had shifted so nimbly to forging tools of war swung quickly to addressing private and public needs.

America generated jobs, goods, and services at an unprecedented pace. In the twenty-five years after WWII, the nation's economy created twenty million jobs and scant unemployment. The process was often rocky. Labor union membership reached an all-time high, approximately 35% of the U.S. work force. Assuming office in 1945, after the death of President Franklin Roosevelt, President Harry S. Truman immediately faced bitter strikes. Nonetheless, the new economy, dominated by manufacturing jobs, flourished as never before. Between 1945 and 1960, median family income doubled; the gross national product grew by almost 250 percent, per capita income by 35 percent. The number of automobiles produced (and purchased immediately) rose by 133 percent.

Returning soldiers had risked their lives on behalf of the country and yearned for normality. Protection of family and country had been reason enough to fight a war; now it was time to pursue interrupted educations, start new families. Peacetime jobs seemed natural rewards for winning a war. One veteran, referring to his time in combat as "the lost years," wrote, "the main thing was to get back to a sane world where the ground would not buckle under your feet, to a world that was not a slaughterhouse."[6]

Women waiting at home were also eager to make up for the lost years. Children represented the new life craved by a war generation grateful to be alive. Veterans soon married, the birth rate soared, and the baby boom arrived in full cry.[7]

Many of the two million veterans in school on the GI Bill lived in Quonset huts, military barracks and plywood houses on and off campuses. In these modest quarters, young families developed patterns of community cooperation and neighborliness that would be taken with them to subdivisions a few years later.

The high post-war birthrate was both cause and effect of the surging economy. New families needed markets for food, clothing, furniture, automobiles, appliances and housing. Fifteen million homes were built between 1950 and 1960. In 1954, a middle-class house cost $7000 for its 800 square feet and knotty-pine paneling. Thus took root a prosperity unmatched by any society in history.

1946
The baby boom begins

Voices of the Silent Generation

1. innovations affecting daily life

Although writers spoke of a sterile and placid age, the late 40s and all of the 50s were a time of remarkable innovation in science, technology, business, and the arts. Held in check for a decade and a half by Depression and war, the can-do American spirit of invention burst forth with a cornucopia of brand-new goods and services. Products inextricably woven into the texture of life today were simply non-existent before the war: penicillin, the Salk polio vaccine, oral contraceptives, the microwave oven, audio books, Scrabble—all were developed in the fifties. The transistor, invented in 1947, would underlie the creation of cyberspace and the breathtaking transformation of communications technology at century's end.

Houses were built for returning veterans in the 40s

With 30% of married women working by 1960, family life was changing. So was dinner.[8] Swanson tentatively introduced its first frozen TV meal in 1954 with an initial production order for 5000 dinners. The company sold ten million more that first year—at 89 cents each. Fish sticks were introduced that year, described by a business journalist as "boneless oblongs roughly four inches long."

Another four-inch object emerged in the 1950s—the stiletto heel. The fashion historian Caroline Cox credits shoe designers Salvatore Ferragamo, Roger Vivier and a few others with offering women a glamorous antidote to the utilitarian footwear of the war years.

After gas rationing ended in 1945, the nation was on the move, relocating for new jobs, leaving the family farm for the city, and taking vacations. Most families owned cars and thousands of miles of new roads were built to accommodate the new national pastime, driving.[9] The abundance of automobiles in the late forties made supermarkets and shopping malls possible. Their significant other, the credit card, was invented in 1950.

Motels such as Holiday Inn, where children stayed free of charge, sprang up to accommodate families newly able to travel. Fast food restaurants arrived, one on the heels of the other: Kentucky Fried Chicken in 1952, Burger King in 1954, and McDonald's first franchise store in 1955. In 1958, a Kansas teenager named Frank Carney borrowed $600 from his parents and opened the first Pizza Hut.

In an age replete with inventions, nothing would match television. During the late forties, advertising, technology, and entertainment arts converged to produce a force that ultimately penetrated every corner of the nation, every facet of American life. In 1947, only seven thousand television sets were sold in an entire year. Just a few hours of evening programs and even fewer daytime shows were broadcast. Television news, as we now know it, had not yet developed. By 1950, almost seven million sets had been sold; by 1956, Americans were buying twenty thousand sets a day. Ten years later, fifty million sets had been purchased, and within a few more years, 94% of all American households would own at least one set.

Television would eventually become not just a primary source of entertainment and news, but tastemaker, town square, arguably the most influential teacher of the nation's children, and certainly its chief peddler. As athletics discovered huge TV audiences, they moved into a financial stratosphere. Network television advertising time sold for $750 per minute in 1950. By 2002 a thirty-second advertisement during the Super Bowl (expected to reach 40% of viewing households) would sell for as much as 1.9 million dollars.

Television became the country's hearth in times of national tragedy. For all its venality, television clearly served as an indispensable vehicle of progress in the civil rights movement. Few Americans outside the South had a deep understanding of Jim Crow laws until the facts were revealed graphically on home screens. Major networks provided information instantly when President John Kennedy was assassinated in 1963. They subsequently broadcast live the murder of Kennedy's assassin. Within days, television then offered a stunned nation the comfort of a funeral mass for the slain president.

Critics feared that television's sheer omnipresence would eclipse other forms of entertainment. It did not. In subsequent decades, a newly affluent nation produced ever-larger audiences for museums, sports events and virtually all the performing arts.

2. social climate

Childhood for a majority of white Americans was spent in traditional families with father at work and mother at home. Most African-American mothers worked, with a higher percentage of black families intact during the fifties than in any period since. Divorce, unemployment, illegitimacy and crime rates were all lower than they would be thereafter.[10] In another contradiction of the fifties, despite the Korean War and the ongoing Cold War, many children spent their early lives feeling secure and protected.

In 1951 my sister and I, ages eleven and thirteen, began to run with a "fast" crowd. The strictest of parents noted our harmless activities and soon relaxed. We rode bikes to each other's houses, complained about homework, and danced to Rosemary Clooney's "Come On-a my House." What made this seem a racy group was the requisite clothing: black turtle-neck sweaters and Levi's (called dungarees by the uninitiated).

It is worth noting that over the next fifty years while fashion rode a rollercoaster, black turtle-neck sweater and straight leg jeans would remain the favored uniform of hip urbanites, its popularity undiminished in the new century, and supplemented only by descendants of Marlon Brando's black leather jacket. (As slang is a child of fashion, it is perhaps not coincidental that the words *hip* and *cool* have also endured.)

Wearing ties and taffeta, 9th-graders gather in a pine-panelled basement recreation room. 1952

Unaware that we were children of a paradoxical time, Diane and I were pleased to change from Levi's to little suits, low heels, hats and white gloves for trips to church, museums or prized excursions to Broadway to see "The Diary of Anne Frank," or "West Side Story."

Strong Women Tell Their Stories

Our summers were punctuated by weekly dances attended by whole families. Floating in organza dresses buoyed by crinoline petticoats, my sister and our friends and I danced to the music of backcountry fiddlers whose artistry we would appreciate in later years.[11]

Lumbee Indian teens Lonnie Revels and Ruth Locklear at a Senior Class banquet in Pembroke, North Carolina. 1954

Adolescents Velma Gibson and Roland Watts, Winston-Salem, North Carolina. 1956

Voices of the Silent Generation

To be sure, segregation and racial prejudice remained ugly features of American life. Yet most of the women I interviewed, regardless of race, spoke spontaneously of the positive community cooperation, neighborliness and structured family life that marked their childhoods. As children, all had respected church, school and parental authority.

Social institutions seemed stable and reliable. Churches, public schools and universities routinely reinforced a sense of shared behavioral norms. Church membership rose from half the population in 1940 to a historic high of over two-thirds in 1959. Most Americans still had confidence in the good intentions and veracity of government officials. With wartime achievements a fresh memory, military leaders were trusted and celebrated to a degree unimaginable ten years later. Essayist Joan Didion wrote in 1979, "I think now we were the last generation to identify with adults." [12]

Children flooded public school systems across the country and soon claimed the lion's share of local tax revenues. Expenditures per student in 1960 were triple what they had been in 1940. Those born before the baby boom, as well as boomers, benefited from increased school spending and building.

High school students volunteer as hospital Candy Stripers, 1950

Strong Women Tell Their Stories

I well recall that on rapidly growing Long Island, some school children were expected to sow as well as reap. Every few years, my parents, ever active in PTA and the school board, recruited squads of twelve-year-olds to deliver circulars urging support for new school bonds. We had collected newspapers and soup cans for the war effort at ages five and six, so trudging door-to-door throughout the school district seemed a natural part of childhood to all of us.

In many parts of the country, white elementary school children were offered programs in music, art, and physical education, along with academic subjects. My own local elementary school (four hundred students) employed an art teacher, five full-time music teachers and three full-time physical education instructors. Black students typically attended segregated, ill-equipped and poorly funded schools in the South, and fared only marginally better in crowded northern cities. Black women's clubs and churches tried to compensate, offering their children opportunities for Bible study, poetry recitation, art projects, choral and solo singing.[13]

The silent generation is the last to recall childhood without television. For many children, even store-bought toys were an unknown luxury until the late forties. Common recollections include reading, Saturday afternoon movies, skating and biking, visualizing radio stories or playing board games, sandlot baseball and pick-up sports. Unsupervised hours outdoors were the norm for city children as well as those in suburbs or small towns.

For most of the small thirties birth cohort, high school was relatively benign and adolescence less perilous than it is for today's youth. Competition for admission to prestigious colleges and universities was intense, but hardly as fierce as it is today. High school and college graduates encountered a bustling economy, alive with abundant jobs and promising new career

Cambridge High School championship basketball team. Cambridge, New York, 1953.

opportunities, the latter drastically more limited for women and minorities. Aware of the deprivation and anxiety of their parent's youth, many young adults felt blessed by their times, and buoyantly optimistic about the future. In fact, David K. Foot, in his 1996 book, *Boom, Bust and Echo*, uses economic indicators to argue that 1938 was the most financially promising year to be born in North America. Foot is known for, among other things, his comment, "Demographics explain two-thirds of everything."

3. stabilizing influences

Given such conditions it is understandable that these young people were not as rambunctious or as eager to change society as those who followed them. Their characters were formed by experiences at considerable variance from those of baby boomers. As one example, the two groups had dramatically different attitudes toward the armed forces. Patriotism and confidence in authority was built into the psyche of those who remembered World War II. Their parents had grown Victory gardens, participated in Civil Defense, and endured rationing of food and gasoline with little complaint. Boomers, on the other hand, were shaped by the Vietnam War, a conflict that produced deep distrust of government and military authority.

Over sixteen million Americans had served in World War II. Old newsreels capture a rejoicing nation as millions of soldiers returned in 1945, welcomed by huge crowds and parades. No celebration could adequately express the country's pride in those who fought--or its relief at their return. The war had created a deep strain of conservatism in most returning veterans. With their presence felt everywhere they became a stabilizing influence on youth entering college even into the early fifties. The conviction that one was fortunate to be an American was still widely shared.

I grew up enthralled by tales told by a family friend, an Army nurse who had served in the Philippines. Bold and tough, she spit out salty language exotic and glamorous to this eight-year-old. My mother's twin, Arthur Gendron, whom I had seen only in his Army uniform, returned from Guam, one of 600,000 soldiers to come home wounded. A quiet man, he told no stories, but we children learned of his bravery and his suffering and were in awe of him for both.

Hollywood studios provided powerful reminders that America was a favored land. Film after film celebrated the heroism of the armed forces and the fortitude of those at home. Throughout the war years, some 85 million Americans a week bought movie tickets.

During the 1944 Christmas vacation, our family stood in a long line at Radio City Music Hall to see Spencer Tracy and Van Johnson in a riveting "Thirty Seconds Over Tokyo." Safe in our seats, parents and children were enthralled by wartime aerial photography (never imagining it was the work of virtuoso miniaturist A. Arnold Gillespie, one of the first great special effects artisans). Two years earlier, my mother and friends wept as a luminous Greer Garson in "Mrs. Miniver" implicitly honored all women who sustain great losses. It would be years before we children could appreciate the intoxicating brew of romance, sacrifice and honor in the 1943 classic "Casablanca." Sixty years later, the film continues to captivate new generations of viewers.

The 1946 Academy Award-winner, "The Best Years of Our Lives," featured the late Harold Russell, who had lost both hands in the war. Another war hero, Audie Murphy, also became an instant film star in the postwar period, suggesting a public eager to keep its heroes visible. [14]

Indeed, who would not admire the young veterans, some, such as my young uncle, permanently disabled. Collegians of the late forties and early fifties studied alongside veterans attending college on the GI Bill. Less than a decade later veterans of the Korean War arrived in those classrooms. Called today the "forgotten war," the fierce struggle of 1950-1953 was not easily forgotten by those who fought it. They too had been forced to grow up (some would say grow old) while still very young. It was natural for both waves of college students to emulate the prematurely wise, yet instinctively conservative, men and women who had served abroad. One historian suggests that the influence was so powerful that those who had not experienced World War II sometimes acted as if they had.[15] As did the war generation, young adults in the early fifties would marry young, welcome more children than was once customary, hold traditional values about family and work, and continue to be relatively apolitical.

Meanwhile, the Nazi Holocaust, genocide of European Jewry barely registered in the post-war American public square. Jewish families in the United States gradually learned of the extent of their losses abroad, but with anti-Semitism still a fact of American life, there was little public discussion, or acknowledgement of the unprecedented catastrophe. Hollywood chose not to explore on film what later became known as the Holocaust, and writers seemed to need time to digest events. Elie Wiesel's *Night,* appearing in 1958, was soon considered one of the definitive works on the Holocaust. Shelly Weiner is an American citizen born in Poland who describes in her Part II oral history an aftermath of war significantly different from that of most Americans. Unwanted by any country, her family and many others lived in camps for displaced persons for three years.

4. learning wariness

For all that was positive about life in the fifties, the Cold War and its threat of nuclear annihilation were never far out of mind and accounts for much of the storied cautiousness of its youth. All knew of President Truman's decision to bomb Hiroshima and Nagasaki in 1945. Debate continues about the wisdom of that decision, though most agree it had the intended effect, bringing the war to a close without invasion of Japan. Truman officially defended the use of atomic weapons at the time, but years later his diary would reveal his own grave misgivings about their use. Physicist J. Robert Oppenheimer, had earlier voiced his own anguish over his central role in developing the bomb. Lacking televised pictures, the public could soon read John Hersey's book

Cold War sailor in the North Atlantic. 1955

Hiroshima, with its graphic portrayal of the bomb's horrifying effects.

Chinese communists under Mao Tse-tung had completed conquest of China by 1949, driving Chiang Kai-shek's Nationalist forces to Taiwan, an island off the mainland. North Korean communists invaded South Korea the following year. President Truman soon made it clear that the U.S. would not stand idle as Asian countries fell to communism. Truman responded with troops and promptly secured United Nations backing for a "police action," to drive out the North Koreans. To Americans who bore the brunt of the fighting, the Korean police action looked and felt like a real war. Before its close in 1953, fighting in Korea took the lives of 36,900 young Americans. No prospective draftees marched on Washington to protest the war in Korea or the draft; military service was an accepted obligation. "American youth, in or out of uniform," observed *Time* magazine in a widely-quoted 1951 comment, "has learned that it must try to make the best of a bad and difficult job, whether that job is life, or war, or both."

After the invasion of South Korea, the Cold War was to be at center stage for almost forty years. A comforting American nuclear monopoly had ended in 1949 when Russia exploded its first nuclear bomb. Soviet development of the weapon was greatly accelerated by scientific information acquired through successful espionage. President Truman soothingly called the new Russian weapon a "nuclear device," but Americans were not soothed. Russia had become an implacable and formidable foe. The arms race was on.

The United States exploded a new, vastly more powerful atomic weapon, the thermonuclear hydrogen bomb, in 1952. Called the Super by U.S. physicists, it was soon matched by the Soviets in 1955. That ushered in the strategy of "mutually assured destruction" (MAD), aimed at precluding first use by Russia. The appalling weapons brought a merciful caution as each side assessed the intolerable consequences of a nuclear war. But such a fragile equilibrium was never guaranteed. The possibility of war by mistake was real and all knew it. Albert Einstein observed wryly at the time that should a US-Soviet nuclear war actually occur, the war after *that* one would be fought with stones. The Cold War haunted the decade.

May of 1957 saw the successful launching into orbit of the Soviet satellite Sputnik or "fellow traveler." Caught off guard, the Eisenhower administration sought without success to minimize the event. An alarmed public and press, watching Sputnik alone in the night sky, proclaimed a "missile gap," and a "technological Pearl Harbor." Not surprisingly, spending for math and science education increased sharply, along with millions of dollars in federal grants for defense-related research.

The explosion of the Vanguard in 1958 exacerbated fears. Later that year a successful satellite, Explorer I, rocketed into space, but did little to relieve public anxiety about Soviet missile superiority. There had been two World Wars in this century; a third was clearly possible.

Several members of Congress offered yet another response: an Office of Defense Mobilization report suggested appropriating $25 *billion* for bomb shelters. Cooler heads later prevailed and the idea was dropped, but hundreds of families were frightened enough to build and stock their own bomb shelters. "Having lived with a nightmare for nearly a year," wrote one observer, "the average citizen is only too glad to grasp at the flimsiest means that would enable him to regain his peace of mind. [16]

In 1955, I thought it only a matter of time before Russian bombs would rain on my high school. I'd heard of grade schools where children wore dog tags for identification should the bombs come. For some of us, these thoughts were so terrifying as to be simply thrust out of mind.

Such denial served for many of us; others report a far higher level of anxiety. Writers responded to the atomic era with works of nihilism and alienation. Theatre of the absurd, with works such as Samuel Beckett's "Waiting for Godot" and "Krapp's Last Tape," and Albert Camus' existential novel *The Stranger* expressed the apocalyptic sensibilities of serious artists.

5. a climate of intimidation

The silent generation did produce Martin Luther King, Jr., Gloria Steinem, Malcom X, Ralph Nader, and others who emerged well after their college years to become compelling social activists. However, another dark side to the decade gave many young adults additional reasons to be wary. Tapping into a broadly shared dread of Soviet intentions, Senator Joseph R. McCarthy of Wisconsin aggravated the climate of fear by falsely branding hundreds of government employees as Communist spies. The press did little to stop him; the senator made good copy. With unprecedented recklessness, McCarthy exploited legitimate Cold War concerns about espionage, and for a few years enjoyed a fearsome success. Factions in the frightened country soon demonized each other, the left accusing all anti-communists of "hysteria," and the right branding all but themselves as communist sympathizers. Finally brought down in 1954 by the cruel extravagance of his charges, Senator McCarthy had by then tainted reputations, ruined careers and badly damaged public confidence in the government.

Senator McCarthy was not alone in abusing his powers. Other measures prompted wariness among the young as they saw their elders branded for earlier political activity. Beginning in 1945, the Red Scare prompted the House Un-American Activities Committee and the FBI under J. Edgar Hoover to make inquiries into the personal lives and political beliefs of thousands of innocent citizens. President Truman's executive order of 1953, responding to public fear of subversion spawned by McCarthy and HUAC, instituted loyalty checks of all government employees. The Civil Service Commission eventually fired over 2,000 people deemed security risks.

The Smith Act and the McCarran Internal Security Act of 1950 were designed to test loyalty and punish persons deemed threats to national security. The new laws convinced many that social activism or public criticism of American values would stamp them "un-American" and "soft" on communism. In fact, challenges to segregation in the South were regularly taken as evidence of disloyalty. Recalling the period, historian Joseph Goulden wrote that the political climate limited "by intimidation what no Western society worth the name can safely limit: the curiosity and idealism of its young."[17] In addition to inhibiting youth, preoccupation with the Cold War held badly needed social reforms in the wings for much of the decade.

Revisionist historians in later years tended to minimize the Soviet threat and subversive activities present in the fifties, some even asserting that the Cold War was a fabrication of an American government intent on its own secret agenda. But most Americans at the time believed that Soviet military power and related espionage were authentic threats, a view eventually substantiated by the opening of KGB (Soviet secret police) files in 1999. The files and intercepted Soviet communications revealed for the first time the names of dozens of Americans who had spied for Russia in the forties.[18]

6. art, not action

The climate of repression drove artists to express social criticism through their work rather than political protest. Indeed, throughout history, artists such as Goya, Daumier, Dickens, Moliere, Swift, and Twain used their art to puncture pretension, ridicule folly, and expose vice in the halls of power. Emerging early in the 20th century, the modernist spirit continues to declare itself subversive and "transgressive." America in the fifties was uniquely ripe for censure by its artists.

European painters and sculptors such as Max Ernst and Andre Breton fled Nazism and emigrated to the United States before or just after the war. Their work infused the New York art world with depth and energy. In no mood for repression of any sort, the Europeans and younger avant-garde American artists created vibrant, iconoclastic art. By the mid-fifties, abstract expressionism was internationally recognized as the first original

American art movement. The center of painting and sculpture gradually moved from Paris to New York, where it remains today.[19]

Black musicians had long pursued a tradition of musical double entendre and encoded political messages that dated back to the songs of enslaved Americans. In a devastating use of music as social criticism, jazz singer Billie Holiday's song, "Strange Fruit," made veiled but clear reference to lynchings of African-Americans in the South. Ray Charles' plaintive love song,"You Don't Know Me," was also a haunting lament about the treatment of blacks in America.

Ralph Ellison's great novel, *Invisible Man*, a 1952 National Book Award winner, served up a powerful indictment of prejudice and segregation in American society. Few other black writers were nationally known, but as the decade progressed, the growing fame of Richard Wright, Zora Neale Hurston, Lorraine Hansberry, James Baldwin and Langston Hughes inspired and encouraged young black artists and writers. Virtually all sought to instruct an oblivious nation on the remarkable vigor of America's black citizens—and the urgent need for reforms in American society.[20] Hansberry's 1958 play "Raisin in the Sun" dramatized those and other themes so effectively that it became an enduring American classic, brought to life over and again on college and community stages.

Arthur Miller's 1953 play, "The Crucible," implicitly drew parallels between 18th century witch trials in Salem, Massachusetts, and McCarthy's brand of witch-hunting.

In 1953 when I saw "The Crucible" on Broadway, I was just old enough to travel into the city with my sister and a friend. Despite our inadequate grasp of contemporary politics, we were overwhelmed by the injustice so vividly portrayed on stage.

The play's power has endured, having perhaps created "the holy resonance" that has been ascribed to it. A revival opened on Broadway in 2002.

Cultural observers agree that while political freedom was compromised, the arts enjoyed a stunning vitality. If endurance is a reliable yardstick of artistic quality, then the decade was indeed a fertile age for most of the arts. Some of the era's popular fiction, and much of its serious literature, drama, music, painting and sculpture are still highly regarded half a century later.[21]

7. "problems have been solved"

Democrat Adlai Stevenson advised a Chicago audience in 1955, "It is time for catching our breath; moderation is the spirit of the times." Suburban families, still influenced by a healthy economy and the war's legacy of conservatism, agreed.

McCarthyism and preoccupation with the Cold War effectively manacled the left and other progressives by creating a climate inhospitable to significant social reform. National attention was diverted from domestic ills to such an extent that one commentator finally wrote in exasperation, "There are only two factors in the political world today, the Kremlin and the State Department, and if one doesn't choose one, one must choose the other."[22] Annoyed by his own government, he nonetheless believed the Kremlin was by far the greater menace. Meanwhile, poverty and the severely constrained lives of American blacks and other minorities remained back-burner issues.

Segregation and poverty, still virtually invisible, received from economic and political leaders far less attention than conditions merited. In 1951, economist Arthur Burns praised the nation's creation and distribution of our national wealth, calling it one of history's great social revolutions. Home ownership reached the highest level the world had ever known; movies, advertising and television showcased a limitless supply of cheerful and well-fed white, middle-class folk. Good times had returned and many believed that the high-tide economy had indeed lifted all boats. President Eisenhower, aware that the entire citizenry did not share in the national prosperity, authorized the creation of the Department of Health, Education and Welfare in 1953. Others remained euphoric and at least one prominent social critic announced his belief that democracy had solved the basic problems of the industrial revolution.[23]

8. student activism: present and absent

The decade's reputation for social serenity had yet another cause. Not only did collegians of the fifties contend with a general suppression of progressive activity, but no long-standing traditions of student protest existed to inspire them. During the Depression, the student body of ten thousand at City College of New York included just a few hundred student activists. By far the most militant student body in the country, they presented too tiny a cadre to arouse their own or the next generation.

Historian William O'Neill noted that as social critics addressed the more urgent issues of poverty and racial conflict, they largely abandoned criticism of the "growing cult of yesmanship," the silent generation, and the organization man. "This tells us," wrote O'Neill, "something about the cycle of fashion, social analysis being no more immune to it than the

Voices of the Silent Generation

fashion industry."[24] O'Neill concluded that while some contemporary critiques of the decade were astute, complaints about college students of the 1950s were insubstantial. More serious than previous collegians, he claimed, they were in most respects little different from those who preceded them. The silent generation is by no means the only group characterized by the absence of social protest, it is simply the first to be so defined.[25]

Many young adults of the 1950s maintained sympathetic connections with older adults throughout the college years, so their conservative behavior is not surprising; they mirrored their elders. Public opinion polls in the late fifties indicated that young and old Americans were "relaxed, unadventurous, confidently satisfied with their way of life, and blandly optimistic about the future."[26]

With television news barely born and television sets rare on college campuses, few students experienced events as viscerally as did subsequent generations. Life on leafy campuses or in pleasant suburbs revealed little about the travail of inner cities or the poverty of rural precincts. Without ample evidence of America's social and economic problems, middle-class collegians had little motivation to seek solutions. Not until the early sixties, with racial injustice vividly displayed on the nightly news in most homes, would student activism begin to emerge on a large scale.

In *The Affluent Society,* published in 1958, John Kenneth Galbraith argued that the country was now more than wealthy enough to start looking after its poor. Indeed, the book is widely credited as the intellectual foundation of the Kennedy-Johnson war on poverty in the sixties. Published in 1962, Michael Harrington's book *The Other America,* featured startling revelations of severe deprivation throughout the nation, and became a valuable supplement to Galbraith's work. For many readers, Harrington was the first to illuminate the true conditions of the nation's poorest citizens.

True to its contradictory nature, the fifties were never as monotonic as reported. Ignoring small but potent pockets of protest, critics exaggerated uniformity in the young. Well ahead of their time, some students repeatedly took action against problems ignored by mainstream America. Ten thousand students massed in Washington in 1958, and again a year later, for the Youth March for Integrated Schools. Students at Cornell University started an affiliate of The National Committee for a Sane Nuclear Policy in 1958; the Ban the Bomb movement was born the same year. Pacifists and socialists at University of Chicago formed the

Buoyant and optimistic, Freshman women at Cornell University dress for a dance in 1956.

Student Peace Union in 1959. Young Quakers volunteered with their elders in a wide range of efforts to remedy injustice. Others were drawn to Dorothy Day's Catholic Worker Movement and its "Houses of Hospitality" for the indigent.

Young black men and women, also members of the silent generation, energetically pursued social reform at Montgomery in 1955, Little Rock in 1957, Greensboro and other southern cities in 1960. Their efforts were neither placid nor unadventurous, and gave birth to a social and political revolution.

With the decade's closing, the struggle for women's rights was a faint glow on the horizon. Nonetheless, heightened awareness of grave domestic problems and the perilous arms race stirred the imaginations of a growing number of young adults. Student activism in the next decade would heat to a fiery intensity as serious issues were more thoroughly reported and graphically displayed on every home screen.

III. INHERITED VIRTUES

Americans born in the Depression did not invent the values and virtues later viewed as peculiar to the fifties. Rather, many of their values were classically American: stoicism and self-reliance, a disposition toward hard work, a keen desire to better oneself economically and socially, and a conviction that an ordered community and personal self-restraint were essential to these goals. Historians and social observers who write disparagingly of Americans in the fifties do acknowledge self-discipline and a willingness to work hard as primary shared virtues of the era. One 1955 college graduate wrote, "As a child of the 50s, I grew up conditioned to put maximum effort into every endeavor because everything counted." [27]

Mindful that a diverse population offered tremendous potential for conflict, Americans always had reason to be concerned with stability and order. The western frontier had been unpredictable, dangerous and unruly. Unmonitored business competition often yielded monopolistic practices and price gouging. Public benevolence often obscured private fraud. Because life in a young country was turbulent, Americans struggled hard for order, even if at some expense to creative expression. Toward that end, children were taught self-discipline, thrift, perseverance, self-reliance and civic responsibility; self-expression was for a later time. Over time families, schools, churches, community groups, local police and government forged successful searches for freedom firmly rooted in civic order.

Inherited values and virtues existed alongside deep and serious flaws in fifties America. Despite early civil rights efforts, segregation prevailed, women's rights were suppressed, and prejudice was rampant at every level of society. Benita Eisler, writing of the personal contradictions of her own early years, speaks unabashedly for her time: "I was, and still am, reliable, responsible, tidy and well groomed...I was polite, considerate, and respectful. I also lied and broke rules all the time."[28] However imperfectly practiced in the fifties, America's traditional virtues and habits, so deeply rooted in the nation's history, formed the character of its young--and underlay the behavior and reticence of the silent generation.

1. stoicism, self-reliance and reserve

Stoicism, arguably both virtue and vice, was deeply embedded in the American psyche. To understand the behavior of young adults in the fifties, one must acknowledge the role of stoicism in American culture. The Puritan ethic maintained that sensory pleasure weakened character; thus for many Americans a legacy of guilt attended delight. Life on the frontier had required endurance. Refusing to bow to danger and hardship had been essential for survival--and would be admired ever after. A red-blooded American could take a punch. When knocked down, he came up feisty. The immigrant experience set ethnic groups apart and bred reserve:

you trusted your own, they spoke your language, and only they were to hear your troubles.

Self-reliance, stoicism's first cousin, was valued in the postwar years. Adults prized self-sufficiency and expected children to amuse themselves. Studs Terkel observed that even during the Depression people blamed themselves rather than the economy for hardship or misfortune. "There was an acceptance that it was your own fault, your own indolence, your own lack of ability. You took it and you kept quiet." [29] What male child has not heard, "Take it like a man," meaning, of course, no complaining allowed.

President Eisenhower, elected in 1952, grew up amidst scarcity, and spent much of his adult life in a poorly paid pre-war army. The inhibitions and cast of mind created by those lean years never really left him. Eisenhower presided over the country as it grew rich, but was not himself a product of wealth. He was conservative, cautious and suspicious of change, characteristics that may have played a role in his administration's ability to end inflation, balance the budget, promote prosperity, and most important, preserve a precarious peace with such tumultuous nations as Cuba, the Soviet Union, Iraq, Lebanon and Indonesia. (Eisenhower's writings later revealed that the decade was never placid or serene for him.)

If poverty tends to breed inhibitions, among them is the fear of being thought foolish, or worse, laughable. Dignity is the more fiercely guarded when the only hedge against despair. For some, ridicule is worse than hunger. By the late forties many American families were no longer poor, but constraints born of deprivation lingered and were transmitted to children. A writer recalled, "I still recognize my contemporaries by our shared horror of appearing ridiculous, a horror no post-fifties form of therapy ever managed to eradicate."[30]

Corollary to such reserve is an aversion to trumpeting one's own successes. No one explores the period's essential modesty better than Garrison Keillor, the brilliant radio storyteller whose heartland Americans were invariably reluctant to make a fuss…about anything, good or bad. Children were taught it was improper to "wear your heart on your sleeve," just as some women had learned that it was "vulgar to wear your fortune on your back." One was expected to suffer in silence, and to be self-effacing regardless of achievement.

In the bustling postwar economy, few excuses seemed acceptable for personal failure. If one were troubled, the family, not a professional, was the first line of defense. "Everyone felt shame and defeat in having to get help," recalls a psychoanalyst. Those who needed therapy feared disapproval, the appearance of weakness. As doctors and psychiatrists witnessed the ravages of untreated depression, alcoholism or marriages gone irredeemably bad, it became clear that excessive stoicism and self-reliance could be dangerous. Said one clinician, "By the time we saw them, they were really sick."[31] Marriage counseling was conducted with little specialized professional training. Until the late sixties, most counselors were doctors, clergymen, lawyers, and only incidentally did they advise couples about marital problems. The 1999 film "Pollock," a biography of one of the fifties' most prominent painters, graphically portrays the dangers of untreated mental illness, its effect on marriage and the lives of others.

Early in 2001, social critic Norman Podhoretz remarked, half-joking, that not only did the silent generation not protest and demonstrate, "they didn't talk endlessly about themselves either. That's the other reason they were called silent!"[32] Podhoretz touched the truth: it seems not to have occurred to the smallest generation to publicly lament or celebrate each new aspect of life as they experienced it. With the largest birth cohort in history nipping at their heels, perhaps they assumed the world did not await *their* revelations. Also, as noted earlier, Depression-era parents had taught children early on that personal life was private: family linen was not to be aired in public. Indeed, few memoirs of personal and family turmoil were published during the fifties.

Individuals may have been reticent in the fifties, but fiction writers did explore family and human failings. Lee Smith's short story "Tongues of Fire" opens with rules for children on how to cope with father's nervous breakdown. Rule # 1: Deny all family troubles. Pat Conroy's popular novel *Prince of Tides,* also set in the fifties, presents a mother who carries denial to apocalyptic lengths. With antecedents in Greek tragedy, theatre classics such as Eugene O'Neill's "Long Day's Journey into Night"*(1957),* Arthur Miller's "Death of a Salesman"(1950), and several of Tennessee Williams' plays all revolved around painful family secrets.[33]

Postwar Americans suffered from a lack of adequate and available psychological counseling, but the second half of the century would usher in an age of therapy. One journalist labeled the new focus on self-help, self-discovery and self-improvement "the triumph of the therapeutic."[34] Television and published diaries and journals eventually provided ubiquitous forums for increasingly exuberant self-revelation. Lacking such vehicles, and bred to self-reliance and stoicism, average folk in the fifties, like their literary counterparts, remained relatively silent about their inner lives.

2. religious belief

By external measures the decade was a religious one, with over sixty-five percent of the population enrolled in a church or synagogue late in the decade. The Bible topped the best-seller list in 1953 and 1954. Among many foreign films available, Ingmar Bergman's "The Seventh Seal" *(1956)* earned popular and critical regard for its serious treatment of religious and existential themes. Unlike previous periods of religious revival in American life, every intellectual level, every class, social and geographic division, every race and age group, and denomination participated in the new religious fervor. Historians suggest that a surge in religious reflection and interest in the transcendent during the fifties was inspired by unacknowledged anxieties about the Cold War and nuclear weapons.

Three of the decade's most influential and popular figures, Norman Vincent Peale, Billy Graham and Archbishop Fulton Sheen combined religious faith with psychological insight. Each reached millions through newspaper columns, books, radio and television broadcasts. They were arguably the first multimedia celebrities.

Before Sunday morning church service.
Lake Lauderdale, New York, 1952

Departments of religious studies expanded as college students enrolled in record numbers for classes on religion. Courses on Buddhism and Hinduism were offered, though widespread study and practice of Eastern religions had not yet taken firm hold in the United States.

Most religions address the mystery and inevitability of suffering in human life. Sophocles offered a universal dictum: "Wisdom through affliction schooled." Humanity's fate and the problem of evil have long been at the heart of religious inquiry. Thus, evidence suggests that while college students failed to mount the barricades of social protest in great numbers, they did not neglect the larger issues of human existence.[35] Recalling her own student days in the fifties, Joan Didion wrote of "the ambiguity of belonging to a generation distrustful of political highs...growing up convinced that the heart of darkness lay not in some error of social organization, but in man's own blood."[36]

3. frugality vs. consumerism

Commentators have long noted the "consumerism" of postwar years. Purchasing habits of the time should be assessed in context, however. At war's end, the nation emerged from a long period of deprivation; postwar consumption was initially a catch-up effort, with real needs to be met. Throughout the fifties, credit cards, advertising and television would blur the line between needs and desires. Still, for many, thriftiness and frugality, virtues born of poverty and passed on from Depression-era parents, held a firm grip well into their adult lives.

Vivian Bussey, who grew up in a segregated southern city and worked for many years as housekeeper in private homes, recalls, "Where I grew up, you made an ironing board cover from a worn-out sheet. When that got all torn up and frayed, you cut it into dustcloths. Finally when those got down to tattered strips, you took them outside and used them to tie up tomato plants. If it was winter, you might use those strips to curl a little girl's hair." Ms. Bussey also spoke of adults she knew who always took the best parts of the family chicken at supper: "Those children didn't know there was *but* wings."[37]

Vivian Bussey, 2005

Family historian Josephine Hoyt Wilson recalls the implications of scarce household appliances—refrigerators in particular—during her small-town North Carolina childhood. Chicken for dinner meant buying a live chicken, keeping it in a pen, and wringing its neck just before cooking time.[38]

A later and urban example

of inherited thriftiness: In the early sixties, a group of post-college friends living in Harvard Square owned not a single television set.

We read the newspapers, and saved our few extra dollars--not necessarily a wise frugality, for we missed, among other things, all television coverage of the early Civil Rights Movement.

Families sought new household appliances with an urgency unknown today. Homemakers of the forties had routinely washed laundry by hand, or with wringer washers. For most, the outdoor clothesline was the only option for drying wet laundry, winter or summer. For women living in Minnesota or North Dakota, this could be a memorable experience.

During the forties, my mother labored over laundry for her family of five, and I well recall her relief and pleasure when our first automatic washing machine was installed. Months later, a dryer rescued my mother, this time from the twin tyrannies of sagging clothesline and unpredictable weather. We never did buy a dishwasher, although my father boasted that he had three, if they could just be harnessed between sports and homework. My mother would have settled happily for the more reliable plug-in variety.

Describing her childhood in the fifties, historian Doris Kearns Goodwin notes that her parents, when prosperous, never forgot the Depression. They "took nothing for granted, and approached each major purchase with a sense of awe." Neighbors also shared such feelings: "Excitement infected the entire block when someone got a new refrigerator...an automatic washing machine, or a television set." [39]

In our family's blue-and-white-collar Long Island neighborhood just a few miles from Ms. Goodwin's Rockville Center home, one saw little evidence of extravagant consumption. Adolescents earned most of their spending money, and typically saved for college, a second-hand car, or both. Credit cards had not yet arrived in our part of the world; whatever the purchase, saving came first.

My parents emphasized activity over acquisition; we were given ice-skates, bicycles and music lessons, but not expensive clothing, portable radios, or large allowances. Friends from the Bronx, an Italian fireman and his Hungarian wife, intent on shaping their children's tastes, carefully built into their family's monthly budget the purchase of one book and one phonograph record.

Having watched banks collapse and jobs disappear during the thirties, many postwar adults feared credit and "buying on time." In 1953, well into the boom years, an average of only one-half of one percent of household income was devoted to interest payments, exclusive of home mortgages.

Voices of the Silent Generation

From 1952 to l956 disposable income increased by 21 percent, and consumer borrowing also began a steady climb. Spending soared as the decade progressed, but purchases were still carefully considered in the early fifties.[40]

Old habits were changing, and each year of prosperity took Americans further away from personal restraint. Adopting tactics from motivational research, advertisers gradually erased the deeply ingrained fear of self-indulgence that initially accompanied the new pleasures of acquisition. Shopping and buying were becoming a national pastime. Credit payments (as a fraction of income) soon rose, to over ten percent by 1998, and fourteen percent by 2001. As the silent generation left adolescence behind, a huge new generation of teenagers purchased records, radios, movie tickets, cameras, cosmetics and clothing, thereby contributing, by l959, a staggering ten billion dollars to the economy. The baby boom had begun to show its muscle.

4. trusting everyone over thirty...

Loath to disappoint their parents, young adults of the silent generation sought to conform to adult expectations. "We cringed at the thought of disappointing our parents—whatever bold assertions we made to the contrary," recalled one writer.[41] Columnist Leonard Pitts noted, in a speech to African-American college students, that most important to him was a mother "who preached certain values and then lived them in front of me."[42] He added that these values then evolved into a moral compass, a set of boundaries that helped him distinguish between right and wrong. A few years later, such firm ties to adults would unravel for many young people, but throughout the fifties most college students still turned to parents and professors for guidance.

Younger adolescent's incipient distrust of adults and reluctance to grow up were pungently captured in the l955 film "Rebel Without A Cause," and J. D. Salinger's 1951 novel *Catcher in the Rye*. Holden Caulfield, Salinger's young protagonist, appeared relentlessly cynical but also vulnerable and likable. James Dean's legendary film rebel was initially more disappointed and confused by adults than actively rebellious. Nonetheless, these works and others spoke to young teenagers, and helped sow seeds of discontent. But children of the Depression were far less receptive than those born in the forties. At decade's end I recall students working two jobs for college tuition who wondered why on earth Holden Caulfield was so cranky.[43]

Collegians read the same literature as older adults. And what a selection they had. *Washington Post* critic Jonathon Yardley calls the fifties a golden age for fiction, citing the unique literary styles of even second-tier novelists. New York's intellectual world was dominated by literary critics such as Lionel Trilling and Edmund Wilson. Ernest Hemingway, F. Scott Fitzgerald and William Faulkner were well-established writers. But the list of other significant novelists publishing in the fifties is long and dazzling, matched in no other period since. Saul Bellow and Vladimir Nabakov are considered by some the century's finest writers; John Updike, John Steinbeck, Flannery O'Connor, Ralph Ellison, Eudora Welty and Philip Roth are still in print and taught in university classes. Harper Lee's 1960 novel, *To Kill a Mockingbird,* won a Pulitzer Prize in 1961 and was made into an Academy-Award winning film in 1962. Both film and book continue into the 21st century as popular favorites. In 1952 Welsh poet Dylan Thomas recorded the first audio book, "A Child's Christmas in Wales," now a classic beloved by children and adults. [44]

Bedtime story. 1955

According to polls in England and the United States, J. R. R. Tolkien's *The Lord of the Rings* is one of the century's finest novels. Published in 1954, the trilogy is revered both for its children's fantasy and the transcendent truths that emerge from the story. W.H. Auden said of the work, "Nobody seems to have a moderate opinion: either, like myself they find it a masterpiece of its genre, or they cannot abide it."[46] The trilogy sold tens of millions of copies worldwide long before Peter Jackson's 2001-2003 trio of films based on the books took their places among the most popular films ever made.

For its inventive, bold artistry and early fictional revelations of a black man's perspective on America, *Invisible Man,* is considered by some to be one of the great novels of the century. On the best-seller list for months and winner of the National Book Award in 1952, the book is still widely read today. While writers of the time had begun to chronicle their rejection of society, Ellison wrote of his rejection *by* society.

Voices of the Silent Generation

Though radical writers of the 1960s criticized the book's ending for being too personal and insufficiently political, Ellison's achievement remains undiminished by time. Two poignant lines still echo down through the years: Ellison's reference to America, "the vast whiteness in which I was lost," and, "To whom should I be responsible when you refuse to see me?"[46]

The silent generation attended the same movies as their elders, and were blessed with some of the century's finest films. The year 1951 alone saw the release of "The African Queen," "A Streetcar Named Desire," "An American in Paris," "Viva Zapata," and "Strangers on a Train." The following year marked the production of "High Noon," Charlie Chaplin's "Limelight," and Orson Welles' "Othello." In 1953, audiences met Audrey Hepburn, one of the most beloved of all film stars, in "Roman Holiday," and Marlon Brando led a fine cast in "On the Waterfront." Lesser films were made as well, but no decade before or since has produced movies of such acclaimed variety and quality.

A common culture spanning the generations was noted by Jacques Barzun: "The hope of a collective enjoyment of the best in thought and art was still strong. It was manifest in the drive to send the young to college...in the free public libraries, in the many series of classics in cheap, well-edited form." Blurred boundaries between high and middlebrow culture made fine art, literature and film accessible to the aspiring nonspecialist, whatever her background.

5. ...or not

As the sixties opened, members of the silent generation had turned to the adult world of work, marriage, family. Those born early in the Depression had become the "over thirty" adults that baby boomers were soon told not to trust.

Literature began to explore a disaffected view of military life. Norman Mailer's *The Naked and the Dead* (1948) was one of the first war novels to depict in graphic detail battle and its corrosive effects on soldiers. Herman Wouk won the 1951 Pulitzer Prize with *The Caine Mutiny,* and James Jones' *From Here to Eternity* was a best seller the same year. Four years later Joseph Heller's *Catch 22* would be both sardonically funny and deeply cynical about the glories of war. In the seventies, the hugely popular television series "M*A*S*H" ran fast and far with the same dark humor as *Catch 22*. These works helped to accelerate growing distrust by sixties youth of military authority and competence.

Strong Women Tell Their Stories

Sociologists and writers David Riesman, C. Wright Mills, Paul Goodman and Vance Packard published books critical of American society. Supplying a keen analysis of "other-directed" conformity, Reisman's *The Lonely Crowd,* published in 1950, was the most influential book of the genre, eventually selling 1.5 million copies. All were widely read and discussed throughout the decade, stimulating a budding critical self-criticism in adult as well as student readers.[47]

A group of young writers called the Beats disdained middle-class values and hygiene, dismissed academic writing and scholarship, took drugs, glorified free expression and the pursuit of ecstasy. Their movement was short-lived but did produce original work such as Allen Ginsberg's poem "Howl" in 1955, and Jack Kerouac's novel *On the Road* in 1957. Kerouac and others celebrated unfettered individualism in concert with youth's typical quests. In a nuanced and sophisticated essay on the Beats, poet and novelist Fred Chappell called Jack Kerouac a "latter-day Huck Finn," and described his writing with gentle parody as "a prose of intoxicated exhilaration, a breathless relentless unstoppable forward-surging impulse."[48]

Kerouac, who in later years returned to the Catholicism of his childhood, was arguably the most engaging of the Beats. Before his death he told an interviewer, without irony, "We were just trying to find truth and meaning in life."[49] Self-destructive as some of the Beats seemed, others remained working artists faithful to their unorthodox ideas. Indeed, poet Lawrence Ferlinghetti, at this writing, regularly holds court and gives readings at San Francisco's City Lights Bookstore.

The Beats were imitated and romanticized by some college students, scorned by others. No one seemed to know whether beat stood for beaten down or beatific. They were true cultural subversives who struck chords that would later be heard by the counter-culture of the sixties and seventies.

Meanwhile, adolescents were profoundly affected by the combined forces of increasing affluence, a nascent sense of societal injustice, a new decline in conventional religious practices, and no memories of war or Depression. Increasingly aimed at the vast group of new consumers, the seductive powers of advertising and television generated rising expectations and an early sense of entitlement in people barely old enough to drive. These elements, mixed with a powerful new music-based youth culture and young women's dawning dissatisfaction with their place in society, led many up-and-coming baby boomers to detach themselves from the adult world. A rising divorce rate, the beginning of the sexual revolution and a restless, generalized skepticism contributed to a "generation gap" with the motto, "Don't trust anyone over thirty." Well before the Vietnam War polarized the nation, a chasm already separated youth of the sixties and seventies from a maturing silent generation.

6. sexual mores: inherited but changing

The silent generation tended to mirror their parents' social mores, accepting that dating, marriage, then sex was the proper order of things. These ideals were reinforced at every turn by religious teachings, books, magazine articles, peer pressure, and fear of out-of-wedlock pregnancy. In a 1957 book, Enid Haupt, editor of *Seventeen* Magazine, urged young women to "keep your first and all your romances on a beyond reproach level."[50] And many did just that. But not all; several feminist writers offer recollections from women who had rejected mid-century mores.[51] Looking back on his adolescence, another writer suggests that young middle-class men were also measured against a strict code. "The ground rules were explicit and unequivocal...You didn't see your wife unclothed until your wedding night."[52]

Summer porch party. Hedges Lake, New York, 1953

Such reports suggest that young people were not all liberated by Dr. Alfred C. Kinsey's studies (in 1948 and 1953) on the sexual habits of Americans. Indeed, critics of Kinsey's work later offered convincing arguments that Kinsey's research methods were seriously flawed.[53] This may explain why the public was so surprised by the reports: many did not see their own lives reflected in Kinsey's statistics. Nonetheless, Kinsey's reports on infidelity and premarital sexual experience were fully accepted and widely promoted, thus helping to build a false foundation for the sexual revolution of the sixties.

Enovid, the first oral contraceptive for women, was approved for sale in 1960. By taking pills on a prescribed monthly schedule, a woman could be assured of a nearly foolproof method of contraception. This innovation became an essential building block in the women's movement, and helped usher in an era of sexual freedom. Women could now plan their careers and families with an assurance previously denied them. The Pill, as it was known, hastened the demise of an already faltering social code.

Sensing drawbacks ahead, not all saw a better future in the sexual revolution. Indeed, sexually transmitted diseases, teen pregnancies, child abuse and abandonment, and divorce rates all rose sharply thereafter. Less than one out of twenty babies were born to unmarried women in 1960. By 2000 the figure was one in three. The century's end also brought widespread sexual activity among middle-school children.[54]

Dr. John Rock, the revered Boston gynecologist who was instrumental in developing the birth control pill, had his own doubts. He told a patient in 1963 that, like Robert Oppenheimer before him, he had great misgivings about what he had "helped unleash on the world."[55] He was concerned that to the extent women were sexually liberated, men might feel less responsibility for their own behavior and any unexpected pregnancies. By 2000, sociologist Barbara Dafoe Whitehead wrote, "Women have been (sexual liberation's) principal advocates, men its principal beneficiaries,"[56] and provided bleak statistics to confirm Dr. Rock's fears about the problematic legacy of the sexual revolution.

IV. MUSIC FOR A NEW ERA

More than any other art form, rock and roll helped to create, define and separate out a brand-new youth culture in the late 50s and early 60s, one that would prevail for the rest of the century and on into the next.

1. rock and roll

Among the many seismic forces separating adolescents of the late fifties from adults, few were more divisive than rock and roll. Parents were startled and irritated by the loud new sound, its pulsing beat and erotic style, its flamboyant performers. The music and all that was to flow from it soon saturated their lives.

Rock music contributed to more than just a spirit of rebellion. Once shaken loose from the adult world, youth of the early sixties began an ongoing critique of the nation. In time that mood of dissent served as a catalyst for both the women's revolution and the civil rights movement. Certainly many adults were leaders, strategists and foot soldiers, but youthful energy, inflamed by injustice, helped propel both movements forward.[57]

Rock and roll was a vehicle of youthful upheaval, inspiring changes in behavior, clothing, hairstyles, and political attitudes. Musically, rock was the product of a natural evolution in particular strands of American music. As one of several forces redefining sex as a form of recreation, rock was an ingredient in the sexual revolution.

Until the mid-fifties, young and old alike enjoyed the same popular music. Musical tastes were not yet subjects of intense debate or avenues of self-definition among adolescents. Singers such as Perry Como, Eddie Fisher, Rosemary Clooney, Tony Bennett, Pat Boone and Teresa Brewer sang of young love, but without sexual overtones. Mel Torme occupied his own velvet niche. Cross-over black musicians Nat King Cole, Louis Armstrong, Ella Fitzgerald, Johnny Mathis and Lena Horne recorded a variety of music, their romantic ballads attracting both white and black audiences.

Rock and roll was a seductive brew of many strains of indigenous American music—rhythm and blues, swing, gospel, rockabilly, folk, country and western. At first offered only on black radio stations, "race music" (as it was then called) was more emotionally charged than mainstream music and used double entendre and clever word play to mask its sexuality. In the early fifties, Alan Freed, a Cleveland disk jockey trained in classical music, began to play and promote the music of Fats Domino, Chuck Berry, Little Richard and other black performers. Moving to New York's station WINS, Freed promoted acceptance of rock and roll among white audiences."[58]

Hearing their music primarily on radio and records, audiences did not expect to *watch* musicians; instead they listened, and danced. But a powerful visual component was waiting in the wings. A new young singer, Johnny Ray, became famous in 1951 when his two hit songs "Cry" and "The Little White Cloud That Cried," sold four million records. Ray was white and his lyrics chaste, but his physical style galvanized teenage fans. He twisted his lean, rangy form, squirmed and all but collapsed on his knees while young audiences squealed at every move, every note. Music historians now agree that although Johnny Ray's flame burned briefly, he paved the way for the sexually charged, intensely emotional music and performing styles that would appear later in the decade and remain a norm thereafter.[59]

The sandpaper voice stirred something, we knew not what, within my friend Marilyn and me. We became obsessed with Johnny Ray's plaintive sounds and soft, falling locks of pale hair. The feelings wrung from each note were mysterious, promising. We did not yet know the word overwrought.

Being dutiful daughters, we first got permission from our parents before we cut school and took two hours of train, bus and subway to the concert at Brooklyn's palatial Paramount theatre. Once there, and intoxicated by Ray's sound cum kinetics, we joined thousands of smitten thirteen-year-olds screaming over every raspy wail.

At school the next day we found ourselves overnight celebrities. For our daring. Parental letters of permission notwithstanding, we were severely reprimanded by the principal. If we'd been horsewhipped, the thought of that voice, those words, ("...if your suhweethahrrt sends a letter of goodbah-ee, it's no suhee-cret, you'll feel be-ht-ter, if you cuh-ry-ee...") would have still made it the noblest, wisest, most loyal choice we'd ever made. The memory of that illicit day in Brooklyn illuminated our lives until we turned fourteen and forgot all about our mournful golden bard.

In 1954 the first rock and roll hit, "Sh-Boom" was recorded by a black group, the Chords, and a white group, the Crew Cuts. By 1955 sweet, popular songs such as "Unchained Melody," and "Cherry Pink and Apple Blossom White," still topped the best-seller list. That spring the film *Blackboard Jungle* appeared, featuring a stunning theme song, "Rock Around the Clock," performed by Bill Haley and the Comets, an all-white group who mixed electric guitars with drums, country, western, rhythm and blues. Their record rocketed up the charts and was to become one of the best-selling single records in music history.[60]

High school youth had found something all its own, an audacious, sassy music that offered a giddy sense of abandon to adolescents who had just begun to challenge conventional society. This was their music, written for them, no adults welcome. Listening to their own loud, dynamic, driving music allowed restless teenagers to feel bold and outrageous without actually having to be rebellious. Yet.

The national climate was ripe for the appearance of a new teen idol. After early success in Memphis and the rural south, nineteen-year-old Elvis Presley burst on the national scene in 1956 with a series of wildly successful television appearances. His undulating, suggestive movements soon earned him the name Elvis the Pelvis. The uninhibited sexuality, florid, sensual features and romantic voice stirred young girls to delirium. The August, 1956, *Look* magazine called Presley, "a wild troubadour who wails rock n' roll tunes, flails erratically at a guitar and wriggles like a peep-show dancer." No entertainer had been in equal measure so worrisome to parents and seductively liberating to youth.[61] In August, 2002, on the twenty-fifth anniversary of Presley's death, magazines reported that over a billion Presley albums and singles had been sold worldwide.

With Elvis Presley, the dam burst and rock and roll flooded the nation. Chuck Berry, Ray Charles, Buddy Holly, The Platters, Little Richard, Jerry Lee Lewis, Fats Domino, Chubby Checkers and dozens of other musicians were soon acclaimed by black and white audiences. Women were virtually unknown on the national rock stage.

Pat Boone's popularity was second only to Presley's. A clean-cut family man, he too, developed a far-ranging career, singing both rock and roll and romantic ballads, performing on television and in films. Some teenagers rejected Boone's avowed Christianity and conventional beliefs about sex, but others admired him for the same qualities. The simultaneous popularity of two men who projected opposing values suggests again the paradoxical nature of the fifties.

The new music was a harbinger of both the sexual revolution and the youth-oriented tastes, attitudes and mores that would not only dominate American culture but spread far beyond its borders well into the next century.

2. but not for all...

The silent generation, with some members just a little older than the rock and roll young, found itself on the far side of the generation gap. They had passed on to college or the working world just as the new youth culture spread its wings. Rambunctious rock and roll was for high school kids. The rock concert, later a staple of popular entertainment, had not yet materialized.

Collegians preferred jazz, classical music or the folk songs of the late fifties. Folksingers as varied as Odetta, Pete Seeger, and The Weavers toured the nation's campuses. The more commercialized music of the Kingston Trio was also popular on college campuses. In the late fifties, the best-attended musical events at Cornell University (which was reasonably typical of the Northeast) were concerts by visiting symphony orchestras or folksingers, and evenings with musical satirist Tom Lehrer. Also drawing crowds were gatherings that featured campus a cappella groups singing in close harmony old standards such as "In the Still of the Night." On the West Coast, campus folk singing was inspired by Josh White, Woody Guthrie and others who sought remedies to injustice through their music. "Folk music was our social currency," said a Californian recalling the late fifties on the Berkeley campus.[62] Young New Yorkers heard jazz greats such as Miles Davis or Charlie Parker playing in local clubs.

In 1961, I was a new teacher living around the corner from the Mt. Auburn St. Coffeehouse, just beyond the walls of the Harvard Yard. One spring evening, friends ran in the door, and in high excitement urged my roommate and me to hurry after them. "This girl, younger than we are, is singing at the Mt. Auburn, you've got to hear her. You've never heard such a voice." The crowd was so thick no gateman took our two dollars; we just wedged in. Packed tight on chairs, tables or floor, the audience listened enraptured as a young woman with long dark hair and a soprano pure as cold winter air sang "Barb'ry Allen." We returned night after night, bathing in that clear water voice and its ancient tales of tragic love and lost honor.

Within a year, Joan Baez would be nationally known. Bob Dylan soon urged Baez to include contemporary songs of protest, and a long career as both singer and social activist followed. In her sixties now, Baez remains politically active and in early 2002 sang in concert at New York's Town Hall.

It is worth noting that many non-rock musicians of the fifties have had astonishing staying power, even posthumously. Louis Armstrong, Ray Charles and Duke Ellington have long been hailed as musical geniuses. Nat King Cole is still revered as both jazz pianist and balladeer; Ella Fitzgerald and Billie Holiday have long since achieved immortality, with Peggy Lee just behind them. Until shortly before her death in 2002, Rosemary Clooney retained a voice untarnished by half a century of use. At age 74, Barbara Cook's golden tones packed houses in New York, London and Washington throughout 2002. After half a century of singing, Tony Bennett continues to draw young as well as older audiences. For those who love musical theatre, the first lyrics presented to Richard Rodgers by Oscar Hammerstein, "There's a bright golden haze on the meadow," open floodgates of memories from a golden age of now-classic works. Indeed, the line opens "Oklahoma," which was revived on Broadway in 2002, almost sixty years after its birth. Written in the fifties, the soundtracks of "Fiddler on the Roof," "Carousel," "The King and I," "West Side Story," and many others are readily available, and the shows still produced across the country. While it has not been revived in other forms, "Singin' in the Rain"(1952) is still considered by aficionados to be the finest of all film musicals.

The "roots music" of singers such as Roscoe Holcombe, Rev.Gary Davis and Bill Monroe was collected in Kentucky and Harlem by music historian John Cohen throughout the fifties. Its "high, lonesome sound" (the term coined by Cohen) of unadorned voices and old-time instruments found a large and appreciative audience in the 21st century, reflecting perhaps a changing popular sensibility.[63]

One can assume that jazz, folk, country, blues, classical music and music written for theatre will always have audiences. But it seems safe to say that, along with television, the new youth music and all it spawned formed one of the most relentless cultural forces of the twentieth century. As the baby-boomers who were rock and roll's earliest consumers grew older and continued to embrace the sounds of their youth, rock and its various descendants and outcroppings became virtually mainstream. For better or worse, rock has influenced music, advertising, film, theatre, television, language, clothing, manners, mores and some aspects of politics and business. At the opening of a new century, the preeminence of pop culture seems secure as its influence reaches down to younger children with every passing year.

IV. RACE, ETHNICITY AND CIVIL RIGHTS

Many Americans hoped that the grand collective struggle of World War II, followed so soon by Korea, would soften lines of distinction among the citizenry. "We're all in this together," had been a wartime slogan. The wars softened but did not dissolve deep strains of racial and ethnic prejudices in America. Cold War anxiety and Korea had distracted the nation's attention away from simmering problems of racial injustice. Obscured too were a host of other serious issues: environmental deterioration, lingering poverty, urban decay, and unequal conditions for women, homosexuals and disabled individuals.

Strong Women Tell Their Stories

1. postwar ethnic issues

Ongoing ethnic, religious, regional, class and racial tensions precluded anything like a harmonious blending of disparate peoples. During and after the war, persons of German and Japanese ancestry were especially subject to hostility. Members of virtually every ethnic group also experienced some animosity. A complex array of state and municipal "Jim Crow" laws dating back to the 1880s (Jim Crow was a minstrel show figure in the early 19th century) effectively segregated black people in every phase of southern life.

While the war with Germany had demonstrated the catastrophic consequences of nationally-sanctioned bigotry, anti-Semitism was nevertheless alive and well in the United States. Jewish writers such as Philip Roth and Saul Bellow were widely read in the fifties, and the film "Gentleman's Agreement" won the 1947 Academy Award for its depiction of prejudice against Jews. [64] Yet private clubs, college sororities and fraternities, and university admissions offices barely concealed their discriminatory policies.

Legal immigration had been reduced by race-based laws enacted in the 1920s. The nation was still a melting pot, however; European emigration including Jews and Gentiles earlier in the century accounted for one-seventh of the population by 1940. African-Americans constituted one-tenth of the population. Native Americans numbered 350,000. During a twenty-year period beginning in the early forties, five million farm workers had come to the U.S. from Mexico, and would constitute 12.5 % of the population by century's end.

Congress had so contained Asian immigration that by 1945 only 100,000 Chinese-Americans, and 130,000 Japanese-Americans lived in the U.S., most of them on the West Coast. Ostensibly for security reasons, the government decided in 1942 to intern 112,000 Japanese-Americans (some accounts put the number at 120,000) in ten western "relocation camps" for the duration of the war. This despite the fact that the majority of Japanese-Americans were naturalized citizens, many with sons and brothers fighting in the U.S. Army. In fact, the 442nd Regimental Combat Team, a Japanese-American Army unit, fought in Europe and was one of the most decorated front-line units of the war. In recognition of the eextraordinary injustice visited on Japanese-Americans, Congress in 1988 offered surviving internees official apologies and financial compensation.

Adolescent children of the Gittleman family, early 20th century immigrants to the USA from Russia. Eldest daughter Sarah, center, is still a practicing sculptor at age 96

Sunday School at Minidoka Internment Camp. Idaho, 1943. Sato Hashizume is at center wearing a plaid coat

Strong Women Tell Their Stories

Japanese culture urges the practice of *gamman,* stoicism in the face of adversity. Thus, until recent years, neither the nation, nor the descendants of those interned, learned much about the camp experience, or of the extreme hardships in returning home to financial ruin, prejudice and derision. Since the apology, reunions of fellow campers are held, children hear the stories, and tears are allowed to flow at last.[65] Sato Hashizume's story of life as a child in an Idaho internment camp is included in this volume.

The story of American treatment of its Native Americans is told in a long march of heartbreaking tales. In *Bury My Heart at Wounded Knee: An Indian History of the American West* (1970), Dee Brown tells the stories of Dakota, Nez Perce, Ute, Cheyenne, Navaho and Apache tribes. In his Pulitzer Prize-winning novel, *House Made of Dawn* (1968), Kiowa Indian N. Scott Momaday vividly portrays the anguish of Indians forced to straddle two cultures. Focusing on the Ojibe people, the novels of Louise Erdrich offer insights into contemporary Indian life, as do memoirs such as Joseph Iron Eye Dudley's *Choteau Creek, a Sioux Remembrance* (1992) and the 1998 film, "Smoke Signals." In the oral histories to come, Lumbee Indian Ruth Revels discusses her family's lifelong struggles on behalf of their tribe.

Individuals of Hispanic ancestry today constitute the nation's most rapidly growing ethnic group. Because they represent many countries of origin and varied histories, Hispanic people in America cannot be readily discussed in a brief essay. It should be noted however, that despite discrimination and language problems, Spanish-speaking immigrants have become leaders in education, business, government and the sciences. The final years of the 20th century witnessed an outpouring of work by young writers, artists and musicians from a variety of Hispanic backgrounds.[66] In her oral history, Californian Marie McKeever, of Mexican descent, describes a happy childhood spent in both Mexico and the United States.

2. black members of the silent generation: civil rights vanguard

Despite early civil rights efforts in the forties and mid-fifties, white America in the late fifties was not yet paying much attention to the plight of millions of black citizens. Young black men and women were largely excluded from the mainstream of American economic and political life across the country. But they too, were part of the Depression-born cohort. Far from being silent, many of their number were at the vanguard of early civil rights efforts. Some of their experiences are discussed here as well

Voices of the Silent Generation

as in the oral histories of Shirley Frye and Velma Watts.[67]

With most white Americans heedless of the urgent need for civil rights reform, black citizens worked on their own behalf throughout the postwar decades. The National Association for the Advancement of Colored People (NAACP), founded in 1909, won an important legal victory in 1946 precluding segregated facilities on buses and trains that crossed state borders. An interracial group of pacifists organized the Congress of Racial Equality (CORE) in 1942. CORE later used non-violent tactics to desegregate several public places in northern cities. Leadership in the forties by Roy Wilkins, A. Philip Randolph, Bayard Rustin, and years of grassroots work by unknown local activists cleared the road to milestone events of the fifties and sixties.

One million American black men had served in WWII in strictly segregated armed forces. Though they enlisted freely, (their 10% of the population producing 16% of the military), for the most part, black men were prohibited from combat and assigned to menial and personal service tasks. A few notable exceptions deserve mention. Needing soldiers in December 1944, the Army brought blacks into the Battle of the Bulge where they fought superbly. Nonetheless, old prejudices prevailed thereafter. An enlisted man observed bitterly, "Just carve on my tombstone, here lies a black man killed fighting a yellow man for the protection of a white man."[68]

The now-celebrated Tuskegee Airmen was an all-black fighter squadron of over nine hundred pilots, and thousands of navigators, bombardiers and support personnel. The Airmen flew more than 15,000 missions under the command of the late Lt. Col. Benjamin O. Davis, Jr. who would become the Air Force's first black general. Well aware of the value of their service to the nation, black veterans convinced President Truman to desegregate the Armed Forces in 1946. A ray of hope and determination began to flicker in black communities.

In the 1954 Brown v. Board of Education case, the United States Supreme Court ruled school segregation to be inherently illegal and unconstitutional. Thus was finally overturned the sixty-year-old Plessy v. Ferguson ruling that "separate but equal" schools could provide adequate education for black children. The 1954 ruling pierced the armor of Jim Crow and signaled a new day ahead for black children.

The importance of the Court's action can scarcely be exaggerated. An important step forward for black Americans, it was also a triumph for the NAACP. Thurgood Marshall, the Special Counsel who tried the NAACP

Colonel Ben Davis preparing for a flight

A few men of the famous "Red Ball Express," convoy drivers who kept the front line in France supplied. 1944

case before the Supreme Court, later became the first black member of the Court.

Despite the Court's efforts, however, segregated schools continued to flourish. President Eisenhower initially provided no leadership or support for desegregation; by 1957, not a single black child in the eight Deep South states attended public school with whites.[69] Another decade of

Not yet nationally known, Dr. Martin Luther King, Jr.
speaks at Bennett College, 1958
(Photo courtesy Otis Hairston)

protest and bloodshed would pass before the nation's schools were integrated and legal segregation finally dismantled.

Congress passed the Civil Rights Act in 1957, the first federal civil rights legislation in 82 years. Designed to protect the voting rights of black citizens, it was seriously weakened in order to appease Southern congressmen. As was the Fair Employment Practices Act of 1945, the 1957 law was also poorly enforced.

The fifties saw two other landmark events on the road to authentic freedom for black people in America. Arguably, the modern civil rights movement was born in Montgomery, Alabama in 1955. After a black woman, Rosa Parks, refused to relinquish her seat to a white man, as required by city law, the city's black citizens united to conduct a year-long bus boycott. Protesting segregation and consistently unfair treatment on city buses, ninety percent of Montgomery's bus-riding black citizens joined the effort and brought strong economic pressure to bear on the segregated city. Speaking at a rally before the bus boycott, Martin Luther King, Jr. revealed oratorical gifts that would catapult him to the forefront of the fledgling movement.

Strong Women Tell Their Stories

Two years later a national spotlight shone on the efforts of nine black students to integrate Central High School in Little Rock, Arkansas. Millions watched on television as a reluctant President Eisenhower federalized the National Guard to enforce court-ordered desegregation and protect the young people. One reporter observed that the nation was finally embarrassed into taking notice.

Revealing the best and worst of human behavior, both events drew heroic action from ostensibly ordinary citizens. The pivotal role of black women in these early efforts is particularly noteworthy. By refusing to give up her bus seat to a white man, Rosa Parks galvanized blacks to take action. In support of Parks and the cause she represented, college instructor Jo Ann Robinson produced overnight some 35,000 leaflets with which she and the women she called her "foot soldiers" would rally a majority of Montgomery's bus-riding black citizens to the cause. Those foot soldiers were aptly named, as they would walk many miles over the next 381 days.[70]

Opposition to the students trying to integrate the all-white school in Little Rock was so fierce that Daisy Bates of the NAACP offered to serve throughout their ordeal as protector of the six young women and three

Lunch counter sit-in at Woolworth's, February, 1960
(courtesy of *Greensboro News and Record*)

young men. As their guide and mentor, Bates reminded the students frequently that their efforts were for the future and for the lives of others. Interviewed years later, one of the pioneers said, "We never thought we'd live through the year. We thought we'd die there." Another, Gloria Ray Karlmark recalled, "It was like going to war every day, like hand to hand combat."[71]

Less-endangered, but also courageous, were Joanne Smart and Bettye Ann Davis who enrolled in 1956 as the first black students at Women's College in Greensboro, North Carolina. Encountering no overt hostility, they were nevertheless required to live alone in a separate wing of Shaw Hall. The four years were, however, ultimately positive for both women. Joanne Smart Drane, a forgiving and loyal alumna, later served on the University Board of Trustees.[72]

On February 1, 1960, four young black students sought and were refused service at a Woolworth's lunch counter in the same city. Declining to leave, they were soon joined by fellow students. By the fourth day, 63 of the 66 stools were occupied by young black men and women quietly doing their homework--while a hostile crowd stirred behind them.[73]

Local newspaper editor Hal Seiber suggests the episode did not degenerate into violence for several reasons: a progressive spirit in the city; effective black leadership; a restrained response by Clarence Harris, the Woolworth's manager; a well-disciplined police force led by an exceptional chief, Paul Calhoun; and the courtesy and solidarity of the black students.[74]

Sit-downs, as they were initially called, had been held in 16 southern cities since 1957, but Greensboro was the first to attract national attention. The courage and persistence of Ezell Blair, Jr., Joe McNeil, the late David Richmond and Franklin McCain galvanized young blacks across the country: within the week peaceful sit-in protests spread to fifty-four locations in nine southern states. The lid had finally blown. An estimated seventy thousand protesters, black and white, participated. Ohio, Illinois and Nevada were next, challenging segregation at lunch counters, in churches, parks, pools, restaurants, beaches and museums. An irresistible force had gained momentum and urgency.[75]

On July 25, 1960, the Greensboro Mayor's Advisory Committee issued a statement that recommended "that all stores...dispensing food serve all customers."[76] By the end of the summer, thirty-two other Southern cities had desegregated some eating facilities, and a year later 126 Southern cities had followed suit.

Once ignited, the movement surged across the country defying discrimination in education, voting, employment and housing across the country. Vivified by Martin Luther King's eloquence, aided by media exposure, court orders and an awakened nation, the passion of America's black people gradually brought an end to legalized segregation and barriers to the exercise of their voting rights. Despite significant progress, the struggle for black Americans to win a secure place in the nation would continue throughout the century.[77]

Tim Moore, raised in a Virginia orphanage, now an independent craftsman who purchased his own home at age 37.

The civil rights movement inspired other marginalized groups to speak out. Women, Native Americans, gay men and women, disabled people, and other minorities began to take action on their own behalf. The modern women's movement had not yet coalesced in the fifties. But World War II had changed expectations for women of all races. Drawn in to the turmoil of postwar events, shaping some, being shaped by others, women and minority groups were prepared by the end of the fifties to begin a measured journey toward their own unfettered citizenship.

VI. WE NEVER KNEW WE WERE A GENERATION

More than one individual has observed, a little wistfully, "We never knew we were a 'generation.'" Although disinclined to call collective attention to themselves, many of those born during the Depression nevertheless went on to make substantial contributions to American life. Men and women distinguished themselves in politics, business, the sciences, literature, the arts, and media.

The nineties saw Janet Reno become the nation's first female Attorney General, Ruth Bader Ginsberg installed as the second woman on the U.S. Supreme Court, and Madeleine Albright named Secretary of State. In 2002, Nancy Pelosi was sworn in as Democratic Party Whip. One third of the thirteen women elected to the United States Senate in the 2000 election were born in the thirties.[78]

Voices of the Silent Generation

As of 1990, the presidents of Brown University, Harvard, M.I.T., Princeton, Stanford, and Yale were all members of the silent generation, as were the chief executive officers of American Express, Apple Computer, Citicorp, General Electric and IBM, and the heads of the Army, Navy and Air Force," [79] After the 2000 election, Richard Cheney was elected Vice-President, Donald Rumsfeld was appointed Secretary of Defense and Colin Powell Secretary of State. Sam Bodman became Secretary to the U.S. Department of Energy in 2005.

Among those who report the news, Peter Jennings, Dan Rather, Barbara Walters, Ted Koppel and Tom Brokaw were all born during the Depression.

That the silent generation represents only ten percent of the population may partially explain why, despite such a record of leadership, it is one of the few birth cohorts never to have had a United States president elected from its numbers. Its men, and now women, have populated Congress, but the presidency skipped from World War II veteran George Bush to baby boomers Bill Clinton and George W. Bush.

One could argue that black men and women were the unsung redeemers of the fifties. While a number of African-American men achieved renown for their civil rights work, southern black women born in the Depression formed the unheralded moral center of many initial reform efforts. Long before Betty Friedan wrote about white middle-class women in thrall to the feminine mystique and the "problem with no name," the fortitude of minority women of the forties and fifties was tested daily as they struggled against discrimination at every turn. Women of color knew the name of their particular problem all too well and had begun to blaze forbidden trails against bigotry and its attendant poverty.

While largely unrecognized at the time, the separate but similar struggles of women of all backgrounds would ultimately play a significant role in the radical transformation of American society.

Some criticism of the fifties is justified—much about the period was deplorable. McCarthyism and its legacy of distrust left an enormous stain on the decade; discrimination against women, homosexuals and disabled persons was virtually uncontested; racial bigotry and injustice were inadequately addressed. That said, other aspects of the fifties are worth defending: the arts, science, literature, civic and community life flourished. The postwar economy offered many citizens unprecedented opportunities to improve their lives.

A full appreciation of the era must incorporate a many-layered and humane view of its men and women and their achievements. Though a troubled time, the decade was resoundingly innovative and exuberant. Its many contradictions and paradoxes were symptoms of inescapable transition in a world that had already begun its metamorphosis.

VII. WOMEN OF THE SILENT GENERATION

Historians and journalists have long described women of the silent generation as compliant victims of a repressive era. A few managed through luck, talent and ambition to transcend restrictions and excel in the arts, business, politics or the professions. The majority of women, however, were barred from full participation in American society by a web of laws and social norms. [80]

Still, for all the limitations imposed, most did not view themselves as passive victims. American women from the beginning have devised imaginative ways to live constructively and contribute to society. Alexis de Tocqueville said as much during a tour of America in 1830: " If anyone asks me what I think is the chief cause of the extraordinary prosperity and growing power of this nation, I should answer that it is due to the superiority of their women." [81]

The notion of a cohort of ineffectual females of the 1950s is gradually fading. Historians have begun to revise earlier unsparing assessments, now acknowledging the vitality and varied achievements of these women. Robert Putnam and others offer reminders that communities and families are sources of social capital—and the self-restraint without which a society flounders. Contemporary scholars note that women labored mightily on behalf of families and communities, and caution that focusing just on the oppression of women presents an inadequate view of history. [82]

Additionally, many more women than is commonly understood combined full-time work with marriage and children. They did so to help support their families, as do many today. During the 1950s, the employment of women soared, at a rate four times faster than men's. Forty percent of all women over 16 held a job by 1960, compared to 25% in 1940. [83]

Statistics show that few women were found in the professions or managerial positions; for example, a study commissioned in 1957 revealed that 95 percent of all doctors, lawyers, architects and natural scientists were male. Such figures tend to obscure the richness of women's real lives. Because their efforts did not mirror those of men, women's actual accomplishments have been undervalued. In fact, most women of the

1950s were not inclined to measure their own lives by the scope of men's achievements.[84]

A fair assessment would suggest that while these women broke few barriers, they functioned with great purpose and effectiveness. Few managed companies or sat on corporate boards, but they did manage families, and raise the nation's children. They planned baptisms and brises, birthdays, weddings and funerals; coped with tragedies and celebrated triumphs. They enriched community life with a host of school, church and civic activities. Volunteers for the League of Women Voters provided information on political candidates and groups of neighborhood women united for action on local issues. In short, as one historian noted, they invested their careers as homemakers with talent, significance and creativity. Theirs was surely an underpaid profession.

Writer and critic Mary McCarthy described in 1951 the typical educated woman as a force in her community: "She is the woman behind the League of Women Voters, ... and yes, the 4-H Club. She won't very often be found sitting at the luncheon bridge table. She'll be found actively, thoughtfully, even serenely playing her role as an intelligent citizen."[85]

Without necessarily expecting to transform society, women of the silent generation made gradual changes in their own lives. By working, volunteering, and raising children with high expectations from life, they provided a semblance of stability just before a new quest for individual freedoms collided with traditional notions of family, community and motherhood.

1. women, work and World War II

Prior to World War II one quarter of women over the age of sixteen worked; these few were typically young and single. It was widely thought unseemly for middle-class married women to work outside the home and only fifteen percent held jobs. Most married women with children who worked did so only out of necessity.

The war fractured old rules and expectations. Wartime labor shortages prompted an unprecedented national effort to recruit women into the work force in large numbers. Employers set aside old biases against hiring married women; three-quarters of the new female workers were married. Factory jobs offered them higher pay than their traditional positions in schools, shops, laundries, restaurants, offices and hospitals.

In 1940, women constituted eight percent of workers employed in the production of durable goods. That percentage rose to 25% by 1945. Over

Strong Women Tell Their Stories

Pvt. Henrietta Ingram, Women's Auxiliary Corps (WACS), 1944

WASP (Women's Air Force Service Pilot) Susie Bain, 1943

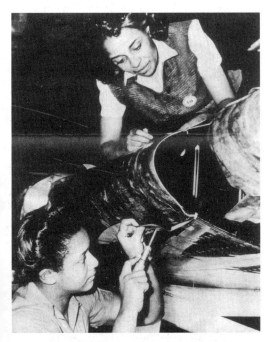

Women factory workers install a de-icer on the wing of a bomber, 1944

Gauging and weighing cartridges, 1943 (all photos courtesy of Women Veterans Historical Collection)

18 million women filled jobs vacated by men or created by the war.

Discarding ancient doubts about women's capacity for strenuous or complex work, companies hired thousands to build urgently needed ships, tanks and airplanes. Laboring in steel mills and factories, they learned riveting, pipefitting and welding-- and performed well. Women operated industrial machinery, drove buses, steered cranes and tractors; they made munitions, unloaded freight, built dirigibles, gliders and bombers.

World War II women's recruitment poster

Black women, previously excluded from skilled industrial jobs at even higher rates than white women, also stepped into the gap. With many working in the chemical, rubber and metal industries, their employment numbers jumped from 60,000 to 200,000 after 1941. Some 12,000 Native American women volunteered for the war effort, with 800 enlisting in the armed forces and thousands of others working in factories as riveters and machinists.

Beginning in 1942, approximately 86,000 women joined the Women Accepted for Voluntary Emergency Service (WAVES). Thousands more joined Women's Auxiliary Corps (WACS) and served as clerks, drivers, telephone operators, medical technicians, cooks, couriers, and mail routers. Nine hundred of the 4500 women hired by the Office of Strategic Services served overseas as spies. By war's end over 70,000 nurses had offered service to the Army and Navy Nurse Corps. The Coast Guard recruited 11,000 women for shore duty as SPARS.

Of the 25,000 women who volunteered for Women Air Force Service Pilots (WASP), just over a thousand were chosen to fly military planes on domestic missions. They logged 60 million miles and ferried over 12,000 aircraft between factories and military bases. The WASPs transported personnel and supplies, towing aerial gunnery targets and ferrying war-worn planes home. Former WASP Susie Bain describes occasional acts of sabotage, and the pilots' need to find their own way home after delivering aircraft. Meanwhile Douglas Aircraft, one of the largest aircraft factories, employed 22,000 women to build bombers and ferry planes to both fronts.

The late Major Charity Adams Earley was one of two black women to hold high wartime rank in the WACS. When the only all-black Women's Army Corps unit to serve overseas during World War II was sent to Europe, Major Adams was named battalion commander for her unit of 850 African-American women. Asked in later years how it felt to have made history, Major Adams Earley replied, "You don't know you're making history when it's happening. I just wanted to do my job."[86]

A *Newsweek* cover story in 1951 highlighted the military career of WAC Col. Mary Hallaren. A former school teacher, Col. Hallaren was asked upon enlisting after Pearl Harbor what someone as short as she (5 feet tall) could do for the war. An adventurer who had already hitchhiked across Canada and Mexico, she replied, "You don't have to be six feet tall to have a brain that works."[87]

Most women initially worked for their paychecks and to support the war effort. But they soon found other kinds of satisfactions: camaraderie with new colleagues, mastery of skills, the discovery of unexpected abilities—and the sheer pride and pleasure of doing work the nation considered important.

In the 1960s, while teaching at a college near Willow Run, Michigan, I first heard of that town's famous World War II product, the B-24 Liberation bomber plane. I would not learn until years later of the unique role Michigan's women had played in producing the aircraft that became the backbone of the U.S. Army Air Force strategic air campaign in Europe.

Liberators were used in virtually every theatre of conflict. The main plant, in San Diego, was producing only two bombers a month when Charles E. Sorenson, a Ford engineer, was brought in to design and build the Willow Run factory. Within a year the women of Willow Run were producing B-24 bombers at a rate of 462 a month. As many as sixty percent of the factory's employees were women working as riveters, punch press operators, and unofficial aircraft delivery pilots.[88]

While working as a researcher in the 1990s for a documentary film, Marcy Gray of Ann Arbor interviewed women who had built B-24s at Willow Run. In conversations so many years after the war, Marcy discovered these octogenarians' intense pride in their wartime work. One woman displayed a well-worn treasure, retained for more than half a century—her riveting gun. (1)

2. postwar years

The war's end changed everything once again. The Selective Service Act assured returning veterans of preferential treatment in the competition for peacetime jobs. As war requirements ended and factories contracted, women were among the first to be let go. Nearly one million workers, most of them women in the aircraft industry, were laid off immediately after VJ day. The Willow Run plant, for example, had employed over 42,000 workers at peak production in 1944. By 1946, it had closed.[89]

Over two million more women left wartime jobs for other reasons. Many sought better opportunities wherever they could be found. Others returned to homes and families, eager to place needs of neighborhood over those of nation. The GI Bill of 1944 enabled veterans to attend college and some of their wives to remain at home with young children.

As industries shifted rapidly to the profit potential of pent-up consumer needs, many women went back to work, with 2.75 million employed by late 1946, a million more than in 1940. Most were in their forties and fifties. If they had been changed by their wartime jobs, so had their bosses. It was clear now to these men that mature women were competent and eager to do good work (but not, they seem to have believed, worthy of promotion at the same rate as men).

Successful wartime work notwithstanding, most women returned to sex-segregated workplaces. Few opportunities for advancement beckoned. "Rosie the Riveter," one historian commented, "had become a file clerk."[90] Average weekly wages for women fell by twenty-five percent and salaried women earned just over half the average salary for men.

Increase in women's employment relative to pre-war levels was a key demographic feature of the postwar period. In fact, historian William Chafe calls it the most striking feature of the 1950s. Working women had learned much about themselves in the war years: they were capable, could learn new skills, put in a full workday, and still manage a home. Most mothers of young children chose not to juggle work and family life after the war, unless obliged to, but a new range of possibilities had been revealed. World War II marked a turning point in the lives of American women.[91]

Wartime work brought a degree of legitimacy to the idea of paid work for married women. Norms for white, middle-class mothers of young children had not yet changed. But behavior eventually eroded custom and convictions. A decade after the war ended, the average wife (including all economic levels, not just middle-class) in America was employed until her first baby was born. She stayed home for several years, returning to work when her youngest child started school. By 1948, 25 percent of women with children between ages 6 and 17 held jobs, and by 1960 the rate approached 40 percent.[92]

Mary Rhodes of Philadelphia was the youngest child in an African-American family in Baton Rouge, Louisiana. Born just before the Depression, she knew hard times, as did her six older siblings. Though an education had not been available to them, the postwar economy offered them jobs and new hope for the future. Seeing the potential in Mary, a bright, energetic teenager, her brothers and sisters pooled their savings and paid all of Mary's college expenses. During a 1991 interview, she recalled, "They never let me down. Those envelopes arrived every single week and just kept me going." Mary went on to marry and combine raising her four children with a long teaching career and a lasting marriage. Ever the educator, she now travels across the nation as a volunteer for Al-Anon. (2)

Most prewar legal and social constraints for women would remain firmly in place for over a decade while the nation repaired itself. But there would be no lasting return to old ways. War and a vigorous postwar expansion of industry had released a new energy into the country and set in motion a drive toward independence for women that would not be reversed.

3. stirrings in the fifties

Two years after the end of World War II, Life magazine's editors featured a lengthy article about a growing discontent they sensed in the country. Entitled "American Women's Dilemma," the piece argued that men and women alike had become disoriented by an emerging conflict between traditional and progressive ideas about the roles, rights and responsibilities of American women. Margaret Mead agreed. "Choose any criteria you like," wrote Mead, "and the answer is the same: women--and men--are confused, uncertain and discontented with the present definition of women's place in America."[93]

The Second Sex, published in 1949, advanced the debate a step. Simone de Beauvoir's arresting portrait of women as second-class citizens was denounced by a number of male critics and hailed simultaneously by female intellectuals praising its accuracy, scholarship and relevance. Though a sound intellectual achievement, the densely written book did not win popular readership. More than a decade passed before a book arrived that would galvanize women to action.[94]

Many young women entering adult life in the fifties inherited from their Depression-era parents a scarcity mentality (be grateful for what you have, don't expect more). They had been taught to respect family, authority and public institutions. Just as young women bowed to conventional notions of marriage and femininity, so too, young men accepted registering for the draft when they turned eighteen. These values seemed reasonable to young people of the time but would weaken later in the decade as hints of future social disruption emerged in film, literature, and rock music. [95]

Working women had already perceived the need for a more equitable basis for relating to men at work and at home. But few were prepared to press for change in a society still resistant to social reform. A small number of educators, political leaders and social critics affirmed the need for better opportunities for women in education and the work place. Others saw any change in the status of women as a threat to established values and the social order itself. [96]

Life magazine took up the same theme again in 1956, this time devoting a full issue to the same problems addressed nine years earlier. The magazine on this occasion highlighted a variety of contemporary choices faced by American women. Articles told stories of working mothers, single women pursuing careers, clubwomen, female politicians, and stay-at-home mothers. Praising all the women's choices, and acknowledging their struggles, the editors nevertheless urged everyone to remember to be feminine. [97]

Members of The National Manpower Commission, established in 1957 to explore the country's workplace needs, were astonished to discover how important womanpower was to American life. In 1957 the commission published its findings in a book called *Womanpower*, which provided details on the number of married women working outside the home. The public was so surprised by these figures that another conference was hastily convened. That conference published its findings in 1958 as "Work in the Lives of American Women," and used the term "revolution" to describe the new patterns in American life. Neither report gave adequate attention to the type of jobs women held, nor to their salaries.

While these studies helped to establish the working married woman as a fact of American life, they did little to change a culture in which such women juggled their work and family lives with little assistance. Professional childcare centers were virtually unheard of, and society insisted on traditional ideas of femininity above the quest for equal rights. Adult women were expected to be primarily maternal and deferential.

Seventy percent of all women in the professions were in teaching, nursing and library positions, all profoundly important work, but considered by some in later years to be typical nurturing women's jobs. Also revealing is the fact that only 9 percent of suburban women worked outside the home in 1950, compared to 27 percent of women in the population as a whole. [98]

The dislocation fostered by new assignments for women in the World War II years persisted and grew, acknowledged by a few but initially neither fully understood nor welcomed by the public at large. Few reforms surfaced in the fifties and most of the traditional barriers to women's equality held firm. However, the number of women at work continued to grow steadily. A tenuous balance was maintained. American society was in a state of fermentation, but few predicted the explosive transformation just ahead.

4. welcome to the sixties

In 1961, Eleanor Roosevelt and Esther Peterson badgered to life a Commission on the Status of Women. Mrs. Peterson served at the time as head of the Women's Bureau in the Department of Labor and Mrs. Roosevelt remained a widely respected public figure. The two were determined to bring women's needs and rights to the attention of a largely indifferent Kennedy White House.

With branches throughout the country, the Commission effectively publicized the breadth and depth of discrimination routinely experienced by women of all ages and in every walk of life. Few collective efforts or laws had yet evolved to encourage the strongest, or protect those in greatest need.

Of all that has been written since 1960 in support of the feminist cause, nothing landed with greater force than Betty Friedan's *The Feminine Mystique*. Brave, fiery and bold, it joined social science, anecdote, history, sexual theorizing and personal philosophy into a passionate argument. Published in 1963, the book instantly found a large, responsive audience.

Women's lives, said Friedan, needed serious re-examination. The happy housewife and mother so exalted by post-war America was a myth. Checked on every side by ancient biases and hobbled by arbitrary constraints that limited professional and personal growth, middle class white American women were suffering acutely from "the problem with no name." They wanted and deserved the same freedoms taken for granted by men. [99]

Voices of the Silent Generation

The Feminine Mystique was bound to be controversial. One early reviewer objected to the book's "sweeping generalities," and many women simply did not recognize Friedan's description of their lives. The book barely acknowledged working class women; women of color, who confronted sexism and bigotry daily, were virtually ignored. Also, the book's theoretical underpinning suffered over time for its dependence upon the work of Alfred Kinsey and Bruno Bettelheim, whose reputations have since declined precipitously.[100]

But none of these criticisms mattered to the millions who saw themselves in Friedan's pages. Traveling extensively while spreading her message tirelessly across the country, Friedan offered a vision of emancipation to discontented women. Soon recognized as godmother to the second wave of feminism, Friedan is today widely credited with igniting a movement that would introduce a radically new way of thinking about one half of the human race.

Circumstances converged in the sixties to set the women's movement in motion. The new feminist vision was so powerful that surprisingly disparate groups coalesced: hardy holdovers from the old Left of the forties, older women in public service, and young white, middle-class women inspired by Betty Friedan's book. Stirred to action by the Vietnam War and civil rights movement, female college students contributed youthful energy and zeal.

Following Friedan's success, dozens of feminist theorists and social critics took up her cause in earnest, creating an intellectual foundation for the women's movement. Among them were Germaine Greer, Kate Millett, Robin Morgan, Ti-Grace Atkinson, Dorothy Pitman Hughes, Shulamith Firestone, Susan Brownmiller and Florynce Kennedy, to name but a few. Later, Gloria Steinem, co-founder of *MS*. magazine, would emerge as an enduring symbol of feminism. Together these writers and many others produced books, essays, articles, lectures, and conferences centering on feminist theory, women's history and the many forms of inequality visited upon women. The finest thinkers on the subject of women—among them historian Gerda Lerner, ethicist Jean Bethke Elshtain and legal scholar Mary Ann Glendon—went a step further in consistently offering a vision of improved conditions for children and men as well as women.

The Equal Pay for Equal Work Act of 1963 was followed by the Civil Rights Act of 1964, the latter containing a provision forbidding gender-based discrimination. The laws did not signify a true change of heart in a nation still largely committed to old customs, habits and expectations.

Strong Women Tell Their Stories

The "second wave" of feminists (the first wave being those who secured the vote for women in 1920) recognized that repair of society on the scale proposed required dedicated advocates, sure of their cause and capable of building a solid theoretical structure to support it. Ardent new feminists met both tests, bringing a prodigious commitment of energy, time and will. More than equal to the formidable task before them, they would gradually win the support of a previously indifferent, often hostile, public.

While it was by no means a seamless struggle, and ended with a variety of feminist factions, forty years of intense effort brought feminist goals to partial fruition. Millions of women and men from all walks of life gradually set aside old notions as one stricture after another fell before the power of an idea whose time had finally come. As a new century opens, the nation accepts women's right to choose the course of their own lives and exercise their abilities across the full spectrum of human endeavor.

Women of the fifties did not view themselves as a political entity; feminist consciousness and the power inherent in collective action were just around the corner but not yet available to them. Still, many lived fruitful, satisfying lives, whether in the context of home or workplace. Some made distinctive contributions to the arts, literature, medicine, science, business and communications. Indeed by 1955, women were employed in every one of the 446 occupations noted in the 1950 census, though few held high positions. Progress was slow in the fifties, but also inexorable. While largely obedient to society's outmoded expectations for them, women of the silent generation nonetheless became quiet harbingers of change.

5. seventeen strong women

Women have long employed stamina, discipline, intellect, love and will to build the character of succeeding generations—and to make their own lives productive. As the oral histories to come testify, many women of the silent generation, whether single or married, toiling at home or elsewhere, struggled to make their lives fulfilling. These seventeen women did so with considerable success.

Their stories portray individuals born into a Depression and while in childhood keenly aware of World War II. They experienced the Korean and Cold Wars in the fifties, and a protracted conflict in Vietnam throughout the next decade. As young adults they were subject to intense social and legal pressures to define themselves primarily as wives and mothers. However, since some of their own mothers or aunts worked outside the home during WWII and thereafter, their new role models were often at variance with society's messages. Indeed, the U.S. Labor Department reported that by 1994 nearly three-quarters of women in their age bracket held full-time jobs.

The sixties brought women of the silent generation to the cusp of change: a reevaluation of roles and relationships, perhaps an implicit reproach to their own life choices. Some guarded old values, while others saw personal and professional possibilities scarcely imagined just a decade earlier. In fact, most women in these collected stories defended some traditional beliefs while also embracing fresh new ideas. They grasped early on that women's roles vary over the course of a lifetime.

As others of the silent generation, these seventeen women were required to be strong, competent—and alternately patient and impatient with a society about to change forever.

Part II
Oral Histories

DORIS BETTS
Introduction

Known for her writing talents and generosity to students, Doris Betts is a beloved figure on the lively Chapel Hill literary scene. She declines to play *grande dame* of North Carolina belles-lettres, however. Her exuberant laugh is the one heard over the din at crowded gatherings and she is as available to students as to celebrated writers.

Younger writers Randall Kenan, the late Tim McLaurin and others have testified to Doris Betts' strong influence on their work. Recent graduates as well as alumni in their forties speak fondly of her as their finest teacher.

Doris Betts has won the Dos Passos Prize, the American Academy of Arts and Letters Medal, and an Academy Award for the short film made from her story "The Ugliest Pilgrim." She is the author of six novels and three collections of short stories. In their astringency, spareness and punch, her early stories recall the work of Raymond Carver or Flannery O'Conner. The novels of her maturity suggest an expanded, more hopeful view of humankind.

A revered teacher of writing for over forty years, Doris also served as chairwoman of the faculty at the University of North Carolina at Chapel Hill, and in 1990 was awarded an honorary doctorate by her alma mater. And all this accomplished by a woman who never finished her Bachelor's degree.

Doris and her husband, lawyer and judge Lowery Betts, live in the country outside bustling Chapel Hill. After their daughter and two sons grew up, Doris and Lowery wanted "something else to nurture together," and bought a horse. Within a few years, nineteen handsome horses roamed the grassy paddocks near the house. Doris enjoys the pleasing contrast between the mental exercise of writing and the physical work of caring for horses. A lover of plants as well as animals, she grows antique roses near the perennial garden. On the day I visited, masses of nodding, fragrant blossoms embraced the unpretentious two-story house. The Betts indeed seem to nurture together successfully.

Family, students, stories, novels, church and service work, horses, garden— each offers a glimpse of Doris Betts' generous nature, appetite for work, and abundant talent. She confesses that the days are too short to attend to all commitments, yet she is known for readiness to take on new assignments.

In her late fifties at the time of our taping, Doris spoke candidly of her uneasiness about the course of her work as a writer. When asked about risks taken in her life, she replied, " Right now feels to me like the riskiest time. The great risk is to not keep going. It's easier to delay writing than it once was and I don't have the same fever to write that I once had. It requires more discipline, but I do have a certain stubborn tenacity."

"Strange, because I ought to feel more secure. It's not so much success that is sought, but to feel each book is better than the one previous. I was disappointed by certain aspects of the last one."

"For a writer it can be so easy to repeat what works well. But you need to test yourself by writing something that is new for you. *Souls Raised From the Dead,* the book I'm working on now, is a novel about medical ethics, and is difficult to write. Many of the issues are so new! We've not previously had to consider some of the problems that have arisen because of advances in medicine. Many situations people must confront are unimaginable. If these issues are to be examined unblinkingly, there will be places where the ethics are not clear. Many of the questions are unanswerable. So all of this is risky for me...."

For most authors, writing fiction is a high-wire walk. Doris Betts, with no small effort of will, continues her lifetime habit of taking just such risks.

Doris Betts
Chapel Hill, North Carolina
1990

I would like to write convincingly about how difficult life is for most people, and how astonishing even so are the courage and achievement of many who persevere and make something of it. There ought to be some place in literature that pays tribute to virtue, that acknowledges something admirable about the human condition without falling off the edge into sentimentality.

looking back

I grew up in a rented apartment near the Statesville Cotton Mill. The apartment was in an old Victorian house with chickens out back as well as peonies, a fish pond and railroad tracks nearby. In that world a child could explore for long distances, whether crawling under the parked

Doris Betts, 2004 (photo courtesy Chris English)

boxcars, walking the tracks, or investigating the sawmill. I also worked with my grandfather on a farm six miles west. Since I had no brothers or sisters, I have memories of being alone on the farm, making up characters and stories.

I went to Mulberry Street School, the same school my father had attended, and we loved to tell one another that the old building had been condemned. I think it's still in use. I dream still of the auditorium with its tin-embossed ceiling, plaster curlicues, draped stage curtain, high ceiling, and those oil-smelling wooden floors. It was the school for mill children, so you didn't have to be very smart to stand out because most came from families with a hard row to hoe. And they didn't necessarily encourage reading. The school was run by a host of maiden-lady schoolteachers: strict, excellent teachers, rather frightening. They scared us to death and taught us a great deal.

I was nine when Pearl Harbor occurred and much of my childhood is associated with having a peaceful, loving life against a background of dimly understood war: blackouts, sirens, the collecting of scrap metal. Certain ranks were earned for collecting scrap metal and I became a second lieutenant. Also played mostly with boys--war games, commandos and the like.

I was very much a tomboy, not happy with being a girl for years yet. Ours was a tough school with many playground fights. I fought a lot and was often in trouble, never wanted to be thought of as a mere girl; femaleness was beneath contempt for me at the time. I absorbed a great deal of Hemingway-style stiff-upper-lip beliefs. Never cry, always fight back, always get up if you're knocked down. And keep getting up. None of which I now consider particularly important! But I suspect that is the way many children survive, by becoming streetwise, tough.

My best friends lived in the mill village but my parents were strict about visiting; I could go for an hour and was quite paranoid about being back home on time. I didn't bring home the stories of fights and bruises; ours was a gentle home and my mother would have been shocked. You didn't say you'd been in a fight—you just said you fell down and skinned your knee. That was part of the code.

I remember one fight in sixth grade; the boy threw me in a ditch and I said that I would get even if it were the last thing I ever did! Recently I saw the man he now is, and after all these years I felt rage come boiling up. But it's a little late, so I guess I never will get even with him now!

My grandfather was important to me and I've written several stories about him. All those memories have fused together in stories about mill town life and that Victorian house. One story, "The Spies in the Herb House," is about the old herb house in Statesville and about war. It's a direct autobiographical sketch, as is "All That Glisters Isn't Gold." The names have been changed a little. The word is glitters now, but glister is the old word and so much prettier, don't you think?

I was very much a loved child, by both parents. I never doubted that love, and didn't know it was a gift. I thought everyone was loved, and assumed the world was a friendly place. If you believe the world to be friendly, you do not guard yourself all the time. I had to learn to be on guard when I encountered the first negative people in my life, but was an adult by then. It's a great gift to grow up feeling valued by the most important people in your life.

I don't think I was as good a parent as mine were for me. My mother was extremely religious, and deep down she thought secular books might destroy belief, were perhaps dangerous. Though her child was in love with something she didn't share, she nevertheless stood aside and actively encouraged my reading, though she must have been apprehensive. My father, who'd had no chance to go to college, might have feared he would watch his child leave home, become snobbish, and never return. Still, unselfishly, he encouraged me. I was just very fortunate. And didn't even know it. I can't even say I was that good a child. And became a dreadful adolescent too. But I got paid back when my children were teenagers!

Going to college was almost accidental for me. We had very little money. Though I had been a finalist for the Angier-Duke scholarship, we couldn't have afforded the costs over and beyond that. But by that time I had been for some time a sportswriter for the high school conference. As I phoned in sports news to the *Greensboro Daily News,* at two or three in the morning, the sports reporters would ask about my college plans.

When I said I couldn't afford to go to college they said yes, you can; you can go to Woman's College, (now the University of North Carolina at Greensboro) and there are many ways to get help. Before this I had just despaired of ever going. So that's what I mean by luck. My mother says never say luck, say Providence.

But why should those sports writers have bothered? It was very kind of them. There are so many people to be grateful to, and I wonder what would have happened had I not encountered this person or that one.

What if I had not gone, for instance, to a college where the writing program was very strong? I went there thinking that I would transfer to Chapel Hill for journalism. But Peter Taylor was there in Greensboro, and Randall Jarrell, and others, all magnificent teachers. That experience turned out to be formative for me. No matter how carefully we plan, it comes down to being in the right place at the right time. There is a moment when you can choose to take advantage of something, or not. When I was looking forward into future life I thought of it as a straight line or progression, something I could plan and then just do. Instead it is rhythm, a sequence of cycles. But it is not true that things work out just the way you believe they will.

As to ethnic and religious influences, my background is Scots-Irish. I'm just now reading a book about the Scots and I didn't realize they were such barbarians when they came to this country! They had an impact on temperament in Piedmont North Carolina. Most were yeoman farmers, workers, doers, not abstract thinkers, but the kind of people who hold the world together.

Most of my early life was spent on farms with rural people in Statesville or with blue-collar people. They have affected my outlook; I have a great fear of snobbery, a tendency to condemn very quickly what I think is snobbery. It's defensiveness, perhaps, for I'm sometimes mistaken.

I almost never saw my kinfolks sit down, and if they did they had work in their hands. They were snapping beans, sewing or repairing something.

Voices of the Silent Generation

religion

My religious background has been significant. Various critics have written about themes in my writing, suggesting that I have a Calvinistic outlook on human nature and the self. My beliefs are there, at some level, in my work, but I would never want the verb "proselytize" used about my fiction.

I am now Presbyterian, but I grew up in the Associate Reformed Presbyterian Church which was much more conservative. They still do not ordain women as ministers or elders. We sang no hymns, just psalms from the old Scottish Psalter. We memorized a great deal of Scripture, and both catechisms. I was there Sunday morning, Sunday evening, Wednesday night prayer meeting, and choir practice.

There were periods when I thought I might have a vocation for the church. That really pleased my mother. I should back up and say that my mother had been born with a cleft palate, which in her middle age was surgically repaired. But she had some difficulty in speaking and was rather shy as a result. As a young girl, she had made a promise to God that if she ever had a child she would give the child to the church. I was aware of that in the vague way that children are, but then one day it hit me like an avalanche. So from time to time I would think of pleasing my mother in the way Samuel pleased Hannah in the Old Testament. I was also caught up in the moral fervor of the times. But eventually I hit teenage rebellion. And young adult rebellion.

Since regular Bible reading was very much a part of life, the King James Bible has had a powerful influence on my love of language. Those early experiences also form one's whole outlook. You may or may not maintain the precise religious framework that you inherited and absorbed. I stayed out of the church for many years, left the faith in college as many do, and didn't come back for years.

But even while I was an expatriate, my philosophy had already been formed; I looked for meaning and purpose, which meant that I wrote a different type ending to my stories than, let's say, Donald Barthelme does. It meant taking ethical commitments seriously and believing that social action is important. It also involved that Calvinist mix or paradox; my parents used to say, "You can't make a silk purse out of a sow's ear, but that's no excuse for not trying."

So in the first stage a young person notices that human nature is flawed. But then comes the realization that we are nonetheless responsible for making the best of everything, of ourselves, of others, of our work. Things may go wrong but it's still your job, your assignment, to contribute, make things better. Such an outlook produces a work ethic and affects whatever you do with your life. If you have a religious background, you cannot assume that things will just happen or not happen. There is either a meaning, or you impose one!

That is in my writing, but in my twenties and thirties I believed I had rebelled sufficiently to be a French existentialist like Camus or Sartre. It turned out I was lying to myself! The bedrock doesn't go away--orthodoxy may go away, thank goodness, but something fundamental doesn't.

In the last ten or twelve years, since I've come back to the church, I've been fairly active. I've taught Sunday School, been an Elder, even preached on occasion. I have orthodoxies about which I'm uncertain; but the big discovery is that the church you return to is not the one you left. The church is full of other seekers, and some have religious doubts of their own. I don't know what happened to all those self-righteous hypocrites. I don't find them in the pew next to me, as I expected as an adolescent. There is a mythical church and a real one; the real one is composed of fellow strugglers and fellow pilgrims. That has been a good discovery, having the stereotypes in my own mind cast away.

When you're young you find fault everywhere--except in yourself! I do believe in the traditional religious teaching that we grow through our suffering. It's psychologically true as well. Another way to put it is: "All wounds heal unless you die from them." And the healing process has therapeutic values. I have not experienced the worst kinds of suffering. So far. But there are always fears and worries for anyone whose life is involved with the lives of others.

Suffering and feelings of guilt should not be sought, but they add a resonance and empathy without which life is mechanical. And guilt can galvanize us into action. The Calvinist view is that when suffering comes, and it will, the only choice is what to do with it. Since few of us get through life unscathed, it's the attitude we bring to pain and loss that matters, and the uses to which we will put them. Otherwise we are at the mercy of our troubles. We can't always control them but we can try to move in some kind of rhythm with the ebb and flow. We can learn patience and sympathy for our common lot.

a natural life

The rhythms of nature, animals, gardening remain important to me. After all those years, here I am back on a farm. People wonder about our having nineteen horses, four dogs, but it is all very calming; it seems the natural rhythm, whereas Chapel Hill sometimes seems very frenetic, artificial, or perhaps it just calls on a narrower part of one's self. Yet I need that larger canvas, too.

In "The Ugliest Pilgrim," the story you asked about, there is a moment when a deer appears and is frozen in time; that is close to a corporeality of beauty--so temporal, so fleeting. I'm very glad to be in the country where as many as ten deer pass by and leap over the fence; it's like a wave of Santa's reindeer. Their grace is indescribable. In time some individual deer even become recognizable.

Animals give meaning and pattern to the landscape. If you love animals, the sad part is that they die. But then the cycle turns and you have others; it renews your feelings that the cycle turns toward life, not just towards death. You are reminded that death is necessary to feed life.

A nest with two baby wrens is up in the barn now. That nest has been in five different places, because the cat has been after it. When I feed the horses tonight, I will tiptoe over there and see that those two birds are still there and warm. One day I will check on them and they will have flown. I will be as pleased as if I had been the mother wren myself. Not because I've protected them, but because I've been able to watch the process. Even without being able to affect the outcome. You can make things worse, but you can't be the creator. You come back to mystery.

There's a black snake living in the storage room under the house. I don't mind him living there; I just don't want to be surprised. In fact, when the summer got very hot, I took water down to him. He's very graceful and very beautiful. He takes care of the mice. So, simply to observe what black snakes do is an aesthetic pleasure as well as a philosophical one.

We've had many cats over the years and have buried a number. After a while, the land you love is filled with graves. Which means it's full of stories. Again, all those cycles turn.

We never planned to own so many horses. But when our children were grown, Lowery and I realized that we would enjoy having some creatures that we could nurture jointly. So we got one horse, and then another--and somehow, here we are with nineteen. But flowers and livestock are so different from faculty meetings, or grading papers. They carry you outward in a different way. For us, physical work is restful; one thing leads to another. And aren't the horses beautiful!

mentors and other influences

A number of people had an impact on my adult life. I married relatively young, at twenty, so my husband has certainly had a strong, lasting influence on me. We are a left brain-right brain pair--he's cool, rational, analytical--a lawyer and a judge. I'm much more instinctive, and impetuous. But we complement each other very well. From him I learned that if I were not to lose every domestic argument, I would have to master logic. It turned out to be very useful.

Lowery is two years my senior. We met at a church camp, Bonclarken, near Hendersonville, and ended up going back there years later for our honeymoon. His family too, were Associate Reformed Presbyterians, from South Carolina. I was only fourteen when we met yet it was instant recognition and we corresponded for a long time. This was ideal because words are my way of knowing and being. We didn't meet again off the written page until college. I broke up with the high school boyfriend everyone was sure I'd marry, and Lowery and I were married at the end of my freshman year in 1952. The plan was that I'd finish my degree, then he would finish his final year. But we soon had two children and law school for Lowery. A story of mine won the *Mademoiselle* contest during that period, but it was a blurred time of babies and not enough sleep or money. We've had a long, good marriage, thirty-seven years now.

Back to mentors: I was scared to death of my freshman English teacher in college. He had a little moustache and a Mephistophelian look. After our first themes for him, Dr. James Painter came into the classroom with a rubber band around our papers, slapped them in his hand and said, "Ladies, these papers are bad--damned bad," and he threw them all in the waste basket. Everyone was stunned. I had always done well in English, but I thought, what am I doing here? I shouldn't even be in college.

Dr. Painter called me into his office after I wrote the first theme that pleased him and I thought I was in trouble. He was not a warm man, but a very serious teacher. I sat down in front of a stack of books and he said with a gruff voice, "Do you see those books?" I replied meekly that yes sir, I did. "Have you read them?" I had only read one, and here I thought I was an omnivorous reader. There was Dostoevsky, Tolstoy, Dickens, Jane Austen, and he said, "Read these books!"

Well, I thought he meant immediately so I read all night long and the next day and night and all weekend until the next class. I went in, scared to death, and said, "I've read the books." He said, "Well, now we'll talk about them." Then he took down more books and I realized I didn't have to rush so. We did go on from there, and so I got a private tutorial in Great Books along with freshman writing class. Women's College then had about three thousand students, and now that I'm a teacher I think, gosh, why did he do that? How generous he was to me!

Voices of the Silent Generation

I had written only poetry in high school. If you were the only person in your class who wrote, it never occurred to you to evaluate the writing; everyone told you the poems were wonderful. I didn't evaluate anything I read, either; I thought every book must be wonderful to get printed. I had no sense of better or worse. So Jim Painter gave me my first serious criticism: he didn't think my poetry was very good, though that's what I wanted to write, but he thought the prose wasn't too bad. I was ready to die because I believed prose was inferior to poetry. So Jim Painter was an important early guide for me. We remained in touch over the years and I still correspond with his widow in Colorado.

I was skipped out of Freshman English and directly into creative writing. That was a great place to be in the early fifties. The writing teachers' friends were big literary names, Katherine Anne Porter, W.H. Auden, Robert Penn Warren. And they dropped in often. I had never seen real writers before and discovered that they are flesh and blood, and will talk to young people, and be very nice. I remember saying as a child that I wanted to live where people speak as they do in books, and here I was in that place: people really did talk in complete sentences; they used adjectives and adverbs, metaphors, different accents...

Outside creative writing I also had wonderful teachers. The fine historian, Richard Bardolph, was certainly a star; he inspired me to become a half English, half history major. There were so many good teachers. Frank Lane taught me to love Greek and to understand what it does to unlock the English language.

As to those stories about my being locked in the library, I did get locked in. But it was intentional and perfectly all right. In those days we had closed study, had to be back in the dorm at seven, with lights out at eleven. We had to be checked in and out and that seemed a hardship. I never violated the rule in order to go out drinking and partying, but did often violate it to read and write.

I spent many a night in a certain room in the Alumni House--it was called the Pecky Cypress Room--because I could hide there until the janitor locked up, and there was the luxury of a typewriter. Other nights I spent in the library, which got more complicated because the lights were all turned out. It was a great shock to discover that to spend the night there I would have to sit in the bathroom to read! In those years I thought sleeping was a great waste of time, and I was able to get along on little sleep.

I studied. I never had worked hard in high school, didn't cheat for myself but did for others. I had no compunctions, sold term papers for money, and charged on a sliding scale to earn people the grade they wanted. So the honor code was entirely new to me. And for the first time I realized that intellectual achievement was for me alone, not just to please my parents and teachers.

I had never before been surrounded by highly intelligent women. That ended my misconception about needing to be like men, because here were bright young women, some from smaller towns than mine. And we had the stimulating conversations that I'd been saving up to have with some man in New York in ten more years. That discovery was crucial, and I often wonder, what if I had gone to college somewhere else?

Any school probably would have been all right, but Woman's College was a particularly good experience in the fifties with so many excellent women professors. They were role models; for the first time, I could see that a woman could be an academic or a writer. I thought an ideal life would be to teach on a college campus surrounded by good books and good readers. And I was right. It's one of the few things I was right about when I was young!

Hugh Holman of UNC-Chapel Hill was my first English professor when I went back to school as a young mother and fledgling writer. He would never tell me a lie even when I wanted him to, which made him a fine teacher and critic. I didn't learn until years later that he, too, was Presbyterian, of a particular cast of mind and experience. He was known as a fine critic of Southern and American literature, but happened to teach a writing class which I took while pregnant with our second child. That began a lifelong friendship, and when I returned to Chapel Hill years later as a faculty member, he was the senior professor and exactly the mentor every junior academic needs.

He kept me from saying foolish things out loud. He taught me the machinery of how the institution works, otherwise I probably wouldn't have been so active in University governance. Through him I began to see that the university is a community with its own network of relationships and a hierarchy of responsibility and codes. To him it was like a church! He took it seriously and I could see that it was worth taking seriously. You don't just take your check and carry it home; you help pull some of the load, do the committees, etc. Even the scutwork deepens your ties, in a pleasant way, to what really matters in education.

Books have been influential in my life, too many to list. I was at war with the Bible for years, but it's been in me too long not to be a powerful influence. As a girl I read much that I was too young to understand. Yet I did return to many of those books. For a long time I read only poetry, then only novels. Now I read more nonfiction and international fiction, and feel more in tune with British, Middle-European and South American writers than with those in America. They are wrestling with large literary or philosophical questions, are concerned with social and political conditions, man in the web of his own society and community. Milan Kundera or Garcia Marquez would be primary examples--because they're not just concerned with self-identity, but have bigger fish to fry.

In Marquez' *One Hundred Years of Solitude*, he deals with mythical or magical reality. A sad book, but very beautiful, conveys his perspective on mortality and destruction, yet is positive in a curious way. You have to be very grown-up to write that way. You have to pass far beyond some of the writing we see here in the United States, so much of it preoccupied with individual neurosis. I tire of that.

I do try to read my contemporaries, especially North Carolina writers. I like keeping up with younger colleagues on campus and watching them grow. I don't want to get stuck in my own generation's work.

social change

As to the influence of social change in the sixties and seventies, I was not so much caught up in the era as I was an observer. Our third and youngest child was born in 1960; I went back to teach at UNC-Chapel Hill in 1966. I had worked locally for civil rights in our small town, but going back to the university was plunging into the sixties full scale. I arrived on the campus in time to see negative effects of the youth culture.

There were more drugs on campus than I have ever seen since and they claimed several promising students. So my hatred for drugs congealed; I never had any illusion that writers were going to have a great vision because of LSD. I don't have the romanticized view of the sixties that some have. There were good things, "flower power" and back-to-the-land and so on. But there was also sentimentality, lassitude, anti-intellectualism, over-simplifying of issues.

On the other hand, when I consider all that's happened since World War II, and the changes in our culture, it's not all been bad. Racially, society is at least now not segregated, if still deeply troubled. Women have made progress; there is less rigid behavior. Still, the family is in trouble. Changes to the culture caused by television are mostly bad. While news coverage can be immensely valuable, all the emphasis on entertainment--as if it were the purpose of life-- is reductive to the human spirit and has trivialized the life of the country.

I've lasted long enough to see the women's movement mature. So many early elements were influenced by television; so much attention was paid to exhibitionists. A lot of nonsense still parades under the name of feminism. But real feminism just allows women to do what they are capable of doing. It is women encouraging one another in their achievement. And that should include motherhood.

children

What have my children meant to me? At different ages of their lives I would have given different answers. Certainly in the beginning I hadn't the least idea of how confining, how time-consuming motherhood would be. And psychically, how all of your self floats out to this little person.

So there's that exhausting phase. Then there's the excitement of their growth, learning to talk, learning to read. And horrible adolescence! Even if they are good adolescents, teenagers just are not very nice people for a while. Then comes the in-between time when they're in college—they're yours and not yours. You haven't quite let go yet, but you have very little say in their lives.

Parenthood is wonderful now. Our grown-up children are a great help to us and we see the balance shifting. Both sons are married now and live nearby with their wives and children.

Our daughter is in her thirties, works in Washington, D.C., but gets back more often now. She has reached the age where her parents have learned a lot, so we have a lot more fun when we get together. Harvest time!

Having been an only child, I had dreams of sibling loyalty. Our first son and daughter were only fourteen months apart but it was several years before the third child was born. The older two brought a parade of children to see the new baby. I thought how wonderful, they've been bragging to their friends about their baby brother. What family loyalty! It turned out they were selling tickets to see him, five cents each!

I did want them to share our love of nature and animals. If you're to learn empathy for other people, other creatures, you have to be taught your kinship young. They were bird watchers and caught snakes and turtles. And loved their animals. None of us could function without a pet!

I'm pleased with their sense of values. They're honest, they don't lie or do damage to others. We enjoy them very much, and see them a reasonable amount but not too much. I'm surprised that they ended up living nearby. I did not especially want to live close to my parents. But our children now say they wish they'd lived closer to their grandparents and want their children to have grandparents nearby.

work

My career choices were not affected by feminism; I had wanted a life on campus since I was in college, but it hadn't worked out. That I began teaching at UNC-Chapel Hill was a fluke, almost an accident that I wound up in academia. But it has been easier for a woman to get ahead on the Carolina campus in my lifetime than for women who preceded me. And though it's easy for me to criticize radicals, they made the way easier for the middlers. I need to express some gratitude for people who were on the barricades.

As to the blending of professional and personal life, I never wanted to choose one thing; I wanted both family and career. I did not work outside the home until my children were all in school, but I was writing at home. I feel most successful when home and career are operating in harmony, but I don't mean to imply that happens all the time. There is always a tension between all the things you want to do one hundred percent: teaching, writing, family; so every day it seems I should have set different priorities--either more or less time to teaching, or the family, or service, or writing or just to learning. I feel troubled when things get lopsided, but know most of us will never be satisfied.

Now that the children are grown things are often harmonious, but sometimes at war; there's still not enough time in a day. Accommodations have been made, in both directions. Sometimes you put your husband first and other times yourself. I'm reminded of the words of my friend Dennis Donovan who said, "It's a matter of which string you pull when; never pull the same string twice in a row!" He was referring to faculty assignments and favors but the principle is broad.

When did I get my doctorate? I never even got a B.A. degree! The University catalogue has my name, date and title, but there's nothing else in between. It just worked out that way. Academic credentials were not a factor while I was a part-time lecturer, but eventually my chairman wanted to promote me to associate professor. I went to tell him, Bill Harmon, "I want to make it perfectly clear that I don't have this degree."

He said, "I know you don't have an M.A.," and I told him I didn't even have a B.A. degree. That did alarm him! He did some research and found two other associate professors of English elsewhere who had no degrees. That way he could cite some precedents if he had to, though by then I had already paid my dues by directing the freshman composition program. But this is why I am so grateful for promotion and why I cannot say that I've been a mistreated female.

The English department did more for me than they did for any male.

Strong Women Tell Their Stories

At one time I did think about going back to school for the degrees but there was never time.

My personal history helps me advise students who say they're thinking of dropping out. They point out that I did. I remind them that I've had to try to be sharper to make up for it. And I have sometimes felt intimidated; I would have enjoyed the security of having those letters. Degrees are not essential but would have been helpful. So I urge students to get the degree if the opportunity is there.

Little in my early adult life came from planning so much as from the way things fell out, just occurred, in many cases because of individuals whose paths crossed mine at crucial times, teachers who took time for me. They influenced my work as a teacher; I'm mindful that we can't ever pay generous people back, instead just try to pass it on.

Part of me wishes I had waited to have children until I'd finished all the degrees. But you can't pull one thing out without disrupting the whole package. If we hadn't married, I might have been off in graduate school at Wisconsin or some such. So it's hard to think of undoing what has already turned out fine. It wasn't the easiest way. But I'm not dissatisfied with the sequence. The price has not been too high.

Being a woman in a man's world has sometimes been difficult. But the great challenge has simply been to persevere. There has always been the alternative not to persevere; I could have gotten along just fine with what I would call a B-minus effort. But to persevere in writing, for which no one is keeping a time clock, where the rewards are so far off—where all the people around you have more than enough to do without writing—that takes a great deal of perseverance. So often, when I'm working on fiction, I'll think, oh, why not just go read a murder mystery, relax, it's summer. So it's not very dramatic, just a daily challenge to gear up.

When my children were small I had to work around naps, and I would get up early in the morning. But now I'm better in late mornings, early afternoons. In the summer I try to write every day and my goal is set not by the clock but by pages. If I finish that set number of pages quickly, I can do something else. If it takes all day to write them, then it takes all day. In the winter while teaching, I grade papers and don't have time for writing.

If you teach writing, you mark papers every night. Occasionally I teach a lit class, which is much easier. I've had three writing classes a semester. Every student will write about 20,000 words a term, so if you have forty to fifty students and mark every page with care, and I do, that's a lot. Some people grade holistically, which can be effective. But I go through line by line as though I were an editor. And that takes hours.

The satisfactions of my working life have been varied. In the academic life, being faculty chairman meant a lot because my peers made the choice. As a writer, to receive the award from the Academy of Arts and Letters meant a great deal because it came through fellow writers. And being promoted without a degree made me feel that my work alone was what counted, that it was judged to be good by people I respected. I like my department; their opinion matters to me.

Gender affected my working life; like other women of my generation, I was so determined not to let being female be a handicap that for a while I thought it was important to think like men and compete with them on their own terms--and to prefer male company. Feminism has freed us from all that. We can admit more about what it means to be a woman and rejoice in what we have in common with other women.

With writing there are few satisfactions. There are moments when the page looks right but an hour later you know it's only so-so. It helps to be perpetually dissatisfied; that keeps you working. The times you feel best are small and scattered. Very often only one sentence goes correctly or one page looks right. I can't say I'm satisfied with anything I've written.

I would like to convey a grasp of life that is "earned," is not sentimental and doesn't falsify, doesn't play the violin, and isn't lazy, because these would trivialize the hard work and achievement of a great many people. Anne Tyler pursues similar themes.

To rise out of that which is difficult, to come out undefeated, why, it's just ordinary! That courage isn't found only in military heroes or great leaders, but ordinary people. A grief that breaks one person will bring out the courage of another. There ought to be some place in literature that pays tribute to virtue, acknowledges something admirable about the human condition without falling off the edge into sentimentality. That's my goal for this book and my writing in general, whereas my earlier books have been described as grim. It's not a matter of switching upward so much as rectifying the balance. My life has taught me to choose, to will cheerfulness and that's the hardest thing to convey in fiction without selling out to Pollyanna. I've been told my short stories were like kicks to the stomach. But that's good. Short stories are meant to be short and punchy.

That's why I tired of the form and wanted to move toward the novel. The short story can be the form of youth, like the lyric poem: you want to get in there and make your point intensely and get out. But the older you get, the less life seems punchy and intense. It is less full of those big events, climactic moments. There's a larger pattern you don't perceive until you look back over the landscape. For that the novel is much better. One flash of insight can make a 3,000-word story, but novels take the long view, get written more slowly, by accretion. A new novel is almost finished now, *Souls Raised From the Dead.* It has been hard to work on this summer, more a matter of discipline than passion.

women

At its deepest level feminism addresses the fact that women, through luck or their nature, have had to cope with the dirtiest side of life. Nursed the sick, wiped up, washed the dead, all the most mundane and difficult things. They have also been the nurturers, told the stories, sang the songs, often against considerable odds. My assumption is that, as women's literature matures, women will contribute from their understanding of that aspect of life, the side that men have not dealt with. The male view of life is more competitive and aggressive, for good and sound biological reasons; but women have much to say about persevering and preserving. I'm not speaking for the little pampered darlings of society. Those haven't much to say.

The people who did exactly what was required of them in a good and decent and steady way are not often considered dramatic story material. They often remain unnoticed until life is nearly over. You and I could list women we know who have been dealt the most unbelievable hand, blows I doubt I could survive. They have something to say, and I would like to celebrate them, pay the tribute they deserve. We can be disappointed with aspects of our lives and still come to terms with them. Such stories require space, time. That's where I am personally, and probably that's where I am artistically. The other views, of unredeemed tragedy, satire and even sarcasm, make for more "interesting" fiction. An entertainment society such as ours short-changes life because it leaves no room at all for the possibility that the shadow of death or pain may ripen the soul. Flannery O'Connor once said, "The task of the novelist is to deepen mystery, and mystery is a great embarrassment to the modern mind."

Our family had another kind of mystery. A distant cousin from Georgia sent me a photo of my real grandmother, Daisy, taken when she was fifteen. She was a rather pretty black-haired girl, looked very innocent. I now know that the next year, unmarried, she was pregnant with my father. I believe that if she had gone to a social worker, she'd have been told to abort the child, to avoid the terrible blemish on her name. There was no future for an illegitimate baby, but in 1911 she didn't, or couldn't, abort him. As it happens, her life was not wrecked and she did keep her baby until he was four years old. She was finally unable to support him and gave him to neighboring farm folks. Although they reared my father, he found his mother later on. A mysterious stranger to me, she occasionally visited our home when I was a child. I would wonder about her, why she stared at me, then left a dollar bill under my dresser scarf. She wrote poems too!

As it turned out, it was my father who looked after her in old age, and at her deathbed. None of which anyone could have foretold. So I don't have that simple a view about human control in life because if modern mores had guided the decision, my father would not have been and I would not have been, nor would any of my children. If you think of your own children, each so different, so unique--no one gets back the one forfeited.

I look at my grandmother's photo now, and realize if this were a pregnant teenager today, she might have that abortion, thereby foreclosing some options, opening others. The fact is, once you have them, all children are inconvenient! With birth control as unreliable as it once was, most of us came along at times inconvenient to our parents.

I don't like the argument about the baby being "part of my body." The DNA of mother and child is totally different. I don't wish to make abortion decisions for other women but I would hope they would have wise counsel, very wise counsel, and take their time. Those who choose it need to think long and hard; and those who have the babies need help with choosing adoption or parenthood. It's an extremely complicated subject.

Women have been, and are, important to me; several friendships have lasted a long time. With close friends, even if we don't see each other often, we pick right up when we are together.

One friend of mine hops from subject to subject but I can follow the associations in what she's saying. To some men, that's like fingernails scraping a chalkboard. Women are better at reading between each other's lines.

looking ahead

There are advantages and disadvantages to being this age. I fear failure more now because there's less time between the present and the grave to make up for it! To write a bad book, one that I thought was bad, that would break my spine now. And it's scary to think that as you get older you may not know when you're starting to lose some of your abilities. For now, I love teaching, and hope to continue until mandatory retirement. In the years thereafter I look forward to having more time to read and write. I've been doing critical writing lately and might do more nonfiction, perhaps even write on gardening.

It's a cliche, but nobody on the inside is as old as their faces and bodies on the outside. Most women when asked, "How old do you feel?" will say from thirty-six to thirty-nine; they just sort of mentally hung there. That's about where I hung too. I'm still a high-energy person. If I don't stay busy I will develop hypochondria. There is a lot of physical work on a farm. I like that; otherwise I'd have to pay a spa. I prefer work because it has a product. Someday we'll build paths and trellises. When you come again there will be roses.

I now have three grandchildren to enjoy as they grow up. Ah, the pleasures of parenthood without the difficulty! I look forward to having the distance that I could never have with my own children, both to evaluate and just to enjoy.

I've watched my mother work at adjusting to widowhood, deafness, failing health. Mother will be eighty in November, but is still a very attractive lady. There have been health problems she hated, but she has handled them with grace, courage and good sense, has never complained or whined. She wanted to be independent when moving here to Pittsboro, so she lives in an apartment a mile from here. And has gotten to know new people. If I walk into the bank, the tellers are apt to tell me the latest witty thing my mother said!

I'm reminded of the Flannery O'Connor story, "Everything that Rises Must Converge," in which Julian is constantly embarrassed by the mother, but the reader sees what a warm-hearted person she is, that she makes friends wherever she goes. Like Julian, I don't think I was as prepared to appreciate my mother when I was younger, but I do now and I am learning from her how to be eighty years old. She is a cheerful person, a quality very different from being optimistic--it requires will, choice.

Eudora Welty was an older woman who was probably never pretty but attained a particular beauty. She captivated everyone who met her. At a reading given by Eudora Welty, Lee Smith and other writers and I were lined up to meet her. She knew we were all writers and she murmured to each of us in that marvelous voice of hers, and with infinite delicacy, "I believe I've read your work, but it was some time ago."

I thought, you smart thing, I'm stealing that line right this minute! Miss Welty was somebody in the fullest sense of the word. She ripened her life, became more of what she was, not less, and without falsifying.

And she has remained so accessible and courteous, never playing the big-and-famous role.

I am grateful that my life turned out as it did; it's almost inexplicable to me. Family life has been satisfying; the three children have all grown up, gone their own ways; they have gifts of their own and good lives. I'm not sure I can take credit; it seems fortuitous, a blessing. Once when I complained to a doctor that a mother is always blamed for how children turn out, he pointed out that if you don't want the blame you can't take the credit! To have ended up doing the kind of work that I love, to have had a durable and rewarding marriage, and three good children, and to come from a home that was unfailingly kind, there are not many more things in life to ask for.

I do have real regrets. I should have written more and better. But mostly I wish I had written more. I'm not certain that had I written more, it would have been better! Most writers have one or two good novels in them, or four or five really good short stories. Much of writing, like everything else, is learning, the part that never shows.

The unanswered questions for me are the great religious questions: what are we doing here, how much purpose is there; whether or not death is final, whether we have invented a benevolent God, or he has invented us.

It's not that I think these can be answered, but simply that on one premise or another you direct your life. I have made Pascal's wager between the two choices, belief or disbelief; if you choose to believe, you have nothing to lose. That choice doesn't mean certainty; I have good days and bad days about faith. I am certain that my life has gone better when I have been oriented one way, towards belief, rather than the other. That pragmatism seems sufficient for the day-to-day part of life. These are the great "plot questions" we can look forward to having answered. I like being here and do not look forward to death. But I am curious, and hope at the end to be alert and still eager enough to have some of those questions answered. And to know the result of the wager.

Postscript, 2005:

As I left Doris on the day of our interiew, she said, "Your questions were so thorough, I don't think I have any life left!" That light-hearted comment throws into bold relief how very much life Doris continues to have left fifteen years later. *Souls Raised from the Dead* received uniformly favorable reviews upon publication, with The *New York Times Book Review* devoting a full page to the book. The next novel, *The Sharp*

Teeth of Love, published in 1998, also received critical praise. Professor Betts retired from teaching in June of 2001. In her honor, novelist Pam Durban endowed the Doris Betts Distinguished Professorship in Creative Writing. Preferring teaching to retirement, Doris enjoys guest-teaching assignments. Two novels are in progress and recent stories were published in *Southern Review, Idaho Review, Epoch,* and other literary magazines.

Doris and Lowery's horses, garden and a greenhouse for seeds and cuttings absorb the hours remaining after commitments to church and local library have been met. Clearly, Doris Betts' definition of retirement includes a more robust schedule than most mortals could tolerate. Reflecting on the careers in politics, horticulture or veterinary medicine she might also have enjoyed, she exclaimed, "We all need about five intense lifetimes in which to gorge on one thing at a time" May Doris have much living ahead in this particular intense lifetime.

A complete list of books by Doris Betts can be found in the recommended reading section.

SHELLY WEINER
Introduction

Shelly Weiner and the few members of her family who survived the Holocaust left a camp for displaced persons in Germany and immigrated to the United States in 1949. It was the last year refugees came through Ellis Island, and the Weiners were among the final group. Shelly was twelve, and had attended school only sporadically. She had never ridden in a car, never seen a telephone or a mirror, never tasted real milk. She thought television was a child's fantasy: "How could pictures come through the air?" Shelly spoke Russian, Polish, Czech, German, Hebrew and Yiddish. As a new seventh-grade student in a Philadelphia public school, however, she spoke no English.

After no small effort, Shelly was speaking unaccented English within six months, and after a difficult year of adjustment, began to feel comfortable in her adopted country. She became a citizen at eighteen and went on to have, as she puts it, "a wonderful American life."

However, half a century later, Shelly still has occasional nightmares of the years she spent in hiding from the Nazis. In June, 1941, Nazi Germany unleashed Operation Barbarossa, the invasion of the Soviet Union. Rovna, Shelly's home city, became a vast killing ground. Virtually all members of Shelly's extended family were killed in an August, 1941 massacre. On November 7-8 of the same year, German soldiers drove between fifteen and twenty thousand Jewish citizens of Rovna to a pine grove and killed every man, woman and child. On July 13, 1942 they killed another five thousand people. One hundred of Rovna's 25,000 Jews survived the Holocaust.

Throughout the years of her busy American woman's adult life, Shelly's thoughts often returned to the grandparents, cousins, aunts and uncles she had lost. As a profoundly personal sorrow, it was not a subject she felt comfortable discussing. In addition to the losses, her early experiences were so painful, so horrible, the nightmares still so vivid, who would care to listen, or even believe her story? Shelly rarely told it.

Until the early 1980's, little public attention was paid, outside the academic world, to the Holocaust as a subject for scrutiny or instruction. Indeed, Hollywood has recently been criticized for avoiding the subject and for over-simplification in the few films that did address the Holocaust, the Shoah, at all.

One day Shelly's daughter came home from junior high school and

Strong Women Tell Their Stories

told her mother that in a history textbook on World War II, the Holocaust had been covered in a single paragraph.

It was time to break her silence. Shelly told her story to the class, leaving the appalled teacher and students with a whole new understanding of the human capacity to endure and prevail. Shelly soon had many requests to speak to student and adult groups. Thus began a new chapter in her life.

Rabbi Arnold Trask, Shelly and others founded the Holocaust State Council with the mission of providing information about the Holocaust. Shelly began to speak at schools, churches, colleges, synagogues and clubs. Telling her wartime story is still difficult, and she finds herself depressed for several hours after speaking to groups. Shelly continues, however, because many of the older people who survived the Holocaust have already died. She believes it is urgent for today's youth to grasp the importance of actively opposing discrimination and injustice.

The movement to teach school children about the Holocaust began in New Jersey in the early 1970s. Five states, New Jersey, California, New York, Florida and Illinois, now mandate Holocaust Education in their high schools, with modified programs for elementary schools. A dozen other states are considering adopting similar programs.

Shelly's work began to include larger projects designed to help other victims of oppression. Starting in 1991, she co-chaired a program sponsored by the Greensboro Jewish Federation to help persecuted Russian Jews emigrate to the United States. Shelly and Frank Weiner had learned something about such endeavors during a visit to Moscow. On that 1974 trip they began to lay the groundwork for the eventual emigration to America of Aunt Sonia and daughter, now Rachel Kizhnerman, her husband and their eighteen-year-old son Jerry. The proceedings took years, but were finally successful; the Kizhnerman family arrived in 1980.

Greensboro's growing Russian community owes much to the efforts of Shelly, her co-chairman, Ina Eisenberg, tri-lingual language tutor Marianne Rosthal, who had left Germany as a child, and dozens of other volunteers. Over one hundred Russian Jews were provided assistance with the details of immigration, and with finding jobs, housing, language tutoring, and transportation. The effort begun by volunteers now has a professional staff that continues to aid Russian Jewish families in their efforts to emigrate to the United States.

Virtually all of the Russian emigres have done well. Many have bought homes and sent their children to college. Now in his forties, Jerry

Kizhnerman owns several popular restaurants, one called Bistro Sofia, named for his grandmother Sonia (who was called Sofia).

I have described Shelly's work in some detail here because she is disinclined to take credit for her own accomplishments, always stressing the contributions of others. In conversations with those who know her work, however, I learned that she is a respected and admired community leader and innovator.

I interviewed Shelly in her home just before she left to visit daughter Donna and grandchildren in Atlanta. Aunt Sonia, with whom Shelly had so strong a bond, had recently passed away; both families were still mourning the loss of their beloved sister, mother, aunt, great-aunt.

The floor-to-ceiling windows offered a view of tulip-tree blossoms ruffled by a late spring breeze. The bright day flooded the room with natural light. Surprisingly, Shelly does not suffer from claustrophobia, but one legacy of her early underground confinement is a love of sunshine. "Light is so important to me! I'll walk into a room, and immediately switch on the lights or open the curtains," she said recently.

In the midst of preparations to leave town for a week, Shelly found time to fit in a fourth interview session with me. She was also baby-sitting for a young friend. Unaffected by daylight, the three-month old baby slept nearby in her carrier. The telephone began to ring frequently; Lula Bowden, long-time housekeeper, called Shelly to the phone for an urgent call or two; another friend dropped in unexpectedly. My tape recorder whirred annoyingly; the baby awakened in full cry. Throughout this modest domestic tumult Shelly remained attentive to all. I watched as Shelly, calmly soothing baby Sydney in her arms, effortlessly revealed the sense of perspective, the deep knowledge of what matters, learned through intense suffering all those long years ago.

Shelly Weiner
Rovna, Poland/Ukraine,
Philadelphia, Atlanta, Nashville,
Cherry Hill, NJ, Greensboro, NC.
2005

I am grateful to be alive. So many European Jewish children my age did not survive. I was fortunate to be young and able to recover.

I was born in Rovna, sixty miles from the Russian border. The city was first in Poland, later became part of Ukraine. Rovna was a large town, with about 25,000 Jews. My father's family had been there since the eighteenth century. The citizens were fairly progressive and Jewish people were integrated into all parts of society.

The Russian army came in 1939 and occupied Rovna. They took a lot of the businessmen, people they considered "capitalists," and sent them to Siberia or the army. My father, Meyer Weiner, was in business and was conscripted into the Russian Army. We knew nothing of his whereabouts for years.

My grandfather, my father's father, had a lot of property and his sons all lived near one another on that property. So I was used to aunts, uncles, cousins nearby all the time. And I remember the agitation of all the adults when the German army marched into Rovna in 1941. I was four years old.

With the Nazi occupation came all the restrictions for Jews: the yellow armbands, curfews, prohibitions against shopping in the big market. But my mother was fair-haired and light-skinned, so she would leave the armband at home and go to the market. I was always frightened that she might not return. If someone had informed on her, she would have been taken away immediately. The killing started right away. I remember seeing the dead bodies in the streets. So we feared the German soldiers from the beginning.

Then there was another decree. All Jewish males were to come to register for "relocation," supposedly work detail. But my grandfather knew better--I don't know how--so he made a hiding place for all the men in the family in the back of one of his buildings and they would stay there during the day. For the mid-day meal, they would come into our house and eat. My cousin and I would play in the front yard and our job was to watch for German soldiers and run in immediately if we saw them coming. The men would run back to their hiding place. This worked for awhile. One day one of my uncles didn't run fast enough and they caught him and started to beat him. They made us watch until he was unconscious. They took him away and we never saw him again.

In the meantime, my grandfather sensed that the situation was growing more and more desperate so he started negotiating with a farmer, Mr. Kostelanitz, in a nearby village where my mother's sister, Aunt Sonia Guralnik, and her daughter Rachel lived. As you may know, this was very dangerous for the farmer. He and his whole family could have been killed. But my grandfather kept talking to Mr. Kostelanitz, and giving him things in hopes that he might at least consider the possibility of helping us when the time came. Then, the Nazis gathered up the sixteen or seventeen

Front page of *New York Post*, September 1939

Cousins Eva and Rachel Woskoboinik (on left) 1937. Eva survived the Holocaust; Rachel was shot by the Nazis in Poland in 1941

Rachel and Yitzhak Woskboinik, shown here in 1937, were among the dozens of Shelly and Eva Weiner's family members who were killed in the Holocaust

thousand Jews that were left—many had already been taken away or killed—and created a ghetto. My mother and I were put in a room with eighteen or twenty strangers and given bread and soup once a day. It was summer and stiflingly hot. My mother was sent out to work detail every day but I had to stay behind in the room. She told me never to go outside, but I was a stubborn child and one day I did. Before I knew it there was a German soldier with a rifle at my head. I don't know why he didn't shoot me, because they did it for sport. He sent me back indoors and I stayed in after that.

We were in the ghetto for about three months. When my mother went out to work one day, one of her old Ukrainian neighbors told her that there was to be "an action" the next day. We knew that meant people would be taken from the ghetto and killed. I never did understand how my mother managed it, but that night we slipped out of the ghetto and walked the twelve kilometers to the farm where Aunt Sonia lived.

The next day the Nazis did take thousands of Jewish people in Rovna and marched them outside of town where they were forced to dig very deep trenches. Nazis shot everyone there, letting the bodies fall down into the trenches. My grandfather, my uncles and aunts and cousins, all of my father's family were killed that day. My mother had come from a family of eight children and, except for her youngest brother who had been taken into the Russian Army, they were all killed that day too.

Mr. Kostelanitz and his family lived next door to Aunt Sonia. My aunt did little favors for his wife and they had a nice relationship. The family had two grown children and two living at home, a twelve-year-old daughter and a son who was eighteen at the time. The Germans offered good pay to the local non-Jewish people and the boy had gone to work for them. He and his friends were put on a work detail to collect and bury bodies. They were so horrified that they ran away and either formed, or joined, a resistance group. They lived in the woods and would blow up Nazi trains and bridges, make any kind of trouble they could for the German Army.

It was our good luck that the son came home at the time we were trying to persuade his father to hide us somewhere on his farm. He not only convinced, but almost threatened Mr. Kostelanitz, and said, "I'll be back to check and make sure you're hiding these women and their daughters." And he did. This was so difficult for the families who took people in. They had to make sure their neighbors didn't notice anything. Unusual activity in a small town is quickly talked about, and fearing for their own lives, people would turn the protectors in.

But the Kostelanitz family was very courageous—they took four of us in, my mother and me, Aunt Sonia and my cousin Rachel. Our first hiding place was on top of their barn in the hayloft. They made a space in back of the barn, just big enough for us to sit and lie down. They made a tunnel by taking out bales of hay and brought food to us through the tunnel. We lived on bread and potatoes and water. That is what the farm families lived on too, because the Germans would take most of their food. We had just one set of clothes each and of course had no way to wash. Once a month Mrs. Kostelanitz would put our clothes in her oven to kill the lice.

The only light we had was from slats in the wall. Mostly we sat in near darkness. There were mice, rats and lice, always. We were there for about eighteen months, freezing in winter and miserably hot in summer. One night I actually froze stiff and the farmer's wife thawed me out with snow. I still have some frostbite on my fingers and toes, and am very sensitive to cold.

Through the slats I could see the chickens and kittens playing out in the barnyard and I remember begging my mother to let me go out and play. But we could never come down. We really couldn't make any sounds at all, because there were soldiers patrolling the nearby woods and looking for Jews in hiding. But from lack of protein I began to hallucinate and make a lot of noise. Aunt Sonia told my mother that unless I was quiet, I would have to be strangled. The danger to the others was so great. And to the farmer and his family as well. My mother, of course would not allow that. Finally, some eggs were found and the protein helped me—and all of us. How did we pass the time? None of us can remember. We knew, even Rachel and I understood, that we had no choice but to just stay there and be quiet.

One day after we had been in the barn for about eighteen months the farmer came into the loft and said, "Someone has informed and the Germans are coming for you. You must come down now." My mother asked him for just a few moments to say goodbye because she knew we would all be separated, if not shot on the spot.

And here is where something odd happened. Rachel and I were so young and yet we understood what was happening. I'm told that we started to beg and cajole, saying things like, "Don't you want to see us grow up, don't you want to dance at our weddings? Can't we take our chances out in the woods?" And we actually persuaded our mothers to slip out and let each of us run in a different direction in the woods. I hid under bushes and covered myself with leaves and debris. We could hear the Nazis and the dogs barking all night. It was terrifying. Then, they left. We never knew why. And for some reason they did nothing to penalize the Kostelanitz family. Something important must have come up to distract them.

We were sure they'd be back so we moved to a wheat field. It was August and the wheat was very high, a good hiding place. We were there for three days in extreme heat. With no food or water we chewed on the grass for moisture.

Finally, we had to go back to the farmer's house or die in the wheat field. The soldiers didn't come back, but none of us could be sure of that. Mr. Kostelanitz was a resourceful man. He didn't dare use the barn for us again so he dug a pit under his watering trough, just large enough for all of us to lie down. Then he covered it with a false bottom for the trough. It's hard to imagine, because it was just like a coffin, but we did go into it. I've come to understand that the human will to live is so strong, and again, Rachel and I understood that we had to do these terrible things or be killed. We came out at night, but during the day we had to just lie still. It was unbearable being in that coffin, especially in the summer heat. We lasted a week and then couldn't stand it any longer.

Lodz, 1945. Shelly Weiner, age 8, wearing clothing sewn from German uniforms found on the street.

All this time, the German army was in the vicinity, and would take all the farmers' corn, wheat and other grains. Our farmer had dug large pits where he hid his grain, covering them with branches and leaves. He dug one of these for us and added a tunnel, just large enough for me to slither out backwards on my stomach each night, to get food or take out waste. We sat in the dark for the most part. We could burn a candle for about an hour each day; that was our only light, except for a little filtering through at the top and a small air hole. But even that little bit of light had a disadvantage because it allowed me to see how sick my aunt was. Mostly we sat in darkness—with the rats, which were larger than those in the barn. And it was damp, very damp all the time. It was truly horrible. Time had no meaning and the four of us have different concepts of how long we actually spent living in that pit. Some say a year or more, others think

Eva Weiner, survivor of Nazi invasion of her home city of Rovna, Poland. As an act of defiance she cut up a Nazi uniform, making from it the suit she is wearing here. 1945

about eight months. How we got through each day is still a mystery to us. Our total time hiding in the various places was three years.

The will to live is so strong, innate in all of us I believe, even in a young child. And if you've seen people beaten or shot and killed in front of your eyes, as we had, you'll do anything to avoid that. When you fear for your life as a child, you learn not to acknowledge fear and to do exactly what adults tell you to do. Even live with rats or lie motionless in the dark all day.

Soldiers prowled about in the woods above us. Our hiding place was covered with branches and grass and looked like a part of the forest. Sometimes the Germans and Russians were machine-gunning each other right over our heads. Our worst fear was that a shell would drop on us and explode. But none ever did.

Finally, liberation! The Russian Army drove the Germans out on February 5, 1944. The war was almost over and we were able to come out of the hole. After so long underground I had to learn to walk all over again. My head had to be shaved and my scalp and body were full of sores. I looked like a little monkey. All this time we'd only been twelve kilometers from our home. We went back to Rovna-- Rachel and I were hidden in a hay wagon--and found our house still standing. All this time, of course we had no way of knowing anything about my father.

My aunt was very ill with

Shelly Weiner (2nd from left) and friends in displaced persons camp in Germany, 1948.

pneumonia. The hospitals were mainly treating soldiers, and my mother felt that people were just dying in the hospitals, not being helped. She managed to find a doctor who treated my aunt and she eventually recovered. I was ill with typhoid, pneumonia and malnutrition but luckily, was also able to recover at home.

Meanwhile my mother had started to cook for the Russian soldiers to earn a living. She offered meals in our house. But then two things happened to end that. First, the bombing continued. There were bombing raids almost every night for nine months and it was just terrible, so frightening. Rachel and I would sit and watch for reconnaissance planes during the day, and then we'd know they'd be bombing that night. We saw people killed by bombs right in front of us. While we were taking shelter in a church one night, our house was hit and destroyed. That ended my mother's meal service. Also, the communists had been pressuring my mother to become an informant. She kept refusing. It was clear we had to leave.

Memorial to the nearly 25,000 Jewish citizens of Rovno who perished in the Holocaust. Built in 1945 by the 100 Jews who survived. Eva Weiner, who initiated the effort, is 3rd from right, front row.

Stalin made a decree that Polish citizens could return to Poland. My mother and I were both born during times when Rovna was considered to be in Poland so we were eligible to return. But Aunt Sonia and Rachel were Russian citizens so they stayed in Ukraine. My mother's youngest brother had survived the war, fighting with the Russian Army, and he found us in Rovna. We worked our way to Poland with him.

My mother found work in a restaurant in the city of Lodz in Poland.

Voices of the Silent Generation

A Gypsy woman took care of me during the day and I liked her, she taught me to play cards and to read fortunes.

Shelly with parents, Eva and Meyer Weiner in Germany, 1949

One day my father walked into the restaurant! He had fought in horrible battles as a Russian soldier, but he had survived. We couldn't believe that he was alive, that he had found us. He had gone home to Rovna and people there told him that we were in Lodz. But we had little time to rejoice because new pogroms started in Poland, and Jews were being killed again. So it was necessary to leave, this time with my father. Somehow we found our way to the American Zone in Germany. No country would take us, so we were put into displaced persons camps and lived in them for three years. The American government and a Jewish humanitarian agency, the Joint Distribution Committee (called "the Joint"), took care of our basic needs. As displaced persons the adults were not allowed to work, so we had nothing. We were in three camps, first, one near Poking, next, another in Bavaria, and the last in the industrial city of Ulm. Sometimes teachers were available and taught the children. I did learn a little Greek mythology and to read and write Hebrew in the camps.

Israel was not yet a state early in 1948, but my mother was a Zionist and wanted very much to move to Israel. We planned to take an illegal boat because the British were turning boats back and putting people in internment camps on Cyprus. But the morning we were to leave I woke up with mumps and we had to give our places to someone else. As it happened, the boat we were to have taken was captured by the British and sent back.

My father, Meyer Weiner, started writing letters to America to find an uncle who was in either Philadelphia or New York. He got telephone books from the Red Cross and wrote to all the Jacob and Louis Weiners in both cities. He actually typed five or six hundred letters, all in Yiddish, but using the Polish alphabet. The uncle in Philadelphia received the letter

Strong Women Tell Their Stories

DPC-219
4-13-49

DISPLACED PERSONS COMMISSION
WASHINGTON 25, D. C.

Dear Sir or Madam:

    The Displaced Persons Commission welcomes you to the United States of America.

    The Congress of the United States of America has established the Displaced Persons Commission to select for immigration to this country, persons displaced as a result of World War II. Under the principles laid down by the Congress, you are among those selected.

    The Congress is interested in how displaced persons fare after settling in the United States. So that the Congress may be kept informed on this matter, it requires that each person who immigrated to the United States as the head of a family or as a single person provide certain factual information.

    The information is to be provided twice a year, for two years. The reporting dates are July 1 and January 1. The first report is required on the next reporting date after you have been in the country 60 or more days. Each of the reports must be in the mails to reach us by the date specified, but may be mailed as much as fifteen days earlier.

    The form for reporting is provided by the Displaced Persons Commission. The form to be used will be available on May 15 for the July 1 report and on November 15 for the January 1 report. It will be available at local offices of the U. S. Immigration and Naturalization Service.

    The Displaced Persons Commission wishes you every success in your new life in the United States of America.

Sincerely,

Ugo Carusi, Chairman

Edward M. O'Connor

Harry N. Rosenfield

Letter saved by the Weiner family from 1949

and sponsored us. The organization Hebrew International Aid Society (called HIAS and still operating) helped us with papers, legalities, passports, all the red tape. We came over in 1949 and I loved this country from the moment we arrived! I try not to take all that is here for granted, all the freedom, the opportunities. The uncle saved the letter my father wrote and gave it to us. I have it in a frame.

We arrived in the United States in 1949 when I was twelve and went directly to the uncle in Philadelphia. I had only gone to school for a week here and there, but I was dropped right into an American seventh grade. Since my parents did not speak English, my father's American cousin took me to register at school. My name is Rachela, pronounced Rah-hela. She told me that didn't sound like an American name and that I should sign Rochelle. I did, then tried to make it easier by calling myself Shelly, and that's what it's been ever since.

That first year was very hard. I was the only immigrant in the neighborhood, so different from every one else with my long braids and hand-me-down clothes. I knew several languages, but not English. At that age, even with my strange background, I wanted to be like everyone else. I tried so hard to fit in, worked at my English and basically within six months I could speak it pretty well, and without much accent. I met nice kids, made friends, and by eighth grade I no longer felt so different.

My mother worked in a factory and at first my father worked in the subway for fifty dollars a month. We were poor but I never felt deprived. We came from people who respected education and fair treatment. My parents were always giving to others and it seemed there was always someone sleeping in our living room or kitchen. I didn't ask my parents for things. If I wanted something I knew I should work for it. I bought all my own clothes by babysitting and doing odd jobs.

As my father gradually learned English he started to work in construction, and moved from carpenter to foreman to supervisor. My parents saved their money and they soon had an apartment, a car, a television set.

But we didn't have a lot of money and when I was accepted at University of Pennsylvania to study medical technology, my parents simply couldn't afford to send me. I went to a smaller school. Actually, I only had one other friend who went to college. Most were married soon after high school. When Frank and I were married I was twenty.

influences after childhood

My mother, of course, saved my life with her determination and courage. She has been a life-long inspiration to me. My father was also my hero. He had suffered greatly during the war, especially at the Seige of Leningrad. It was so horrifying he could not talk about it. A legacy of his service in the Russian Army was that he feared authority of any kind. For the longest time just the sight of a policeman would make him tremble. He was a very hard worker and worked his way up to become supervisor of large construction. So he did very well for someone who came here not speaking English. My father was an active and vigorous man till the day he died in his sleep at the age of eighty-two. He lived a good life and we miss him still.

I don't have any sense of being Polish, but I do have some sense of being European. And American-Jewish. My parents and their friends were insistent about maintaining Jewish values and strength from our past and our traditions. It wasn't religion so much as history and culture. The feeling of a debt owed to those who perished made those things that much more significant.

Other people influenced me too: I was also inspired by a young girl who got through the war living in the woods alone. My mother took her in and we all loved her. I have found other close friendships with women very helpful throughout my life. I have always been grateful for encouragement given when I needed it by a nurse and doctor at the college for medical technology that I attended. And, of course, my husband. He has been my best friend.

At a very early age I had a sense of self-reliance and independence. Before the war, it was not unusual for mothers to leave their children to play alone or with a friend for long periods. I was an only child and took care of myself to some extent. Then, when we came to the U.S., all of us speaking Yiddish, I was able to learn English quickly because I was so young. I worked very hard at it too. But it was much harder for my parents and so they had to rely on me for a long time. That gave me a feeling of being a responsible person, not just a child. Later, my husband traveled a great deal, so though I was only twenty when we married, I soon was making many decisions for our family.

I still have nightmares, but not as many as I once did. And I have a strong sense of overcoming all that horror. That helped me to believe I could handle whatever came along.

The social changes of the 60s and 70s didn't affect me deeply at the time because I was so busy with three young children. And we moved several times in those years, four different cities before arriving in

Greensboro in 1972. Of course, living in the South we were very aware of the civil rights movement. But with my husband traveling and the children to care for it was impossible to be actively involved. Later, I realized I needed to pursue at least some of my own goals. And that's when I took courses at the University for several years. It was mainly for my own development and education, not for professional goals. I studied art, psychology, literature and education. I needed to prove to myself that I could write papers, take tests and make A's.

virtues and abilities
I think whatever personal virtues or talents I have blend into one quality and that is self-reliance, the sense that bad times will pass, we can endure. Also, I can put together big projects. I enjoy seeing the whole picture of an endeavor, then figuring out what needs to be done and how to do it. With partners I started two of my own businesses and kept them going for five years or so each. That was in sequence, by the way, not both businesses simultaneously!

risks, guilt
I don't always do the safe thing. I tend to do what I think needs to be done. I have started a number of volunteer programs. The plan to resettle persecuted Russian Jews was a big risk. There was so much to be done. And Holocaust Education was not really accepted in this area in the 1980s. People did not seem that interested at the time. So getting started with something that meant so much to me, but not perhaps to others, was also a risk. I was lucky to work with good people on both programs.

Holocaust survivors feel enormous guilt; we have to do more than others to make up for all those who perished. You always want to contribute all that you can. I would say that is probably my only regret—that I didn't do more.

As a teenager I tried so hard to understand all that occurred during the war and especially, *how* and *why* it had happened. Why would the Nazis do such things to other human beings? And not just a few atrocities, but systematically, over and over again. But where to even begin to understand such things? I read everything I could find, but I felt overwhelmed. That was a very hard time for me. Eventually I found some peace by concluding that most of us will not be Mother Teresa but we can influence the people around us, our friends, family, neighbors. We all have a responsibility to speak up when we witness injustice. We can't be indifferent, just passing it on to others. And sometimes we do have opportunities to persuade a larger group.

I used to feel guilt over our family's material comforts. My husband came from a poor family, has worked extremely hard, and I am happy for him that he has been rewarded with success in business. And we are very philanthropic, we give to many causes. For myself, I never felt I needed or wanted anything beyond the basics. I didn't need jewelry or special clothes, just a comfortable home with plenty of light. And I am especially glad to be able to travel. But if we had to leave our home, I think I could adapt.

Shelly Weiner in 1987

children

As with most women, children have given me my greatest satisfaction. Also, our daughters have five children among them who have also been a great joy to us. All three of our daughters, who are now in their middle-thirties and forties, and my husband, are wonderful people and have helped me to believe in the kindness of humanity.

Since I didn't have a childhood I didn't know about so many things children learn through play in childhood. When I had my own children I realized I didn't know about nursery rhymes, games, toys. I had to learn about normal childhood. It should be said that despite the circumstances when I was a child, I knew I was loved, and then later developed a clearer understanding of what my mother and aunt had done for their daughters. They were truly heroic.

I tried to teach our children to appreciate differences among people, differences in economic circumstances as well as race and religion. And to stand up for what is right, even if it is uncomfortable to do so. I'd like to write an ethical will for my grandchildren, to pass on my ethics, my values and hopes for them.

work

I wouldn't say my personal and professional lives blended with complete success. My husband traveled frequently so it was hard for me to push for my own goals, hard to prevail over daily requirements of home and children. I regret that I didn't assert myself more. I feel that I have not fulfilled my full potential though I have done a lot of different things. I'd like to have done more in a concentrated way.

I worked part-time mentoring mothers who had abused their children. We tried to build their confidence and teach them other ways of handling their children. After two years I became so discouraged with the Social Services system, and its inefficiencies, that I had to leave. The experience did help me to improve my relationship with my own mother, to be more patient with her need to be somewhat controlling. Though I understood that my mother had to have a powerful will for us to have survived, still, as an adult I have my own will too!

I went into business with a partner, Kathy Treanor. We leased and maintained tropical plants for offices and department stores, and had people working for us all over the state. We were pretty successful and continued for about five years. After we closed that business, I started a restaurant with my husband. I liked doing the menus, the décor and training the staff. But over time I realized this business was not for me. It took all my time. I really needed something part-time and with flexible hours, even after my children were grown and gone. I began working with the Multiple Sclerosis Society as a special events planner and coordinator. At first I was a volunteer, but for the last five years it was a paid position. That work was perfect for me. Working on behalf of those who suffer from MS was very gratifying. I coordinated the activities of two hundred volunteers. We raised money and awareness of the disease with a variety of events.

I mentioned the resettlement project earlier; the Greensboro Jewish Federation also developed a twin city program with the city of Beltsy in Moldava, which is one of Eastern Europe's poorest countries These people were so very poor, yet warm, lovely people. They were just emerging from seventy years of isolation and repression. We established a family summer camp for Jewish people in Beltsy, and we have ongoing programs to assist them. A computer lab has been installed, and the Jewish cemetery was restored. We have dentists and doctors who volunteer their services too. On one trip over I was so surprised to meet a woman who spoke Yiddish with the same accent as mine. Doing these things, meeting these people, have been wonderful experiences.

Strong Women Tell Their Stories

The work in Holocaust Education has been important to me too, as you can imagine. When I speak to young people, I always emphasize, just as we did with our daughters, the importance of being able to recognize bigotry and injustice. Then take a stand against them. So much that is bad in the world happens because good people don't stand up against evil. I tell school children the story of the King of Denmark. You've probably heard it. When the Nazis came to Denmark they demanded that all Jews wear yellow armbands with the Star of David. The King, in effect, said if the Jews must wear the yellow armband, then so will I. And he strode out in public wearing it. He has gone down in history as one of the few European leaders who stood up for the Jews in public.

Our Council on the Holocaust also commissioned the Touring Theatre Ensemble to write and produce two dramatizations of stories from the Holocaust. "Let the Children Tell" was for elementary students, and "Who Will Carry the Word?" was for high school students. TTE is a wonderful theatre group that adapts literature or letters and memoirs of actual events for theatrical presentations. Its founder, Brenda Schleunes, discovered a packet of letters in Israel that she adapted to create "Letters to Leokadia," about a real Polish woman who sheltered a Jewish girl throughout the war. These programs are a unique way of teaching children things they might not otherwise learn.

Shelly Weiner, 2000.
(Courtesy Abby Santamaria)

Every year or so the Congress of Holocaust Remembrance Day is held for high school youth from all over the world. The event is called the March of the Living. Yom Hoshoa. Last year when I attended, three thousand young people walked from Auschwitz to Birkenau. I was shocked to see swastikas painted where we could see them from the march. After all that happened! That tells me our efforts are still necessary. One of the things you come to understand when you go there is that Maidenek, where the crematoria were, is just a short distance from the camps. Ordinary citizens would have seen and smelled the clouds of smoke. They must have known.

The young people's emotions are very intense. They too, wrestle with the same questions I had as a teenager. I was on the bus approaching the march to talk with teens from Rhode Island and North Carolina. I tried to explain to them that you can not live with it all every day. Some survivors do carry it every day. I was fortunate to be young and able to recover.

looking ahead

Like most people, I hope to continue to be healthy and productive for as long as possible. I'm not ready to just be retired and "play." I enjoy being a part of a vibrant and varied community. Things change and evolve and we never know quite what's coming next. And that's certainly true for my husband and me, and our health, and that of our family. We've had some surprises, not all good ones.

My mother is eighty-eight and has never felt old. In her mind she's sixteen years old and loves to be with younger people. I admire her spirit. She doesn't admit she's aging. In her mind whatever aches or pains she might have are always going to be fixed next week. I've learned to accept such things too, not give in to them.

The great unanswered questions? I have periods of sadness when I think about the suffering in the world, not only in Nazi Germany, but Rwanda, Bosnia, and now Darfur. And so many other places. Will humanity never learn? But I have to come back from those periods, and I do, for my family. I've found there is much goodness around us. We just need to look for it.

I am convinced that the will to live is a deep part of us. To think that we can go through such terrible times and still grow into people who lead good and productive lives. It is absolutely amazing what the human spirit does for us.

I am grateful to be alive. So many European Jewish children my age did not survive. Then to come to the United States, to live without restrictions and with so much opportunity! And to have not only raised our children in freedom but now to enjoy our wonderful grandchildren…I appreciate it all very much.

Editor's note:
Because Shelly Weiner's story was added to the collection of oral

histories in 2005, no postscript is needed. She was in her mid-sixties when her story was recorded, rather than early fifties, as were the other participants. This discrepancy seemed a small price to pay for a remarkable story.

VIRGINIA SEIPT
Introduction

Widely acknowledged as a television pioneer, Virginia Seipt was the first woman to produce sports programs for network television. Beginning her career in New York City during the early sixties, Ginny was intimately connected with sport as it evolved into the entertainment giant it is today. For decades she traveled for the network, often at a moment's notice, to cover major athletic events anywhere in the world.

After twenty-five years with NBC, Ginny was summarily fired along with a host of other production staff. The networks decided in 1987 to avoid health insurance and benefits associated with salaried staff. Ginny and others turned to free-lance work; life in their fiercely competitive business became even more precarious.

Shortly thereafter, Ginny was struck by a car and her leg was broken. An unwieldy cast precluded a return to her apartment for months. Ginny's sister, Barbara, lived nearby and offered a more convenient residence and help with a long and difficult recovery.

I spoke at length with Ginny a few years after these events, and discovered, as in several other oral history interviews, a substantial gap between image and reality.

Ginny and I were in the class of 1960 at Cornell University. We never met, but I knew her by reputation. Ginny looked like a film starlet: petite and pretty, her face framed by wavy blonde hair. The phrase "beautiful people" was not yet invented, but Ginny Seipt, from Darien, Connecticut met the test. Or so it seemed then.

Over the years, Ginny's picture appeared occasionally in the *Cornell Alumni News*, receiving a distinguished alumnae award, or serving on a panel to discuss women in television. I visualized a glamorous woman prevailing in a man's world, doing so at a time when doors were closed to most women. Ginny made a name for herself in television production long before married classmates began to wish they'd started earlier on that graduate degree or job search.

My sister, Diane Meakem, knew Ginny and encouraged me to invite her to participate in the oral history project. Diane assured me that I would find Ginny unpretentious, candid and good-humored.

We first met in New York City and I found Virginia Seipt to be just as Diane described her. Soon after we began, a call interrupted the interview. NBC was offering an assignment and the usual rules applied: drop everything. Ginny invited me to accompany her, explaining as we hailed a cab, that television free-lancers must respond immediately. We worked on her oral history exactly as Ginny lives her life: on the move.

Minutes later, as I trailed Ginny through the labyrinthine corridors of NBC, we glimpsed Tom Brokaw, surrounded by technicians, cameras and a jungle of cables, giving the evening newscast. We smiled at the contrast between my humble taping equipment and the high-tech gear surrounding us. We passed Gene Shalit's open door as he prepared a film review, and tiptoed across the empty "Saturday Night Live" set, which resembled a high school gym set up for play night.

The impromptu backstage tour included watching Ginny and her assistant (who had somehow materialized) as they edited videotape for a news program. To observe the editing process is disconcerting; one becomes aware that events as captured on the videotape are then filtered through the mind of the tape editor. What the viewer later sees is only in part chronological reality. In Ginny's experienced hands, the process seemed artistic: she made choices to enhance meaning, highlight one aspect and not another, and created, as accurately as possible, a new whole.

Virginia Seipt, a conscientious, modest and unassuming woman, is a craftsman in her chosen medium. She calls upon experience, judgment, technical knowledge, taste and integrity to present a defensible version of events. Knowing that viewers will accept her version as literal truth, Ginny takes her responsibilities seriously.

When the work is seen in that light, it is not surprising to discover that her favorite forms of relaxation are knitting and a needle craft called counted cross-stitch. Ginny finds it calming to spend hours doing needlework, which requires, as do her professional endeavors, meticulous effort and concentration. Relaxation surely comes from the practice of a craft unattached to true stories.

By late 1996, having covered the Olympics in Atlanta and a lavish wedding in Bucharest for gymnast Nadia Comanici, Ginny was serving ABC as associate director for news magazines.

A pioneer who settled on the frontier and found that survival required great struggle, Ginny discussed her questions about whether survival in a difficult business had been worth the price paid.

Virginia Seipt
New York City
1992

Suffering is a relative term. The trauma of being hit by that car, and all that followed, made me realize how lucky I was to be alive. Rather than feeling bitter about what happened, I'm more appreciative of life itself.

I am best known for the career I stumbled into. The sense of who I am has been determined by the career more than anything else, and my feelings of accomplishment have come from being a pioneer. It was not something I chose, but through luck or genes, I seem to have been able to make the best of it. In recent years, circumstances have changed and I have had to look again at my life.

Surviving in a tough business has been the big challenge of my life. I am essentially defined by my job. Which is why it was such a rough go when the job was taken away after twenty-five years. At that point I looked at myself and asked, is there anything at all to me other than my job?

Just going from event to event and getting through each was hard. Every production was a challenge and then you got ready for the next one. That's how my life at NBC was measured: one event after another: taking a plane to China, getting on another to watch Diana Nyad try to swim from Cuba to Florida. Most sports events don't take place in NYC. They happen elsewhere ninety-nine percent of the time. So I was always on the move. You don't go in advance of an event and prepare for it. You go, do it, get on the plane and come home; there is no built-in rest or planning time. Or maybe I just didn't create it.

I started off in television news, then was assigned to a children's program and an adult magazine program. When both were cancelled after a year or so, I wound up in sports production. Three times before beginning in sports, I came close to being fired by NBC. The third time, the sports assignment came as pure chance, but I reached for that opening when it came. Having grown up in a suburban community with many opportunities for sports and summer camps, I had participated in all kinds of sports while growing up and I understood the basics. I knew baseball games had nine innings and football games had four quarters!

Strong Women Tell Their Stories

I didn't have high expectations. None at all, in fact. I majored in English and my only career model while in school was my mother. She had trained to be a teacher, but spent one day substituting in a classroom where kids were throwing erasers and decided she didn't want to teach after all. She became secretary to the editor of *Field and Stream* magazine. I thought that being a secretary was a fine job for a woman. I learned to type and later took shorthand during my senior year at Cornell.

Wanting to get away from the East, I went out to San Francisco after graduation and spent about nine months there working as a secretary. But I missed my friends back East and came home to New York.

The San Francisco job was not for me. I worked for two executives in the underwriting office of an insurance company: deadly boring. Maybe if I'd had a different job I would still be in San Francisco at that insurance company. I came back to New York ready for adventure but with no career goal in mind. Television seemed exciting....

I walked in off the street to ABC, NBC and CBS, applied, took the tests, and was offered jobs at all three. I didn't know a soul.

At the time, Jules Bergman at ABC was starting children's programming. His first question in my interview seemed rather rude, "What do you know about office procedures at ABC?" I said, "Absolutely nothing, I've been in the building twenty minutes," and concluded that this man and I were never going to be soul mates. Strangely enough, he later offered me the job. Meanwhile I had gone over to NBC where three jobs were offered: production secretary on "123 Go!" with Jack Lescoulie as host, secretary to John Chancellor, and secretary to Craig Fisher, associate producer of the "Today Show." The job with John Chancellor was the glamour job, but something told me it was not for me. I went to the "Today Show."

Five or six years later, secretarial jobs were no longer given to college graduates. But at that point they were, and the person you worked for determined how far you went. Craig had an idea for a children's program. This was the time of Newton Minnow's pronouncement on the "vast wasteland" of television. Under fire for low-quality programming, the networks bought Fisher's idea and overnight Craig became a producer of a new show. I went with him as his secretary.

At the time we made this move, he said I didn't know enough to be a production assistant. But I set up the offices and did the research. We moved in June, started taping in September, and by then I was the production assistant. The show was "Exploring," a program for children in a magazine format. The format is found everywhere now but was

Voices of the Silent Generation

revolutionary then. It had storytelling, music, mathematics, social studies and science. It was a classy show, with Dr. Albert Hibbs as host. And extremely successful--we won a Peabody Award that year. We did thirteen shows one year and twenty-six the second year, then worked all summer and taped ourselves right out of jobs! Our work for the year was complete as the first shows were aired in September. There was no reason to keep us around.

We were about to be fired, when a man named Shad Northshield arrived on the scene. He later moved to "Sunday Morning" on CBS, but was then at NBC. He suggested a show that would become the very first magazine program (for adults) done for television. It grew out of the *New York Times* newspaper strike in the early sixties when Shad Northshield brought in columnists to read their columns on the air.

Shad was then promoted to NBC News president and left. The magazine show was scheduled but there was no production team to do it. So they took Craig's group from "Exploring," the children's show. We swapped in and did the same thing for adults. We had segments on classical music with Martin Bookspan, and folk music with Oscar Brand. Richard Shickel, who now reviews movies for *Time*, did books for us, and William Zinser, who wrote for *Life* magazine, covered movies. Ailene Saarinen handled art and architectural design. It was aired on Sunday afternoons and was called "Sunday," a brand new concept.

The program was cancelled after about a year and a half. In June of 1964 we were all once again fired. Craig Fisher went on vacation while we all floundered about trying to find jobs in different corners of NBC.

Sports coverage in those days was part of the news department. The

With a mobile unit at the 1969 World Series

executive producer of sports programs also handled special news programs such as "Sunday." I went to him on a Wednesday, and said I was fired as of Friday. He said "Oh, I just got a call from the "Sports in Action" people in Washington. They need a production assistant to do a rodeo in Laramie."

I got on the first plane to Wyoming and did the Laramie show. "Sports in Action" was based in Washington so I moved there and worked for its producer, Stuart Shulberg. While in DC I heard that "Sports in NYC" was looking for a production person to coordinate commercials. I applied for the job, got it, and that's how I ended up in sports.

I spent the next seven years coordinating commercials for sports events. It worked out well. My skills are in systems and organizing so I quickly figured out a foolproof system to get commercials where they needed to be for weekend sports programming. I was also able to do the production work I'd been doing in the news area. I could type endless routines with commercial numbers with half my brain, using the other half to do production work. In 1971 I was offered a job in management as a unit manager, in those days work never offered to women. I turned it down because I wanted to go to Japan to do the Winter Olympics. I had always been more interested in the Far East than Europe.

Looking back, I can see that pushing numbers around for management was more secure than production work. It's different now, but in those days it was an honor to be offered a unit manager's job.

I was made associate producer right after I came home from the Olympics in Sapporo, and in 1972 I became a producer. I was thirty-four years old. My first assignment as a producer was in the fall. I followed Hank Aaron around waiting for him to hit his 715th home run to tie, and then break, Babe Ruth's home run record. I went to the ballparks or to the nearest NBC affiliate to record his games, then turn around and play them as instant specials to the network. Aaron hit number 715 in the spring but for various reasons I didn't get the credit. Thereafter I was associate producer for Joe Garagiola's Monday night pre-game shows and produced the World Series pre-game shows.

I was the only woman doing this kind of work. Technically, there was another. Eleanor Sanger, Roone Arledge's secretary, had done some production work. When I was named an associate producer, NBC did all sorts of press releases about me. Not to be outdone, Roone named Ellie a producer the very next day! Since I was an *associate* producer, technically I was not the first woman producer but the second.

I was made an associate producer because I told the division president that I had been doing someone else's work. That someone had been a wonderful unit manager and everybody loved him. He was supposed to be writing on-air promotion but was monumentally unqualified for this. In his soul he was a disorganized person, so I ended up doing his job for him. They finally figured that out, and *he* was promoted to associate producer just to get him away from the job I was doing for him!

That's when I went to the division president and said, "Wait a minute! If this is going to happen for him but not for me, then tell me so I can leave. I'm finished with doing other people's work and not getting the credit." Five days later I was an associate producer. Someone in personnel told me the speed with which that happened was record breaking. So without ever telling me they appreciated my work, they did show it by giving me the job, and that was how I ended up with the title of producer.

I can't remember exactly when guilt over the treatment of women began to spill over. NBC used me for that at a time when giving women an equal opportunity was a new idea. I was the "token woman" and didn't resent it. I did the work and earned the job, after all. I was then fed to the press to be interviewed as the "first woman sports producer." Many years later, those same reporters found out that NBC was letting me go and called for my story. The executive who let me go was upset that it appeared in the newspapers. I said "Look, you fed me to them all those years ago, what makes you think they won't write about it now!"

looking back

I don't actually have much self-confidence. It has a lot to do with upbringing. I find it interesting that I remember so little about growing up. It's all gone, repressed.

I still don't have a very good sense of self. At what age I couldn't tell you, but it got lost somewhere along the way. What I do have is an overdeveloped Puritan sense of responsibility, wherever that comes from. I have a sense of humor and a certain perspective on life; both have gotten me through. I have an even temperament, but I think there is a lot of anger hidden down below somewhere. That I have controlled it all my life is probably miraculous and perhaps a virtue of sorts. I also have great patience with people who try hard, but not with those who don't.

My family moved to our house in Darien, Connecticut when I was three. My parents lived there until fifteen years ago, so we had one home all those years. My father was a mechanical engineer and worked in a factory in Glenbrook. He was home for dinner every night. At six every evening he would drive in the driveway and we'd all sit down and have dinner together. There were four children, one sister three years younger than I am, another thirteen years younger, and a brother six years younger.

My mother made sure we had piano lessons and figure skating and many other children's activities. If working had been acceptable my mother would have worked. She had live-in help and led an active community life. She was president of her Cornell Alumni Class; my parents and my brother all went to Cornell. We attended the Presbyterian church and I was devoted to the church choir. I continued that in college, and have retained knowledge of music and the church from those days. But I don't know that I actually paid much attention to religion itself.

For some reason, my mother was always competing with me, although I didn't know or understand it at the time. I was the oldest, the trial balloon and the good little girl; her competitiveness was just with me, not with my younger sisters. My parents didn't know what to do about our sibling rivalry. Throughout our childhood, my sister Barbara and I fought physically; we actually punched each other. Maybe that's a clue to how I wound up in sports!

Although he was physically in the house, my father was actually an absent father. I wish I could tell you more than that, but I've forgotten so much. I don't let myself think deeply about it; for whatever reasons, he functioned as a provider, not as a father.

I have a reasonably high IQ so school was not difficult for me, but I had a weight problem as a child and teenager, so until I got a grip on that I was mostly miserable. I did no dating at all in high school until my senior year when I had a date for the prom. Toward the end of high school I got diet pills from our doctor and was able to lose and keep the weight off. That's why I wasn't heavy at Cornell.

I was the butterfly coming out of a cocoon at Cornell. That was the magic moment for me. Someone even put me up for Freshman Queen, though I didn't win. I also discovered what I was good at. I found that I could organize things, that I could be chief in charge of this-or-that and get people to cooperate. I had not done that sort of thing in high school; I thought of myself as a fat little kid and didn't even try. When I got to Cornell, I even changed my name. I'd grown up as Gail. My middle name was used because my mother is Jinny. As I left for college I told myself it was time to decide. I started calling myself Ginny and became a different person in more ways than one on that first drive from Connecticut to Ithaca.

As to my relationships with men in general, I think the problems trace back to my relationship with my father, or lack thereof. I'm sure it's not a coincidence that neither of his daughters is currently married.

As to coming to terms with that, well it all just sort of happens, and before you know it, people are asking, "Why didn't you ever get married?" The years when I might have married were years when I was working all the time. Very few men were interested in waiting for me to return from wherever I was. That was problem number one. The other was that I did date and had relationships with people at work that never really developed into anything. Friendships suffered from the inconveniences of my travel and work; not many people understood when you couldn't show up for things. There was something bizarre about a woman doing sports in those days. When I was introduced to men, all they wanted to talk about was my job. It was as though they wanted to hear about a job they might like to have. As to what I was besides the job, they weren't interested.

Ginny Seipt. High school graduation picture, 1956

mentors

There were a few men who helped me along the way. I worked closely with two extremely creative men. I've mentioned one whom I more or less kept organized. When I moved to Sports, I became associate producer to various people. But I worked mostly with a man named Don Ellis. Like Craig Fisher, he was a lovely, decent, kind human being. I was a godsend to both because I kept the bus on the road and on a straight line. I worked with them for major chunks of time and they encouraged me. It was with them that I became a producer myself. Then Carl Lindeman was not afraid to promote me when I squeaked about being treated unfairly.

The next person who appreciated what I could do and was supportive was Don Ohlmeyer, who came from ABC to NBC to be the executive producer for the Moscow Olympics. My work was not appreciated by the existing staff at NBC, but Don could evaluate people's ability. He doubled my salary and gave me a contract. When Don came in 1978, NBC had no sports anthology like "Wide World of Sports." There were two people in the department who knew how to edit shows. I was one and Teddy Nathanson was the other.

Don figured out early on that I was the only person who knew how to make a twenty-minute segment out of a seven-hour event. It was he who acknowledged this, then promoted me and that made me professionally equal to the men. I don't know if I ever made as much as the men, but I made a decent salary. I was the first woman ever to produce an NFL football game and Don gave me that assignment. It got him a lot of press but I was seen as the token woman.

With Freshman Cynthia Ferris at Cornell, 1958

For us, during every football season in the middle of November a sort of doldrum time arrives when we were still a very long way from the Superbowl and yet trying to get the ratings up. One year they did a game without any announcers, using just the cameras and the cheering. That got a lot of attention, and the next year it was my assignment to produce that football game.

Whatever the reason was, I didn't have much life outside of the job. I really gave my life to NBC because that's what it took to do my particular job. Women married to men who are sports producers raise the children by themselves.

There wasn't time to do anything outside of NBC. At first I tried some volunteer work and inviting people to dinner. But I so often had to call and cancel; it all became too difficult. Finally, it got to the point that if I were going to a town where I knew someone, I wouldn't even tell them I was coming because I'd spend so much time just trying to get together, usually without success.

With Gerry Post, editing profiles of athletes for the ill-fated 1980 Olympics

But it was also fun! It seemed the best of all possible worlds. It's inherent in the business of television that you don't ever know what you will be going to do when you come in through the door in the morning. Some people cannot tolerate such a life; I found it all fascinating.

There are problems with trying to do every show well. How many times can you produce, for example, a good gymnastics competition and come up with something just a little new? Just for myself I have to do a different opening all the time. I can't do the same thing I did last time or two years ago. Department management wouldn't know the difference if I used the same openings for a particular championship. But I would. I never wanted to repeat myself, although I could have and nobody would have been the wiser.

social change

I didn't develop much of a feminist consciousness during those heavy work years. I was just too busy and was also doing fine, though I was aware that many women were not. By the time I left NBC Sports in 1987, I was getting calls from women wanting to be sports producers. I talked to many of them, gave speeches, sat on panels and spoke to all kinds of people about television and sports. To this day, I say, "If you're a woman and you want to do sports production, know that for women the road to executive producer in a sports division is long and may be a dead-end. It is a brutal thing that isn't going to change. And if you bitch about it, it only gets worse."

Strong Women Tell Their Stories

Even today, young women just out of school come to me and say, "I want to be in television; how do I do it?" And my advice is about the same. I was lucky, though it took eight years to move from production assistant to producer. Today it happens in two or three, yet women in sports television now are still frustrated. I didn't start out with any particular ambitions; the women I've counseled have far greater ambition than mine for whatever they want to do. Their frustration must be monumental. At cable and places other than the networks there are more and more jobs in sports production, and there will be more women. But whether there will be real opportunity or women will be stopped at associate producer, I do not know.

Getting angry in this business doesn't usually work. The last thing I'd ever do, no matter how angry I got, would be to take somebody on. I'd never work again. If I had sued at the time they let me go, I might have won, but I'd be eighty-two by the time the case got anywhere. Corporations are pretty good at defending themselves. One woman sued and the process took ten years. They were not allowed to fire her so she had her job all through this, then ended up losing. Actually, she didn't have a good case.

My life has been so specialized and focused I can't even tell you how much I was affected by social changes of the last thirty years. As far as I know, I have never been rejected simply because I was a woman. When I was asked to do something I did it as well or better than any man. I have, by and large, been treated as an equal. I've been told that certain men think I'm tough. Some people think I'm tough because I can distinguish between a person who is jerking my chain and someone who has a real problem.

setbacks

Losing my job after twenty-five years was the shock of my life. They gave me a watch in December and in January told me that my contract would not be renewed. So the dilemma is that if your whole identification is your job, when you lose your job, you lose your identity. I was given six month's notice. In the present climate there are no permanent jobs in television for people who are doing what I do. Companies are getting rid of people to eliminate overhead. Thirty percent of the cost of an employee is life and health insurance and companies just don't want to be bothered with that. Everybody is freelance; there are no benefits, no health insurance. I take care of all that myself.

I was lucky though. My last day at NBC was June 30th, 1987. On August 1st of that year a strike began at NBC involving all writers and the technicians. That meant programs were without writers. The ongoing shows were fine; they had enough people. But NBC was just starting a show called "Sunday Today." They called me and I went to work on the show.

You can do a story that's more than two and half minutes long with this format. I got to hire the crews I wanted and work and leave whenever I wanted to. I delivered the pieces to the length that they wanted and everyone loved what I did. Now, a few years later, I have been able to move out of sports and into news and can earn a living as a news producer. In the process, I've spent time in the halls with people who do remember what I've done. Others, younger people, think they have a new idea and it's what we introduced decades ago.

Most of my sports colleagues have since been let go, including many of the highly-paid experienced ones. In most cases they have no alternative identity. Four or five men have not yet found employment. Unless you have the right connections there is no solution. Cable will hire them but pay one-eighth of what they had made. One has since become a travel agent.

In many respects, I am numb. But I am not bitter or immobilized. I realize I'm not alone in being a freelance struggling around in the world. Others face the same situation.

So that was one major jolt for me. A second was being hit by a car that broke my leg. That changes your perspective fast! I'd never had anything life-threatening happen before; I was totally unprepared for it. My leg was fractured in the accident and I was in a cast four and a half months. First, a hip-to-ankle cast, then a fiberglass cast just above the knee, and finally a Velcro shoe with cut out circles....

I used to walk for exercise but since the accident I have a problem with how my body has been repositioned. I get bizarre spasms, not in the broken leg, but in the other one. I don't understand it. Talking about aches and pains is a total bore, but the truth is, my physical activity is reduced.

After being let go, then the accident, I began thinking more and more about myself, that I should treat myself better. In the next ten seconds I could be dead, so I had best live well. That's the wrong motivation for being nice to yourself, but at least I now have one.

We all learn from the good and the bad. Some of what I have experienced has made me a bit cynical; I don't think I have grown much in a positive sense. But suffering is a relative term. The trauma of being hit by that car, and all that followed, made me realize how lucky I was to be alive. Rather than feeling bitter about what happened, I'm more appreciative of life itself. I am fortunate in many ways: my parents are both alive, though frail; my sisters, brother and nephews are healthy and happy.

looking ahead

So far I'm surviving. I've come to realize that I need to be watchful. Experience has turned me into a person that I was not raised to be, but at this point there isn't an alternative.

Hindsight is really terrific, isn't it? I probably should have chosen a more secure and less all-consuming career. Traveling the world to do shows broadened my life, but the trade-off was that my world at home was narrowed down to edit rooms and crazy schedules, leaving me rather isolated. But perhaps it's my nature to be inward and self-absorbed. If I had required a large circle of friends I might have found a way to make them.

I don't have many close friends. Being a friend is a two-way street and I've never felt that I could do my share. I've been reluctant to commit myself to friendships because I always wind up being the recipient and never the giver. My work got in the way of many things. But now I do see a small group of people. Some are my sister's friends; she is more outgoing and social than I and has a group of people that she calls on a regular basis.

We do sometimes discuss personal problems at the office; how we cope, that sort of thing. I have people who keep track of me and that I keep track of, but not as a regular sort of ongoing call-me-every-day. And, however much we hated each other as children, my sister is the one I find myself calling now.

As to the future, that's a tough one for me. I can't envision the day when I won't be working. I don't know where I want to be or what I want to do if I decide to stop working. I'm not sure I can even afford to stop working. Or if I actually would stop if I could. Perhaps teaching in a college or university lies ahead.

Aging is the problem I worry about most. I fear the time will come when I will not be able to find work in my field. As a single woman there'll be no one to take care of me should I be incapacitated. My sister would probably get stuck with me, and I hope to avoid that. The same would be true for her, of course, since she is not currently married either. Old age is the time when being single is a problem. The retirement place where my parents live seems a good solution for them. Planning for such a place is the answer to this problem, but I worry whether I will be able to face that decision in a realistic way at the right time. My parents didn't for a long time and most people don't. I have to admit that I'm probably like most people.

I wonder why people who know what should be done, don't do it. What is it about the nature of man that allows us to lie, cheat, steal, kill and all those other ways humans fail one another? Why, why do we do it? If we knew the answer, could we change?

I haven't the foggiest idea of how to solve such problems. Does that make me, and all of us, failures? The situation in our country, and the world, does not look very promising. I never used to be afraid to live in New York, but every day something happens that says I'd better get out before I'm a victim too.

I'm grateful I was born with basic intelligence, got an education and was able to use it in a way that was satisfying to me and, I hope, entertaining to others. Despite the changes in the industry and my work, I have been able to survive, at least for now, and still have a rather nice roof over my head. And I'm glad to have my health and sisters and a brother to help deal with our aging parents.

NBC Sports Reunion with Sandy Koufax, 2004

Strong Women Tell Their Stories

My approach always was that I do my job the best I can, and if I'm not as good as somebody else, maybe I deserve to be fired. That's my overdeveloped work ethic. I would say to a young person today, try for success in this field, but don't throw yourself off a bridge if it doesn't work out. It's not your fault, but the temper of the times. And these are very difficult times.

I keep wondering whether I should have left the bustle of NYC and gone elsewhere. Then I think of all the people outside NYC who said their lifelong ambitions and dreams were to succeed in New York; you know that old saying about success not being real unless you make it in New York. I just appreciate what I've been able to do this one time around.

Postscript I, 2005:

Fifteen years after the initial interview, Ginny is still working, if less frenetically, after four decades in a demanding business. She has fewer doubts today about the price of survival in television production. Working three days a week, rather than all hours, all days, she now sees more friends and does volunteer work. Alterations to the apartment purchased many years ago have created space for her needlework projects. Ginny wrote recently, "There's actually no better place to grow old than New York City! Great health centers, good public transportation, lots to do, and always interesting new people to meet."

Postscript II:

Mark Moore, a student who helped transcribe the oral history tape recordings, answered Ginny's question, "Does that make me, and all of us, failures?" Though he never met any of the women, Mark grew very fond of them, and often responded to their commentarys in print while he typed the oral histories into the computer. Deleting his many remarks from the transcriptions made extra work for me as I began the editing process, but it was also an entertaining and often moving look into the mind of a sensitive young man:

"No, Ginny, I think it makes us all part of humanity, afflicted and bewildered from the "git-go", as they say in the Southern mountains, but still trying to carry on however we can, usually with a hole in the bucket."

Mark Moore

SIDNEY CALLAHAN
Introduction

Combining career and motherhood since the nineteen sixties, Sidney Callahan has lectured or led workshops at over two hundred colleges and universities, Columbia, Harvard, Yale, Dartmouth, Johns Hopkins and Notre Dame among them. She has won awards for her columns and books, published dozens of articles, essays and reviews, and has been awarded several honorary doctorates.

Sidney Callahan's first book, *The Illusion of Eve: Modern Woman's Search for Identity,* was published in 1965. Affirming the value of faith along with a certain independence of thought and imagination, the book was greeted as the first feminist book for religious believers. Sidney was soon offering her message on the "Today Show," "Firing Line," "CBS News," and other television programs.

I first read Sidney Callahan when she was writing for the progressive newspaper, *The National Catholic Reporter.* I was a new mother, my husband was a graduate student, and the sixties were upon us. Sidney Callahan's columns and articles offered a new role model: a fine, imaginative writer who was also mother to seven young children. Struggling to live a life of mind and spirit as well as diaper and carpool, she treated each facet of her complex life with respect and humor.

Twenty-five years later, as I planned this book, I sought out the woman I'd long ago admired from afar and she kindly agreed to participate in the project. On the bright fall day of our first meeting, a friend drove me to Ardsley-on-Hudson, north of New York City. As we approached the Callahan's apartment house on narrow roads, dense foliage concealed any hint of our proximity to the Hudson River. I took the elevator to the top floor. Entering Sidney's apartment from the dark hall I was dazzled by light and a sense of dislocation: every window offered broad, bright vistas of blue sky and water. Late afternoon sunshine sparkled on the river and poured into the apartment. Surely I had walked into a beach house? Or an impressionist painting? No, just the upper reaches of a tall building perched on a hill overlooking the Hudson River.

Appropriate to the mythic status I had assigned her, Sidney, as she opened the door was encircled by a halo of sun, sky and reflected river light. I recalled certain aristocratic heroines in 19th century French novels and memoirs--animated, intensely feminine, the stewards of formidable intellects.

The imagination strains to accept the fact that Sidney, so delicate in appearance, gave birth to eight children in ten years. Without maids, nannies or housekeepers, Sidney and Daniel, married since 1954, raised six sons and one daughter. A seventh son died in infancy. In her sixties, Sidney returned to motherhood, helping to raise her granddaughter after the death of one son's wife.

We spent long hours taping her oral history, but also took time for tea, for visits with several Callahan sons and friends, a walk in nearby woods and a fine dinner with Dan. Also the author of numerous books and articles, Daniel Callahan founded the Hastings Institute for the Study of Bio-Medical Ethics, and travels widely as lecturer and consultant.

The next morning, Sidney prepared breakfast, taken as first light played on the river. The locale was the Hudson River, but the hospitality felt decidedly Southern. At the end of our time together I opined to Sidney that, given the seriousness of her writing, she seemed to possess a surprising streak of merriment. She laughed and said, "Yes, I come from a merry family."

Of the myriad pleasures to be found in this project, one of the finest was to spend an overnight in this little village on the Hudson River and to be amused, provoked and nourished by the hearts and minds of Sidney and Daniel Callahan.

Sidney Callahan
Ardsley-on-Hudson, New York
1990, 1993, 2005

It's never over. We're always in the midst of the transitional phase— we're never going to get there. We're never really going to be grown-up; there'll always be something we'll need to work on!

The sixties and seventies were a time of great trial for us. Our life was the soapiest of soap operas; we seem to have gone through everything.

Raising children was sometimes hell. Ours was the first generation of middle-class people to cope with drugs, and in our town it was the adults who seemed literally to go mad! They fell for open marriage, had affairs, and started smoking marijuana.

Here we were, parents trying to hold things together for our children, having so little support anyway. Then drugs swept in and just devastated the town, our family included. It was horrible, just horrible. And it was all so new that none of the adults, including the police, knew how to fight back.

Sidney Callahan, 1990

Children had to cope with drugs and a brand new sexual permissiveness for themselves and their peers. And a lot of "enlightened" parents in our town concluded that early sex was healthy and good. I knew that could not possibly be right or work out for anyone. It didn't. Everyone I knew was leaving the church, including my husband and my children. I wasn't tempted to leave, but it was hard being around alienated people. Our church was not helpful then either.

It hurts a lot that I was unable to pass religious faith on to my children. It's like having a beautiful diamond that no one wants. If I had it to do over, I would find a town with a strong church and a good religious school. All of us need a community with values similar to our own and plenty of support in raising children. We foolishly believed we could do it with our own strength alone. We hadn't fully measured the power of peer group influence.

Our children were so disillusioned by Watergate, Vietnam, Kent State. Their idealism was shattered. I had been brought up to be patriotic, and it became impossible to maintain that, much less convey it to our children. Then, too, a recession made it terribly difficult for our oldest son to find a job. That period in the seventies demoralized a great many people.

looking back

I had an unhappy childhood but a good adolescence. My parents had a bitter divorce when I was very young. Shortly thereafter my mother had a breakdown. So my father set about raising my sister and me. That was good for me, because his temperament was like mine. But he was called off to war, and that was my second great loss.

I was super-sensitive, highly irritable, very dogmatic. I was also intelligent but didn't know that for several years. We were treated like little princesses by the relatives who raised us. Actually, we felt halfway between waifs and princesses.

It was in many ways a privileged childhood. We were given everything we wanted, went to good schools, traveled, and were given all sorts of training about character and good manners.

We were taught perseverance, to struggle through to the end. It took persistence to eventually overcome my fears and difficult temperament. In time I developed a deep sense of gratitude. If you're grateful, you tend to be undemanding because you so appreciate what you have.

I learned much that was valuable from my father: about making do, being a part of a community, having a sense of filial piety, self-reliance, not complaining. All good stoic virtues. There was the sense that you can do it, you can work it out. I remember my father saying, "If anyone else can do it at all, it should be duck soup for you."

He gave us a sense of family honor, a sense of being part of a long, ongoing family community of shared values. He was a Southerner, after all, from Alabama, an interesting mix of the pioneer and chivalrous gentleman. He was a romantic populist. Sir Walter Scott was a hero in his family. The grown-ups seemed to understand rules that we young people were expected to learn. Much simpler than today!

We were raised in Virginia, during the Second World War. Children were taught to be extremely patriotic, perhaps the last generation of Americans inculcated with patriotic pride. Religion was interwoven with school. In our public school, a gold star was put on your chart if you'd gone to Sunday School that week. As a little girl who loved to receive gold stars, I, of course, went to Sunday School.

After my father remarried, he and my stepmother went out to parties and dances, and we always had a sense of fun and merriment. It didn't seem such a workaholic world as today. Prejudice and racial discrimination were taken for granted by many people, and yet in other ways the times seemed so innocent.

I had wonderful aunts. One in particular, an intellectual, started me on a lifetime of reading. She was very kind to us; it took years for me to fully appreciate the depths of her gifts. Unhappy children often find solace in books. I certainly did, and loved those wonderful literary women—Jane Austen, Louisa May Alcott. I still feel like a 19th century person from all that early reading. George Washington was a hero when I was young, also Robert E. Lee, Franklin Delano Roosevelt, Madame Curie, and Scarlett O'Hara. How is that for a combination? And later I read lives of the saints, especially St. Thomas More and the two St. Teresas. As an adult, Dorothy Day seemed to me a living heroine.

My stepmother also loved books, culture, and religion. When my father went to sea, she stepped in. She taught us to sew, gave us a sense of enterprise, and taught us how to persevere just as my aunts had: make mistakes, but press ahead anyway.

Having those wonderful women, as well as a sister, in my early life made me always want women friends. My sister was and is extremely important to me, and as a child I always had girl friends and little clubs. I went to girls' schools and to a women's college. So women friends have always been an important foundation of my life.

I acquired some confidence in adolescence, had good friends, and grew to be pretty, which I had not been as a little girl. So I have lovely memories of being a bit of a belle, going out a lot, and just having a wonderful time! I was a Miss Goody Two-Shoes, but very sociable, went to many parties, and got A's in school. It was lovely. We were all happier without all the early sexual involvement of today. It just *worked* so much better. There was an air of romance and fun, but also the understanding that a system was in place to protect young people. The sexual revolution has robbed more recent generations of innocent playfulness.

My father had been raised in a strict, narrow-minded, anti-intellectual denomination. The sabbath was a horrible day where everyone sat around being glum. So he did not want us raised to "be religious" in that way. In my rebel phase I wanted to upset him, so, of course, my rebellion was to become very religious. At fifteen, I became an ardent Christian, though not a Catholic, and attended the Church of the Savior in Washington, D.C. Anna Freud once said that the great defenses for adolescents are being somewhat ascetic and intellectual. I can tell you, she was right! They work! They keep you out of trouble, and produce self-disciplined, idealistic, happy, self-confident people.

At eighteen, I met my husband Dan. He was a little older and had a deep influence on me. We married when I was a junior at Bryn Mawr. We grew up together, influencing each other as we went along. I started early in my adult life to combine marriage, children, and academic work.

My way of dealing with fear and timidity is to plunge in. I feared having babies and had a lot of them, with natural childbirth. If I am afraid of something, I push myself to do it: go back to school or write a book. I'm timid physically, but socially and intellectually, I will charge in. I was afraid of being poor; we pressed ahead, insisting that we wouldn't care about money.

children and family life

Having children has meant everything to me! They were such a gift, such a privilege, such a training school for life, such a joy. Even with all the trouble and suffering we had, it was all such a drama, such an enlargement of life. You create an on-going soap opera. You create the family community with all the connecting, the reaching out to each other over many years.

I know what I would have been without them: a selfish, neurotic little intellectual! Having children saved me from all that. It was the greatest thing in my life. Having lost my own mother, and then having a child who died, our children were a reaffirmation of life and its fruitfulness.

My own father was authoritarian, but oddly enough, we were raised rather permissively. He believed in us, talked to us, gave us a lot of freedom and responsibility, and used a bit of guilt to keep us in check. As a hypersensitive child, I would be crushed if I thought I had displeased him.

But my own children were not at all transfixed by their parents! Perhaps because there were so many of them, our children were more attuned to each other than to us. But I did read to them, sometimes for hours at a time. It was the one thing that would keep all the boys from jumping around and hitting each other over the head!

Those early baby years were exciting and wonderful, but I sometimes felt that my children paid a price for our having them so close together. I thought that was a wonderful way to do things, but I later realized I may have been taking risks with their development. I wanted a big family, and I wanted them quickly. But I was so young! I can see now that it actually was taking risks with someone else's life, a risk that is not worth taking.

One winter in Cambridge, just out of desperation, when I needed to take the other children out, I would leave the baby sleeping alone in the house. It kills me now to think that I actually did this. Today, of course, I would have been reported for child neglect . . . and convicted, I'm sure! So I always feel for young mothers who out of desperation leave their children sleeping while they go to work or on an errand.

A woman I knew frequently left her children alone and would say, "The angels will care for them." I thought that was horrible! And yet sometimes I felt pushed and left my own baby asleep, to get the others out to play, or whatever else. I should *never* have done that.

I often felt like such a terrible failure as a mother, but perhaps many mothers feel like that. I tried as hard as I could, but the times and my own expectations made it difficult.

Dan did his graduate work at Harvard in the fifties, when Catholics were just starting to be assimilated into academe and faced prejudice. Perhaps people thought we couldn't think for ourselves! We felt isolated and so different from others. To survive, we had little reading groups and a club. Of course, the married Catholics had many more children than anyone else, and we helped each other a great deal. We had a grand sense of community that was quite wonderful.

We admired Dorothy Day and her Catholic Worker movement and visited her Houses of Hospitality. Dorothy's work with destitute people inspired us to volunteer for groups promoting peace and nonviolence and, later on, with those protesting the Vietnam War.

We were connected for a time with a group of families trying to live in the Franciscan manner, very sparse and ascetic. Learning to be poor as an adult was difficult. I wasn't able to overcome my materialism, but did at least fend it off for awhile. But we found that, though one might sacrifice and go hungry oneself, it was not something we wanted for our children! Still, the fifties offered new ideas, new possibilities for young believers. And as the children grew older, they could see that we were committed to various causes. We wanted them to be aware, to develop their own social conscience, and, if possible, to love and respect each other along the way!

When Dan finished his degree, we left Harvard and moved to a small town with no religious community. I had just lost our fourth child to Sudden Infant Death Syndrome. That was horrible, and we suffered intensely. I didn't even know that I was supposed to allow myself a long grieving period. So it was a pretty awful time.

Slowly over twenty-five years, Dan and I built a bit of community, PTA and such. But never the same close-knit religious group. And, as described earlier, it was during that period, the sixties and seventies, that our family life became so turbulent.

Now we have a community in a larger sense, people we know all over the country, some in New York. But everyone is so busy, we don't get to see them in easy, informal ways. Perhaps four or five times a year, that would be a good year; there isn't the sense of a day-to-day connection. Dan and I tried Christian Family Movement, and made other similar efforts at different times. But as you become a specialized person, the harder it is to find, outside of your own family, a whole group who can become soul mates.

Sometimes it seems as though all of this happened to someone else a long time ago. Was that me? It must have been someone else!

religion

I became religious and an intellectual at the same time; faith inflamed my curiosity. That's a good fit because the quest for meaning and the desire to know are fed by worship. Catholics worship and confront great mystery all the time. I converted to Catholicism as a young adult, but I've always considered myself a Christian humanist. God wants us to know, wants us to learn about creation. I've heard this expressed as "Yahweh is the head of the Science Club!" Yahweh is the transcendent being, and we must seek His order and truth. In our time and country, most intellectuals are not religious, but that is not the historic norm; it's an oddity. Throughout history, religious and intellectual quests have usually been closely allied.

Spiritually, I've not been much of a risk-taker. Since my mother was schizophrenic, I feared getting into religious areas that would prove more than I could handle. So I always resisted unusual religious experiences.

Emotionally, my religion has fed my spirit and kept me wanting to love and be alive. You ask the Holy Spirit to make your heart more alive, more tender. We can become very callous, but religion and worship help us to stay sane and find balance and peace. Also community, a way of life.

I believe one can grow from suffering. Some forms are so debilitating, demeaning, and make people so unbearably miserable, that degree of suffering often does not bring growth. My own experiences did make me grow, become more empathetic, more humble, more appreciative, and closer to God. I have tried not to enshrine my own experience, but there were times when I was so broken and in need. Losing our fourth child was truly terrible. But we were forced to reach out in our need and learn how to accept help, to give and receive.

It was another jolt to find my children weren't like me. They just weren't! They've gradually come around as they've grown older, but for many years they didn't do anything I had hoped they would do. They weren't interested in school, they rebelled, they were involved with drugs, misbehaved in different areas of their lives. It broke my heart in so many ways, the mistakes, the shame . . . some of that seemed worse at times than losing our child.

There was a time when I was thought to have a terrible disease. I recovered but the physical pain did show me how much I'd taken good health for granted.

Dan and I both found it extremely painful to watch our children struggle, to have to stand by sometimes, unable to help them. Through all of this there were periods of stress in our marriage during which Dan and I had terrible difficulties with one another. We both suffered greatly. So those were all times that forced me to grow and become a different person.

surprises

I had many surprises as an adult. If you are conscientious and life has gone reasonably well for you, there's an inclination toward the "good person's" sins, being proud and judgmental. I was an arrogant person, with much to learn. I'd always think after each terrible shock, well, now I know everything! Then another jolt would come along, and I'd think now I *really* know everything. POW! There'd be another. As a parent, one is soon humbled. Children and life do that for all of us, bring us to our knees!

I was surprised by my strengths and by my weaknesses. It was a shock that I did as well as I did, and that I could be so weak. I stopped drinking because I saw the beginnings of a problem with alcohol. If anyone had ever suggested to me years ago that I would have a problem with alcohol, I'd have laughed at the idea! But I did, so I stopped altogether.

It's paradoxical that we are so complex, good in some areas and so bad in others, sensitive and also tough. That we can be so calm on the exterior and a mess inside. I was stunned to learn all of this.

Then falling into success, and a little money, another surprise! We had thought we'd always be poor. Dan took a risk in founding the Hastings Center, but it has gone well. His writing was successful, and eventually we were both in demand for our writing and lectures. It was money from heaven. Finding that the things we wanted to do anyway turned out to be "valuable" was a great relief. We're all created by our times, but if your interests just happen to fit into the times, it is a tremendous advantage.

working

I was stultified, thwarted during the first ten years of our family life, before I started writing. I was extremely happy with our children during that period, but frustrated with the sense of having gifts and not being able to use them. Writing at last was just the right thing to do. It was a way out for me; I wrote about what I had been trying to work out for myself. My first book, in 1965, *The Illusion of Eve: Modern Woman's Search for Identity*, came out of that period.

I actually wrote the first book before all the social changes of the sixties and seventies. Those changes were already happening within myself. When I was first married, women with children simply weren't even accepted in a graduate school. That I finally got into graduate school as an older woman is evidence of the impact of the woman's movement. But I would have become a psychologist no matter what. I've been interested in the same questions my whole life. Questions about consciousness, conscience, values, why people are the way they are, what makes people do what they do, character, fate. I was originally an English major, interested in those issues from a literary standpoint, but later shifted over to psychology.

That first book was an example of fitting into the times--people in the church were just ready for a feminist book in 1965. It seemed a revolutionary clarion call at that moment, and I was invited all around the country to give talks. Then the book about birth control came at just the right time. After that, I didn't quite hit the right moment again with my books, but those two were enough to give me a national reputation.

With family and time pressures, my personal and professional lives did not blend successfully at the beginning. Being an intellectual and a writer is at variance with being a mother. Writing and reading take solitude, concentration, and time. People in more extroverted fields probably blend their work and home life better. But being a social, available, nurturing person conflicts sharply with being a quiet, withdrawn, intellectual person.

I believed that being at home with my children was better for them. But all day, every day was stifling to me. I needed more. So after ten or twelve years of family life, I closed myself in a separate room for part of the day to write. Writing was ideal work for me because I could do it at home.

In 1972 I wrote a little book called *The Working Mother* after first asking a number of women how they had combined their work and private lives. This was long before it became the rage to write about these issues. I found combining work and family very difficult, and yet it seemed that everyone else solved these problems so easily. As I spoke to more and more women, I found it was in fact hard for everyone.

I was lucky to find that I was very schizoid! I would go into my study and be completely engrossed in my work. Then I came out and boom! I was completely into the children's lives, wiping the tears, applying the Band-aids. So being able to shift gears rapidly was my great advantage, my secret.

I had to struggle with my husband, though, over pursuing my own interests. He wanted me to join him at the Institute instead of going to graduate school. There were other things, too, so we had great battles and struggles during those years. Who'd have thought we'd be enjoying tennis with each other at this point? And reasonably well-matched, too!

Basically, though, as the children got older, I did more and more. Wrote more, went back to graduate school, began teaching, did some therapy with children and families. I should have gone back to graduate school earlier. I postponed it for too long, because I was in so much conflict about it. It would have been easier when I was younger; I could have gone to classes at night when they were all in bed. It was too hard when I finally did go; the children were old enough that they needed me there more or less all the time. If I had been more astute, put that goal a little higher up in the hierarchy of family needs, I could have done it earlier and without so much stress.

I'm finishing a book now about being the parent of adult children. What should our relationships be now? What do parents owe their grown children? Should they live at home as adults? Now there's the blend of private and professional life, right in that subject!

I would love to see some sort of unity arising out of all this work. It has seemed to me at times that I just wandered from place to place. I would like to see a theme coming forth. I wrote about women's problems, and sex, mothers and families, abortion, spirituality. Yet it has all been about moral choices and values, questions of conscience and moral development. I try to write about that place where psychology, religion, and ethics meet and overlap. That's why it looks like I've been wandering around intellectually, but perhaps I have been focused but haven't known what to call it. You can be interested in many things and try to work across a wide spectrum, but then you're left feeling a bit scattered and dispersed.

It's helpful that interdisciplinary work is coming back into academic fashion again. Psychology is becoming more philosophical, and philosophy is becoming more applied. So it has become easier to do the work that appeals to me.

looking ahead

Turning fifty didn't have much impact on me; I feel the same inside as I did when I was about four! Age is connected with how other people make you feel, and I've been allowed to just feel like myself, not a particular age. I do remember thinking, ah fifty, I should be grown-up! Well, maybe I'll feel grown-up at sixty. . . .

I think you do become more and more yourself as you age. We are creating our old age all the time, as we go along. The people who have been spiritual seekers seem to grow old the best. It becomes more and more clear that the spiritual way is the way to grow old; all the rest withers. But even that can't protect you from illness, and when illness comes, it becomes your road of suffering; there is no choice. I fear that greatly. But to the extent that one can choose, I think becoming more spiritually attuned is important. I see people reaping what they sow.

Inertia is the enemy, that sinking down and becoming more and more safe. It seems essential to stay connected, reach out for new experiences, new friends. Being healthy is important, too. When I was about fifty, I went to a health club for advice because I was a bit heavy and out of shape. I worked at that for a while and am much more active physically and feel better than ever. As a young adult, I was always so busy and tired! Having the children off on their own makes me feel free and ageless.

My appearance is important to me; I'm a Southerner after all! That was one part of the message, how you looked and how you presented yourself mattered a lot. I have wasted thousands of hours on appearance in a way that I wish I hadn't, but I know I'll always be that way.

Still, I'm glad I wasn't a beauty. Getting old must be terrible when you've been a beauty. I had the right amount of attractiveness in that I wasn't so good-looking that it was all-important. I had been an unpleasant-looking little girl, so I did appreciate getting better-looking as I got into my teens. But most women struggle when they pass out of that young twenty-five-year-old look. Aging is certainly a blow to the vanity. But you learn to play a different game with it when the game changes. The challenge as you get older is how to look like a distinguished person when you're not cute and pretty anymore.

A funny thing was that I transferred my narcissism to my children. Their bodies were young and beautiful and such a joy to me. Then what a blow it was when my sons started to turn grey or lose their hair! This was true mortality up close, my beautiful boys beginning to age. . . .

I spend loads of time dyeing my hair, putting on makeup, shopping for clothes which I love. Mind you, this is my own perception of myself; perhaps someone looking on might say, hmmm, too bad she doesn't pay more attention to those things. But I think I pay a lot of attention. I love jewelry too! I know it isn't the real me, and I could do without it all, but it's something that is important to me, say, in about the mid-range of importance. It's being Southern, and just plain vain. Now is the first time in my adult life that I've ever had a little money and been able to buy clothes, so I'm enjoying it! It's like the first time we ever had a nice house; before that it had always been a big wreck!

All my friends are getting very Zen; they just want to live in little white rooms with a single teacup. But here I am into things, this is my thing period.

Yet I do feel guilt about the material comforts in my life. I feel it very keenly, all the time. Dorothy Day said that whatever you have above the subsistence level is stealing from the poor. So I do feel terrible guilt because I believe so deeply in economic justice and that we all need to work toward it. And yet I just cannot give up living comfortably. So I do feel guilty and in bad faith. Getting more and more comfortable just sort of creeps up on you.

Beauty is important to me. It was hard when we were young and lived in ugly places with awful furniture. I like fine architectural design, good furniture. And a view, a vista. For the last twenty-five years, we have had a beautiful view of the river. I find that very sustaining. That was something about Dorothy Day that I marveled at. She could live in poverty, amidst disorder and ugly surroundings, because of her love for the people she served.

I once took Rosemary Houghton (English writer and founder of the Wellspring communities in Massachusetts and Scotland) to visit Dorothy Day. Even Rosemary, who is so religious and rather ascetic, came away saying, "Oh, I could not live that way, the disorder, the lack of privacy." That made me feel much better, because I certainly couldn't either.

questions

For me the great unanswered questions are the same ones others think about. So much suffering and evil. The great metaphysical and religious struggles: Why is there evil in the world? Where do we go when we die? And how do we think? Coming from a generation that came into consciousness during the Second World War, we were aware of so much evil. How could human beings do such things? You can become obsessed with it. I think many people of that time feel this way.

The new science and the universe are fascinating: the old pictures of the world are changing, yet we understand so little. Where is it all going: matter, space? It's provocative, particularly from a religious standpoint.

There is so much to be grateful for. Being born in America,

knowledge, life, health, family. Self confidence came from several of the same resources: the gifts of religious faith and intelligence, a good education. I have been showered with riches. It feels like too much sometimes.

I am still an outsider, caught between the separate worlds of family, church, work, university. That prevented my feeling captive to any one of those worlds. I always worked against the grain. Yet the lack of belonging, the instability have been sources of creative energy enabling me to have a large family, convert to Catholicism, get a degree later in life.

My family and my intellectual work give me the deepest sense of accomplishment. Having survived my family (and it was by no means always certain that I would!), and making it work while writing books, gave me a sense of triumph. Finishing the graduate work was so difficult, so hard. But I'm glad to have done it and been able to continue writing. Being a Catholic intellectual in a secular world is not easy, but it's satisfying to grapple with it all, to feel like the underdog struggling against the system! It's important to me, for some reason, to be witty and lively, too.

The major challenge of my life is to really love other people. To love the people we've been given to love. That's the basic statement. And to discipline myself to work. Love and work, that's it! And very difficult it is.

I would like to be remembered not so much for my work, but for what kind of person I was. That doesn't sound very grand, but there it is.

It's never over. We're always in the midst of the transitional phase; we're never going to get there. We're never really going to be grown-up; there'll always be something we'll need to work on!

Postscript, 1993:
Now I've turned sixty and I'm still not grown up . . .

Postscript, 2005:
My son and his daughter Perry are still with us; she was born on my sixty-third birthday and is a gift beyond compare. We have lived through her baby years and are now reaping the delights of a nine-year-old. I am still writing and lecturing, but not for a college. All our children are flourishing and making us happy and proud, so this is a very good time for our family.

SHIRLEY TAYLOR FRYE

Introduction

At the age of fifteen Shirley Taylor Frye left her family's tobacco farm in rural North Carolina to attend a state university. Her mother was concerned that it would be difficult for Shirley to "leave home and still be a lady."

On a winter afternoon many years later, I sat with Shirley Frye near a picture window in her sunny living room as she reminisced in the soft, modulated voice of an experienced public speaker who is very much "a lady." There is no artifice, no facade, however. Gentle, gracious, and hospitable, Shirley has long known who she is. Her record reveals years of unstinting work on behalf of others. She grew up under segregation but the focus of her adult life has been reconciliation of the races. Always optimistic, Shirley voices a firm belief in human progress.

In 1956, after graduating magna cum laude from North Carolina Agricultural and Technical State University, Shirley married Henry Frye, who graduated from the same university with highest honors. He served in the Air Force in the Far East, earning a law degree thereafter. One of twelve children, Henry also grew up on a farm in rural North Carolina. He was known in his family as the boy who worked from "cain't to cain't," from when you can't see in the morning until you can't see at night. Relating this bit of family lore, Shirley smiles knowingly at its life-long implications.

Henry won his second bid for the state General Assembly in 1969, becoming the first black legislator in the state since 1899. One of his first efforts was a bill to eliminate the literacy test as a requirement for voting in North Carolina. At the time, questions were so arcane that prior knowledge was a virtual requisite for passing literacy tests. To the surprise of many, the bill passed both the House and Senate easily, a credit to Henry Frye's legislative skills.

During the debate preceding the vote, Henry described his own experience.

An honors university graduate who had served the nation as an Air Force lieutenant, he had been denied the right to vote in Richmond County, because he couldn't pass the "literacy" test.

The voters of the state were offered a constitutional amendment to remove the literacy test. The North Carolina Bar Association did not support the measure and voters rejected it. The United States Supreme Court stepped in two years thereafter and ruled the literacy test unconstitutional. It was finally abolished.

In 1983 Governor James Hunt saluted Henry Frye's professional achievements and his years of community service by appointing him to the State Supreme Court. He was subsequently elected to two terms on the court and in 1999, Henry Frye was appointed the first black Chief Justice of the North Carolina Supreme Court. While serving on the Court, Henry commuted at regular intervals between the State Capital in Raleigh and his home in Greensboro.

Shirley Taylor Frye, 1990

After earning a Master's Degree in Special Education at Syracuse University, Shirley taught in elementary schools for several years. While her children, Harlan and Henry, Jr. were young, she served city and state in various capacities as a volunteer. When the children were older Shirley became an assistant professor of Education at her alma mater, and, some years later, development officer at Bennett College. The list of Shirley's local, state and national activities and numerous awards fills several pages. She makes no references to such a list, providing it only upon request.

Shirley's leadership proved to be especially valuable in the early 1970s as Greensboro made the transition to integrated schools. She helped devise a plan that brought together students, parents, and teachers in retreats and discussions. The process helped to calm and inform anxious citizens. Greensboro's transition was so successful that it became a model for other cities.

Today, Shirley recalls, "One of the reasons Greensboro was calm during school desegregation was that people from all parts of the city joined the cause." Throughout the city bumper stickers on cars, pick-ups and trucks read, "We're all in this together." And too, the February 1, 1960 lunch-counter sit-in was a proud legacy and reminder to citizens that people could indeed work together.

Since 1992 Shirley has served as Vice-President of Community Affairs for WFMY, a local television station. The work calls on her communication skills, perfected over many years. She dips often into a treasure trove of experience in community service, devising new ways for the station to serve the city's poorest families. Under Shirley's leadership the station has sponsored food drives, worked extensively with the public schools, and raised funds for a variety of non-profit organizations. It should be noted here that several years after recording her oral history, Shirley received the national Athena Award from the Chamber of Commerce in recognition of professional excellence and commitment to the advancement of women.

The pale rays of December sun begin to fade, reminding Shirley of a dinner meeting an hour hence. The afternoon of recollection ends, but the slanting winter light recalls a previous visit to the Frye home. The Frye's gathering every New Year's Day features several distinctive elements. The invitation is written in the comic rhyming verse with which Henry Frye enlivened legislative and court life for many years. Shirley makes an outstanding clam chowder, New England style, but with a southern touch. Finally, and still unusual at North Carolina private parties, people of various races mingle easily at the Frye home.

Shirley Frye's early years might be labeled, in today's language, as economically disadvantaged. Yet she had an unusually happy childhood and has passed on a rich heritage of love, hope, and faith to her sons, their wives, and their beloved grandchildren. Drawing on a strong character nurtured in youth, Shirley combined her many virtues with dedication to public service. She has emerged not only as the lady her mother hoped for but as one of the state's most distinguished women.

Shirley Taylor Frye
Greensboro, North Carolina
1990, 2005

When we saw the drinking fountains with the signs for whites and for 'colored,' my dad would tell us, 'In ours, children, they have Kool-aid.'

My parents always said we could do whatever we chose to do with our lives. My mother taught school for a short time but my father had only a third-grade education, formal education that is. Yet he helped me with my college algebra, and played the organ beautifully. He taught us that school was important and that we owed it to ourselves to take it seriously. That stayed with me. He was a tobacco farmer and I watched his struggle, the way he managed it all, without an education. I had an education; I knew I must use what I had been given.

looking back
I've always had a pretty strong sense of self. Growing up on a farm, we all had basic responsibilities, tasks to complete. My job before I took on milking the cows was making the beds, all the beds. My other sisters helped Mother with the cooking. When my Dad marketed the milk and butter, I went with him to keep his books. He also sold hogs, hams and I was right there with him. I watched how he worked with people...he did it all. He was a very smart man to do all this with a third grade education.

One year, my Daddy got the mumps and his face was swollen. I heard people say, "You'll go down." They meant the swelling of course, but I thought they meant he was going to go down and die. I wanted to help him with his work so he wouldn't die and I begged him to let me do the milking. I had to get up at 4:30 in the morning to do the milking. And can you imagine, on a grey rainy morning, with that cow's wet tail swishing...then to go to school and keep sniffing myself to see if I smelled like the cow. And wondering if my friends smelled the cow on me. I don't drink milk to this day, because I still smell the cow's udder! It's silly, of course.

I had taught myself to do the milking incorrectly. I had been holding my hands in the wrong position while milking, just a slight variation from what it should be. I developed something like carpal tunnel syndrome from incorrect use of those muscles and nerves. There was a kind of spur-like growth that eventually had to be surgically removed when I was older.

At school in that little town, I had a teacher by the name of Miss Jessie Beasley. I can remember her saying, hold your stomach in and your shoulders high, let people know that you are somebody. Miss Beasley had us do Negro History to develop pride in our heritage. She was ahead of her time. I made more scrapbooks of Booker T. Washington and Langston Hughes! If people of that time accomplished so much, she told us, then so could we! And my mother added how unfortunate it is that people determine the kind of people we are by our manners and what we wear. "Still, you must always be at your best," she would tell us.

The black teachers at our charismatic church gave us more positive reinforcement. They offered opportunities to express ourselves that we did not have in school. I was writing and delivering speeches in church when still quite young.

In the country we were all poor, though we always had enough food. We grew our own vegetables and never had to worry about what was sprayed on them because they came out of our own back yard. And they were so good. I've always loved fresh vegetables and fruit.

We children said we'd never eat raccoon. But one night at dinner after Daddy had been hunting, Mother told us, "You children finish up and I'm going to tell you something after dinner." After we'd eaten she told us we'd had 'coon and never knew it. That was her way of "coaxing" us to eat something we didn't want! All the while, she also wanted to be sure that my father wouldn't think his hunting had been wasted.

Working on the farm and then going to church--that was our life. My parents were able to shelter us from certain aspects of segregation. We couldn't go to the movie, there was no separate room for blacks, but my parents wouldn't have let us go anyway. Mother didn't go downtown alone. We went downtown only with Daddy and then we came right back. Daddy would play the organ and we would sing and enjoy ourselves at home.

My parents were what today we'd call fundamentalist Christians. They were, perhaps, overprotective; we weren't allowed to go to a dance, for example. We had to be at least sixteen to start dating, which meant I did not date at all until I went to college. One year my sister begged to go to the Junior-Senior prom at the little high school. My parents finally let her, but insisted I go with her, the two of us together. My father sat in the car and waited for us the whole time!

Working in tobacco, black and white people worked side by side, ate together in the field, and the children all played together. And here's something odd: a white family lived down the road and when those parents went away, their children stayed with us. If my parents had to leave, we stayed with them. It was that kind of relationship, even though we went our separate ways when we went to church or town.

As young children, we had to walk several miles to school and watch the white kids ride the bus. Now that was disturbing, we just couldn't understand why it had to be that way. It didn't make any sense.

Sometimes our father was able to take us to school in a horse and buggy, but mostly we walked and it was a long, long way. We had to cross a railroad trestle going to school. And we were so young. But our mother would say to us "Don't worry children, it won't always be this way."

When we saw the drinking fountains with the signs for whites and for "colored," my dad used to tell us, "In ours, children, they have Kool-aid." That was his way of shielding us. My parents did a good job of protecting us, keeping us isolated from the worst of what went on in those days. And too, I left in 1949 at age fifteen, so my time there was limited and I didn't have the terrible experiences that many black people had in those days. It seems to me that in the forties and fifties, people seemed to be more caring. You knew all your neighbors. You went outside and stood and chatted. Now our lives are all so busy and scattered, we hardly even know our neighbors.

Also, there was the closeness to life and nature...my mother raised chickens, and as we'd watch the hen sitting on those eggs, she'd tell us that life was developing. We children could compare this with our own growth...such wonderful ways to learn. My father raised hogs and you could see the females growing large with their baby pigs.

My mother loved flowers, especially her snapdragons. We always had them freshly cut in the house. Then there was the struggle with grass. I laugh about it now, but where I came from, you would chop off the grass because the idea was to have a "clean yard" instead. You swept and raked the dirt.

mentors

People other than my parents also had a profound impact on me. Going way back, I knew that Henry was the person I wanted to spend the rest of my life with. But I'm not so sure that he knew that or felt the same way early on. When he graduated from college, he went away to the Air Force. I didn't know the future of our relationship. But I decided that I would take the risk and wait for him. My family and close friends were worried about me. All those years! Henry was very focused and knew what he wanted to do. There wasn't necessarily a particular person in his plan at that time.

I knew that I wanted to marry and have a family. And I wanted to marry Henry. Thirty-plus years later, I know that was a risk well worth taking!

Henry is my best friend. I talk over everything with him. He recognized strengths I had before I understood them myself. In some of my civic work, there were some delicate and difficult times and he helped me to have the courage to see them through. In the early 70's I was able to prevail in situations involving a number of white civic leaders. This did a lot for my confidence and belief in my abilities. If I started to tell you some of the stories, we'd be here all night!

I stayed with Mrs. Bessie Lee when I went to school at North Carolina Agricultural and Technical University in Greensboro. She was a cafeteria manager for the schools. Her husband had been ill for about eighteen years and she took care of him herself. She would go to work and then come home and take care of him. She had so much determination and goodness. She was a true inspiration to me. And she convinced me to stay in Greensboro for school, which turned out to be an extremely important decision in my life.

John Leary was the principal of Washington School where I did my student teaching and later had my first teaching job. He was in his forties at the time and he was like a father, big brother and good friend all in one. If you saw him, you wouldn't necessarily know that he is black. There was a black association for teachers and a white association. He took me under his wing and brought me to the black teacher's association. I later became a delegate from our school. We'd stop on the way to meetings at restaurants where blacks weren't served. But he could get by, "pass," and go in and get food for us. He'd advise me about how to deal with that kind of situation. He was a wonderful guide and inspiration to me.

I was inspired by people who didn't have many advantages. Still, they were able to respond to their environment and their background with determination and hard work. Sometimes the capacity for hard work is greater than any privilege. I've known people you might describe as down and out, and yet they raised wonderful children. I have tremendous respect for them. They are heroes and have inspired me. They had so little and did much with what they had.

When I was a child, Pauline Frederick was my role model. I would listen to her on the radio every morning before going to school, and I thought that's what I want to be. But my mother was very firm about my being a teacher.

work and marriage

Except for the teaching I had been trained for, my career choices were not planned ahead. But I was prepared to accept opportunities. The work for the YWCA had a tremendous impact on my life. That was one of my more deliberate choices; some of the other things came through my involvement with so many people. Through working on the National

Board of the YWCA and dealing with such a variety of people, I developed the skills that led to the work in higher education.

I regret that I did not get the PhD while I was young. That limited my academic career. You might have experience and ability, but not having that degree can stand in your way. Who knows, I may still do it!

I worked so that Henry could go to law school and into politics. I felt our children needed me too, so there was some juggling at different points. It was a challenge to be involved in activities that made me happy and gratified while also keeping my family intact. Combining career and family is possible--with a husband who supports your efforts. I am happy with what I have been able to do.

My personal and professional lives do blend successfully, especially now that our children are grown. It helps, too, that Henry and I get along so well and enjoy many of the same things. We have been careful to spend time together, especially on weekends. With Henry spending most of the week at the State Capitol in Raleigh for so many years, I've traveled back and forth and been a good supporter for Henry. But now that my work keeps me from preparing meals every night that he is home, he is supportive of me. He doesn't cook, but he will fend for himself or go out without complaint. That's just a small example of the many ways he helps and encourages me.

As a college student, my goal was to get married and have children. At first, that is. Soon I realized I wanted to work with those who couldn't help themselves. My first work was with mentally-handicapped children, and to a great extent I have continued to work with disadvantaged people. I enjoy helping others find success. For me it's a way to use my own creativity. I love the behind-the-scenes role.

During the social changes of the sixties and seventies, I began to recognize my own independence. In 1973 I decided to accept the nomination for the National Board of the YWCA without discussing it with Henry. It was to involve trips to New York City and the meetings would be on weekends. We had made a pact that we would always spend our weekends together. Also our children were still young. So it was a big commitment.

I didn't plan not to discuss it with him, he was just out of town when the decision needed to be made. Usually I'd say I need to discuss it with my husband. Now my mother did not make major decisions for herself, so that is what I had grown up with. When he returned, I told him that I had decided to accept the position. But it didn't upset Henry in the least that I had made this decision on my own. I discovered that I really could be myself, do the things I wanted to do and it wouldn't be in conflict with my marriage at all.

There is a funny little extra chapter to that story though. Years later, Henry was asked to speak about the legislature to a group of professional women. To my surprise, he spoke to them about how hard it had been on him the first time I made a major decision without consulting him. And, of course, that was my decision to go on the National Board of the YWCA. He told them how upset he was with me at the time, but that he'd also realized great changes were taking place and that he would have to change a little, too. He went on and told them how proud he was of the work I had gone on to do.

After a few of my weekends in New York, I could see he was not happy about my being away. So I told him I was uncomfortable up there all by myself, and couldn't sleep. I asked if he could possibly arrange his schedule to come with me. He did and would work in the hotel while I was at my meetings. But he would always walk over and accompany me back to the hotel when my meetings were over. I would sometimes deliberately keep him waiting outside my meetings. That was an experience I believed he needed to have. For his own development! I had always done the waiting, and it was important for him to be on the other side of that. He took it well and I believe he did learn from it.

Also, in the world of the North Carolina Legislature, it had always been "I'd like you to meet my wife, Shirley." Now I could say, "I'd like you to meet my husband, Henry Frye." So this was healthy and good for our growth as human beings. Years later, I finally told him I actually slept like a log in New York before he started coming with me. We laugh about all this now.

During all the turmoil of the sixties, people often made remarks they later regretted. I learned to be careful, to think before speaking out. I seldom make a speech without writing it beforehand. I want to know later just what I said and be sure that I can later say no, I did not say this or that. When you speak extemporaneously, people can so easily misinterpret what you've said and you have little recourse.

During that period I came to realize there were good and bad people in every group— you just could not generalize. I learned that you can't judge a person until you have talked to him and discovered what he thinks and believes. We all speak out of our own experience. We all come from such different backgrounds and sometimes those differences prevent us from seeing that we actually do agree, or want the same things. We just use different language. We need to work to understand each other; it doesn't just happen.

At a National YWCA Board meeting I was talking rather freely, in a social situation with a group of people. I told them how important it is to me to look people in the eye, that I always think anyone who doesn't is just a coward. There was a Native American woman in the group and she said "Well, I beg to differ with you on that, Shirley. In our culture, it is considered to be too personal to look a person straight in the eye."

Well, you can imagine what I learned from that! I realized how important it is to listen, observe, learn about another culture, and not be so sure we understand things at a quick glance. I learned to be very careful about seemingly innocuous statements.

Back in 1954 a professor at Syracuse University told a racist joke right in class. He used the word nigger without thinking about it. I went up and spoke to him afterwards. He hadn't even realized how offensive that was. I don't think he had even noticed me; I was the only black in the class. Then later in the semester, after we had submitted a long paper, he asked me to stay after class. He wanted to know who wrote my paper for me.

But as it turned out, he eventually apologized. He thanked me for bringing all this to his attention. It was his first experience with a black person; he just didn't know anything about us! It was my first time away from home and my first experience of that sort, too. I did finish my Master of Arts degree with honors at Syracuse.

In later years both Henry and I worked with a variety of groups and encountered many people who had never had much contact with black people. We could see in many cases that they really were trying. In other cases people had a basic "attitude," and we saw that our job was to try to change their ideas by having direct contact with us. We never really allowed these things to bother us. Perhaps we were ignorant! But, to some extent you teach people how to treat you. And having our own self-confidence helped a great deal, too.

My current position, Community Affairs Manager of the major television station in Greensboro, is one of the most exciting things I've done. It's a real challenge; when I started I didn't know much about television, but from my years of volunteer work I know a cross-section of people from all ethnic backgrounds in the city and have earned their confidence and trust. Now people can come to me with their complaints about the station, or suggestions for improvements, and know I'll listen, not be defensive.

Through this office come requests from all corners of the Triad area.

We respond to requests for organizations or individuals to bring their causes to the television audience through our community affairs programs. You find people doing things for others that you wouldn't believe. It has made me feel so good to be part of this region. The different ways people help each other are truly remarkable.

One of the main satisfactions of my job is in helping community agencies to co-sponsor various events. Friday, for example we are co-sponsoring a health fair with Physicians Health Plan. We have an AIDS awareness event coming up and a Minority Task Force Breakfast the same day. We provide publicity and television personalities for these events. One of our people might be the MC, another might moderate a panel. We try to demonstrate the station's interest in the community. I'm beginning a food drive, working with the state farm agencies, to culminate at Thanksgiving. My goal is to coordinate the food drives of various organizations, so that we don't duplicate each other. The station tries to be the catalyst for bringing competing programs together, so that each can be more successful.

I do feel a sense of service, and having been a fund-raiser for so much of my life, it's nice not to be calling people for money! I also like having the choice to work or not. At other stages of my life, I had to work.

religion

Religion has played an important part in my life. I grew up on the Bible. I don't take the Bible literally, but it has had a tremendous influence on my philosophy of life.

As young children growing up in rural Eastern North Carolina, the church was the focal point of our lives. We went to church every Sunday, we went to prayer meeting every Wednesday, and every Sunday night. One grows up and gets a little tired of the regimen, especially if you are a bit independent, as I was. So when I left home to go to college at 15, I decided that I would not spend that much time in church. But I realize now the importance of all that early training and focus.

When Henry and I married, we were both working hard. I was teaching and Henry was commuting to Chapel Hill for Law School. I would get up at four o'clock in the morning to prepare his breakfast. Sunday mornings were the time I could rest. But one weekend, Henry said to me, "Shirley, church and Sunday school have always been an important part of my life, and I always hoped that the person I married would feel the same way."

He had not been brought up quite as strictly as I was, so he didn't have the same need I had to break away a bit. Eventually, I did become very active in the church as an adult and participated in many ways. We are members of Providence Baptist Church. I was director of the Bible School at one point, chairman of the day care program, church clerk at another time. And of course, we went with our sons to Sunday school as we felt it was important to raise them in the church.

When I have difficulties in my life, that is where I turn for strength. God has been very good to us. We have had many challenges and having that support and faith has been very important. I don't think we would be where we are today without our religious faith.

trials and sorrows

Our sons have had several serious accidents; one son was hit just over the heart with a baseball. When he was a little older, he was in an automobile accident. Both times the doctors told us it was a miracle he lived. As adults our sons each had a serious automobile accident. In both cases the car was demolished and they walked away without a scratch. I know the Lord was taking care of them. Those experiences always bring you closer to God.

Perhaps because I was so carefully sheltered during my childhood, I've remained very close to my family. The major struggles of my life have involved family members. This past year has probably been one of the most painful and difficult of my entire life. Within a three-month period I lost three people who were very dear to me. My nephew who was like a son to me died of bone cancer at age thirty-one. A month later the sister who was like my twin growing up died, also of cancer. And soon thereafter, my mother, who had been in good health for her years, died, I think of a broken heart, from these two losses.

All of this coming so suddenly was almost unbearable. I credit my husband with getting me through it. He was wonderful.

Going back a bit, our older son was eleven when we learned that he had diabetes. He was very ill; I didn't know anything about diabetes. It was terribly difficult and I almost lost hope; I thought he would die. I stayed at the hospital with him constantly and neglected the rest of the family very badly. Gradually, we all learned to live with it. But it was a very big challenge. Today he has three children of his own and is a public defender here in town. He has given himself his own insulin all these years.

When my husband first ran for the legislature and lost, in 1966, I was devastated. We had all worked so hard. How could people not know that he was perfect for the job! He took it much better than I did. He knew even then that you win some, lose some. So I was forced to grow up a lot in that experience.

Men have their sports (most women didn't in those days) and they learn a lot about winning and losing. Years ago women did not have many of those short-term goals to work for and enjoy. Their goals were traditionally of a more long-term nature. Raising children is certainly a long-term experience.

But in the political life, with which we were involved for so many years, you do learn a lot about those short-term, win some, lose some situations.

As to problems of growing up in the segregated South, I do believe in the teachings of Jesus; I believe in forgiveness. And once you have your own self-confidence and know who you are, you are able to rationalize the lack of understanding of others. Bitterness? I don't remember staying angry for a whole day. I don't hold grudges. Even on a personal level, I try to follow that; my husband and I made a pact long ago that we would never go to sleep angry. So there's no pile-up of anger.

Early in our adult lives we did not allow ourselves to be in situations that would hurt or embarrass us. My parents had protected us when we were young in more or less the same way. We always said we came from the quiet generation, we didn't challenge things, we followed the rules. That old saying "you knew your place" really did apply. In time, of course, we worked for change and still do.

We were not able to go to restaurants, but when our children were small, we didn't go out to eat much anyway. It was painful to go to a movie and not be able to sit where you wanted to.

During the mid-sixties, Japanese friends at Wake Forest University invited us to spend the day at a park in Winston-Salem. We called ahead and learned that we would be denied admittance on racial grounds. Our friend Hideki suggested we come ahead anyway and attend church with them. We were readily accepted by the white congregation at Knollwood Baptist Church. The only discomfort I felt, if you can even call it that, was that I wore a hat and the other women did not. Hideki reported the incident to the Human Relations Commission.

children

Our third child lived only one day. That was hard, very hard. I didn't have all the children I wanted. I'd have liked six children, but wasn't able to. I've thoroughly enjoyed both of our sons. It has been a joy to watch them grow and become responsible adults. Children do make a home, along with all the joys and sorrows. All the good times in family life help you through the difficult times.

Our sons' childhoods were certainly different from Henry's and mine. Our children thought milk came from a box! Farm life versus city life: as a child, I had to participate in all the work of a farm. Our children had none of those responsibilities. They were allowed to be creative and they were allowed to express disapproval; I was not. Henry and I did not use corporal punishment, but it had been used on us.

One day when my mother was here, I let the boys play with a basketball down in our basement recreation room. Moments later we heard a crash; they had broken a lamp. My mother said I should spank them right away. But I said no, it was my fault for letting them use the ball in the house. That was a typical difference between my mother's generation and mine.

Our children attended integrated schools and most of their activities were integrated. In my childhood, except for that one neighbor family, everything else in our lives was all-black, strictly segregated.

Our children grew up in a political family, a political atmosphere. There was always so much concern with the outside world in their childhood. When I was young, I never even saw a Republican until I came to Greensboro!

The most important quality I tried to instill in our children is honesty, keeping your word. My father never signed a contract and yet he did everything he ever promised to do.

living

In each period of life there has been something different to enjoy. Now, I want to be sure to save plenty of time for my grandchildren. I missed having daughters and am taking special pleasure in two daughters-in-law and three granddaughters. Henry also takes each of those little girls, ages three, five and seven out for a day with him, one at a time, just so they'll know how special they are to him.

We have had a strong sense of community in Greensboro. It has problems, like any city, but it is a good place to live and work. I expect to be involved in civic affairs after retirement, perhaps just not as much.

I have a few women friends whom I cherish. And I am close to my sisters. But I don't go to lunch regularly with women friends; I'm usually working. Henry really is the primary friendship of my life.

We enjoy tennis in a nearby park and swimming in the backyard pool.

When Henry's family comes they all play a card game called Bid Whist, similar to bridge. We like to drive around the state, to the little towns. Most of all, since we have so little time at home, we just enjoy being home, listening to music for an evening

I relax by cooking. You've had that clam chowder we serve at our New Year's Day open house. I make that by the gallon. If I feel stressed, I'll bake a batch of cakes and freeze them. That's where all the cakes came from that you saw along with the clam chowder.

Personal virtues? I'm a determined person. I have learned from every experience, then looked for new opportunities. It takes a long time for me to get angry, and I do forgive immediately. But I need to be able to go to the person and discuss the problem. I like people and I observe them closely and try to focus on the good in them. I try to understand that hurtful comments aren't always exactly what's intended. You need to look at body language to determine actual meaning.

As to talents, I can't sing, I can't dance. But I think I can communicate. I'm pretty up-front, lay my cards on the table. I cannot deal with hidden agendas. I'm a good listener and in fact, I am bombarded by people who just want someone to listen to them. I spend an inordinate amount of time listening to people, especially young people. I once asked my husband if I look like a nanny! But I must enjoy it, because I do take the time.

My appearance is very important to me. I diet 365 days a year! Unfortunately, we are judged by the way we look, more than by what we are. I'm not extravagant, but I do want to please my family and myself with the way I look.

looking ahead

Turning fifty was not a major change; I really don't feel different and still go at the same rate that I always did. The main difference is that I am freer now that our children are grown. We often think how hard empty nest would be if we didn't enjoy each other's company. And now with the grandchildren, we enjoy them, and then they go home! I like this stage of life.

As to the future, I might start a small business. I'm still thinking about it. Right now, some people are encouraging Henry to run for a political office. But with both of us being fifty-seven, we feel it is time to be not quite so heavily scheduled by others.

I am grateful for good health, for a husband I love, and for our grown sons who are now making their own contributions. And my precious granddaughters! I am grateful for loving parents and the support of my husband in whatever I have chosen to do. I've had the opportunity to "be." I've had no restrictions.

I often feel guilt over our material comforts, very often. We have been so fortunate, so blessed. But we have tried to dedicate our lives to public service. And our older son, as a lawyer in the public defender's office, helps many poor and homeless people. Still, when I see others who have not been as fortunate as we have been, I find myself thinking, why them, why not me? Why was I so lucky?

Postscript:

By 2005, Shirley and Henry were both semi-retired and enjoying a little free time for the first time in their lives. The word little is used advisedly as both remain engaged with life in their adopted city. Both sons and families live nearby and the Fryes continue to enjoy their grandchildren and a full family life.

DR. MARILYN LOCKWOOD
Introduction

Marilyn Lockwood knew from childhood that she wanted to have both children and a career in medicine. To achieve those goals she deployed raw ability, determination, numerous jobs and scholarships, marriage and successful family planning. Whence came such precise focus in an era that offered so few women doctors for a small-town girl to emulate? Only seven percent of American physicians were women by the end of the sixties. Surely, Marilyn revealed in youth an early thirst for knowledge and experience. Perhaps readers will find in Dr. Lockwood's commentary other keys to the path she discovered and followed so early in life.

Marilyn treated children in public health clinics for the first phase of her medical career. The second was spent tending the complex needs of students at a university campus clinic. A third phase was still unfolding at the time of her oral history interviews.

Divorced after ten years of marriage, Marilyn continued to raise her three daughters, and saw each of them into college. Their departures permitted a dramatic change in professional direction. In her early fifties, while working full-time as a campus physician, Marilyn earned a Masters Degree in Business Administration. Leaving the clinic, she agreed to serve as a *locum tenans* physician. The Latin term refers to doctors sent out for weeks or months by medical corporations to substitute as needed for primary care physicians. Assignments may last weeks or months.

Substitutes are often necessary in cases of a doctor's prolonged illness; also, for doctors in solo practice, a *locum tenans* physician may represent the only means for taking a study leave or vacation. Requests for such services pour in; although medical specialists are numerous in the United States, primary care physicians are in short supply.

Marilyn gave me her oral history as she was about to embark, with some trepidation, on the life of a *locum tenans* physician. I caught up with her again two years later. In the course of those two years, Marilyn lived in rural areas, small towns and cities in New York, Illinois, Arizona, North Carolina, and Virginia. She had served a Native American community where she was the minority person. In several back-country enclaves one-third of her patients were illiterate, and some adults could not tell time.

I wondered whether these were lonely years. "Only rarely," Marilyn responded, "I seem to have enough maturity, or insight into myself, that I manage to keep myself company." She enjoyed the patient contact, but, after being with people all day long, she was glad to have a little time alone. Then, preparing the evening meal in her furnished apartment seemed a pleasant contrast to the day's efforts. The weekends might have been spent exploring a new part of the country, or sampling regional foods, reading a good book. Or all of the above. Vacation trips with Marilyn's three daughters and visiting European exchange students took them to Georgia and Florida, Maine, North and South Carolina.

When I spoke with Marilyn on the second occasion, she had sold her house and was about to leave for a year in Germany. Under a civilian contract with the U.S. military, she would serve adolescent children of American servicemen at a large base in Heidelberg. Before returning to a practice in Erie, Pennsylvania, she would travel throughout Europe and visit one daughter in Belize. ("I hoped my daughters would grow up with a global orientation, and they did.")

As she flew to most assignments, Marilyn learned to take necessities only. Which things were sufficiently important that they would go to

High school graduation picture, 1954

Europe with her? Along with spices for cooking, there would be books, a family crucifix, the King James Bible, a very old Book of Common Prayer—and a potato peeler.

Marilyn Lockwood's gentle manner belies an independent nature. Her self-confidence is not immediately evident. She is modest and unassuming; a distinct quality of reticence, not quite shyness, characterizes this supremely capable woman.

As others blessed with wide-ranging curiosity, Marilyn is a life-long student. She loves the arts, as well as science. She is rarely dogmatic: her opinions are measured, and temperate, yet her life offers ample evidence of strong values. Life seems to unfold steadily before her grave, attentive eyes. She can find humor in absurdity and unblinkingly note the extremities of human behavior.

During many hours of recording Dr. Marilyn Lockwood's oral history, I found great pleasure in the serenity and keen intelligence of a seasoned physician and deeply compassionate woman.

Dr. Marilyn Lockwood
Washington, DC
1991, 2005

I've been so fortunate that I wonder if something extraordinary will be required of me. My God might say to me, 'You had it good! What did you do with it?'

A crucial turning point for me, and the most difficult experience of my life so far, was my divorce. My husband and I separated after ten years of marriage. I was forty, had three young daughters and the last five years of my marriage were my ordeal by fire. It took me five years to arrive at it, but once the decision was made, it was a benchmark. I should have come to those conclusions sooner, but wanted to wait for the children to reach a certain age. So much of my energy was drained in trying to resolve a variety of issues. When it was finally over I had much more to give the children.

They have maintained good relationships with their father, who lived nearby while they were growing up. He was faithful about child support, a crucial issue. Our children probably have better relationships with him than if they had gone through all that fighting for another ten years.

But those were some very painful years, certainly the hardest thing I have had to go through.

looking back

I grew up in western New York State. During the years I was ages ten through seventeen, we lived in a dairy-farming area about sixty miles southeast of Buffalo. It was, and is, a beautiful valley, but can you believe we called it Hog Hollow? Named after the groundhogs, of which there were many.

The farms were a half-mile or so apart, yet it was a close community. An elderly couple next door became "Grandma and Grandpa," and the people at the next farm over the hill were "aunts and uncles." Social activities were well-organized; someone would have a Christmas party, someone else a Fourth of July party. Whole families would be together-- parents, elderly people, and children. As a child I experienced a lot of warmth, a kind of nineteenth century ideal that I've never seen since.

I also had the blessing of several family members nearby. I have fond recollections of my paternal grandmother. She was quiet and steady and I could always rely on her. My mother's father was a good-natured Irish man who died when I was about two and a half, but I remember sitting on his lap while he taught me to read headlines from the newspapers.

My parents had their four children when they were quite young. I was the oldest. My mother had left school after the eighth grade, my father after high school. But they were bright people and had done well in school as far as they were able to go. Back in the days when people could skip grades, my father had graduated from high school at fourteen, but was always bitter about not going further. He remained an avid reader and could speak on many subjects.

Our family was extremely traditional. My brothers were not allowed to wash dishes, for example, and of course my father never did. My father was very much the dominant figure in the family, and accustomed to being cared for by women. My mother was submissive. Actually the male-female polarity was so extreme in my family that it wasn't hard to rebel against it later on.

I was spanked until I was fourteen years old! My brothers were never spanked but my sister and I were. One of my greatest triumphs was that, at fourteen, I realized I could outrun my father. He was a big man, over six feet tall, and strong. On this particular day my father was intent on punishing me, but I ran away across the field surrounding our house. He chased me across the field. I'd run, get ahead, then stop and taunt him...talk about taking risks! Then I'd run and tease him some more; it was exhilarating! Finally I just ran away for a few hours. After that, we got along well and he never tried to spank me again.

One of my early memories is of our kitchen. I'm told that at ten months I started making up little imaginary people who lived under the kitchen table. Their names were Dada and Peru. Dada evolved, as I grew older, into a glamorous woman who went out on dates. Even though she lived under the kitchen table! Peru was my baby talk for perfume. I'm sure I was trying to imitate my young aunts.

I still remember the jingle from "Let's Pretend" on the radio on Saturday morning. I would hide behind the kitchen door, frightened by fairy tales, while also fascinated. I've kept some of the old books; my favorite poem was "Custard the Dragon," by Ogden Nash about a cowardly dragon. Custard— isn't that a great name— was a bit fearful, but when a crisis came he was able to be fierce and save the day. Then he went back to being his old, Custard-like self again!

How fortunate to have been born in 1937 in Buffalo, rather than, say, Berlin or Leningrad, and to have grown up sheltered from the wars that were raging then. Because of the Depression and the dip in the birth rate, ours was a smaller age cohort, with fewer people competing with each other than was the case later during the baby-boom years. That's more significant than many of us realize. College admissions, finding jobs, all were less difficult for us.

Stable family life and early success in school help develop a sense of who you are. I always did well in school, am still a perennial student and could go to school forever. I was fortunate to grow up in New York State during the golden years of education. Throughout the forties and fifties, the state just poured money into public education. Our small, centralized public school in western New York had a wonderful theatre, large gym and cafeteria. All thirty-four students in my graduating class took music, art and physical education throughout our school years.

I had three sets of aunts and uncles who were younger than my parents. My grandmother moved to Washington, D.C., and so did they. I took the train all the way from Buffalo to Washington every summer to visit. The aunts and uncles would take me, and sometimes my sister, everywhere. We went to Annapolis, to the beaches, restaurants, museums. They gave me a lot of attention. I seem to always have had a kind of mental hunger. I drove my parents nuts asking what's this, what's that? An intense, persistent little creature. We all benefited from having those relatives in our lives, but I think I did most of all.

Strong Women Tell Their Stories

Taking the family as a whole, it was nurturing and stimulating. Here I was an electrician's daughter from Buffalo, yet every summer I would go to Washington for enriching experiences that I would never have had otherwise. I'm told I was responsive to everything. I actually remember seeing the Monet cathedral paintings at the National Gallery at different eye levels, because each summer I would be a little taller than the previous summer.

When I was six, one uncle took me to a restaurant over the Potomac and I remember the balcony was especially thrilling to me. My uncle handed me a raw clam and told me to dip it in clam sauce. I did, chewed it up, said, "Yum, yum!" and asked for another. He was impressed that a little child would eat raw clams. His degree was in education and he apparently thought I was a very educable little kid.

But there was a dark side to those times too, and by 1952 I was truly frightened by the atomic bomb and all its possibilities. Another uncle worked with civil defense and was trying to predict the fall-out if a bomb should hit Toledo. His maps showed the fall-out cloud would be directly across the area of Western New York where we lived.

This was terrifying to me and I went through a period of great anxiety. I wanted my parents to dig an underground shelter in the woods and stock it with food. My father said, "I won't do that...if the bomb comes, I'd rather die." I was very angry; I was only fourteen and didn't want to die without living my life. My parents had always given me a great deal of independence; perhaps that's why I felt so strongly that I should do something, fight, protect myself, protect all of us.

By age sixteen, that anxious period was over and I knew I wanted to do something special and different, perhaps combining art and science. I decided to become a physician that year.

When my mother died last June, a lovely funeral was held in that little New York valley town. Many neighbors attended and afterwards I went around visiting them, spent an entire evening with one family, and had a wonderful discussion of political, social, moral issues with an eighty-six-year old farmer.

A little story from that time gives a flavor of farm life. While I was visiting a family I'd been especially close to as a child, one of their cows gave birth to a calf up on their hill. They couldn't get the cow to bring the calf down the hill to the barn and had to go up for it. My youngest daughter, our Danish exchange student, and I rode along in the hay wagon behind a huge tractor. Off we went, bumping and banging up that rugged hill, clinging to the hay wagon, every bone in our bodies rattling.

Voices of the Silent Generation

Here was the big Holstein cow up on the hill refusing to budge. So the farmer ties the calf in the wagon and starts down the hill. We suddenly realize the wagon has no brakes. So we're going lickety-split down the hill, and here comes the mother cow, who had given birth that morning, desperately mooing and running beside the wagon, very concerned about her calf. She runs up beside the wagon, gives the calf a lick on the cheek. Then dashes behind the wagon, slipping in mud along the way, comes around the other side and gives the calf another lick. Now that was ardent motherhood!

heritage

I've tried to learn about my ethnic heritage, which is a potpourri. My father was English, French and German and my mother was German and Irish. Our family's name and any English name with Lock in it, like Whitlock, or Lockey--these are old pagan names that go back to the Norsemen honoring Loki, a Norse god.

Some of the family came to Boston in 1630 with the Winthrop Fleet. Others were indentured servants. About twelve years ago I went to an old cemetery in Western New York where my great-great-great-grandfather Ebenezer Lockwood is buried. As an adult he took his own family across New York in a covered wagon. He and others are buried there, and, as I was trying to find out about all of this, I met a man named Newton who lived next to the cemetery. He turned out to be a descendant of Maria Newton, my great-great-grandfather's sister who was one of the children who went on that wagon train. So this man and I were related too!

The seventeenth-century Puritans were sturdy, vigorous people. I had always thought they were stuffy, but they weren't. I especially like one ancestor's old death head tombstone. I have a rubbing of it; it's really medieval art. To me it suggests the energy that you associate with earthy people. Descendants of this ethnic origin have gotten very intellectual, so they've lost that link to the soil.

Just this week I read "A Model of Christian Charity," from the 1630 Winthrop Papers. It's the sermon or treatise that includes "we shall be as a city upon a hill." He was talking about the nation to come. It's masterful, and if you strip it of the old theocratic language, it's clear he's talking about social cohesiveness: the sum is greater than each of the parts. Connectedness, cooperation--those gradually were superceded by the American ideal of individualism. We need to rediscover that spirit of community for today's world. We discuss the same topics in the MBA courses I'm taking now. So Winthrop was up to date!

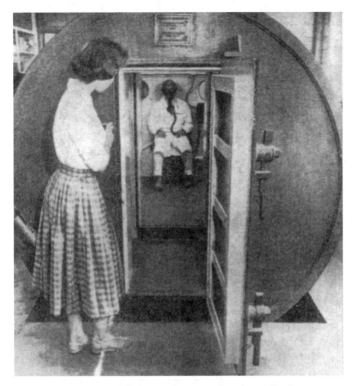

Newspaper photograph on work wth medical
researchers in high-altitude chamber. Buffalo, 1958

mentors

I majored in English Literature at the University of Buffalo, had scholarships, but also always worked. Later, in the middle of medical school, I ran out of money, dropped out and worked for a year at the Mayo Clinic.

I was fortunate in finding teachers and mentors. While going to college and medical school, I worked in the physiology department at the medical school. It was headed by the late Herman Rahn, an outstanding respiratory physiologist. He worked with compression and decompression chambers; we walked on the moon because of Rahn's work! He had a magnificent department and attracted many intelligent people. He had a great deal of personal integrity, was a brilliant scientist, but was also good at encouraging creativity, inspiring and organizing people to work together.

One of my jobs was to prepare lunch; then I sat down with these wonderful scientists, even participating in their discussions a little. And they always treated me as a medical student, not a servant (which I had been elsewhere). I did not become a respiratory physician myself because

Voices of the Silent Generation

of difficult math requirements, and because it would have taken too much time away from family life. But I was glad to be part of that group at that time in my life. If I have known a great person in my life, it was Dr. Rahn.

I took my children back to meet Dr. Rahn years later. We visited him in his office and he was so kind to my three little girls. At one point he talked to us about the respiratory system of the egg!

social changes in the sixties and seventies

As historians look back, I think they'll agree that one of the most important changes for women of this generation was oral contraceptives. To me that has been the major social change, more significant than any laws. Because I could protect myself against unplanned pregnancy, I was able to plan the major events of my life almost as well as a man can; that makes a tremendous difference.

I was actually able to plan precisely the birth of each one of my children. Some people are uncomfortable about this, like their father, who thought it was unromantic. I didn't use any exotic scientific knowledge for this...almost anyone could do it; it wasn't because I'm a physician. I had the advantage of being very fertile and able to conceive very readily. If there had been no oral contraceptives, I'd probably have six or seven children. Not every woman can plan that precisely; I was fortunate to be so fertile. But people do still resist making use of what is available to us.

I'm a great planner. I didn't get married until I was close to the end of my training (had always hoped to marry at twenty-eight!). I'd planned to have children since childhood but wanted to delay it until the time was right. I was almost thirty when the first came and then had two more close together--part of "the plan,"--so they could go through similar stages together. It was also easier with three girls (though I didn't plan their sex) because they had similar interests. I loved my time with the children.

I spent the early sixties in medical school, finishing in 1964, then going on for more training in 1967. Medical school was such an intense experience and I was so preoccupied that I was oblivious to many external events.

Some nasty things happened in Buffalo during those times. An English professor, an extremely fine man, was physically brutalized by students and held hostage. And yet I was so wrapped up with life at the hospital that I barely knew about it. A Vietnamese man sought sanctuary at the Unitarian church, and I remember the unpleasant crowd around the church. I was sympathetic to him, but, with my baby there in the carriage, was more worried about her safety. I would take risks for myself, but not my children.

In 1967 when I was pregnant, we lived in a rough neighborhood in downtown Buffalo near the hospital. I wanted to get out of there to protect my baby. I felt vulnerable living in an upstairs flat, wondering what to do if a riot broke out. My husband bought me a huge gun, an M-1. We went out in the country so he could show me how to shoot it, but that gun made such an impact, I feared for the unborn baby. The noise was loud enough to cross the abdominal wall and the baby jumped violently each time I fired the gun. I mention that just to indicate the lengths we were driven to by the climate of the times.

The feminist movement had an impact on my marriage. When we married, I was already a physician. Many of the issues being brought out nationally also came up in our marriage and there was a lot of arguing. Strangely, he approved of women's rights on an intellectual level, but on a deeper personal level, couldn't quite cope. A lot of couples of that era had similar problems.

I did participate in major family decisions. We left the state for a change in his employment and I fully agreed with it. We agreed about having children, and I was involved with building our house. But then we would get into endless arguments about what brand of peas to buy! Theoretically we agreed, but on a gut level there were problems, and so we would get into these impasses about trivia. The public issues probably made things a little more difficult, but did not actually cause our problems.

The hostility and anger generated by women's issues in the sixties and seventies did affect my daughters and me in one particular way. I am wary of special interest groups, women who are concerned about the rights of women only, and not about liberation for all people. I'll join a women's social group, but not a women's political group. If I get into a political group, I want it to be mixed.

I have serious doubts that we are better off with the sexual revolution and all that has come with it. The birth control pill turned the tide. Appropriately used, it is beneficial, but the way it is used to enable unwise sexual behavior, is very questionable.

Much has been lost for today's young people. My first kiss was so simple, innocent and dramatic. It seemed far more wonderful to me than these full sexual encounters. The young women at the university clinic spoke very intimately to me, and I rarely sensed real love or passion or joy in their relationships. Just problems, and an almost mechanical servicing.

Even young men have confided to me that they felt pressure to perform, that this was expected of them, and they were not really happy about these relationships.

Society seems to be on a locomotive with no way to control it. Young people are taking awful risks with their health and their lives. Physicians see the overwhelming evidence: all sorts of STDs, sexually transmitted diseases, not to mention pregnancy and abortion. Many young people will not open their minds until they are simply unable to deny their situations. The physical problems and diseases transmitted by all of this activity are a much bigger problem than most people realize.

People can become very angry with a physician who tries to tell them what they need to hear. I just try to give information, but it must be delivered in an unthreatening way—which isn't always enough because there is so much denial and projection of blame on others. Those may seem the only tools available for some young people to get through life, but they severely inhibit growth.

I was telling you my fears as a child of nuclear war, and now it's AIDS. There are things about AIDS which make it worse than the Black Death, because it's something people can carry for a long time and transmit unknowingly. It's moving into the general population...maybe a vaccine will be developed, but it's so late now that there will still be devastating effects. The world of medicine thought it was close to conquering infectious disease, but we are not. Infectious disease is a greater threat to mankind than ever before.

religion
Religion is important to me. But I moved across the full range of Christian denominations and had difficulty settling down. I became a Unitarian in college after being influenced by an outstanding minister in Buffalo.

I remained a Unitarian for years but eventually resigned; Unitarianism can be very interesting and a way to participate in a church community, but can also seem purely intellectual. I need a more religious dimension, also missed the old Gregorian chants, the beautiful rituals. I'm now a member of an Episcopal church, and it seems like the right compromise for me.

Jesus somehow stays with me; I think of Jesus as a metaphor. There is something so satisfying in the image of a being both divine and human as the only way to bridge God and humankind.

I don't think I diminish Jesus by thinking of Him as a metaphor. Jesus is very real and of utmost significance, yet there is more to understand. In the final analysis, I think metaphor is the only way we have to comprehend some of the dimensions of divinity. His human image helps our dull human minds to grasp a little more.

One of the few things I'm taking with me during this period of moving around a lot is an old crucifix. I found it while looking through my mother's clothes to dress her for her funeral. I know my mother, who was Catholic, cherished this cross, though my father was Protestant and we had a Protestant household. One of my regrets is that I didn't pass much on to my daughters; they were raised Unitarian.

Virtues? One of the issues I struggle with is narcissism and here I am with a whole afternoon of indulging in it! I'm sure one of our major tasks is to try to reduce our own self-absorption.

It's hard to assess one's own virtues. I am persistent. But persistence can move a fraction of an inch and become obsession. When I get an idea in my head, it's pretty hard to shake it. I try not to move into rigidity and hope I am reasonably moderate.

In the Meyers-Briggs test, the category I'm in is nurturing, somewhat introverted, but democratic, not interested in controlling people.

I read a lot and have a broad range of interests. It is possible to spread oneself too thin, but generalists are needed; I like being a primary care physician rather than a specialist.

children

I knew from a young age that I wanted children. But I had a great deal of energy, and was afraid that without a career I would smother my children with attention. I remember being concerned about that, even as a young person.

I loved that period with little children. But I'm glad they're grown up! Seven straight years of lifting babies was enough.

What happens to my children is extremely important to me. Their lives are just unfolding, and if things don't go well for them, that will be very hard. Yet those things are unwritten— we just don't know.

I like to think that there are many different pathways by which one can have a satisfactory life. A woman doesn't have to have children. But I'm glad I did. And I'm looking forward to having grandchildren. I've saved many little things, books and some of their baby clothes, even bought little books for future grandchildren.

My children's childhood was different from mine in many ways, the first being lack of an extended family for them, and city life rather than rural. And their education was different. My children attended a public high school considered one of the finest schools in the state. They were fortunate to each earn 19 college credits through an advanced placement program.

Nevertheless, I believe their education did not approach what I got in my small rural high school in a well-developed community of the fifties. They experienced neither the depth nor the satisfactions that I did. Schools today are just in terrible trouble. My children had some good teachers, but these teachers are working desperately against huge handicaps. That's another long chapter....

The other big difference we discussed earlier: the dating and courting. It's difficult for young people today because they are expected to jump into extremely intimate relationships. It's especially difficult for an intelligent young person who is aware of the risks. There's less romance than in courtships of the past.

Some of my child-raising practices were different from those of my parents. My parents considered me permissive. I did not spank my children, except in cases of extreme danger. I waited until each of them was three before toilet-training them. We sat across the table, and I said I know you would like to go to nursery school, but you can't go unless you use the toilet. So they did. And that was it! Discussion is better than physical methods of changing behavior. That isn't permissive, just reasonable. And role modeling is by far the best way to raise children: what you say does not matter as much as what you do.

I've tried to help my daughters learn not to blame their problems on others. I've tried to instill the idea of cooperation rather than competition and that jealousy is destructive. And that denial as a defense mechanism does not work.

I like being a catalyst to inspire or foster their well-being. Sometimes they would like me to give them a script. But I'm not directive; it's burdensome to try to control others. In the MBA program they put great emphasis on understanding oneself, that you cannot understand another until you understand yourself. We live in complex, difficult times and it seems that few people reach adulthood before the age of twenty-eight. And many never reach it at all.

work

Some women today are as compulsive about their careers as women of earlier times were about their families. I've often talked with my daughters about the need to understand the different choices, and also the importance of motherhood, the value of being with your children.

My career happened to be a nurturing one, so being a pediatrican and a mother were complementary. Much that I learned from raising three children I was able to use as a physician. I finished residency in June '67, had my first daughter in September, and had a few months of taking care of the baby and not working. That was just like another year of pediatric residency! Then as I went into young adult medicine, my own were moving into that stage too. A relative says I spend too much of my time with twenty-year-olds. Well, I've had three daughters, three exchange students, and most of my patients are in their early twenties. So it's very efficient if you want to put it that way! And lively and fun! You can do worse things than spend all your time with twenty-year-olds.

A fellowship in pulmonary disease began several months after the maternity leave, followed by work for a county health department. My board certification is in pediatrics and much of my pediatric work has been with low-income children. I worked with children in youth clinics for seven years, then with adolescents and young adults at a university clinic for thirteen years.

Working as a physician offers an almost infinite look into human beings and their behavior. It's not an all-encompassing window, but you do get an inside look. You ask a lot of questions and receive many insights. And you see so many people, thousands! By now I say hello to any twenty-year-old in town and chances are they've come to me as a patient. It's hard to say I've had a major effect on people's lives; you just never really know.

It's funny, there seems to be no correlation between how much effort a doctor puts forth and its impact. Sometimes you knock yourself out for a patient and they hardly notice. Other times you'll do some simple, routine thing and they will just shower you with profuse gratitude.

Here's a concrete example. During a little talk I gave in another city a young man stood up and said, "Dr. Lockwood showed me how to stop smoking!" I didn't even remember him and yet that impact had taken place, unknown to me.

I always wanted contact with people and didn't go into research for that reason. I like dealing with ambiguity and love literature for that reason, too. I so appreciate my college English Literature major; literature is a wonderful preparation for medicine. And also for an MBA degree!

looking ahead

My life will change in the next twenty-five years. A career change is one possibility. I'm getting an MBA with the idea of becoming a sort of "bridge" person--one who knows about medicine and business. This is important to our national problems of distribution and financing of medical care. There is a tendency for doctors to become obsessed strictly with medical care, while business people have no concept of medicine. I'm trying to look at what society needs.

When I think about a way to make a modest contribution toward the latter part of my life, this seems to be what I'm best suited for. I like medicine and am not burned out at all. My daughters are more independent now. I look forward to being able to focus on career now that they're grown. My grandmother worked until she was seventy-two. At fifty-two, I would like to work for another twenty years, maybe more realistically fifteen. A great many things could happen to prevent that, but I hope to have some time.

I'm trying to loosen some of my attachments to possessions. You can ask me next year how it works out! My house is up for rent, and the furniture has been given to the children and others. An 8x20 warehouse room stores the special things that I don't want to give up. This has been a comfortable house with the garden and all the familiar things. It was good for my children to be in one house all these years.

But I've reached a stage where possessions require too much attention and upkeep; the time has come! In the next few years I'll be living in a series of efficiency apartments and won't need much. I'd also like to free up time for reading and possibly professional writing. I'm not creative enough to do fiction, but maybe some social/medical writing.

I guess what I'm doing now, leaving my home and clinic position in order to go off and get business training in medicine, is a risk. It's not a reckless, foolhardy risk, but a considerable risk, especially emotionally. I'd like to think that my inner self is well enough developed that I can leave familiar surroundings and still maintain my self. I'll be leaving soon; it's time to get shaken up a bit...and I hope it'll be just the right amount. I suspect that I will not live in this house again.

growing older

I do get little signals that say I'm not going to be immortal! But I still have a lot of energy and feel a lot better than I expected to at this age. Since turning fifty I haven't noticed much loss in thinking or academic ability; both are stretched in the MBA program.

During the period of the divorce, I confronted the facts of aging and mortality. Some, not all, of those issues were resolved in my own mind. I don't mean to sound oblivious to the possibility of illness and death in the future. I feel so good sometimes I wonder if I'm denying something. I'm glad to have reached fifty-two. Not everyone does. I picked out my grave this summer. Now, that's the opposite of denial! It's beautiful, two graves adjacent, and there's a place where I can plant a tree. When I was young, I thought getting older would be horrible. Maybe it will be, but not yet!

I've got two good role models. I know that my grandmother enjoyed the latter part of her life even more than the earlier parts. And I can't remember my mother specifically saying so, but I think she did too. My father died in 1981; they had a good marriage, I think, but it was kind of the classic old-time male-dominated relationship. When my father died, it turned out she could indeed handle things like writing checks, which she had never done. She was good at managing her own life and, I think, enjoyed her later years.

My mother died just this past June at seventy-six. Her mother had died at sixty-one. My mother took good care of herself, and was able, with a medical history of diabetes and high blood pressure very similar to her own mother's, to live for fifteen more years. She also functioned normally and looked wonderful right up to her final illness. My mother had a sort of radiance about her in death.

My grandmother retained a very pleasant appearance well into old age. She had the Victorian ideas...a lady did not expose her skin to the sun! She was a brunette with an ivory complexion. She would never go out in the mid-day sun and always wore a hat. She washed her face with dew and tried to get me to do that...put a washcloth out on the grass at night. Her lovely complexion was largely genetic and from sun protection...probably not so much the dew! She had deteriorated mentally before she died in her late eighties, but she still looked very nice.

Prolonged decline is the universal concern, so those are my fears too: poor health, helplessness and dependency. Being in a nursing home with unkind people.

I've had a lot of good luck, and I hope it stays that way. I'm grateful for my daughters, my abilities, and excellent health. I feel a little guilty to have been so fortunate, and wonder if something extraordinary will be required of me. My God might say "You had it good! What did you do with it?"

rewards

I am pleased to be a physician. In light of my background, what I did was most unusual. Most of my relatives had not gone to college.

Voices of the Silent Generation

By the world's standards, being a physician is something to be proud of, but going to a deeper, more personal level, what pleases me most about myself is that I can foster growth in things, in children, in plants and animals. It's a good quality for a doctor to have. That's where I get my deepest sense of accomplishment--from a growth response. I'm not sure where that comes from, maybe from an above average degree of health and energy. And I'm *biophilic;* I love living things and seem to sense what they need.

Gardening for me is a method of stress-management. It's relaxing and really quite meditative. As I work in my garden, I pretend I am in a large painting...all those colors and textures, the grasses, the flowers, proportion and balance.

I try to avoid the sense of pride and accomplishment with my children, but of course I want them to do well. They are in their twenties now, but it's all still evolving for them. Julie, the oldest is a trust officer for a large bank, and it has been wonderful to watch her develop and grow in this work. At twenty-five she is supervising people my age and seems to handle it with tact and empathy. My middle daughter, Susan, is trying to decide whether to pursue art or science, a choice I once had to make too. Sarah, my youngest, is a college junior and hopes to become an archaeologist. Her summer job involved digging at a 17th century Indian village site.

questions

The question we all grapple with is, why does evil exist? There is suffering from illness and natural disaster, but then there is human evil. The intertwining of good and evil is almost impossible to understand.

I've been interested to read Erich Fromm, M. Scott Peck and others on character disorders as a source of evil. Fromm has studies of people like Hitler and Himmel in the book, *Anatomy of Human Destructiveness.* He tries to get at reasons for such personalities but finally admits evil on that scale just passes human understanding.

I do wonder whether there isn't a fairly large segment of our population that does not develop a human character with all the dimensions it should have.

At one time I thought that for the latter part of my life I should be monkish and go to the top of a mountain and be alone because I couldn't develop my soul unless I were isolated. But I finally realized we are social creatures and we have to work our way through life together. So I chose more involvement with people.

Strong Women Tell Their Stories

In medical school a line from my biochemistry book jumped out and has always stayed with me. The subject was entropy and the line was, "An organism in stable equilibrium with its environment is dead." And what I took from that is that life is a struggle, a constant struggle until it is over. I don't really ever expect to stop working and struggling. That is what life is all about, after all!

Postscript, 2004, 2005:

In 2004 after retiring from her last position as a physician in Erie, Pennsylvania, Marilyn made a choice that some might find unusual. Decisions inspired by love are often surprising. The doctor made a welcome move to Washington, D.C., home of the arts and science she enjoys, and began a new chapter as delighted caregiver for her first grandchild, a baby girl. One can imagine that, with such a companion, baby Alison will be unusually healthy. Happy too. Having done similar stints for months at a time, I can well understand Marilyn's choice and the joy it brings her.

During many hours of recording Dr. Marilyn Lockwood's oral history, I found great pleasure in the serenity and keen intelligence of a seasoned physician, deeply compassionate woman, and now, devoted grandmother.

Marilyn Lockwood with her daughters.
From left to right are Susan, Sarah, Marilyn, and Julie. 2005

GLORIA KITTO LEWIS
Introduction

Gloria Kitto Lewis was thirty-seven and the mother of three young sons when her husband John Kitto died after a long illness. After a period spent consoling her children and coping with her own grief, Gloria, a respected teacher and fine violinist, eventually returned to work

A second tragedy struck the Kitto family. Eighteen-year-old Michael, her middle son, was struck by a car. Michael remained in a coma for months before his death. Family friends, John's medical colleagues, Gloria's friends from the university and her work in the arts all kept vigil with the stricken family. In her oral history, Gloria discusses both ordeals and their aftermaths with rare eloquence and hard-won wisdom.

While the two cruel blows left Gloria drained and depleted, she did manage to go on. She gave high priority to ensuring that her two surviving sons enjoyed their lives. Today they are grown men with satisfying careers.

Gloria was to endure yet another blow, not one concerned with life and death, but a serious setback nonetheless. Having earned the degree that enabled her to secure a teaching position, Gloria had established herself as a valued teacher and member of the university and local arts communities. State cutbacks and the dire financial climate of Michigan in the early eighties then left her without a job. She was obliged to return to school for another degree, and find yet another position.

Several features of Gloria's personality make her a particularly interesting figure for the times. Though I knew her only slightly, it was clear that Gloria possessed a strong sense of personal worth. Certainly, early and overwhelming sorrow sets one apart, in a company of the initiated. So too, does the disposition to "work like a racehorse," as she puts it, to make the most of her gifts. Gloria's life-long study of the violin, the discipline required, and rewards accordingly reaped , no doubt helped form her character. Music, painting, sculpture and the writings of Thomas Merton remain beloved companions on the path she has chosen toward religious and spiritual growth. Gloria's natural elegance, whisper-soft voice and gentle manner contrast with a fierce sense of purpose. One perceives, beneath an appealing filigree of femininity, a backbone of well-tempered steel.

More than two decades after the events described above, I returned to

Michigan to record Gloria's oral history and found a woman profoundly marked by her experiences, yet still deeply engaged in life, work, family and music.

In 1982, thirteen years after the loss of John Kitto, Gloria married Ralph Lewis, a professor of music at the University of Michigan. As might be expected, Ralph shares Gloria's love of music and performance.

After Gloria and I completed our day of recording, Ralph joined us for dinner at a small restaurant tucked into one of Ann Arbor's narrow streets. It was not just the good sauvignon blanc that made so evident their ongoing celebration of each other. The banter, the humor, the debates both light and serious, the very youthfulness of this mid-fifties couple, left no doubt about the quality of their marriage.

As I left the Lewises later that evening, I was filled with a sense of the marvelous. So it is indeed possible: to suffer so much in life and yet again find a large measure of happiness. Perhaps resilience is our most valuable ally after all.

Gloria Kitto Lewis
Ann Arbor, Michigan
1990

My belief that I can get through adversity and survive, even prevail, is now based on experience, not youth—I learned of life's terrible uncertainty, how to sustain unspeakable losses and go on. Sorrow becomes a part of the fiber of one's life. And now it is a sweet sorrow, gentle and abiding.

There have been two major losses. My husband died in 1969 at the age of forty-three. I was thirty-seven. In 1978, my son Michael died at eighteen. Each of these losses changed my life forever; I had no choice but to accept them, try to gain strength from them, and go on.

Jack was thirty-three when we learned he had a brain tumor. It was 1960, and he had just started his medical practice. Our oldest son was four years old, our youngest five months. Jack subsequently had three operations, but between 1960 and 1969, when he died, he established a good practice in pediatrics and we lived years that were often filled with great joy.

Voices of the Silent Generation

Jack was an extraordinary husband and father and a kind and devoted doctor. He was also very courageous. I truly loved him--and still do--and the possibility of his dying was immeasurably painful to me. It was like losing the other half of myself. He truly loved me and being a father to his three sons was very natural to him. He took pleasure in time with us. We enjoyed taking the boys to museums, concerts, to baseball and hockey games. And we enjoyed time alone. Often I would go with him to the hospital when he made rounds, just so we could talk along the way.

At the beginning of his illness I had to reconcile myself to the possibility of his dying, to live with all the uncertainties and insecurities of his illness. I think our priorities were straight. We went on, raised our children, found joy in them and in each other. We each had our own road to walk as well as the one we walked together; mine gave me a deeper sense of what life is about. There is actually something exhilarating (for lack of a better word) about living life on a level where you come to understand the depths. Other fears fall away, some things are no longer as important as they once were.

Then to learn to live without him. Death is quiet, even serene and sometimes strangely natural. And yet it cuts and brings you to the center of what life really is. It took me a long time to deal with losing Jack. You find yourself responding from levels deep within.

I had to figure out what to do with the rest of my life. I knew I could take good care of the boys and myself. I had been admitted to the doctoral program at Michigan State University, but found that I just could not continue after Jack's death. Eventually I joined the English Department at the University of Michigan campus in Flint where we lived.

The death of a son is simply beyond comprehension, beyond one's ability to respond; there really are no defenses for a mother. Michael was injured in an automobile accident just before his eighteenth birthday. Before dying he was in a coma for five months.

To live through this with my other sons, who loved their brother dearly, was very hard. Peter, the younger son, was in a kind of ongoing shock for some months. We lived often hour to hour, day to day, not knowing how he would be feeling from moment to moment. With Jack I had stayed at the hospital most of every day. Yet with Michael, I just couldn't; the fatigue was overwhelming. We did have good support from friends so there were others who also came and stayed with Michael.

Towards the end of his life, there were times when I would simply faint when seeing him, something I had never done in my life. It was just beyond what I could handle. I think the body has a kind of protective circuit-breaker that kicks in when the situation threatens to push one to points too difficult to cope with. I also think the body has remarkable abilities to rise to occasions. When called to the hospital that rainy night at two o'clock a.m. when Michael was hurt in that car accident, I felt my body shift into another gear. I was able to summon the energy to get through Michael's five-month stay in the hospital, but when it was over, I experienced a profound exhaustion that went on for six months.

David and Peter and I will always have times when the pain from those deaths comes to us. We are all scarred and strengthened by what we went through together.

The need to protect your child is so powerful, I know I would kill to protect my children. Michael was in a coma, so I could not protect him. But I believe he did not feel pain, and I felt that Jack was near Michael. There is a feeling of continuity--of loss and yet, not loss. They are both near— the bond is not broken. They are in pain no longer, are whole and at peace. I believe they are near one another still and that gives me a sense of comfort and peace.

Gloria, sons David, Michael and Peter. 1962

Strangely, having Michael near death in the hospital was like going back to a part of life I already knew about. Because of going through a similar experience with Jack, I felt as if I were somehow in familiar territory and that made everything less terrifying. In the end, I learned that in my earlier experience with Jack I had had as much pain as I could feel. It is as if one has in life one cup of sorrow and when that is filled, all the subsequent sorrow is part of that single cup.

Then, it was simply a matter of going on or not. I did have a job after all. The wonderful people in the English department offered to cover all my classes for me. But I wanted to set an example for Peter, that we had to go on, so I went back to teaching. It was important to me to keep busy with parts of my life that I could control and to keep a sense of continuity in my life. I felt somehow that this would help us all.

Those deaths changed our lives in tremendous ways. We did not recover quickly or completely. We kept going, even built a new house, but we never felt whole again. In our midst was an abiding sorrow. We had been an especially blessed family and I can only hope my sons will feel a sense of a whole family again when they marry.

I was never a well-adjusted single person. And I was angry with God for a long time. Why take someone so deeply loved, so needed in the community? Why? But gradually, acceptance does come.

My life now incorporates a sorrow that makes me feel closer to heaven. The sorrow I feel is quiet and ongoing. In strange ways, heaven and earth seem one for me.

Albert Schweitzer referred to those who have suffered greatly as "the company of the initiated." Perhaps it is the sense that I am in such company that makes me wish to write about my experiences. I hope to find time to write as I feel a responsibility to share what I have learned about life; it is a way of making some sense out of what happened to my family and me.

looking back

My father's name was Onofrio De Feo. He was born in Trani, Italy in 1881 and came to New York at the age of sixteen, thinking there was money on the streets. He found only a dime, once. I think of him when I find a coin in the street. He began as a tailor, but then worked to become a designer of custom men's clothes. He moved to Chicago and became the designer at Marshall Field & Company. His clothes were beautifully made. Occasionally he would make skirts or jackets for his daughters using those fine British wools. I sat near him on Sunday afternoons as he listened to Italian operas. Later in my life, I realized I knew most of them from beginning to end.

Being with Italians helps me to understand myself and rejoice in all that I am. Because I never met my father's family, I went to Trani as an adult to find them, to learn a little about our family heritage. I would so love to learn Italian so that I could speak to his cousins! I identified with the Italian's sense of spontaneity and honest emotion. And I admired their devotion to family, the wonderful kind of arrogance in the men, their charm, vitality, the beauty of their church, art and opera. And I loved their vulnerability, softness and sensitivity along with an outrageous ability to do what they wish. I admire the elegance of their art, clothes, architecture. And I could eat pasta at every meal, every day!

Our family lived in Evanston, Illinois. It was a comfortable, socially-aware, upwardly mobile life. I knew I wanted to "marry well" and have children.

Much in my childhood was predictable, rigid and programmed, governed as it was by routines, maxims and a protocol based on my mother's Scandinavian upbringing, and what society prescribed, at least to her mind. My mother was both rule and role-bound. Her role as mother was clear to her and she found that role to be consuming. She found definition in her role as mother; her sense of self came from activities as wife and mother. She was a meticulous housekeeper and taking care of the house and family occupied her every moment. She was devoted to her daughters, selfless really, and her fulfillment came through our achievements.

Fortunately for me, my father was very creative, unpredictable and far less rule-bound. He did not fully understand or agree with my mother's style of raising children. My Italian father freed me. Because I had this other model for living, and because I was essentially like him in spirit and temperament, I was able to move to the beat of my own drum. I learned to look at the world through my own eyes, to learn from experience.

It was an ordered time; you could major in something in college and know there'd be a job in your field if you wanted one. I was expected to take a practical major, so I started in music education at Northwestern University, but that was not for me, and in any case I did not work right after college.

In those days you finished college, married at twenty-two and had children soon thereafter. (I grew up in the generation before the pill, and was expected to be a virgin before marriage. I was, and that was pleasing to Jack. He was older than I and helped me to grow up in many ways.) I did not think seriously about careers even as an insurance policy. Later, when I began work on a Master of Arts in English, I knew I had found the right field.

I had a sense of self when I was very young, a wish to create and excel. I identified strongly with my father. He was my soul mate and we were alike in spirit--ambitious, proud, religious and emotional. He was very proud of himself and me. I understood him because we were alike, and I learned great lessons about how to live, not so much from what he said but how he acted and reacted. From him I learned how to be true to myself, to care for and value myself. Like many very young people, I had an unshakeable confidence that I would always land on my feet.

My belief that I can get through adversity and survive, even prevail, is now based on experience, not youth. And yet being able to sustain those unspeakable losses and keep on going was probably rooted in early life. I'm sure all the early training in the violin gave me the sense that I was disciplined, hardworking, and perhaps even courageous.

I brought that strong sense of self and confidence to my work as a life-long student of literature, music, the arts. I have always had the need to learn, and to develop an inner life. We must take care of ourselves in order to bring love to others. I have been fortunate to have two husbands who understood that, and helped me to explore and grow.

religion

The work of Thomas Merton is important to me, especially his idea of the "hidden wholeness" of all creation, the Living Spirit, and that one can be nurtured spiritually by religions of both East and West. I've read Joseph Campbell and been intrigued by his incorporation of Buddhism and other eastern religions into his thinking.

I grew up an Episcopalian, the compromise between my Scandinavian mother's religion and my father's Catholicism. That was comfortable at the time. But it was the music and beautiful ritual of Catholicism, its art and architecture, that spoke to me as a child and where I first came to understand the concept of God. My father would take me on the feast days to the grand Gothic Catholic church in Evanston. Listening to the great organ there, hearing the priests chant, I knew for all time that God was near.

The Episcopal denomination, the "high church" that is, is very close to the Roman Catholic in significant ways: the service, the level of intellectual sophistication, the fine sense of ritual and tradition. Art aids the search for the spiritual. I rejoice in the Gothic cathedrals, the great religious music, especially the beautiful Easter hymns. The Easter season assures us of life everlasting, a precious hope. Where there is death, there is inevitable rebirth. That is why I love springtime and find Easter the greatest festival of all.

Most religions teach that growth comes through suffering and that was certainly true for my sons and me. Jack's illness was a true baptism of fire, the major growing experience of my life. Such suffering does make you stronger, if you aren't broken by it. Thank God, I wasn't broken. I learned that I was able to accept the pain and sorrow, to let all permeate my being. In that way, I could accept, deal with it, and eventually, live with it. But I know I could be hit again where I am most vulnerable.

Through that travail I learned what life is all about and how to cope and prevail. I learned of life's terrible uncertainty, and how to lose and go on. I learned what sickness and death really are like and found that times of great illness have happy times as well, that everything does not fall apart. One does hold on to oneself; the human spirit has a great ability to heal and grow stronger.

But one's values change forever; that is true for my sons as well. You learn to focus on what is important, not fuss over trivia. You learn to be very grateful for what you do have. Sorrow becomes a part of the fiber of one's life. And now it is a sweet sorrow, gentle and abiding.

mentors and women friends
My musical interests were recognized early and I had the good fortune to work with extraordinary musicians and teachers. Perhaps that is why I was willing to work so hard. In fourth grade I practiced at least one and a half hours a day and in high school practiced three and a half hours each day. When I was a child, my heroes were violinists such as Nathan Milstein and Jascha Heifitz. I remember hearing the young Patricia Travers and wishing to play as she did some day.

Clarence Evans of the Chicago Symphony was my first "big" teacher. I began studying with him when I was eight. He encouraged me to play, not for fame or fortune, but because I loved the music. That was an invaluable lesson. To this day, I love the sound of my violin, a Guersan. After Mr. Evans died, I began studying with George Perlman, another great teacher of violinists. I was only in the eighth grade, yet he taught me how to perform as a professional and also how to teach. I often think of him, because now I teach writing as I was taught the violin.

The mentors of my adult life have had a profound impact. Jack helped me to live with a kind of freedom through those dangerous times. He taught me to have a sense of proportion and humor. He believed in me and with him I blossomed and began to accomplish more.

James Downer was my mentor at the University of Michigan where I got my Doctor of Arts degree. He helped me discover my strengths as a student and taught me a great deal about how to teach and how to analyze and criticize literature.

I was forty before I learned to get along with women. The artist

Voices of the Silent Generation

Shirley Essex was the first woman I met with whom I did not feel I was competing. Most of my life I had been around very competitive people, men as well as women, but mostly men. Since I am like men in my drive to excel, I usually got along well with them. But I had to learn how to be close to other women.

Gloria Kitto Lewis in 1987
(Photo courtesy of Barry Edmonds)

I met Shirley Essex because I commissioned her to do my portrait. I was finishing my degree and my life was beginning to take some shape for the first time since Jack died. At forty I felt special and lovely, with a Mary Cassatt hairstyle that made me feel feminine.

Shirley Essex is widely recognized as a fine portrait artist. I had no models for being a woman or a professor, but I did find a friend in Shirley. She is an artist, not a cold intellectual, and was very kind and honest with me. She was very perceptive; I was coming out of all of that intellectual work for the doctorate, and was still dealing with a lot of grief. And Shirley, who was so intuitive, would make me talk. There was never a feeling of performance, which was all I'd known. She wouldn't let me not tell her the truth and when I was hurting she wouldn't let me move away from it without talking about it. I needed that.

Through Shirley I learned to stop the performing, the competing, and really talk to women and trust that I could talk with them about things that mattered to us all.

I have a few close women friends now for whom I am very grateful. In academia and in music, women are often very complicated, ambitious and career-centered; one needs friends outside those worlds.

The social changes of the 60s and 70s did not affect me in terms of my own choices. I did what had to be done, given my interests and abilities.

But I have become more and more interested in what women have to say about their experiences, and in observing social change everywhere.

Over the years, I have learned more about how the politics of the university work. My husband Ralph directs three departments in the School of Music at the University of Michigan, and he has been especially helpful to me. Yet, I do not think I have the brand of toughness and assertiveness of my colleagues in their thirties who are so well attuned to any kind of discrimination.

work

Early in my adult life work expectations were clear and I fulfilled them: I was a good mother and stayed home with my children in the early years. I could find some life of my own, which I discovered I needed after the boys were born, by playing the violin and taking one course at a time in graduate school. Jack believed in me as a wife and mother, but also knew I needed a way to grow on my own. But he also needed me, and going to school full time would not have been true to our life together. Even just getting the Master of Arts in English, one course per term, was at some cost to our family. Certainly the boys learned not to expect homemade apple pie! But Jack did respect my efforts, was never competitive and, in fact, was proud of what I accomplished along the way.

In those years I played in recitals and chamber music concerts. I learned much of the major orchestral and chamber literature for the violin. I did a great deal of volunteer community work in those years, often with substantial responsibilities in arts organizations and events. I was comfortable in this work and felt fortunate to be able to contribute as Flint, with major infusions of General Motors funding, began to grow up culturally.

It was a natural evolution for me to want a career. I knew I wanted to continue to grow and to take responsibility in the professional world. By my late twenties, I knew I

Gloria with violin, 2005
(courtesy of Patrick Adams)

needed to do more than volunteer work. I had finished the Master's degree in English and was ready to build on that, to go on for the doctorate. I am grateful for the luxury of being able to enjoy my children when they were small and later on, when they were settled in school, to go on to teach and finish my graduate work. And I was fortunate not to have to support us during the years of graduate school.

My professional life began after Jack died. Being a teacher in a college works well with school-age children because I could teach early in the day and be home two full days a week. I could also work at home on weekends. There were sacrifices made by all; teaching does take an immense amount of time. But it was, after all, our livelihood at the time, along with what had been left to us.

My tenure review came up three years after Michael's death. It was 1981 and financial hardships throughout the state of Michigan required funding cuts to state universities. Though recommended for promotion by my department, I was denied tenure. It was a terrible blow. I loved teaching and I believed I was a good teacher. But many people lost jobs then, especially in the auto industry. That affected everything else in the state, even university budgets.

That interruption to my career in my mid-forties was substantial. Jobs in English and the humanities were hard to find. I needed to stay in Flint so that my youngest son's high school years would not be disrupted.

After earning another graduate degree, this time in Communication Studies, I had the good fortune to join the English Department at Wayne State University in Detroit. I direct the Technical Writing Program and teach composition and technical communication. I've enjoyed working with students in engineering and the sciences as well as liberal studies.

I think combining work as wife, mother, and professional can be done. But there are costs and benefits. One simply cannot have everything. If a man's career is unusually demanding and the children are young, it probably is not possible for the wife to work at a demanding career and have everything go well.

But that stage does not last forever. Later a successful blend involves each partner recognizing the other person for what she or he is; that means knowing the other in essential ways.

Now I have the good fortune to be married to a truly liberated man who is proud of my work. There is a cost to working outside the home, but Ralph is used to professional women and would not really wish for another kind of wife.

My work has always been a mix of being very solitary and then sharing with people. I have spent many of my waking hours practicing violin or studying. The major satisfactions for me have been in helping students to nurture their own spirits, to awaken strengths that will sustain them throughout their lives. Teaching is, after all, missionary work. It is also gratifying to help students develop skills they will use professionally.

It was thrilling to me to write papers and see them published. The recent paper on Thomas Merton gave me special satisfaction.

Now the concerns of my work are the terrible amounts of time it takes to teach well and the difficult problems in departments. As a faculty member I have only known university life in times of trouble. The whole state of Michigan, since the early eighties, has had dire economic problems and these are reflected in the universities. So it has been a time of struggle for most of us in the academic world and the politics are often wearying.

children

Motherhood felt very natural to me and I believed that I cared for our children as no one else could. I must admit that nothing in my life had prepared me for three sons in under five years. I learned that boys hit each other all the time, when happy, when angry, whenever! One could argue that raising boys helps one earn points toward Paradise.

I value children more than a profession. Having children and pursuing a profession are simply not in the same league. I also value being a wife and the profound experience of marriage, so natural and energizing.

It is important to have a life of one's own. While raising the boys, I always took at least one course toward my degree in English, played violin recitals, and worked on community arts projects. As a mother, one can accomplish goals, such as finishing a degree, though one cannot do it as quickly as some others. There has to be compromise and patience.

However, there are some costs to everything. Certainly in the academic world, there is no question that most of us who start in our forties cannot go as far as people who started their careers in the twenties.

Both Jack and I had been precocious, sensitive children and we learned on our own to protect our individuality. We wanted our boys to grow up knowing and liking themselves and having freedom to explore, create, and define for themselves. So, unlike the home of my childhood, there were minimal rules and lots of encouragement. We thought of the family years as a time of sharing life with our sons. We introduced them to what each of us knew and cared about. Jack knew about medicine, politics, sports, and the outdoors. I knew about music and the arts. And we both knew about our Episcopal faith. I wanted to share the art and religion that meant so much to me, just as my father had done. Jack took them camping and to sports events and we all did many things together.

Friends and I had observed huge gaps between the educations of our parents and our own fortunate selves. We were provided with more opportunities, money, sophistication, and education. That was the case with both of my husbands as well. That difference between my generation and my children has been erased and I rejoice in the experiences we were able to offer our children.

When Jack died, I took care of myself as well as them, rather than sacrificing myself to them. They knew that I had a life separate from theirs, knew they were always first, but not everything, in my life. That turned out to be good for us all. My sons told me in later years that knowing I had concerns and interests of my own made them feel free of me, not as responsible.

Mothers have many sides, many needs. My sons also told me that it was helpful to them, after their father died, that I went on and carved out a professional life. It allowed them to grow, have their own aspirations.

We always taught them that they are precious people, loved by their parents, welcomed before they existed, as it were. We taught them to be courteous and respectful, genuinely so, to all people; to be honest about their feelings, to acknowledge them to themselves in particular; to be grateful for goodness and beauty; to welcome and nurture a family, knowing that our gifts to others are central to life; to seek a sense of accomplishment, yet strive for a balance in their lives.

looking ahead

Turning fifty was not a time of unabashed rejoicing for me. Mainly, it sounded older. Turning fifty-five was even less fun, a kind of mild shock! I had a revelation that I do not have a whole lifetime ahead of me and I needed to take a closer look at what I was doing and why. For the first time in my life, I discovered that I passionately want to have time to myself. I wish for quiet time to read and meditate, free time to walk, to garden, to ride my bike. I want to go to more lectures and more concerts. I want hours and hours to learn more violin repertoire. I want time for fun with my husband as well as with my grown children and their children. No longer can I in good conscience allow my university work to consume so much of my time.

As to feeling older, the deaths and other losses that have been mine to accept have taken their toll. A part of me is spent, tired. And yet, I still have a great deal of energy and drive and can work like a racehorse...when motivated. But now I do want to choose. More than ever, now in my late fifties, I do want to do more of what I enjoy.

I feel that I am at a fork in the road now. My sons are raised and in the world, each doing well in their respective fields. Peter is a physical therapist here in Ann Arbor and I am told he ministers to his patients with skill and sensitivity. David is the marketing manager at Carnegie Hall, and teaches a course at Brooklyn College. I feel free now to turn my attention to my husband, Ralph Lewis. This is the turning point that I feel most significantly.

We share a love of music and the pursuit of knowledge, wisdom. We are in tune spiritually and find peace together. We have been married since 1982, but we are still romantic and never seem to tire of one another. He always makes me feel lovely. The pressures of our work sometimes make life a little tense, and that makes us especially treasure our summers together in Northern Michigan.

When we married, it took a couple of years to stop living metaphorically with my hands clenched. Until then my work had been a holding strategy, a way of making life tolerable. When I met Ralph it took me quite a while to calm down on the inside. There was an amazing feeling of lightness. I had lived so many years alone, and now to rediscover the joys of being married! At times I still rediscover it and think, "My God, here he is upstairs, we have such fun, and work is not all there is."

I look forward to time with my sons, and Ralph's adult children. I am certainly ready to have grandchildren; I long to have babies around the house again.

I learned at a fairly young age that life can be short, unpredictable and hold much pain. So one really ought to live each day as fully as possible. Living that and learning it firsthand is quite different from learning it intellectually.

You prepare for age by the way you live your life. Old age can be lonely, filled with worry about money and illness. Early in life one needs to plan carefully for the later years---habits of using time, of taking care of needs for friends, for spiritual, artistic and intellectual nourishment. One must find pleasure in solitude. And be grateful.

rewards

I do not have so much a sense of pride as a sense of humility in the face of all my good fortune. I have lived in the best of several worlds in that I have been able to be a wife and mother, play the violin seriously, and have a teaching career.

I tried to be the best mother I possibly could to David, Peter and Michael. They have grown up to be genuinely humane, principled, loving and dependable men. They care a lot about others, and themselves, and I think that the world is better for having them here. We grew up together in many ways. My sons are reminders that I have lived life in a way that matters.

Also I believe very strongly in being as good a wife as I can be. What a blessing to find Ralph, such a gift to find someone who not only loves me, but needs me as well.

Finishing an advanced degree and going on to teach in colleges and universities gave me a great sense of accomplishment. I know that I have touched souls, made a difference in the lives of some of my students.

I did not grow into an adult friendship with my mother, yet I feel that I have been a good daughter. I am most grateful for my parents, my children, Jack and Ralph who have all brought me deep happiness, for good health in body, mind and spirit, and for the abilities given to me. And I am most humbly grateful that I was able to prevail under difficult circumstances and somehow be strengthened by them.

And music in my life! I feel truest to my self when I play the violin and speak through the music. I love to play works by Mozart, Bach, Beethoven, Nardini, Pergolesi and Tartini. The sonatas of the Baroque violinist-composers, who wrote so beautifully for their own instruments, are a special joy to play.

I think I know how fragile life is, and I value what comes from experiencing birth, marriage, death. I do wonder why some are sent such enormous tragedies to bear and why those most needed by the world are chosen to die. Yet these questions become less burning for me as I get older. I can live without answers for the present. Perhaps that is because I believe in another realm of existence and know that angels are near.

Postscript, 2005:

After retiring from Wayne State University, Gloria resumed her study of the violin. In recent years her faith and music blend as Gloria plays chamber music at Thomas the Apostle Church and other recital spaces. In February, 2005, she played at the Basilica of San Spirito in Florence, Italy. Her son David still resides New York City, while Peter and family live nearby in Ann Arbor. Gloria rejoices now in two fine grandsons who surely help to redeem past sorrow and complete the joy of daily life.

SATO HASHIZUME
Introduction

Born in Oregon, Sato Hashizume was the daughter of a tailor who had emigrated from Japan. Her mother died when Sato, the youngest of six children, was a small child.

Shiro Hashizume might have distributed his children among relatives, but chose to keep the family intact. Of the many difficulties he faced during World War II, none matched the forced internment by the United States government of his family and other Japanese-American citizens.

After Japan's attack on Pearl Harbor in 1941, hostility towards Japanese-Americans intensified. In February, 1942, President Franklin D. Roosevelt signed Executive Order 9066, authorizing the removal of 120,000 persons of Japanese descent from their West Coast homes to internment camps. Sixty percent were women and children.

The years in the camps formed the core of Sato's childhood and altered her family's life for years thereafter. Sato is a reserved and dignified woman, disinclined to ready discussion of difficult times. But as Sato peeled away layers of memory and time, she spoke eloquently of the camp and its effects on her family. For an independent woman accustomed to maintaining her composure and poise, this was no simple exercise. I am much indebted to Sato for allowing me to accompany her as she returned in memory to painful events.

Sato offered the words of scholar S.I. Hayakawa to summarize the responses of many Japanese-Americans to their experiences:

"Since their words would not have been believed, especially in wartime, they communicated by action and behavior. 'We are good Americans,' they said. 'We are good neighbors. We are useful and productive citizens. We love America and are willing to die for her.' This message was communicated by the industry of the workers and businessmen and farmers, by their service to the communities in which they live, by their behavior as good citizens, and by the war record of the 442nd (editor's note: a U.S. Army unit in which many young Japanese-American men served). It was a form of communication for which there is no verbal or symbolic substitute."

During the years immediately following internment, Sato's family suffered as grievously as they had in the camps, in some ways even more so. The family faced bigotry, poverty to the point of hunger, and with her father's illness, no possibility of returning to their former comfortable life. In early adolescence Sato found work as a housekeeper to support her disabled father, while also holding herself to high standards in school. She later earned degrees in nursing and community health, pursued postgraduate work in psychiatric nursing, taught at the University of California, and served in Sri Lanka aboard the hospital ship Hope. Sato recently retired as liaison coordinator of the Home Care Program of geriatric nursing operated by the University of California, San Francisco.

Reflecting on her career, Sato is most pleased with being a master clinical nurse. As a home care specialist, she visited patients in their homes and made comprehensive evaluations. She had access to a variety of specialists for treatment as needed. She also enjoyed teaching these clinical skills to nursing students.

Sato retired soon after our first meeting. As might be expected, her retirement life is full. The group of "Hopies" with whom Sato served on the hospital ship gather regularly for reminiscence and fellowship.

Separated from Japanese culture at an early age, Sato now studies Japan's art, literature and history with enthusiasm. She volunteers for extensive work with the city's elderly Japanese population. Her unaccustomed leisure also affords time to develop the garden below her snug San Francisco townhouse. As long as he lived, Sato's cat Sinbad offered his own idiosyncratic assistance with planting and weeding.

Sato attends reunions freighted with emotion and memory. In 1990 the first evacuation reunion of Portland area Japanese-Americans attracted over a thousand people from the United States and Japan. When I met Sato for the first time, she had recently returned from the second reunion, held over several days. Almost fifty years had passed before Japanese-Americans could speak freely to one another of their wartime experiences.

Sato introduced me to the fine artistry of the *tansu*, antique Japanese chests which she now collects, and together we leafed through books of Japanese and family history. After years of suppressing her Japanese heritage in order to "be American," Sato has rediscovered her family's ancient stories, language and customs.

The Hashizume family is descended from Oda Nobunaga, who was Shogun during the mid-1500s. When he was assassinated in Kyoto, his clan escaped to the mountains where they remain today. The Hashizume cemetery, located close to the ancestral home of Sato's father's family, dates back five centuries.

In her early fifties, and bolstered by three semesters of Japanese language study, Sato visited relatives in Japan. At the family shrine her second cousin showed Sato a fragile, gilded, fan-folded book of ancestor's names, including those of her own parents. She was then taken to the location of the clan's castle during the feudal period; nearby the Buddhist temple houses Hashizume family tablets of the dead dating back to the seventeenth century. Sato had visited the ancestral home twice before, but had not previously been shown family treasures. These disclosures of family history brought poignant resolution to Sato's search for her heritage.

The long morning of recollection had passed quickly; hunger pangs brought us sharply back to the present. We went out for Sunday brunch overlooking San Francisco Bay, the present filled by fine seafood, sunshine sparkling on dark gray waves, and seabirds swooping overhead. Sato's memories had been somber, but now there was lighter talk and much laughter. Sato most certainly possesses the quality of gravitas, but her wry sense of humor peeks around corners unexpectedly.

As demanding as much of her life has been, Sato Hashizume eagerly embraces the future. I have no doubt Sato will continue to conduct her retirement years as she has her life: with skill, persistence, purpose and grace.

Sato Hashizume
San Francisco
1990

When I think about the Issei, I remember the Japanese Daruma, a doll without hands or feet that bounces back every time it's knocked down.

When World War II began, the other school children would throw stones at me and call me "Jap," but it never occurred to me to stay at home. Instead I traded a bag of penny candy for a large "I am a Loyal Chinese-American" button and went safely to school wearing that button as my shield.

Education has always been highly valued in Japanese culture. Regardless of how poor we were, there was always money for books, pencils, paper and school clothes. I always went to school unless I was so ill I couldn't climb out of bed.

Voices of the Silent Generation

looking back

My mother was killed in a hit-and-run automobile accident when I was two years old. My brothers were then four and six, and my sisters, twelve and fourteen. My oldest sister assumed the role of mother and managed all the household tasks while going to high school as an honor student. My twelve-year-old sister took care of the three youngest children. We struggled together and became a close-knit family. My father, Shiro Hashizume, provided the security that was so vital to all of us. He showed us that even if we were poor and discriminated against, we could still be proud.

Children need two parents. We had only one parent, but my father was exceptional. He kept our family together and raised five children. And he did have other options. He could have sent us all to Japan, or he could have farmed us out to other relatives here. I found out recently that there were also people in the community who wanted to adopt the older children. But he chose to keep us together. I've always been thankful for that.

My father was always very encouraging. If I wanted to do something it was always "Sure, okay." He wouldn't give me a lot of verbal praise; his encouragement was mostly nonverbal. I could tell when he approved of something I had done because he'd have a big grin on his face. Or he'd say simply, "Good!" The communication was there. I think that my family in general was proud of me, yet there wasn't direct praise to let me know. I usually overheard someone in the family talk about the achievement or it would come back to me through others. This is the indirect way Japanese people often communicate.

Since before World War II there has been a Japanese-American community in Portland, Oregon, where we lived. Everyone belonged to a Japanese school, church, club or other organization, so we all knew each other. Before the war the children addressed the adults as "uncle" or "aunt" and could count on them for help. For the adults there was mutual support. And later there was the Minidoka camp community consisting of the Japanese-American population of Portland, Seattle, and parts of Alaska. Even today, older Japanese-American strangers will ask each other which of the ten camps they were in as a way of starting a conversation.

The first challenges of my life were all connected to the concentration camp experience. I was ten years old; I remember everything. We were given seven days to sell almost all we owned and leave with what we could carry.

Strong Women Tell Their Stories

But, to a ten year old, it was exciting at first--to see real FBI agents standing in front of our apartment house, interviewing all the tenants who went in and out. We had an eight o'clock p.m. curfew imposed on us, and it was great fun to sneak outside late at night to see if we would get caught. It was just like "Gangbusters" on the radio on Saturday nights. And it seemed exciting to be moving.

As I began to understand what was happening, I became anxious about my father. Everyday we would hear that someone's father had been taken directly from his place of employment to the FBI; their families did not see or hear from them for months. Although no evidence of subversive activity was ever found, many families were separated for years.

For my father, I thought I had a solution. Anytime my father went out for any reason I would go with him. I would thrust my hand deeply in his coat pocket and hang on tightly. Surely, the FBI wouldn't know what to do with a small child clinging to her father; of course they couldn't take him away. Fortunately, my father was never suspected, but my aunt and uncle in Los Angeles were considered dangerous because they led a sect of a Shinto church. They were sent, without warning or notice, to Crystal City in Texas. We knew nothing about them for a year. Finally, we heard via the grapevine where they were and that they were safe.

Because the camps were not ready, we were sent first to an assembly center in Portland. We were placed in the Pacific International Livestock Exposition center. Many of the assembly centers had been facilities for animals before Japanese-Americans became the unwilling tenants. The Japanese people of San Francisco, for instance, were sent to the Tanforan horse-race track.

We were forced to live there until the camps were ready. There were about four thousand people from the Portland area crammed into one building. It was terribly crowded and very hot. We lived there for about three months, caged-in and not allowed to leave the Center. The large spaces were partitioned with plywood into individual cubbyholes that became the living quarters for whole families.

There was very little privacy. The tops of the rooms were open to a skylight roof, and a flimsy curtain covered the doorway. The toilets were lined up in a row without partitions. You were lucky if you happened to go in alone. There were about twenty showerheads in one room where all the women would shower. With the hot weather, the stench of the former animal tenants was overwhelming; and the food was terrible. But we could cope with all of that; the worst thing was that we were surrounded by barbed wire. I remember one man died. I don't know if he was shot or not, but he went berserk, and I understood that a soldier killed him.

Finally the camps were ready. Our camp, Minidoka, was in Hunt, Idaho, about twenty miles from Twin Falls. It was in the desert, very hot and dusty in the summer, bitterly cold in the winter, and incredibly muddy during the rainy season. The camps, they called them relocation centers, were built like army camps; there were fifty-two blocks for the ten to twelve thousand people in our camp. Each block had a mess hall, laundry and bathroom facilities in the center with a row of barracks on either side. Each barracks had six rooms of varying sizes, and each family was assigned to a room based on family size.

Our family of six shared one small cramped room, furnished with six cots and bedding. The barracks were not insulated, just wood frames and tarpaper, and it was freezing cold when we arrived. The toilets were not ready so we used outdoor facilities the first winter. We did get potbellied stoves later, and carried the coal to our room for heat. But there was no way to cope with the mud and dust storms in spring, and oven-like heat-- sometimes over 100 degrees Fahrenheit in summer.

It was a very difficult time for my parent's generation, but for me, still a child, I played, met new friends, and went to a school there in the Center. Children's perspectives can be very different from that of their parents. But, as a consequence of the camp experience, I never learned to swim or ride a bike. There were no bikes or pools in the camps, though some men in the camp did dig a muddy swimming hole. And I was just the right age to learn those skills. There are certain times in your life that are prime for developing specific motor skills; later in life it's much more difficult. I know because I've tried! So I have hidden deficits which I later realized came from those times.

The adults tried to keep everyone occupied. We had a Sunday school and there were music groups. Men in the camp built baseball diamonds and small parks for picnics. That baseball team was topnotch! They even managed to publish a newspaper, the *Minidoka Irrigator*.

And *Irrigator* was certainly an appropriate name, because residents cleared almost a thousand acres of desert and dug ditches and canals for irrigation. So there were vegetable and flower gardens. People even collected pebbles and stones and made traditional Japanese gardens. These Issei and Nisei were very resourceful people! They also worked outside the camp in local sugar beet and potato farms and in canneries, so they contributed greatly to the local economy.

Ironically enough, there were Japanese-American soldiers in World War II. My own brothers were drafted later and served in the Korean conflict. Tom served overseas, while George, a third-year engineering student at Ohio State, went to Huntsville, Alabama, to work with Wernher von Braun. These contradictions were astounding, then and now.

While we were in Salt Lake City, my oldest sister married a man who had just returned from the U. S. Army. He had been drafted into the Army just two days prior to World War II, but it was not uncommon for the young Japanese men to enlist in the Army directly from camp, because they wanted to prove they were Americans. Of all the camps, Minidoka had the highest number of volunteers, about a thousand. With some exceptions, most of the men from Hawaii and the mainland were placed in the now famous 442nd Regimental Combat Team, a segregated troop of Japanese-American men. They fought in Italy and France at great cost and proved themselves over and over again. They were one of the most highly decorated combat units in World War II. My brother-in-law was honored with a Bronze Star and two Purple Hearts. He carries the shrapnel scars to this day.

One memory I have of camp was the almost routine ritual of the block manager standing in the mess hall announcing the names of the latest casualties from the battlefield. We held our breath not knowing who would be next. Seventy-three soldiers from Minidoka were killed in the war and two received the Congressional Medal of Honor.

Yes, there was a blatant inconsistency in government policy regarding the evacuation of the Japanese-American families and the drafting of their eligible sons. The government was not concerned about the Japanese-American people, only that it was politically expedient to remove them from the West Coast, and draft their able-bodied sons to fight the war. All were expendable.

There were a few young men in camp who would not sign the loyalty oath; they were called No-No boys. But in general there was somber acceptance of the evacuation and enlistment or drafting of the young men. People were still loyal to America, despite the internment. Two-thirds of us were born here after all!

How could this happen in America? It's important to remember that this took place before the civil rights movement, and the Japanese in America had few rights. We were not allowed to vote or hold property. We lived in restricted areas and, in some locations, went to segregated schools. The older generation spoke little English, and with a few notable exceptions, were unsophisticated about politics and bureaucracy.

We label ourselves by the generation into which we were born. "Issei" are the first generation of Japanese residing in the United States. The

Voices of the Silent Generation

"Nisei" are the second generation, and "Sansei" are the third generation. We are the only ethnic group who do this; I can tell you how it came about. In the United States there was extreme hostility and prejudice against the immigrant Japanese from the beginning. After several discriminatory laws were passed, the 1924 Exclusion Act stopped Japanese immigration completely. From the 1890's on, young Japanese had come to work and start families. With no further immigration allowed, a fairly clear generational demarcation was established.

At that time, members of the American-born younger generation were either adolescents or in their twenties with very little experience to guide them. Many of these Nisei were well educated, but held menial jobs or worked at their parents' place of business because discrimination was common, and few employers would hire them. Culture also played a role in allowing the forced removal to take place. The Issei wanted to be good Americans and not cause trouble. They were used to a hard, unyielding environment, and always made the most of it. They would prevail! And they did.

Gamman is an important Japanese cultural value. It means forbearance in spite of adversity, the ability to come through tough times successfully. My parents' generation endured harsh times with remarkable grace. *Gamman* helped me as well.

It has been stated in several publications that because of the war record of the 442nd infantry, and the recognition, at last, that a terrible wrong had been done, the Japanese-Americans were more quickly accepted and assimilated into the American mainstream. But at what cost?

We were away from our home for about three years, from 1941 on; then the government closed the camps, and we were displaced again. By 1944, the war was not yet over, so the West Coast was still what I would call a hot area. Some of the Japanese people who went back found their homes firebombed, and there was prejudice and ugliness. In fact, when I went back to Portland a year later, some restaurants still had signs saying "No Japs Allowed."

Because of the attitude toward Japanese-Americans in Portland, we moved from the camp directly to Salt Lake City. When we left the camp, we were given fifty dollars each for relocation. We found a two-room apartment without running water in someone's home. Fifty dollars paid for the rent, and fifty for some groceries, with a little left over. My father had been a tailor, so he went to find work at a particular dry-cleaning establishment. Unfortunately, just the day before he got there, someone else got the job. My father was then fifty-eight, and couldn't find a job until he went to the University club and told them he could cook. Well, he never cooked in his life! The next morning when they told him to fry the eggs he broke twelve before getting one right, so they shifted him over to the dishwasher.

Then winter came. He slipped on the ice and fractured his pelvis or hip. Actually, it was never clear which it was because we didn't have money for x-rays, much less hospitalization. The doctor came to our home for one visit; then we cared for him at home for the next six weeks.

One sister and one brother had moved from camp to Cincinnati. This left my father, my oldest sister and another brother in Salt Lake City. None of us were employed. I knew the situation was desperate, so I applied for a job as a domestic at the home of a man who was the editor-in-chief of the *Salt Lake Tribune and Telegram.* The woman said that I looked too young. I had just turned fourteen. But they were desperate too. They asked me if I could cook and I said, "Oh yes!" I thought that I could cook since I had learned to make muffins in the seventh grade! Although we used chopsticks at home, I had learned to set the table in the seventh grade as well, and as for child care, I had done some babysitting in the camp. I thought I was prepared, and she hired me.

Sato Hashizume, high school graduation photo, 1949

Since education was so very important to our family, I went to school full time. Before going to school, I got up early, did all the cleaning and vacuuming and made breakfast. The family wanted only fresh-squeezed orange juice so I squeezed oranges every morning. After school, instead of taking a study period, I would rush home to do the ironing, take care of the two children, and cook the evening meal. I would serve dinner and clean up afterwards. I worked until about seven every night, then started my homework.

It was in that home that it occurred to me that there was a difference between us, a difference in class: I was a servant. The first night, I set the table for them and included a place for myself at the table. The woman took my setting off the table and told me to eat in the kitchen. That was the most painful part of the entire experience.

They never showed any compassion for a little girl doing all this. I was definitely a domestic servant and to them I had my place. But I wanted to prove myself. I worked like the devil, polished all their silver, cleaned all their crystal, and did ten times more than I had to. I never really felt appreciation until after I left and they had to hire someone else. Then they begged me to come back! I said no, I was moving to Oregon.

I learned from this experience. I learned about people and how I would behave if ever I were in a position to have people working for me. And I helped solve the financial problem with my family, and I do have strong emotions about that.

When my father was able to walk again, we went to Portland, and he tried to start a business. He was about sixty, an age when he should have been able to think about retirement. But we didn't have much money. The hotel business he found cost three thousand dollars. In order to raise enough money, he cashed in his life insurance policy, and a small award that was granted when my mother had been killed. This was painful for him because he had hoped he could leave something for his children. He also needed to borrow money from his best friend to cover the purchase. These heavy sacrifices bought for us an old, dirty, third-class hotel business on Skid Row.

We rented to many elderly pensioners who had little money but were very decent, and frankly, we also had prostitutes. We were not supposed to rent to them, but as long as they signed Mr. and Mrs. we closed our eyes, because we needed the income. And then we would have drunks who would come and start fires in their rooms, or urinate and vomit on the stairways.

I was a teenager and was very sensitive about living in this environment. But my father said let's just try it for three years and see if we can make a go of it. Before the war we had lived in a very nice part of town right across the street from the Ambassador Apartments that were later converted into expensive condominiums. We had lived in an area restricted to Japanese; but that's another story. Our apartment house had a beautiful, heavy oak door with beveled glass windows, and a spacious lobby with fine furniture. And here we were in this old hotel without running water in the kitchen. I did not want to stay in that place.

There were many unexpected expenses. Unknown to my father, the hotel had already been condemned by the city inspectors, and the person from whom my father had purchased the business stripped the hotel of all supplies and stole all of the bedding not already on the beds. We had to put everything we earned back into the hotel to quickly bring the place up to code or lose the business. That first winter, my brother and I slept under our coats because we didn't have enough blankets. We had very little food so we would go into our tenants' rooms after they moved and check to see if they'd left an onion or a potato.

The saddest part was that after we got the hotel, my father had to work day and night. He was the day and night clerk, the carpenter, the plumber, the paperhanger, the painter. He did everything! He was one of those people who always got up at six in the morning no matter what. Then he went to bed late when all the work was completed. He had a heart attack soon after that, but couldn't stop working. There was too much to do.

By this time, only my older brother, then seventeen, and I, then fifteen, were with our father. My oldest sister had married and stayed in Salt Lake City. My brother and I cooked and kept house, and tried to help our father by making the tenants' beds and cleaning the halls and toilets. Of course, we continued to go to school as usual and tried to maintain a social life. Fortunately, there were other Japanese nearby who were in similar straits, and we were all very supportive of each other.

Sato with father, Shiro Hashizume, at Capping Ceremony, Providence School of Nursing. 1950

Things opened up after the war, but there was still overt racial prejudice. In high school there were social clubs sponsored by the school that were closed to Japanese-Americans. Also, I remember going with other students to a local restaurant where a waitress would not serve us because I, a Japanese-American, was in the group. As it happened, the whole group stood up and walked out with me.

Some years later, when I had almost finished nursing school, my father had a massive stroke. I came back to take care of him. The brothers who had been in the army came home. My unmarried sister was there as well to help. Our father had taken care of us all those years, now it was our turn. With effort we were able to rehabilitate him from bed to a wheeled walker. He lived four and a half years longer.

heritage and religion

I have an unusual religious background. My father was a lay minister of a Shinto church, although he was raised a Buddhist. He allowed me to go to a Methodist Sunday School because my friends were going there; and that was fine with him because as far as he was concerned, God was God!

So I would go to the Methodist Sunday School in the morning and then to my father's church in the afternoon. I've always thought his religious beliefs kept our family together. For a man to raise five children by himself took faith and strength. Although he belonged to a specific religion, he accepted all religions. This left an indelible impression on me.

I attended a Catholic nursing school for three years during the fifties. I went there because of their scholarships and their beautiful new dormitory. In that nursing school, we were all treated like nuns. It was strict, with lights out at ten-fifteen. Recently I encountered one of the nuns from that school and we laughed about those days. We took medical ethics, learned how to baptize babies, and were well indoctrinated in Catholicism. We were told that if we were not baptized as Catholics we would certainly go to hell.

When I finished there, I thought, something doesn't quite fit. Catholics think they are the only ones who go to heaven; Methodists think they are the only ones who to heaven. But the Shinto religion had a more liberal perspective. I took college religion courses and tried to come to my own conclusions. I think that people can believe as they wish. What's important is that they gain ethical values and a philosophy from their upbringing in a religion. I have traveled extensively throughout my adult life, have seen many religions practiced, and have strengthened that belief. If a particular religion seems appropriate and makes sense to you, then it is probably right for you.

The questions of suffering and injustice are the great, unanswered questions of life for me. Now, as I mature, I'm examining Buddhist beliefs and I like much of what I see there. The Buddhist philosophy seems wise and I plan to spend more time studying the teachings.

Strong Women Tell Their Stories

What appeals to me is the idea of finding answers and strength from within. And treating other people as if they were Buddhas; that is, to have respect for other human beings. Also the acceptance of life and death as part of a natural cycle. Many of the pieces seem to fit. But my thinking is still evolving.

I accept the Buddhist belief in reincarnation. I can come back and keep doing it until I get it right! I've learned some things in this life but I'll learn other lessons in the next. I still wish I hadn't had some of those experiences though. I can't say I have regret for my own choices; I did the best I could.

As to the Japanese cultural influences, before the war years I went to Japanese school every day right after American school, then half a day Saturday. We never had time to get into trouble! But when the war broke out, we wanted to be American so badly, to be accepted, that we stopped speaking Japanese. So I don't speak Japanese very well now. My older siblings do because they had enough early Japanese school education. But I tried to block that, and speak English so well, articulate so clearly, that now people don't know I'm Japanese until they see me face to face. For years I was closed, clamped down against the whole idea of being Japanese.

In 1981 there were congressional hearings on the evacuation and the camps; the Japanese people finally began to talk about their experiences. Then it dawned on me: I was a part of all of that! So much had been suppressed in my mind; I needed that awakening. I am a product of both cultures: still very much a Japanese, but also a product of acculturation. The younger generation was already asking questions and many of us began to rethink these issues.

The civil rights movement of the sixties and seventies profoundly affected me both directly and indirectly. It was because of that movement, I believe, that the Sansei, or the third generation Japanese-Americans, took up the cause of redress and reparation for the unjust incarceration of their parents and grandparents. The Issei, the first generation, and the Nisei, the second generation Japanese-Americans, did not talk about their wartime experiences. It was too shameful and painful. But, the younger generation, well educated, articulate and incensed about their parents' and grandparents' concentration camp experience, decided that justice had to be served.

Through a long, arduous process of congressional hearings, legislation and education, both of the Japanese-Americans and the leaders of this country, the Sansei, in 1988, achieved their goal of reparations for the evacuees and an apology from the President of the United States. The amount of the reparations was small, but significant in recognizing that great harm had been done. The 1988 Civil Liberties Act also set aside funding to educate the public to prevent future massive violations of constitutional rights. Hopefully, it will never happen again to anyone.

The dynamic changes of the sixties and seventies also promoted more openness and honesty. I was influenced by the nursing students I was teaching; they challenged "the system" and made me look at myself. I am more open now than I had been, a little less reserved, but the influence of my cultural background is still pervasive.

I have some of the virtues of my ethnic/cultural background--being able to stick with something in spite of the difficulty—working through it, enduring, hanging in there. The other is hard work. That's a cliché, but with the kinds of prejudices we encountered, there was no other way to get ahead.

In fact, what has given me the deepest sense of accomplishment is the ability to solve problems, cope with hardship, go beyond, grow and learn from experiences. As I look back on all that has happened, I appreciate what I have learned.

friends and mentors

My sisters are my good friends and wonderful people; they listen and help through rough times. Over the years women friends have been important in the same ways.

A number of people are my heroes and heroines. Of course, my father is one. The group of people I admire most are the Issei, first-generation Japanese-Americans. They toiled long hours at menial jobs and businesses no one else wanted, and were frugal so that their children could have what they needed. Laws were passed to exclude them from the mainstream and they faced poverty and racial prejudice. Not until 1952 could they own property or become American citizens. Some made gains in the twenties, but lost heavily during the crash; then, just as they were beginning to get on their feet, the evacuation to the camps took all their material possessions again.

Whenever I think about the Issei, I recall the story of the Japanese "Daruma," a doll which has no hands or feet, but bounces back each time it is knocked down. The Issei bounced back time and time again, always stronger and more determined that their children and grandchildren would have a better future. I often think of the sacrifices made by my parents for our family. They were truly heroic.

Strong Women Tell Their Stories

I've been fortunate, in my career, to have people who recognized some potential in me and encouraged me to take on new challenges. I wasn't always ready to jump into new things, but with encouragement I would try. I seemed to have small successes along the way, enough to tell me I was doing well, and could go on to take the next step.

This was the case when I was a staff nurse in a public health department; the nursing supervisor, a stern, imposing, woman who at first scared me, took me under her wing. I eventually became a clinical instructor, my first teaching position in nursing.

A teacher in high school also left a deep impression on me. He gave the commencement address on the nature of success. He told a story about four high school boys who decided that in twenty years they would have a reunion and pick the one in their group who was most successful. When the reunion was held, three of the men came and began to talk about their accomplishments. They were all wealthy, though not happy in their home lives. When the fourth arrived, he told of many trials and career disappointments, yet spoke with great joy of his wife and children, and his pride in his younger brothers and sisters, whom he had raised after their parents died. At the end of the meal, the first three decided the fourth was the most successful man because he had coped best with what he had been given.

That story was tremendously important to me; I heard it long ago yet I still reflect on it. It means even more as I grow older. I found in my life that success was not so much wealth or position as the ability to cope with life's problems.

work

My career choices were not influenced by the social changes of the sixties; I decided in the sixth grade! We were instructed in school to make a career choice. I read a book about Clara Barton and liked the idea of becoming a nurse. Career choices in those days were simple. Women went into nursing, teaching, or became secretaries. I had a brief stay in the hospital when I was in camp, and thought this is a nice place to work. I'll be a nurse. I've never regretted it. There have been times when people have made me feel that nursing is a low status job, but it takes much more skill than many people understand. At long last, in the past five or ten years, nurses have begun to be more fairly compensated for their education and for the complicated care they provide. You would not believe how low my salary was when I first went to UCSF.

I have worn many hats during my career and I'm grateful to have

Sato teaching nurses on board
hospital ship HOPE, Sri Lanka, 1967

experienced many aspects of nursing. I've always felt interested and challenged. I look back at the landscape and wonder, did I do all that? There have been many satisfying moments in my career. Two stand out. One was the tour with Project HOPE to Ceylon, now known as Sri Lanka. The whole experience was unforgettable. I was the coordinator of the public health program; our staff of public health nurses, a nutritionist and health educator, worked with counterparts from the Ministry of Health and its departments. Polio, diptheria, and malaria were rampant at that time, so we organized large screening and immunization programs in the communities. I learned so much, both professionally and personally, and received much more than I gave. After twenty years, many "Hopies" remain my good friends.

The other career high point was the period when UCSF had a home care program primarily for student education in the Division of Family and Community Medicine. The faculty/staff of the program was an interdisciplinary one with a medical director, pharmacist, social worker and nurse, myself. The staff was close knit, competent and dedicated to ideal patient care. The students, from the Schools of Medicine, Pharmacy,

Social Work, Nursing, and occasionally from Dentistry and Podiatry, made individual and joint visits to the patient's home under staff supervision. Interdisciplinary patient care conferences were held; the patient's multiple problems would be discussed, and the best thinking of the staff would be brought to bear. We made miracles happen with extremely complex, difficult cases. The staff learned from each other and the students learned from all of us. I still have former students of all disciplines tell me how much the home care rotation meant and that their career decisions were shaped by that experience.

The last half of my professional career was at the University of California, San Francisco. I was a teacher of undergraduate senior nursing students, a nurse practitioner, an administrator of the home care program, and the liaison coordinator for the home care service. I did a little writing too--a couple of articles in nursing publications, and chapters in two different nursing textbooks. I was in community health all my professional life, and still love it.

In February of 1962, I was selected from several candidates to work for a year as a public health nurse with Project HOPE in Trujillo, Peru. I took Spanish lessons, stopped teaching at the University of Oregon School of Nursing, was interviewed by all the newspapers, royally partied by all my friends, and had my trunk packed. I was riding high and full of enthusiasm for the adventure.

Then the ship was delayed for three months; during that time, I developed shortness of breath and chest pain that turned out to be tuberculosis. I was devastated. How could this happen to me? I was sure I would never have another opportunity for anything so wonderful again.

Instead of going to Peru with Project HOPE, I went to a tuberculosis hospital and stayed for four and a half months. What I thought was going to be an unbearable experience turned out to be meaningful. A thoughtful physician said to me, "It's not everyone who has a chance to think about her life, and what she wants to do. This can be an opportunity to do just that." I thought about what he said and decided I needed to make some plans when I got out of the hospital. I had just enough time to apply for graduate school, and by the fall of the same year, I was going to the University of Minnesota. As I mentioned earlier, I did finally join Project HOPE five years later for work in Sri Lanka, not Peru.

Difficult experiences mark you forever, but they force you beyond yourself to learn and grow. And risks! Every step of life has risks. With every new job I started I felt a little anxious, especially if it entailed new challenges and learning new skills. I was never certain that I would be able to become a teacher, but I tried and was successful, I believe. Opportunities to try supervision and administration came along, and again despite trepidations, I acquired new skills and learned much about myself along the way.

looking ahead

Turning fifty was a time for thinking through how I wanted to use my life in the future. I considered obtaining a doctorate. At one time, a Master of Science degree was the standard in a nursing career; now it is the doctorate. Many of my colleagues, most much younger than I, were going back to school.

Always in the past, once I made a decision to further my education, there was no question. I would do it. This time, I went through the process of completing an application, obtained references, and then, at the last minute, called and canceled my application. I had never done that before in my life.

But, I still wasn't sure. I interviewed instructors at two other programs and began the application process again. Then it finally dawned on me that my priorities had changed. The piece of paper wasn't important to me anymore, but how I used my time and resources were very important. I preferred to stay close to my friends and family and develop in other ways. Having my life dictated by assignments was no longer appealing. I haven't regretted that decision.

I think about aging. I believe I show my age more than many people, but I've chosen to leave my gray hair alone.

The Issei have aged with such style and grace that I would love to be able to emulate them and be dignified in my aging. They have taken life as it came to them and made the most of it, and accepted aging and dying as natural events. As they became frailer they acknowledged and accepted their aging bodies. They preferred to be independent, but accepted their children's help when needed.

I do fear total physical or mental dependence and the depletion of my funds. I hope that one day we will have adequate long-term care insurance at a reasonable cost. With insurance, I could get enough assistance in the home, and not be a burden on my family or friends.

Retirement is wonderful. My working friends ask what I do with all my free time. Others, who took early retirement as I did, wonder if we can adjust our busy schedules to find time for lunch. I love the time with friends, doing volunteer work with elderly Japanese people, studying Japanese and looking into my family's Samurai history. I have traveled extensively, but there is still so much to see and do. Too many choices!

At the risk of looking silly, and also risking some physical harm, while on vacation in Hawaii, I went boogie-boarding for the first time! It's like a surf board but broader and shorter, and I had to watch the kids to figure out how to do it. I don't know how to swim, but I had a friend nearby, so I went out until my toes barely touched the bottom. I was the only gray-haired person out there, but I had the time of my life! One time when I came up out of the water, there was a group of people watching me. They were grinning and applauding my efforts!

I am glad to be living in San Fransisco. I love the ocean in any kind of weather, stormy or calm. I love the clean air near the ocean and the quiet days when you can hear the ocean sounds a mile away. The sunsets on the Pacific are spectacular. The air-conditioning, that is, our fog, is welcome when it gets too hot. And when it gets too gloomy in the summer, our heavy fog season, then a five-minute drive will take you to sunshine.

Sato with Sinbad, in San Francisco, 1990.

I enjoy long walks on our lovely bay area trails, and along the beach. We are lucky to have symphony, ballet, opera, ethnic dance festivals--so much to choose from. And, with such an ethnically diverse city, we never run out of wonderful places to eat!

Meanwhile, Sinbad is doing well. At his annual exam last month, the vet gave him a clean bill of health, but said Sinbad had tartar on his teeth. Have you ever tried to brush a cat's teeth?

I would like to write a book, a legacy for the third generation of our family. Many are out-married, and will lose their Japanese-American culture. As they get older and become interested in history they will be ready to appreciate their own heritage. I've been to Japan, I'm studying the language and family history, and I would like to make connections for the next generation, help build that bridge for them.

Postscript 2005:

Sato wrote that she has been encouraging other Japanese-Americans to write their own history before their generation is gone. She visits elementary and high schools as well as universities, reads from her own and other's work and holds discussions. "I had not planned on a second career after retirement!"

The fruits of Sato's retirement include contributions to two books. *From Our Side of The Fence: Growing up in America's Concentration Camps* is an anthology written by twelve Nisei, second generation Japanese Americans. As last living survivors of the camp experience the Nisei feel an urgency to tell their stories. Sato's writing is also included in the anthology *Only What We Could Carry: The Japanese-American Internment Experience,* edited by Lawson Fusao Inada and Patricia Wakida.

SISTER MARY BARBARA PHILIPPART
Introduction

Raised in Detroit, Sister Mary Barbara Philippart lived for over twenty years in Manazo, a rural village 14,000 feet above sea level in the Altiplano, the High Andes, of Peru. Her love for the people of Manazo, coupled with robust good health and a talent for community organizing, assured her a stay in the Andes far longer than any other missionary nun.

Few other sisters were permitted to stay in Peru when the danger posed by the Shining Path guerillas was at its peak. Early in 1990, Barbara was bound and robbed at knifepoint in her Manazo home.

I met Barbara, as she prefers to be called, through a friend whose church supported her efforts in Peru. In addition to funds, they sent volunteers to serve Manazo in a variety of ways. Barbara's visits to the church were festive times, with parties and picnics arranged by the group of Manazo alumni. Her ready laughter, good-humor and gentle manner tend to obscure the firmness of purpose underlying her visits. She is an irresistible fund-raiser. Her deep love for the poor village people among whom she lived and worked for so many years was obvious. She is one of them.

Barbara's successes in Peru testify to organizational skills, physical stamina, energy and fearlessness. Her soup kitchen serves lunch to five hundred children daily. Another program pairs villagers with Americans who write to the children and support their education. Under Barbara's guidance, a village library, reservoir and church were built by village people. They dug trenches and laid pipe to bring the village its first potable water. Additionally, as Manazo's church grows in vitality, more townspeople live faith-centered lives.

In 1985 Barbara organized village women into a knitting cooperative, Artesiana Pachamama (Workshop of the Mother Earth). Their handsome alpaca sweaters, hats, vests, mittens and scarves sell through a non-profit collective in the United States. Sixty-eight women sold, in 2003, over 400 sweaters for $75 to $150 dollars, the prices varying according to whether they are sold at churches or specialty stores.

After a sabbatical year in the USA, Barbara returned to Peru in 1992. The countryside was still dangerous, but after a long period of thought, prayer and consultation, she concluded that Peru was still too much a part of her not to return. Barbara told friends she had spoken Spanish so long she sometimes had trouble finding the correct English word.

Shortly after Barbara's return, Manazo was again raided by guerillas. One parishioner was shot, another killed in an explosion. Barbara and the village women bathed and prepared the bodies, then performed the burial service. Meanwhile, two village men were kidnapped. Later released, they eventually made their way home.

The efforts of then-President Alberto Fujimori brought some order to the troubled nation soon thereafter. Guerrilla incursions were fewer and American investors began to return. Peruvians hoped that Fujimori's promises for reform would bear fruit. The constitution he submitted explicitly endorsed free markets and foreign trade. But in 1992 the nation's hopes were dimmed by revelations of intelligence advisor Vladimiro Montesinos' illegal government activities. The decade ended with Montesinos under arrest and Fujimori fleeing the country, unwilling to face corruption and human rights abuse charges. In 2001, Alejandro Toledo was elected on a platform of political reform and economic progress. Terrorists again menaced the countryside.

Barbara's efforts were not political. Her goals were to ease suffering and offer villagers opportunities to improve their own lives. Her work extended into her vacation leaves. One was spent at her order's motherhouse in Cincinnati writing a textbook in Spanish for the children of Manazo.

Upon returning to Peru after that leave, Barbara was reassigned and became director of a new radio station. Tackling the unfamiliar work with characteristic zest, she soon had the station up and running, staying on as *directora* for several years until the entire operation was stable.

It was clear from our earliest conversations that Sister Barbara's spiritual strength is at the core of her work and her courage. I believe she is indeed heroic.

Sister Mary Barbara Philippart
Sister of Charity of Cincinnati, Ohio and the High Andes, Peru
1992, 1997

I love adventure and I love to get things done! My philosophy of missions is that you help to get good things started, then teach others to lead by showing a way out of hopelessness...But the wisdom that you think you have must be offered carefully to others. Even it you know how to offer it, they still may or may not want it!

Strong Women Tell Their Stories

Throughout the 1980s, Manazo was randomly attacked by Shining Path guerrillas. They entered the town one night, broke into my house, tied me up in bed and held me there with one knife at my throat, another at my back for over two hours while they robbed the house.

Other than that they did not touch me and I was not actually afraid, though I did pray for the Lord to help me face death if that was what was to happen. In fact I actually had a good conversation with my guard. When they were ready to leave, all four young men came into my room to say goodbye. They tucked my sleeping bag up around my neck and tried to explain what they were doing and why they believed in it. But they left me to struggle out of the ropes when they left, and when finally free, I found they stole almost everything in the parish office and house, including our bedclothes and food.

It is true that living in Peru during the last eleven years of terrorism was a risk. But I had lived and worked there for many years. Some may have questioned my volunteering to go to Peru in the first place, leaving everything I knew to go into the unknown. But I always wished to be a missionary. And life is full of risks. It is a risk to love, to serve and to drive on any road.

Sr. Barbara (then Nancy, upper right), with siblings Janet, Mickey and Kay, circa 1940's

My first true risk was joining my Congregation. I came from a comfortable, secure and loving home and leaving was very much of a risk for me. Taking vows, first and final, is taking a chance: "I give my life to you, Lord, and I will live my vows to the best of my ability, relying on your help."

Voices of the Silent Generation

looking back

My self-confidence comes from my parents, their love for, and confidence in me. We had a beautiful family life and strong religious values. We loved one another very much. My brothers and sisters have been wonderful, supportive people all my life. From a young age on, I put a lot of expectations on myself. My parents always made it clear that they were not putting those expectations on me.

My dad wanted to go to college but his father did not believe in college education--this was in the 1920's--so Dad won a football scholarship to University of Detroit, graduated a star, and eventually became a lawyer. He practiced law, but was also a coach in an inner-city school long before other volunteers came in from the suburbs. He learned sign language as a teenager and became the lawyer for deaf people in Detroit. They consulted him at home because he felt his office was too formal a setting. He loved people, enjoyed working with and encouraging young people, and he was very religious. Dad was my ideal. He taught us to respect others and to be generous.

My mother was a woman of deep faith who quietly helped and supported others. She taught me much about peace, love and concern.

The contact my father had with the inner-city children gave us a very strong sense that other people out there were not as fortunate as we--and in other countries as well. We lived in the Northwest section of Detroit, and we didn't have a lot—I was born during the Depression—but I can remember my mother giving out food. Our house must have been marked because almost daily Mom gave someone a sandwhich and coffee. We didn't talk about it. Mom's concern for others was just one of those extraordinary/ordinary things in our lives.

I have been a Sister of Charity all of my adult life. From the time I was in the second grade and made my First Communion, I wanted to be a religious. I wanted to attend the Sister of Charity Aspirant School for my high school years, My parents said, "Not yet. You need an ordinary high school life. Make your decision when you graduate." So I enjoyed high school very much, was involved in many things. We had so much simple fun. I dated and danced a lot, had a very good time. The craziest thing young people could do then was smoke and drink. I didn't smoke because I was in competitive swimming; my friends didn't drink because nobody had the money for it.

We were also keenly aware of World War II. We made bandages and quilts in school for the soldiers. My brother was in the Navy and family friends were drafted. A number of young men in my neighborhood were killed. The war made me think about death more than I ever had before.

Sr. Barbara in Manazo, Peru. 1979

It also made me think about the utter stupidity of war and of how very many parents were sick with worry about their children.

I also owe much to the sisters who taught me in high school and college. The Sisters of Charity had missions in China and we worked hard in school to help those missions. My dream was to become a missionary in China, but it was then fulfilled in an unexpected way. My first foreign mission was to the Chinese, but in Peru!

religious life and work

My faith has been the most significant power in my life. It is my life. My religious heritage gave me meaning, purpose, and made my world a secure place. We were a religious family, though not in an ostentatious way. Religion was built into our lives, but just in small ordinary ways. We would all go to Mass. We wouldn't think of eating without praying just as we wouldn't leave the house without kissing our parents goodbye. We didn't go to bed without saying our prayers.

In March of my senior year, I told my parents that I wanted to join the Sisters of Charity. They said I could go with their blessings and that my vocation was a blessing to the family. I have never regretted it even though at times there were problems. I know that I am living my call and I love the life I lead.

It is a tremendous challenge to take what Jesus told us and interpret it for today's world, for the USA and for the people in Peru. To live as He told us to live is a constant challenge. Most people share, but out of their abundance; they don't usually give if it hurts. We must learn to share what we have--knowledge, skills, resources, to be really concerned about others in the world. Popular culture constantly presents false values--values of having instead of being, selfish values. Those who have lived amid great poverty must tell other Americans what materialistic values and patterns of consumption are doing to the world.

But the most difficult part of my work and life has been to discover ways of walking with the poor and making God's love apparent to them without creating dependency. I was raised with the idea of giving, but had to learn that giving opportunities for work, development, learning, and for community organization is much more important than giving things. And to respect all people, their culture and their knowledge, while working for social justice and structural change. To do this in a balanced way, while keeping a reasonable perspective, is very hard.

Given the type of life we lived, separated from what was happening in the world, it was difficult to keep up with and understand young people, to know what was going on, and to make my teaching relevant to their lives.

After two years as a Postulant and Novice in the Congregation, I finished my first degree and taught school for twelve years. In the early sixties, I went to Peru with two other Sisters who had volunteered. We founded a trilingual school for the Chinese colony in Lima called Collegio Juan XXIII. Now that was a challenge! The school still exists and is one of the best in Lima.

In 1965 I had the opportunity to study for three months in Cuernavaca, Mexico under Ivan Illich, the great teacher, priest and social activist. Missionaries sent to South America in those days received excellent training in language, culture and history of the countries south of the border. In Cuernavaca we had the best of theologians; many of those returning from the Second Vatican Council stopped in Mexico on the way home. It was an exciting time in the Catholic Church, a time of tremendous renewal and change.

In 1968 I returned to the States for a few years and taught Spanish and Religion at Seton High School in Cincinnati, thereafter in team ministry in Fremont, Ohio, with migratory farm workers. There I learned the principles of community organization under other great social activists such as Jack Eagen and Gino Baroni. My actual work there was not too successful, but it was a time of much important learning for me. In 1976, I returned to Peru with two other Sisters of Charity, this time to work in the high plain, the Altiplano.

I began work in the Peruvian Andes first in an extremely poor rural town called Manazo, and later combined that with work in a neighboring town called Vilque. Our purpose was and is to evangelize in a very practical way. Loving the poor means working together to better the lives of everyone. It really means organizing community projects that can be accomplished and will benefit everyone. We work with the people. Each small community (we have fifty-two communities) selects two Christian Community Leaders who work with the parish in teaching the Gospel and in organizing projects according to the needs of the community and the available resources.

Our people are poor and the poor are like everyone else; they have good and bad qualities. Often in the communities there are power struggles, fighting, jealousy or envy, and we are called upon to be mediators. We try to teach forgiveness and human relations, how to interpret what people are saying, and how to relate to one another in Christian ways. I still have much of that to learn too. I've always been more or less successful, but in the missions I had to learn not to focus entirely on the end result of a project. If it is not fully successful but people have grown, and learned in the process, then the effort was not wasted.

I love adventure and I love to get things done! I'm a workaholic in a lot of ways. Either the need I see before me is so great, or it is very interesting, and I become involved in it for one of those reasons. My philosophy of mission is that you help to get good things started and then teach others to take over. In Manazo and Vilque they are now taking over their own parish and government. The leaders take great satisfaction in helping others to see there is a way out of hopelessness and helplessness. And it is a great reward for me to know their faith is much deeper now and that they understand their faith very deeply.

For fourteen years I have been responsible for running the parish; that includes education, response to poverty and organizing. That's the way I divide up the work. So education means working with the schools and community leaders. Also working with the youth groups and women's clubs on health matters.

One principle behind all of this effort is that I don't ever do anything that the people will not take responsibility for. Even the children in the Educate A Child program are required to maintain a certain average in order to "earn" the support that is provided.

A second principle, a corollary of the first, really, is to try to do nothing that creates dependency. For example, one year some of the people suggested that they needed a grist mill, so I helped them organize the effort. But I wouldn't do all of it for them and take full responsibility for the project. They don't have a grist mill today because they didn't follow through. But many other projects did succeed, such as the building of a health center, rebuilding the church, the irrigation project, smaller projects like wells, gardens, greenhouses These were done in the context of forming basic Christian communities.

Next to the education component of my work is the response to poverty; that involves determining who is poor and who isn't. We help the people to look for jobs and be responsible for themselves. We try to show them that they also have to look out for others, that they can organize to help their own, as do the women in the soup kitchen. If the community is organized, they get food for "common cost," as it's called. We also help them to get capital to organize small businesses. It's important for us all to discover the root cause of a particular need. If it is lack of water, then we help the people find capital for irrigation projects.

Dancing with Chinese children at the Collegio Juan XXIII, Peru. 1964.

A good example is the cooperative organized by the women: Artesiana Pachamama-- Mother Earth Artisans. We worked for six years to help the women produce sweaters and other sewn articles of export quality. Besides learning the necessary production skills, they learned to account for the value of their labor as they price their goods, to write their association by-laws, to obtain licenses, and to export the goods. The women in the *campo* (rural areas) of Peru are not well educated. About 40% of our people are illiterate; anyone who finished five years of grade school is fortunate. These uneducated women formed the cooperative and keep it running. And it is doing well! They learned to be businesswomen. I am very proud of them.

Life in the Altiplano is extremely hard--poverty, hunger, no employment, an unpredictable climate, unstable political conditions and eleven years of violent incursions by the Shining Path guerrillas--all this make great faith and hope necessary elements for sustaining life.

It is difficult for many of us in the United States to understand the degree of poverty in developing countries. The children of Peru, and elsewhere in South America, refer to their sandals as "Goodyears." They make their own sandals from discarded rubber tires.

Here's a little story about the relative nature of poverty. We get movies from the embassies, and show them in the village once a month--there wouldn't be any movies otherwise. One film was about community development and how people in a poor section of Chicago had organized and cleaned up their community. Afterwards, during a discussion, one of the men asked, "Were those mattresses and old chairs out in front of that house being thrown out?" The answer was yes, to which he replied, "If that's what they throw away, I don't call those people poor." So even the concept of poverty changes depending on your perspective. I've lived without water, sewers, electric power and know what that feels like. We simply cannot comprehend how little the people in the Altiplano villages have.

We struggled for years to get enough food for the village children. I see people in the States throw out food, just waste it and it makes me sad. Clothing too. In the States people can go into a Goodwill or thrift store. But in the villages we simply don't have enough clothing. Or anything else: a father makes a hoop with a piece of vine, the child pushes it down the street and that's a toy.

When you leave your own way of life, and enter completely into another, you are forced to examine and evaluate everything in your own culture. Having returned to the States, I want to be careful to retain what the Peruvian poor taught me for so many years. I am afraid of losing that! I don't want to be swallowed up by the mainstream American culture. I don't believe in *consumerismo*. I do love beautiful clothes, lovely things, but I don't want to become attached to them. I returned to the States with one small trunk and hope to live out of that one small trunk for the rest of my life. But that is not easy for me!

mentors and influences

The strongest impact on my adult life came from Mexican-American migrant workers and my Peruvian *campesino* friends. The priests who guided my education also taught me a great deal. I still receive support and encouragement from men and women who have been friends for many years, some since high school. My sister-friends in religious life have also been helpful and important to my life.

There is no better teacher than experience to help one to think, to grow, to mature. Before I returned to the States in 1968, I went through a painful and difficult time. I can't give you the details on it but I decided to return to the States, took a plane from Peru, and called our Superior General from Miami. "I'm back!" was the first thing I said to her.

That was probably the first real decision about my life that I had made since entering religious life. It was a major turning point for me. I think I lost part of my maturity in the structures of religious life as it was lived then. I felt I had to take my life in my own hands at that point. I thank God for all the difficulties and pain because they made me more my own woman, more self-reliant, more independent. But, I must tell you that I do not really like independence. I like and believe in *inter*dependence.

social change

The Second Vatican Council of 1963 introduced significant changes into the practice of Catholicism and coincided with the dawning of an era of enormous social upheaval for the nation. Our order was influenced by the great secular social changes of those decades. Most of us developed a much wider view of social concerns. Vatican Council II also affected us. We had a period of friction and pain because of the changes. Some were confused about what religious life should be, and had to rethink our three vows—poverty, chastity and obedience.

We had to re-evaluate our community life and all it included, our works, our prayer life. There have been many changes in religious life. Not wearing the habit is a small part of it. The changes coming out of the Council caused problems, but I think the result was a great deepening of faith for all Catholics. Since Vatican II, the majority of women religious have responded to the need for the church to be more socially conscious. They choose to work with and for the poor people of the world, in the United States and other countries. There is also a new type of priest who has integrated spiritual life with social concerns.

Since the election of John Paul II, the right has retrenched, but I think the church does that. We surge forward on a new wave of change and then we stop, look back, evaluate and give people time to adopt and to institutionalize the changes that have taken place. And then there's a new surge. But I hope it won't take eight hundred years as it did last time.

We did hold on to the essence of religious life and spirituality in Catholicism. The attitude is no longer, "I go to church, send my kids to parochial school." It isn't that way anymore. More people today are saying, "How do I grow through my religion?"

Liberation theology has given me a stronger sense of commitment. It is not strictly concerned with Third World social issues. For instance, black liberation theologians are concerned with conditions in the USA and feminist theologians look at many religions. The idea is that Jesus came to redeem us not just from sin, but also from the effects of sin. The effects of sin are hunger, war and poverty and injustice. And if we are going to be Christian, we have to fight all of the causes and effects of sin.

It isn't spiritualism. It's the fight for justice. If you're really going to be redeemed, you have to fight for justice; especially for the developing nations who are affected by our way of living and our ignorance of other peoples. I like to imagine three different streams coming forth--Vatican II, liberation theology, civil rights--all flowing together as a river bringing needed changes to the world.

A wonderful legacy of all that upheaval was the freedom of thought and movement that opened up for women religious. On one visit from Peru, I returned to Ohio for a homecoming celebration of our chapter and was surprised by the unity and spirit, intelligent questions, the search for ways to promote social justice. This was a beautiful surprise and made me feel humble and grateful.

Today, each sister decides, in the discernment process I mentioned earlier, and with her superiors, where she will live, and what work she will do. Each community or house decides on its own Horarium (prayer schedule). There is no regimentation and each sister has much more personal responsibility for her own life, for living her vows and the rules of her congregation.

I believe that if you are forced into a mode of living, there is no virtue in that; you must have the freedom to choose to practice virtue. If you have a choice between an expensive purchase or one that will leave you with more to share with others, and you choose the latter, that is virtue. But if you are simply told what to buy, there is no real virtue.

looking ahead

As our physical powers decrease, we hope that our wisdom will perhaps increase. But the wisdom that you think you have must be offered carefully to others. Even it you know how to offer it, they still may or may not want it! I've also discovered that when the time comes to stop your work, that you've done certain work for long enough, then it won't be easy; it's going to hurt. But I'm not finished yet!

Voices of the Silent Generation

Sr. Mary Barbara Philippart, 1997.

Postscript, 2005:
 In January of 1997, Barbara concluded her career in Peru and returned to the United States. A number of assignments awaited her, and she wrote to me at the time, "It's reassuring to know there are so many jobs out there that others believe I can do." Barbara spent six months studying theology in Cambridge, Mass., and in 1998 was assigned to found a radio station for the growing Hispanic population of Little Rock, Arkansas.

With the help of volunteers, Barbara wrote and produced six weekly programs that were transmitted to seven stations across the state. Five years later, in 2003, she became Pastoral Associate at Our Lady of Guadalupe Mission in Port Huron, Michigan. In her early seventies now, Sister Mary Barbara Philippart's productive career is by no means over, just continuing to evolve.

MARIE MCKEEVER
Introduction

Marie Grider McKeever, of Fremont, California, spent much of her childhood shuttling between California and Mexico. Though Mexican culture predominated in her early life, Marie married Neil McKeever, of Scots-Irish heritage. Neil was promptly folded into Marie's large, high-spirited family.

The variety of jobs Marie has held throughout her married life is perhaps evidence of versatility born of life in two cultures. She has been typist, police clerk, and rectory housekeeper, among others, enjoying each position in its time. When we first met for her interview in 1990, she took time off from her job as customer advocate at a local newspaper.

Two of the McKeever's three adult children have serious handicaps. Marie's sustained and effective efforts on behalf of special needs children and their parents made her a celebrated figure among Californians dissatisfied with state management of their children's records.

Verbally energetic and passionate, Marie speaks directly to the point. Words cascade from her, yet she is pithy and forceful on fundamentals, and her humor is often irreverent. Marie insists intelligence or courage were not the keys to badgering the California legislature into submission. "You would do it too," she says, "if you were as desperate as I was."

During the nineteen-seventies, Marie formed Bay Area Coalition for the Handicapped (BACH). The group drafted new legislation on a variety of issues affecting California's children and their parents. The premise was simple: parents should be directly involved in decision-making for their own children. For no good reason, until then it had been extremely difficult, for example, for parents to gain access to their own children's records.

BACH changed California law dramatically. Their draft became state law, and Marie found herself in demand soon thereafter as speaker for parent and school organizations. After an unusually compelling testimony before Congress about the needs of California's children, Marie was offered the post of Director for the State Office for the Handicapped, an offer she reluctantly declined. The close supervision required by the complex disabilities of her two children, Helen and Paul, mandated a flexible local job for Marie.

In the course of our time together in Marie's walled patio garden, I met her husband Neil, a gentle man devoted to his family. Helen was then in her late teens, Paul and their daughter Heather in their twenties. Paul worked and attended school part-time. Heather was a store detective in another city.

In the years following our initial meeting, Helen had two brain surgeries for the rare disease Moyamoya, the cause of her strokes. The close-knit McKeever family stayed with Helen throughout both ordeals. She recovered and is now able to work part-time.

Though I had not previously met Marie, her reputation preceded her. I expected to be impressed by a woman who had prevailed in a long-term battle with legislators and bureaucrats, and I was. But knowing in advance of her family's travail, I was not prepared for Marie's exuberant manner, her warm hospitality, her mordant, ironic humor and the well of sorrow behind her ready laughter.

Marie McKeever
Fremont, California
1990, 2005

Somehow I was given the tools to help protect my children; I could make someone listen. It never occurred to me that you cannot just pick up the phone and call the governor. I've done that.

My paternal grandfather was born in Bordeaux, half French and half Mexican; my grandmother was born in Tarbes, France. Along with a number of other French people, they migrated to Mexico and settled there; he worked for the French Consulate. In the early 1900s, their son, my father, won a scholarship to Mexico City College and lived with a Mexican family. Eventually he married their daughter. As a young girl, she had to give up her room for him. He was very strait-laced, a prude! Years later he wrote, "I slept in your mother's bed before she slept in mine." Isn't that dear? I know he was tickled with himself for being so risqué!

We moved every two years when I was growing up, but the real home base was Mexico where we often visited my mother's aunts. She grew up with five sisters, a brother, and wonderful aunts. It was a Mexican-French family, and the warmest, most loving atmosphere. My brother's nature is French, but mine is Mexican. I was pampered and babied, and they were all such wonderful teasers—they would kiss my dad on his bald head.

My husband never had this as a child, so he loved being kissed by all the cousins. They never thought of him as the "in-law." When we married, he became "family," and he loved being smothered by all of that!

The French way is matriarchal; my grandmother, Tia Martha, sat at the head of our table; at age forty you were still accountable to her. We spoke Spanish at the table, but when they didn't want us (the children) to understand, they switched to French. My mother was eager to become the matriarch; it's hard for her to know that she still can't be that when she is with my children and me. If we talked back to our mother, we always reported it as a sin at confession. I don't feel that way about my children. We are much more easygoing.

Brother Carlos and Marie, age 5. 1942

I would not feel comfortable telling my children how to raise their kids, but that is not a problem for my mother! Mother will say, "I am eighty years old and I am wise and I will be part of the decision-making," and sometimes I have to say no, you may not.

My father was an engineer in the army during WWII, building dams, which is why we moved so often. People said it must be terrible to live like a gypsy, but it's not true because it's comfortable living among other service families. Everyone you knew lived nearby. Psychologists say I should feel as though I don't have a home. But our family was intact, and my mother always made our moves exciting. I never heard her say, "I wish we didn't have to leave." I would cry when we'd leave, yet I was always excited to see the next place, too. I can be packed in an hour!

We lived in Korea and Germany, traveled in Japan and all around Europe. In Korea our family lived in a house with no heat. My father would teach us poetry to keep us from thinking about how cold we were, and so I can recite to you every verse of the "Road to Mandalay." Years later he gave that book to each of my children. Helen learned to read with *A Child's Garden of Verses.*

We became aware of world affairs at a young age. I remember my father packing the car in Korea in case we had to move when the communists crossed into South Korea. My mother is a naturalized American citizen and always read the paper and kept up with world events. That was unique at that time among her circle of friends. Because of my mother and her strong character, I had a sense of possibilities, that I could do things. And yet, growing up in the fifties you accepted authority; if the school had a rule, then that was that.

My father always backed the standard, but he would also tell us to think for ourselves. It seemed contradictory. So it was hard to find the happy medium between accepting what is and trying to change what's wrong. I follow the law of the land until I think it's wrong; then I try to change it. But he taught us that certain laws are not negotiable: Do not lie, do not be unkind, and do not give away the respect you have for yourself.

I was raised to believe that you work hard, do good, tell the truth, and things will be fine. Then you find out that's a big lie! As a young adult, I confronted my father with that and said none of that is true; the color of someone's skin or the social status or luck can determine so much. I felt betrayed by this realization.

Later another great surprise followed: that there is a gladness in doing what you think is right even if it doesn't work out perfectly all the time. This is an exciting realization, and I was helped to see all this because my father was so honorable and steadfast.

I was a Daddy's girl. My father died two years ago, and I miss him. I'm mad that he's gone. I take pleasure in remembering what I had in him. He knew I liked poetry; I grew up on it. And when I was an adult, he would find a poem in the *Atlantic Monthly* and mail it to me. We would go for a ride or a walk. He was not directly affectionate, but he would take time with me. Those memories are in my head, and I can draw them out anytime. And I'll never be charged interest! I try to remember that.

I had been angry with my parents as a child, but I still never doubted their love and my role in the family. They were very clear. I never had a voice, but it took a lot of hard decisions off my shoulders and was easier. My life was so similar to everyone else's life; you did chores before you listened to the radio. There was a nice uniformity in what was expected of you as a child. I remember my daughter Heather saying, "Jamie has two sets of parents, and she has clothes in both houses!" And I said, "Well, I'm not going to divorce your father so you can have another wardrobe."

I think it's harder for kids now. I would not want to go through being a teenager again or being the parent of a teenager again. My husband was drafted as a young man and was in the Army. But now he works for doctors who were not in the service, never had to live in those circumstances. Sometimes he says, "I wonder if what we see as selfishness in some people might just be that they never in their lives had to dig a latrine."

My senior year my dad was in Chicago and I was sent to a small Catholic boarding school in LaGrange, Illinois. That was the first time I'd been away from Army life and out in the civilian world. It was probably the first time I ever encountered ethnic and racial prejudice. I was shocked. I also realized that, because of all our moving, we army brats were more sophisticated in some ways. Seniors in my Chicago school didn't know there was a Berlin Wall (no television everywhere then), so I sometimes had a sense that I didn't know what to talk about. My life was so protected until then.

Marie Grider leaving Heidelberg, Germany, 1954

The military life had been a shelter. There are ranks, but everyone knows what everyone else makes, so there's no pretense. With army kids, friendships are very important because they know they'll be moving in two years.

A senior year journalism class was the toughest, harshest class I've ever taken. Sister Joanne had this horrible colored pencil, and she would scratch up my papers and say you could write this in ten words instead of fifty. "Let's get to the heart of the matter," she would say. She never let me get away with silly stuff. Sister Joanne's lessons have stayed with me.

In 1957, after high school, I went home and attended classes at Roosevelt University. But I felt out of touch, as though I didn't belong anywhere. I went to college for a year in Texas, and my world opened up again. Here, too, the "social attitudes" cropped up. I lived in DuBois Hall, and since most of my friends lived in another hall, I tried to switch. Someone told me that I "really belonged in DuBois Hall," and that's when I realized for the first time that most of the people in the other hall were Mexican-Americans! Since my last name was Grider, it was assumed I had no Mexican blood and would not be associating with Mexican-Americans.

Talk about being naive. I had traveled all over the world, and here I was suddenly made aware of the prejudice in our own country and that it could affect me.

Eventually I took a bus to Los Angeles where my grandmother lived. I didn't know anywhere else to go. I worked as a typist and lived in a boarding house with a wonderful assortment of people; I wish such places still existed. I felt at home with all these different people: college students, engineers, secretaries, a marvelous assortment. It wasn't segregated at all. And I remember thinking, "Maybe here I'll find what it is I want to do."

I met Neil McKeever the day I moved in. I came out to the stairwell, and he was sitting on the front porch. We were married four months later. I was twenty, and I remember Neil wouldn't take me to a place where they served liquor because I wasn't old enough.

Neil was at UCLA studying to become a dental technician. We were married in 1958 after he finished school. Over the next few years we lived in Seattle, Los Angeles, and Palm Springs. It was a wonderful time in our lives. In Palm Springs I worked as a police clerk and Neil as a technician. He loved to come to the police station during my shift and visit.

During this time I had miscarriages. A lot of them.

We adopted Heather, our first daughter, who is now in her late twenties and in good health. We discovered we could avoid the waiting list for a second child by moving to Sacramento where my parents lived. So we moved there and adopted our son Paul. We didn't know then of his health problems, that he was hyperkinetic. I'm not sure Minimal Brain Damage (which is not really minimal at all) as a specific set of characteristics had even been identified at the time. So it was a very difficult experience to gradually become aware of the extent of his many problems and disabilities. There were times, not knowing what his situation was or how to cope with it, that I thought I would go crazy.

After all the miscarriages, when I became pregnant with Helen, I didn't even buy maternity clothes. But this healthy, gorgeous child was born; it was like a miracle. In her early childhood we could see those

Marie (2nd from left) and Neil Mckeever (far right),
Edgar Grider and Alberlina Beguerisse Grider, 1959

slivers of brightness. Later we learned that Helen had a heart defect. When Helen was five, she was operated on for the heart defect and, prior to surgery, she suffered a stroke. Suddenly I had another child with a disability, two children to protect.

There were certain things Helen couldn't do, but she just kept on with life and adjusted. We finally discovered that she'd had a massive stroke. She has had several strokes since then, each reducing her abilities a little more. To see our beautiful daughter afflicted with these strokes—I can't begin to describe it. And I'm terrified of dying with no one to take care of my children. I fear for them, that they will be lonely or victimized.

It's a hurtful world out there for both Helen and Paul. Paul did finish high school, and he has a job; he takes the bus back and forth. But as a young person he needed an enormous amount of supervision and support.

Doctors are doing a long-term study on Helen. She won't have a wide range of possibilities as her condition continues to deteriorate. And yet Helen remembers the time before these problems. The neurologist's scan showed that she lost a lot of ability last summer, and she knows it. She's a bit confused and less willing to venture out. She has wonderful common sense, and, if she understands the information, she can keep up a good conversation.

It is difficult for her to cope with numbers— making change, concepts of time. She can't retrieve certain words at will, especially if there's pressure. She has lost a lot of visual perception. She can make terrific judgments sometimes, but it's awful for her because she knows that people think she can't solve problems due to a lack of intelligence. It's frustrating because she knows that she could once do more.

I'm proud of the hard work I did for Paul and Helen. I'm glad to help children and parents pull together to do what they can for their children. The parents' advocacy group we formed, The Bay Area Coalition for the Handicapped, or BACH (we thought we'd try to sound classy!), has made important breakthroughs.

California law used to say, along with Florida and other states, that we had to wait forty-five days to get a copy of our children's records. Our parents' group wrote the new law that says you can get them in five days. We wrote it and now it's the law! We thought the old law was terrible, stupid, and so we went to State Senator Gerry Smith, who is a very nice man. He helped us and it happened! No one should ever say, "It's not done that way." That makes me angry!

There was a policy in which very negative methods were permitted in teaching handicapped kids. Like locking them in boxes. Horrible! You wouldn't believe these things actually occurred in our own times. But they did. We were able to write a new policy prohibiting those methods.

People are paid big bucks to say this or that is too hard, it can't change. I can't control those men who think there is something humiliating in dealing with plain facts. And then they expect mothers of disabled children to be these perfect people who don't sometimes just heave with disgust over their situation. But I do have control over myself, and I just keep heading in the right direction. I am a diehard and say, "Let's fix it!"

Isn't it sad that people have to make strategies about how to deal politically with suffering? My dad gave me focus. He said do what's important to you because there is not much time out there. He said delay is the deadliest form of denial.

So much sadness and hard work—parents of handicapped kids have to be incredible survivors. We are constantly walking on eggs and facing questions. Children and parents both need tremendous courage.

I got that courage from pure fear! I had to do these things for my own children. The sense of family, the parents and children, all pulling together—that also gives me courage. My husband has given such wonderful support. For myself, I call it persistence and perseverance when I feel good, and other times lightheadedness! My father instilled in me a need for justice and fairness. And to remember the name, the signature, that defines you. There is always that sense of honor.

Courage. I remember when I was trying to teach my son to read and he would say we had to try hard —his courage inspired me. And every time my daughter gets through one more migraine — that's perseverance and courage.

But sometimes I'm not sure who I am. I'm lots of people. I feel as though I have no confidence. And yet I do know that if I don't do it, it won't be done. If you feel passionately about something and you're truthful and honest, at the end of the day even if you lose you can feel good. You don't always have to succeed. Success is often just the pursuit of something important.

I had to overcome the fear of speaking before large crowds. Now I would not be afraid to speak to anyone. I'd go before the President in a second, to talk about the needs of children.

I was invited to address the United States Congress, but I am terribly afraid of flying. But I went, and Hubert Humphrey and Senator Jennings Randolph, both such dear people, tried to make me feel at ease. When I told them how relieved I was just to survive flying, everyone laughed and I wasn't at all nervous. Someone said later that mine was a most unusual testimony because I didn't read notes. After flying, testifying before Congress was easy!

On the plane and at dinner our group was discussing what to say if we're asked this or that. They asked why I wasn't concerned, and I said I've done my preparation and I'll answer them sincerely. My dad once said, "Marie, if you always tell the truth, you don't have to remember what you said."

My religion has been important to me. To be able to go to church and feel that you can set aside everything else—it seems not so much a reflection but an emptying. But it has created conflict in my life because, though I feel very warmly about my church, parts of it seem unjust.

Catholicism is interesting; you can't grow up with it and not be Catholic, even if some things make you furious. I've known priests who are wonderful, and there's the steadiness of it all, and the order. That's what helped me to work within the state government, going step by step by step. That's very Catholic. My father kept his little notes in his pocket and was very organized. Though I am scattered in my conversation, I am well-focused and have a good ability to analyze and be quiet in my head.

The Church makes me angry because that's where I would look for justice and fairness, and yet they do stupid things. But I can't live without it! In my family, if someone needs braces, we don't go to the movies or we make other sacrifices for whatever is needed. The Church does not do that—they do what is comfortable and looks good. Catholic schools don't even have special education classes: once a year they hold a mass for the disabled and everyone cries. I don't—it makes me angry.

When the children were still young, we moved here to Fremont. Paul had a lot of problems and I thought I was going crazy. The school didn't help, and I felt I'm obviously doing something wrong here. So I decided, I'm probably losing my mind, I'll go to church for some help for *me*.

Being Mexican-French-Catholic is probably like being Jewish in that it really isn't just a religion, it's part of you; you don't say, "I'm not going to be Catholic anymore." I was lucky. I started going to daily Mass, and at that church there was a wonderful priest and we would all visit after Mass.

I hadn't been to church in a long time; the priest spoke English and faced the people. What was this? When he spoke, you could speak to him in return. I loved this; I only remembered priests talking to you about sin. I would go back day after day, and after Mass we would all have coffee and talk about many things. That was the time when a whole new spirit came into the Church. After about two months, one of the women had a birthday lunch for me and even made chopped chicken livers, the love of my life!

During this time, Paul went into a major seizure, and we took him to the hospital. We went home about two o'clock in the morning, and Father Joe called up to ask about Paul. He said, "You're going to sit up with him all night—I'll come over and sit up with him and you can go to bed," and I thought, "Now, that's a priest!" He could have just called up and offered to say Mass for us in the morning. I remember being touched by that.

I experienced several changes within myself during the sixties, and it was paralleled by what was happening in the church. I was affected by the social changes of the sixties and seventies; it began to be possible to speak and work for change when you saw the need for it. You didn't worry quite so much what other people thought. Songs about Vietnam and oppressed people had a great effect on me. I still cry when I think of some of them.

I learned a lot about people, life, and politics working at the police department. I'm still six years behind the feminist movement, though! Bobby Kennedy helped me to have a sense of my own ability to create change. He came to a Sacramento shopping center and gave a little talk to a bunch of housewives. His eyes were piercing and he was inspiring, not at all condescending. The way he spoke to us made us glad we were housewives, and for the first time in my life it surfaced that I had the ability to create change. I didn't know exactly what I wanted to do, but I remember having a new sense of possibilities. What a wonderful gift to believe you can make a difference.

I'll tell you the story of BACH. At five, Paul was tested and the pediatrician said he's very bright, but because of his learning disabilities he may never learn to read or write. But I thought he might be able to read. The doctor also said you might want to think about some kind of care situation, and I said, well, he drives me crazy but he laughs and he's loud and fun and he can do some things and not others.

We finally found a wonderful psychologist. And I can remember he took one look at Paul and said, "Paul is an unusual young man . . . he will challenge you." Whew! I'm not crazy. That in itself was a relief. And he advised us to find a new pediatrician for starters. We did, and the new doctor said Paul should live at home, but go to a good school. And yet how to manage, where could he go to school and have even some of his needs met?

I realized that I'd better start to educate myself about disabilities and the way the state handles families and children. So I started reading and investigating everything I could find on the subject. And I discovered that in many ways the legislature and the education system definitely were not working for families with disabled or handicapped children. We had been misled in a number of important ways.

I joined the Association for Neurologically Handicapped Children and went to a conference on writing laws for special education. It was very exciting; they talked about parents having some say in how their children are educated.

Having a handicapped child is not half as hard as going through the system. That's what was driving us all crazy. Parents didn't know about alternatives. We all talked about the law and decided there needs to be something better. That's when we founded the Bay Area Coalition for the Handicapped.

A wonderful spirit developed, and we're all still very close. The house would be full of people because the BACH office was in our family room. Neil always just naturally shared in the effort. And Helen answered the phone when I wasn't there: "Now my mother would tell you to get the child's records." Isn't that wonderful? She was only thirteen!

People came from various walks of life, but there was real respect for

(L-R) Paul, Neil, Helen, Heather, Marie. Helen's high school graduation, 1991.

each person. If you could see some of the sophisticated professional people at our office chewing carrots! All pretenses disappear. But there was something else…you could be yourself; you didn't have to be the perfect person that parents of handicapped children are expected to be. We're supposed to be so perfect, but you wouldn't believe the awful jokes we tell on our kids and ourselves. If anyone else told such jokes, it would be cruel, but coming from us it was, and is, a great way to release some of the pressure that builds up.

And the bonds are still intact. I see members from years ago, and it's as if it were yesterday. I know that if I died tomorrow, there would be people who would still do the work.

The point was that an expert does not necessarily know what's best for your child. Individual cases must be in the parents' own hands. The idea was participation; you didn't advocate for another parent. Parents have to know about alternatives, then seek out what's best. You take part of the child's burden off and say, "I'm going to help you carry this." If each set of parents will be advocates for their own child, then each child enters a stronger system.

My commitment was to tell parents, "You know your child. Every child is unique and their needs are different." No parent should fear sending their child to school. It seems so obvious today, but people at that time needed to hear these things. I remember comments at conferences that were so condescending and unfeeling for the parents. Now we all had some support.

You could see parents who thought they were crazy at one point begin to gain confidence. It's marvelous to help someone to understand that they already know what needs to be done and that they can indeed do it. So it is funny to me when I hear the various interest groups talking about empowerment. It's a simple concept: it's not magic, just hard work.

Meanwhile, after much searching for a setting that would be right for Paul, we found a teacher in the town of Saratoga. Neil was willing to move to Saratoga so that Paul could have this teacher, a Japanese woman. I noticed that she pasted words on the wall at the children's eye level so they could walk around learning them. Within two weeks Paul was reading. The tools had been made *available* to him, which was not the norm in those days.

I was asked to go down to the farms in the valley. The people were predominantly Mexican-American and they laughed at my Spanish, because I don't speak it often anymore. But we all laughed and that made it fun.

A woman there had a little boy who had problems, and as usual they placed his class in a unit across a field from the main building. The boy got spanked all the time for wetting his pants. But he wet his pants because by the time he could get out the words to tell them that he needed go and they got him all the way over to the main building restroom, it was too late. And he would get spanked. I thought, that is so wrong; he simply needs to be in a class that has access to the bathroom! Children should never be punished or spanked for what they can't help, especially handicapped children! That should be so obvious, but it wasn't to some people. But three years later when we returned, we found that the child had never been spanked again. Imagine, when the boy's mother sees that change, she knows she can continue working to protect her child.

Now, when I talk to school administrators about parents, I tell them that when a parent says I want speech therapy for my child, that parent is also saying I'm afraid that after I die, my child will be unable to tell someone, "I'm hungry."

One friend would say I have perseverance, and someone else might say it's hard-headedness. But I do have a sense of humor, and I try to remember to laugh at myself. When Paul was small, he had been put into a regular class in Saratoga part of the time to see how he would do, and the first few days were a disaster. So I called the teacher, Mr. Smith, and told him he didn't plan well for these children, was not organized, and that I was going to come down and talk to him. And all the while I'm thinking that I'm a co-author and have all of this background and experience with these problems. I got there and he was very nice and cooperative. When I went back to the office where I worked, someone said to me, "Marie, did you know that you had your smock on inside-out?"

I called Mr. Smith and said I was testing to see how observant he was! He laughed and was so nice and gracious about everything. It was a good lesson for me! I learned not to be so pompous.

Another teacher once complimented me on how clean Paul always was. You may not know this, but hyperactive children's hair is never right and they don't stay clean. But Paul loved being in the bath, and it was the only peace I ever had. I didn't really earn the compliment! So I try not to be too quick to judge on appearances.

If I had an easier life, I may have been nicer and less sarcastic. I don't know. I hate to hear the saying, "God never gives us more than we can handle." That saying makes me angry. These challenges have come into our lives, and I hate the pain it causes for all of us. I don't see it as a Godsend but as a tragic joke.

If this was designed to make me grow, I would say that's a cruel joke for God to inflict on a human being. That part of Judeo-Christianity I don't like! I love my children with every fiber, but I wouldn't wish these things on them for any reason. Maybe it magnifies what we are, the graciousness or goodness. But I would not like to think there's another purpose in all of this. It would be a mean purpose.

I'll tell you something else all this has meant to me. Being tired! Well, not always, but family life sure brings out the best and the worst in you. And you do learn not to be so selfish. You can't get away with being selfish. It's a mirror, where everything comes back to you. I hear myself saying things and then I wish I had never heard my mother say them to me. I do want my children to be kind. And I want everyone to have Neil's sense of humor.

I once had a pediatrician who said between the years of fifteen and twenty-five, no matter what you say they're not listening. But if you all survive those years, later you will see how much they did learn from you. That was very wise.

Heather called me from Washington, D.C., the other day; she was going to a barbecue and she wanted my apple cobbler recipe. Now that gives me more of a thrill than any committee meeting! Oh, I loved that! Paul will work very hard for something that's important to him. I've learned a lot of perseverance from Paul and Helen. From Heather I learned how fragile and gentle the human spirit can be.

Strong Women Tell Their Stories

Raising children takes away all semblance of privacy, and yet being a woman you lose that eventually anyway!

As to the future, what I look forward to most in the next twenty-five years is just getting through it! That's a luxury question for me. I would like to have some peace of mind, the sense that, when I die, Helen and Paul will be safe. And that's difficult because I don't know the course. I also worry about our oldest daughter Heather. She is a store detective with Marshall's and is very good at it. She is so pretty and talented and can do so much. And I pray that she will be able to relax and be happy and find peace throughout her life.

I don't worry for myself because Neil gives me so much. He has been the main influence on my adult life. There has never been a wavering of kindness—we can get mad and there will still be a flower for me. No matter what goes wrong in the world, he is always a part of me. And gives me the hope it takes to survive in the world.

I like to be in the same room with Neil, even if we're doing separate things. This may sound odd, but I love to read Supreme Court rulings. I love the laws, and it's relaxing, stimulating, and reassuring to learn about them. But sometimes if he's working on something, I will just sit and watch him work. He's my grounding and makes me feel as happy and safe as you can be anywhere.

There's so much trust and we always support each other. Certain classes and groups invite me to come and speak to them. And I have my standard joke: When they say that it was nice of me to come, I say, well, my part is easy. My husband is home watching the kids and cooking the dinner; I get to come and have doughnuts and coffee.

Neil knows how much I love flowers. As I awakened last Mother's day, he called me to come outside. He and the kids had built a window box and filled it, so the first thing I see when I wake up in the morning is flowers.

So if you have that, you can go out and slay the dragon. I feel fortunate to have those traditional things, home and family, and a good marriage. I remember a priest once saying that the best gift a father can give his children is to love their mother. I never once doubted that my parents loved each other. And my children have had that, too; they've had a wonderful father.

It's been exciting to live in an era when you can go out and accomplish a lot. Somehow I was given the tools to help protect my children; I could make someone listen. It never occurred to me that you cannot just pick up the phone and call the governor. I've done that.

Voices of the Silent Generation

The major challenge for me now is to remember what's important and not to take myself too seriously. To remember that certain things will always be hard, and to keep an eye on the children's future. And the subtler things: reminding myself to enjoy my flowers, take time to call a friend. You still need to water all the plants or they die.

Postscript, 2005:

Marie wrote in 2000 that her daughter Helen had undergone two more brain surgeries that year, but had recovered and was doing reasonably well. Daughter Heather had moved to a city near Montreal and was continuing her education. Paul lives nearby in his own apartment and comes home for a home-cooked meal at least once a week.

In 2005, Heather had graduated from college and was starting a new life. Marie described family camping trips in the California foothills. The McKeever home has been modified to provide private living quarters for both Paul and Helen. Though more or less retired, Marie reports that she still hopes to change another law or two.

VIVIAN SHAPIRO
Introduction

Harold and Vivian Shapiro were children of Russian and Polish emigres to Montreal, Canada. Both were among the five percent quota of Jewish students admitted by McGill University in the nineteen-fifties. After McGill, Harold and his twin brother spent their early adult lives managing a large Chinese restaurant inherited from their father. Following graduate work at Princeton, Harold taught economics at the University of Michigan and soon acquired a national reputation for his scholarship.

Vivian Shapiro at her Ph.D ceremony, 1991

Vivian was able to create a professional life of her own while she and Harold raised their four daughters. After she earned a graduate degree in social work, Vivian conducted research under renowned child psychologist Selma Fraiberg. When the children were all in school, Vivian became an associate professor of social work. All of the four Shapiro daughters have followed their mother's example: each is married, and combining a family with career. Anne is a hospital planner, Marilyn does research in internal medicine, Janet is a psychologist, and Karen is a business consultant.

Harold Shapiro became President of the University of Michigan in 1979. He knew the campus intimately and was well prepared to take its helm. According to those who know her best, Vivian was an ideal president's helpmate; "born for the job," said several friends. She remains warm and gentle, always herself, regardless of the company. There is no sense of pose, of social role; the authentic person is always present.

Voices of the Silent Generation

A university president's wife is offered no trial run or training ground. One day the mantle is deposited on her shoulders and she is expected to perform her duties expertly from then on. Overnight, Vivian became hostess to hundreds of people attending fall pre-game football luncheons in a tower high above Michigan's one hundred thousand-seat football stadium. She entertained visiting dignitaries from all over the world. Great artists and generous patrons of the arts dined at the President's House, while students strolled to class just beyond the back garden gate. Faculty, staff, students, alumni, benefactors, business leaders and state government figures needed attention--as did four growing daughters.

President Shapiro took the reins of the university just as an economic earthquake shook Michigan's automobile industry. Shock waves rippled through all state-supported institutions, including the Ann Arbor campus. During his term of office, severe budget cuts, student unrest, a Regent's suicide on campus and racial tensions added to his burdens. The Shapiro integrity and quiet competence were hallmarks of those quicksand years.

In 1987, Harold accepted the presidency of Princeton University. After twenty-four years in Ann Arbor, the couple moved to New Jersey. Although he had earned his doctorate there, Harold was the first Princeton president who was not an alumnus of the undergraduate college.

During Princeton University's 1989 commencement and reunion celebrations, I noted the activities of the new president and his wife as they sailed through three days of a dizzying array of speeches, parade, and social events, all culminating in a seated dinner for one hundred guests in their campus home.

In addition to her duties as president's wife, Vivian accepted a research appointment at a New York City hospital. With some trepidation, she began a new professional life, combining several familiar elements with many yet to be discovered. Vivian later began work on a doctorate in social work, commuting to Smith College for the program. She earned the degree in the spring of 1992 with a dissertation focused on the many-faceted losses experienced by families moving from one culture to another, and the difficulty many have in communicating their stories of cross-cultural loss and dislocation.

Although Vivian Shapiro's life demands stamina and superior management skills, she reveals no hint of self-satisfaction. Indeed, she speaks candidly of the depression she experienced and her dismay at how hard it was to find adequate treatment at the time. Vivian's careful listening habits blend with a fine sense of humor and a unique mindfulness, like a light fragrance in the air. Initially, I could not tell whether these qualities were inevitable results of maturity--or of living so public a life--or both. Vivian's memories of a difficult childhood offer additional insights into the character of an extraordinary woman.

Vivian Shapiro
Princeton, New Jersey
1989, 1994

One of the hardest things to give children is an understanding of the significance of struggle. Even if things do come easily to you, hard work and struggle are still important.

My memories until the age of six are vivid. I was born in 1937 in Montreal into an intensely European and Jewish environment. There were many immigrants in the Mount Royale section, and colorful figures, some in my own family. My parents and other family members had emigrated fifteen years before, speaking Russian, Polish and Yiddish. They had to learn both English and French because of settling in Montreal, and the entire experience was difficult for all of them. They suffered from losses in culture, family, language, identity. They were still trying to adapt to their new surroundings when the Depression hit. They were all interdependent and there was a strong overall sense of everyone caring for one another. But there was still a great deal of tension and turmoil in our home; it was hard for them to manage, both financially and psychically.

My maternal grandmother was an important figure in my life. My father's parents were also nearby and we cared for them as they grew older.

My father had a small clothing factory. He hired everyone, cousins, uncles, all his relatives, whether they knew the business or not. It's a wonder a suit ever came out straight!

World War II began and there was deep concern for family members who were still in Europe. There was a tremendous sense of anxiety and loss over whatever it was that was happening in Germany. I remember my mother constantly listening to the radio for news.

My grandmother lost five sisters in the Holocaust.

Children were expected to cope with the adult's problems as well as their own. The adult's burdens were so great that they were not able to make allowances for the fact that we were children. In today's world some of the family members would have sought medications or counseling to relieve some of the distress they were experiencing.

I was a grave, serious child. I felt myself to be an observer to all that was happening. And I remember thinking, couldn't there be an easier way? If only people could talk and listen to one another they could manage better. I also had a strong feeling of needing to take care of myself.

We children all developed different ways of managing for ourselves. I managed by retreating, investing myself in what I knew I could do, which was schoolwork. I felt myself lucky that I could create small islands for myself where I could concentrate.

But I did develop a sleep disorder. I could not sleep, and it has remained with me. Even today I will work out various anxieties or concerns at night.

As turbulent as our family life was, I did receive encouragement. My mother had published poetry; she was very romantic in her writing. My grandmother was also encouraging. And my father's greatest desire was that his three daughters would go to college and learn to speak "British."

From an early age, I knew I wanted to work with children. And I always did. In high school I worked with the children in a neighborhood settlement house.

I was selected for a special school, an opportunity school, which I attended from fourth through sixth grade. I took the streetcar early in the morning and didn't return home until six in the evening. So this separated me for long periods from the family traumas and also gave me a special status in the family. I was considered a little odd, but that was okay. This gave me space and permission to pursue my own goals, a chance to be in my own world.

In seventh grade I returned to the regular school and was elected head monitor. These were British style schools. In high school I was head prefect. I was still serious for such a young person. I also formed two lifelong friendships in high school, women to whom I am still close. They came from difficult family situations too, and that helped form a strong bond among us.

I won an essay competition and, as the prize, was sent for two summers to Masad, a Hebrew-speaking camp. The name of the essay was: "What Every Jew Should Know." My mother helped me with mine, and I basically said that since Jews had suffered so much, what they needed most to know was that they must never pass this suffering on, never transmit it to others.

The camp was cohesive and encouraging for me and opened

doorways to new experiences, new people. Some of them are still my friends today.

Out of these experiences came a deep belief in the importance of education and an interest in the profession of social work that I eventually chose. The reinforcement I received from school and the camp was critical for me.

"Ghosts in the Nursery," an article I worked on with other researchers at the University of Michigan, developed the same idea I had used in that early essay, though the article dealt with the needs of infants rather than a whole ethnic group of people. But the ideas are the same. Psychoanalysts know that terrorized people will eventually identify with the aggressor and adopt his behavior. The abused will usually become abusers. By contrast, one develops empathy by receiving empathy in childhood. We also know that people who manage not to repeat destructive behavior usually have had numerous opportunities to think and talk about their experiences.

Growing up female in those years, the forties and the fifties, it wasn't clear what would be possible for a woman. That wasn't clear at all. As a student at McGill University, I had a sociology professor, in Criminology, who said to us one day, "I must say to the women in this class, that even though you're working hard, I can only envision you at home in a few years with your children. And I'm not sure what all this is for." I thought about that a lot, because I wasn't sure either. I don't think there was much support for finding work outside the home. Especially in Montreal, which was even more traditional, perhaps, than some places in the States.

There was a separation between education and life, one just had nothing to do with the other. The professors didn't raise any questions or suggest that there would be problems. I was ahead of my time and I knew it, but I didn't have any definite plans. And one didn't ask parents for help, nor were there mentors of any kind. The women professors, especially in social work at that time, tended not to be married.

For me, the major challenge in my life has been dealing with a core sense of self. I have been subject to depression on and off, with one major crisis. I have needed to work as a way of making sure that I am connected to others. I have a tremendous fear of aloneness.

I wanted a family and have cared deeply about Harold and our children. But I needed to balance the issue of survival for myself with caring for others, to balance as mother and wife and professional. And that's difficult.

It always frightened me not to have an immediate goal. As a professional, I always felt that I needed to continue learning. I alternated periods of working with periods of learning. At a conference recently, a speaker said this alternation of working and learning is the way it will have to be for most people. It's not a bad design, actually.

mentors and influences

Several people outside the family were important to me. I met my husband Harold when I was sixteen, and he has had a profound impact on my life. Though we came from very different families, we were both focused at a young age on how to construct meaningful lives. We were supportive of each other as undergraduates, discussed many ideas with one another. He really has cared and he is an unusually thoughtful person.

My father loved my husband; Harold developed strong relationships with both of my parents. Over the next thirty years, Harold became a true best friend for my mother. At the same time, we sustained good relationships with his family as well.

Another mentor was a psychiatrist in Boston, a wonderful woman from Ceylon. She was bright, feminine, beautiful. She raised a lot of questions for me and offered ways to expand my thinking. She helped me to put many things into a broader perspective. I had come from such a closed community, at a time when there were few options for women.

At each stage I've had wonderful friends; during the family years there was that special camaraderie with other mothers. Also Selma Fraiberg, a professor at the University of Michigan, had a strong impact on my life. I worked under Selma Fraiberg for ten years and she provided professional opportunities I wouldn't have had otherwise. She was a Freudian psychiatrist, perhaps the finest interpreter of Freud of her generation. She is known for her best-selling book, *The Magic Years,* and for a later book, *Every Child's Birthright: In Defense of Mothering.*

work

Selma Fraiberg demanded complete loyalty and was a firm disciplinarian. But it was a privilege to work, write, and travel with her. All of this was an unexpected development in my own academic and professional life in the seventies. Our team was doing groundbreaking work. We all happened to be simpatico, and worked hard in a tightly-knit group. It was something I never even hoped to do in my life.

Selma Fraiberg was the theoretician; I was doing some of the field development, good mental health development. Studying children at risk, we looked at how to assess the mental health development of the infant. We, the research team, published a book with Fraiberg called *Clinical Studies in Infant Mental Health.*

We studied affective emotional development, cognitive development. At the clinic we got referrals of the most extreme cases and we began to see children whose mothers were very depressed, or who, for some reason could not spontaneously nurture their children. Out of those experiences came the article I mentioned earlier. "Ghosts in the Nursery" became an important article. It looks at what kind of nurturant behavior gets transferred from one generation to the next and what is brought from the past into one's own parenting behavior. Why do some parents repeat negative experiences, while other parents can protect their children from aspects of their own lives that they don't want to see repeated?

One outcome of our observations was learning that becoming a parent evokes feelings and experiences that one doesn't even remember in a cognitive sense. For those parents who did not experience positive nurturing, good parenting, and who also shut down the feelings of what that was like, there is a tremendous amount of denial of the pain of those early experiences. These are the parents who seem to be unable to be empathetic with their own children. So we developed a method of treatment that involved helping the parents to uncover those things from the past. Then separating that out from the baby.

Our work was done in conjunction with some of the work that was going on at the same time at Yale and Harvard and in Washington. It was part of the groundbreaking work that led to a greater understanding of the impact of neglect on children's mental health.

We saw fifty families over ten years, so we were able to help the people over a long period of time. But then the funding patterns changed in the eighties. This type of research was no longer funded by NIH; they turned to biological issues. But people like Berry Brazelton and Stanley Greenspan have continued their work from a medical perspective. The problem of inadequate parenting is an ongoing national tragedy, which the nation has only begun to acknowledge in the last few years.

work and family

I would say the combining of career and family life has been successful for me, but there were choices made, conscious choices. For one thing, I have never worked full time. Also, it has taken an enormous amount of effort. I would say my work has always had to be in third place, after husband and children. I chose not to travel with Harold as much in the child-raising years, nor to go out at night as much. It was always important to our children that I be available to them in the evening and I tried, as much as possible, to honor that.

Even now, at Princeton, with the children all out on their own, I don't quite feel that I could go out and get a Monday to Friday job. We entertain students, faculty and others two or three nights a week. We have a fine staff at the Lowrie House, but there is still much that takes my time, and much that I enjoy doing for Princeton. I feel that one of the most important contributions I can make is to be company and support for Harold. I felt fortunate to have the two-day a week research position in New York when we first arrived, then the graduate work. It is important to me to have that complement to my involvement here at the University.

The cornerstone of my work has been to help children who start off with disadvantages. This is so important, especially today. I think I have skill as a teacher. And I've also enjoyed writing in my field. I haven't ever made a whole lot of money, but I feel respected in my field and I believe that what I am doing is important and worthwhile. It's that vision that gives you the drive to continue.

social changes

My career choices were somewhat influenced by the social changes of the sixties. Betty Freidan's book certainly encouraged many of us then. The climate of the times helped to crystallize my goals. I went back to graduate school in 1964 and then again in the late eighties when we moved to Princeton. But I would certainly advise younger people to get as much training as possible while they are young, before they have children.

The social changes of the sixties and seventies affected me in another way. I had always considered myself to be a liberal person, in terms of my work, my aspirations. But I was frightened for my children, especially since we had daughters. One daughter in particular, I could see, wanted to be out marching. She's now a doctor and probably will practice in public health. But I had great concerns then that the children could easily be swept away, lost. That was a conflict for me, because I believed in some of the issues of the sixties, civil rights for example.

On the other hand, I was concerned with the excesses, especially drugs. And the anger that was being expressed. So much of it was sort of aimless, in terms of tearing down authority. That concerned me especially because I think children need a sense of order, of boundaries and protection. So that was a time of some conflict. I couldn't really go with my heart, because I was very concerned about what would happen to children. So I got through the sixties being stricter and more conservative than I might have during another era.

That period was difficult for Harold; the students with whom he had always had good relationships suddenly started looking upon him as "the enemy." He was then head of graduate studies at Michigan and one or another of the famous student radicals of the times were always threatening to sue him...they had various running battles. I think Harold did wind up actually being rather collegial with them, but nevertheless it was a turning point. There was no longer the same rapport between students and their professors. It did affect him deeply, made him worry more.

We spent some of our time in Canada during those years; I felt protective of our children. Our older daughters were already in their early teens then, and the junior high school seemed to be out of control for a time.

We saw an Arthur Miller play in New York a few years ago. It's called "Danger" and deals with these concerns. A man's daughter is eventually killed in the play. The father is someone who had been active in the sixties, a liberal. She was a young woman who wants to "save" everyone. She befriends a convict, who later kills her. Arthur Miller's point in the play was that her father never taught his daughter to distinguish between liberal ideals and real danger.

That was the type of concern that I had then, even though I did not know how to articulate it at the time. One of our children had some difficulties. She's fine now, but we had some rough times. It was a mistake during the sixties to let so many children imagine that they could actually take care of themselves, independently of parental concern, at such a young age.

risks

Risks are very personal and hard to talk about. But probably the biggest risk was moving away from Michigan after so many years there, to come to Princeton, a very different place. Leaving a close community of friends and leaving one's children...very difficult. Actually they were grown and leaving us, but we were leaving the home they grew up in. When you get a little older, it is harder to make big changes. It was a risk because I didn't know that I would be able to start in new directions again, make new friends, learn about a new community, make a life on my own without the children. On the other hand, Harold and I have grown closer together because we have had to start over, just the two of us.

I think this must be what happens to a lot of women. Harold and I are fortunate to start over together, but I often think about what it must be like to be fifty, go through a divorce, or a death and to start over alone at this age. It is possible and if your health is good, you can go forward. But it did scare me, and was a big risk in the sense of being severed from one's surroundings, many relationships, a sense of order, knowing what you can fall back on. None of that scared me when I was young.

It was interesting too, because, at age fifty-one, Harold had no need to slow down at all. And my own feeling at the same age was that I wanted to hold on to some of the past, yet I was ready for some changes. The idea of moving...so many things were going to change so much! I could see that for me, my life was going to take a different kind of focus and energy. It has turned out that it was important to our daughters that I was able to move on, that they didn't have to "worry" about me.

That is one difference between our generation and our mothers' generation. After fifty they changed very little, though my own mother, who died last year, did go to work after my father died, and was still working at age 75! In our generation and in our children's, if we have good health, there actually can be a different life. I didn't want a new life, but it was going to come anyway!

I do miss my original family; perhaps everyone does. It's nice to go home, and hard not to. When we left Canada, we did not know this would be a risk, that it would be so hard for me. We were so full of confidence. I don't have any regrets about having four children, or about adapting my work so I could raise my children. It was so different from young people today who think so much about what they want. They make choices in such a rational way, which I don't think we did. We let things happen more.

When you lead a public life, as we have, you spend a large percentage of your time on the public part of your life. Perhaps not quite as much needs to be spent that way. It may have been more important to spend time with close friends and family. Making sure there is a little respite, that really is important. There is a risk in not saving enough for yourself. I did go through a time when I did get very depleted. You can get so physically exhausted that you are actually a bit depressed. I'm not sure that everyone realizes there is that connection, between fatigue and mental condition.

I've often wondered about learning through suffering. I've been so fortunate and have such a good life. Just how much does one need to experience in order to learn, to grow? Sometimes people suffer too much and they just don't make it through. Their lives are just too hard and sad. I have seen that up close in my own family; it is too painful to talk freely about it.

surprises

The big surprise of my adult life is that I didn't end up as a total nerd! I'm optimistic. I believe in the possibility of change. And I know when I've done the right thing. Almost everything I've done has been a surprise. We've had a privileged life in terms of the varied experiences we have had, the travel, the people we've met, the opportunities to do meaningful work. I never expected so much.

A negative surprise: I did have a serious depression that I never expected to have. I wasn't hospitalized, though it was close. It was very humbling, taught me a great deal. I've changed my life significantly in the sense that I used to think one could will oneself to do almost anything. I don't think that anymore. There is a limit for each of us, and one can reach it. Then you go through the hard time, and in a strange way, it can improve your life. It has to do with a sense of mortality. I have heard this from others as well. It makes you look again at your life.

We're only just now beginning to work on relaxing a little. Buying a house in the country was an attempt to address those needs. There were years when we simply had no time to ourselves. This year, we're saying we'll take Sundays for ourselves. It hasn't quite worked! There's always something. We are trying, just to go to a movie, or have a quiet time. At least we have both managed to read a lot. It will be an effort to develop some real friendships; that's hard at this point, and friendships do evolve in different ways over the years. I still have close friends from Ann Arbor and high school in Montreal. And now I have four grown-daughter women friends!

One of my realizations when I got sick was that I needed to take some time to have fun! One of the best things about our little house in Michigan is that we both have to do all the hands-on things. That can be very restful and restoring if you are doing desk work all week.

children

Having children has been creative, on the most basic level: the creating of life! A lot of trouble, but a lot of pleasure. We enjoy our family so much. One thing happened recently that summarizes the experience, as if anything can! Our little sixteen-month old granddaughter was visiting us with her mother and our other three daughters. We were all sitting about talking when she came in and joined us. She looked up at us all, as if to say,"Here I am, I'm part of this group of women and I'm happy to be here." I had such a sense of kinship, of all three generations together.

Our daughters' childhoods were much less ethnic than ours. Ethnic in the sense that we, their parents, had many friends who were not Jewish and they themselves had friends representing a wide spectrum. We did observe the holidays with our children, and identify ourselves as Jews, but our whole family life was much more culturally assimilated than Harold's and mine when we were growing up in Montreal. The Bible, for example, was so much a part of my childhood, much less so for our children.

I'm not sure how hard we worked at it, but our daughters are kind to one another. It was important to us that they be responsive and responsible. They are very good citizens with strong social consciences. We tried not to overindulge them. One of the hard things to give children is an understanding of the significance of struggle. They would look at Harold and see that he seemed to do things with such ease. But they needed to understand, and they eventually did, that he also works hard, very hard. So the idea is that even if things do come easily to you, hard work and struggle are still valuable. Your choice of work is important, as is the struggle that may be required just to do that work. Also we tried to convey to our daughters that we valued what they did.

setbacks

I felt both older and younger at fifty! It can be difficult to go through "the change of life," as they used to say. I did have some surgery and I'm all right now, but it did take about two years to recover fully. Physicians seem totally unaware of the physical impact of the mid-life problems.

A friend in Ann Arbor is a psychiatrist. After a hysterectomy she was angry at how tired she felt, how much energy she lost. Her doctors had not warned her, nor did they know how to help her. She felt so strongly about it that she began a whole research project on this. She found that there are significant hormonal reactions and that there are ways to help. There is medication, proper advice on expectations for rest, exercise. Others have since done more research in this area.

I can't tell for myself whether it was being fifty or just my own health at the time that broke down. It took two years to get my physical strength back and to be as active as I had been. I don't think we get excellent medical advice for this age.

I am typically more optimistic than I was when I was not well. I think women do hit a physiological changing point which some people have more trouble with than others and often go through menopause without any anticipatory guidance or advice. The physical problems should not be divorced from psychological well-being. I had always looked down my nose at the idea of these changes, but I had my own difficult time and learned much from those setbacks.

Now that I have my health back, I'm finding that it really is a nice time of life. The children are independent and that feels good, even though I do miss the family together. The fact that our children and their families are all right enables us to think of another kind of life for ourselves. If your health is good and you have the energy, there are many years left and things to do.

looking ahead

The Ph.D was an unfinished piece of my life. I'm looking forward to writing, developing some aspects of my dissertation research, perhaps doing some consulting, and to spending time with our family. I don't want to work all the time anymore. There should be some fun! Fun for me is travel, seeing children and grandchildren, just the normal things. We feel lucky, Harold and I, because we do have a good time together, we enjoy many things together.

As to aging, I think loneliness is the hardest part. It's so important to do all you can to take care of yourself, to stay healthy. Loneliness is so hard that we need to plan ahead, help ourselves. I do not want to live alone— I would like to make some sort of plans to avoid that.

It feels strange to say this, but my appearance has become increasingly important to me! I was not very vain when I was younger. But in recent years, I've realized that I do care about my appearance. I have become very conscious that I would like to be an attractive person for as long as possible. Sometimes effort in this area can be comical though!

questions

I've always lived my life as though there were a purpose. But I'm not really sure about it. I had a conversation with an astronomer at Princeton last year and said, "Astronomy is so remote, so frightening," and he replied, with a heavy accent, "My dear, it's not astronomy that's so frightening, it's tomorrow I'm worried about."

I do think about good and evil, life and not-life. It's hard to keep the fragility of life in mind, while still living life with tremendous optimism and caring. Most of the time, I do that reasonably well, but it can be difficult. One needs a religion and a philosophy to address those issues.

Some of the discourse on these subjects can be pretty sterile.

In the Montreal immigrant Jewish community where I grew up, the Bible and our religion were central elements in our lives. I believe in the continuity of life and that it's important for people to think about religious issues, concepts of faith, of God, of religion for the family. It has been important to me that our daughters married Jewish men, and that they will pass these things on to their children.

The rise of the fundamentalist religions in recent years shows, I think, that people are desperate for something to believe in. But it's hard for people to accept differences and some of the radical groups have become dangerous. This is such a terrible time in the world and some of the issues are intractable. One must be very thoughtful. In Judaism, I don't think we have really recovered from the last fifty years.

rewards

I am grateful that I was born with the capacity to make it through. My early life was not easy. I was fortunate in the way my life evolved. I'm grateful to have met Harold and to have been able to sustain a vital marriage, not an easy task! And to have raised four daughters who are healthy and engaged in life. I'm glad to have been able to participate with Harold in university life. And I'm thankful to have been good friends with my mother until she died. We were very close when she needed it.

I can't yet believe I've finished my PhD. One of our daughters said recently, "Mom, I don't think you realize what you did." And that's probably true. But I do feel that I've made a contribution to my field. I would like to publish the research I did for my dissertation on Russian immigrants. It examines their perceptions of the losses sustained through the immigrant experience, including the gaps opened up between themselves and their more assimilated descendants.

The work we did at the University of Michigan in the seventies was significant and is still read, so I'm pleased that I was involved in that work.

But I have come to realize that what we are able to accomplish over the years becomes a part of us. An important part. And if it has been something that allows us to learn and grow, it can be used in various ways over time. Women wear so many hats, have so many roles, that most of us cannot give everything to a profession all the time. Some years we need to turn in other directions, then later approach our work in a slightly different way. If one can set aside the need to be competitive, and appreciate one's own work for whatever it may have meant in the world, and to you as an individual, then that should be very gratifying.

Postscript, 2005:

During thirteen years at the helm, both Shapiros earned places of honor in Princeton's long history. President Shapiro decided to close his distinguished administrative career in 2001. The Shapiros moved to a house near campus and began a new chapter in their lives, with Harold returning to the research and writing he had always enjoyed. Vivian completed a book (see recommended reading list), co-authored with her daughter Janet Shapiro and Isabel Paret, just before being diagnosed with cancer. Losing a year of active life to the illness, she was successfully treated, and is grateful to have regained her health. Her reflections, borne of a year of illness, merit at least another chapter. Perhaps in time Vivian will write it. For now, she has typically chosen work that goes beyond what she has done before. Undaunted, Vivian is developing a remarkable new project that examines the way ideas enter a culture, with particular attention to art as a conduit.

RUTH LOCKLEAR REVELS
Introduction

Along with 45,000 other Lumbee Indians, Ruth Locklear Revels lived all of her early life in Robeson County, North Carolina. Segregation there was multiple, with three separate school systems: white, Indian and black. Restrooms, drinking fountains, bus and theatre seating also came in triples. Separation of the races in Robeson County was so complete that Ruth and most of her family had no black or white acquaintances. Nor did they know whites as employers because no jobs whatsoever were open to Lumbees during the forties and fifties.

Many Lumbee families crumpled under the weight of displacement, discrimination and poverty. Ruth Locklear had the good fortune to be born the oldest child in a large and loving family. Growing up on her grandfather's farm, she worked hard and learned at an early age to assume substantial responsibilities. Today her kindly and modest manner offers little hint of the enormous drive, energy and intelligence that took her so far from home.

After graduating from college, Ruth and Lonnie Revels were married. Throughout their adult lives the couple provided leadership to their fellow Lumbees while raising two children and operating a successful printing business.

Lonnie Revels died in 2003 after a long illness. Newspaper editorials across the state offered praise for his bravery in youth, and steadfastness in maturity; and for his many contributions to North Carolina and the well-being of its native people. A large extended family and many friends mourned the passing of Lonnie Revels while celebrating his exceptional life.

As witnesses to the needs of their fellow Indians, the Revels helped lead a long and disputatious struggle for federal recognition of the tribe. Congress finally recognized the tribe with the 1956 Lumbee Act, but denied its people the benefits and privileges granted to other federally recognized tribes. Such assistance, as requested in 2003 by state Senator Elizabeth Dole and Representative Mike McIntyre, could provide more than $400 million over four years to help the tribe with education, economic development, housing and health care. Consistently blocked by the Eastern Band of Cherokees, by early 2005, Lumbee efforts had not yet been rewarded.

Strong Women Tell Their Stories

Lonnie and Ruth helped to establish the Guilford Native American Association and its Center, dedicated to assisting Indian people struggling with problems traceable to centuries of deprivation and displacement. The Center also offers counseling and referrals, and sponsors the Guilford Native Day Care for young children. One of the Center's primary goals has been to raise the high school graduation rates among native young people; related aims are to impart cultural knowledge to youth while elevating their expectations for themselves. In 1977, Ruth Revels became executive director of the Association, the first Indian woman to lead a state tribal organization.

A high school teacher for sixteen years, Ruth has strong convictions about the place of the arts in education, and stresses their importance to poor and minority children. Ruth's special joy has been the Native American Gallery, which she founded while director of the Association. Now housed in a handsome new civic art center, the Gallery exhibits Native American art and offers lectures and programs of music, dance and storytelling. Ruth and her staff aim to delight, but also to teach the community about the breadth and depth of Native American culture. "We want people to know that it's not just beads and moccasins," she tells visitors.

Because the initial recording of Ruth's oral history occurred during her work day, I witnessed the variety and scope of requests she fielded on a typical day. Calls came in from the Center: would the budget cover extra blankets at the day care facility? Could a team be formed to visit elders? A staff-member requested information about a painting; an artist called to report a cancelled flight, another to negotiate fees.

Ruth is round and smooth, her clothes bright and colorful. She was herself a work of art, in constant motion as she delegated, soothed, managed. Clearly, Gallery and Center took precedence over interview and we laughed at the folly of our plan to record her story on "a quiet day" between exhibits. Privacy and quiet being rare commodities in Ruth's life in those days, we never did reschedule the interview, just pieced it together over time.

I attended many Gallery events and we spoke often, adding to her story with each visit. I learned of parallels between creation of the Gallery and Ruth's own evolution from sheltered farm girl to forceful civic leader. Initially uncomfortable speaking in courtrooms or corporate boardrooms, her natural leadership skills and passion for the Lumbee cause gradually carried her to the highest levels of civic and tribal leadership. The idea to provide a home for Native American art grew apace with Ruth's confidence; in time both came into full flower.

The Gallery and the Guilford Native American Center were the focal points of Ruth's work. To some extent, family life was integrated with work; while still in her teens, the Revels' daughter Jennifer regularly helped out behind the scene. Having inherited her parents' dedication to the Lumbee Indian cause, Jennifer gradually took on more work, becoming director after Ruth's retirement in the late nineties. Several years later Jennifer gave the reins to new hands. The Gallery continues to flourish, its founding spirit now in the wings.

The Center's social and educational programs continue to aid Lumbees and other native families. Much has been accomplished, much remains. Though denied admission to state universities until the mid-twentieth century, Lumbees now count many doctors, lawyers and educators in their ranks. Legislation has advanced the cause to be sure, and many other Lumbee leaders deserve high praise. But Lonnie and Ruth Revels' lifelong efforts on behalf of their people will long be remembered as central to Lumbee progress.

Ruth attributes her achievements to her family's tribal heritage and ideals—religious beliefs, pride in work and family, emphasis on education and commitment to society rather than self. By serving with courage, stamina and imagination, Ruth and Lonnie Revels earned places of honor in a world never imagined fifty years ago on grandfather's farm in a segregated rural county.

Ruth Locklear Revels
Pembroke, North Carolina and Greensboro, North Carolina
1990, 2005

One of the men at the Indian Council meeting said, 'Ruth would make a good secretary,' and I said, 'Absolutely not! Ruth would make a good president!' ...The irony for us is that here you have a people who have been discriminated against for hundreds of years because of being Indian, and now we have to fight to prove that we are 'technically' Indian!

My husband Lonnie and I were in ninth grade together, dated in high school, and married a year after college. I am the oldest of ten children and Lonnie is one of six children.

Ours was a large extended family, not just the ten of us, but many other relatives as well. My brothers' and sisters' lives are going well, and we still have wonderful get-togethers. We grew up on a farm, poor and certainly materially deprived, though we didn't really know it. I was grown and married before my parents had indoor plumbing or a decent, nice house to live in.

We lived out in the country. The Methodist church was the center of our Union Chapel community and part of the Lumbee River Indian Conference. My grandfather, on whose land we lived, was a leader in our small rural community and in the church. He owned some of the farms, including those my father and uncles worked. The ten children in my father's family were all very close so I grew up with nine aunts and uncles. We had a strong sense of community and, except for one year, lived in the same place throughout my childhood.

Growing up as the oldest in a large family, you are given a lot of responsibility early on. From the age of nine on, it was, "Take the children and do...," so I learned to cook and do various other household chores. I must have learned to like the responsibility.

We were given a strong work ethic from my grandfather. He would say, "If you can't make a dollar, then make fifty cents." He was a great believer in preventive maintenance although he didn't call it that. But he always told us to do things right the first time. And if you're going to do something at all, do it well. He took great pride in his fields of tobacco and corn. The rows were straight and "clean" which meant no weeds or grass between the rows.

The traditions of extended family life were significant. You grew up with a sense of belonging to everyone! Anyone could discipline you; everyone was an aunt or uncle. And a child would never call an adult by the first name. There was a great sense of respect for one's elders and of course that extended to the very elderly as well. There have only been nursing homes in Robeson County for the last ten years or so. We had no access to social services, but families had always taken care of their elders anyway. And I never heard of an older person being abused.

There is also great respect for the land. We lived frugally in order not to lose the land. We ate and lived off that land; it was sacred. The men took great pride in "running a row" on the farms, keeping the fields well-tended.

We have lost many specifically Lumbee traditions. The language, tribal government and arts, crafts have all been lost. When the French Huguenots and Scottish settlers encountered Lumbees for the first time in the 17th Century, they were already speaking a broken English. We have learned basket and quilt-making but these were not our own distinctive tribal crafts.

When I realized this I was deeply disappointed that so few traditions have survived. But I have come to appreciate what was saved, the reverence for land and creation, for Mother Earth, the belief that the Great Spirit was a part of all of creation. Christianity--and we are Methodists--teaches that God is omnipotent. That is not so far from the Indian beliefs, and yet when the missionaries came they misinterpreted and thought we worshipped trees and rivers and rocks. It was not worship, but respect for these things because they were created by the Great Grandfather, God who is, in turn, a part of all creation.

The sense of frugality was related to respect for nature. Everything was utilized. Before anyone was allowed to hunt for rabbits or squirrels he had to know how to hunt so nothing would be wasted. The hides and the meat were always used. The pillows and mattresses were stuffed with feathers that we collected.

Respect for elders is found among other rural people, but I especially loved the old expressions and basic values that were passed down for generations. Our people always speak of going to pick "huckleberries." Others call them blueberries. I like those little old-fashioned ways.

A few years ago, I went to a meeting of Indian Councils at Warm Springs Reservation and I was impressed by other tribes' values, stories, expressions. Passed down to them, but identical to ours. They said "huckleberries" too!

Robeson County, where almost all Lumbees lived (it's now about 80,000) had three-way segregation while I was growing up. Even today, the churches are self-segregated along the same lines.

My parents' generation was so obliging and submissive. I don't remember anyone speaking out. But our parents protected us; they would see to it that we used the bathroom before we went into town. I don't recall that I ever used a segregated public restroom. At the movie theatres blacks and Indians had to sit in the balcony, with a partition separating them from one another. But we never went anyway. And as for restaurants, we couldn't afford to eat in them. So those of us who were lucky did not have a sense of discrimination because our parents protected us so well.

But there were others, children of Indian tenant farmers who lived even further out in the country, and were desperately poor. Life was much harder for them and they did not have the protection of a community or an Indian church the way we did. They were among the first people to leave for factories in the fifties and sixties. That's why there is a large Lumbee population in Guilford County. During the fifties and sixties the tenant farmers went up to Greensboro or High Point for the textile and hosiery mills. The wages were very low but they made far more than they had as tenant farmers. A program called Upward Mobility paid the moving expenses in order to encourage them to go.

The worst thing about prejudice and segregation is not just all the blocking of opportunities, but what it does to the spirit of decent people.

I remember being with my grandmother when she went to a doctor's office in town, and of course she didn't go to the doctor unless she really needed to. She was turned away, treated very badly. And when we talk about such times, my mother still says, "But they're nice to us now in town!" as though this was something special that we should be grateful for.

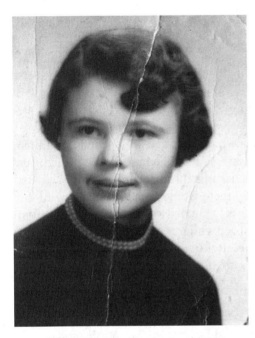

High school yearbook photo, 1954

The Ku Klux Klan was active in the South when I was growing up, but they did not bother Indians very much. We "knew our place" and pretty much stayed in that place. Until about twenty years ago, one town even had a big sign saying "Welcome to Smithfield, Home of the Ku Klux Klan!"

In 1958, the Grand Wizard of the Klan, Catfish Coles from South Carolina, rented land for a rally in Robeson County. Our sheriff warned them to stay out, but he was ignored. They strung up lights for a night meeting and brought in carloads of women and children. I listened to it on the radio, because Lonnie was there with some other students from Wake Forest University and I was concerned for him. As the first Klansman started to speak, an Indian shot the lights out with a shotgun. Then a lot of people started shooting. You could hear women screaming, children crying, the shotguns zinging and popping, people scrambling for cover, the sheriff's deputies ordering everyone to leave. It was a miracle that no one was injured, especially since they were all shooting in the dark.

Catfish Coles was tried and convicted for inciting a riot. No Indians were tried in the case. In fact Indians earned some respect for putting the Klan to rout. They never came back to Robeson County after that.

Lonnie was part of a group of students who confiscated the KKK flag and he was photographed holding up the flag. Before we knew it reporters from everywhere were interviewing him and the photograph was on the cover of Life Magazine! The picture is now on display at Pembroke State University.

My mother did not work outside our home and she spent a lot of time with us. She was not educated but was a refined person and taught us poems, songs and stories. My father's nine brothers and sisters lived just a few miles away, so every Sunday there would be a big gathering of the family. My aunts were like big sisters to me. I also got extra attention from my grandmother. As the oldest of ten children, I wanted more than my mother could give me, so I spent a lot of time at my grandmother's house next door. She was a matriarch, very strong and she talked to me about many things. She too, had many stories. So, poor as we were, it was a secure, comfortable way to grow up.

In school I was also given extra attention because I was a good student. My papers were pinned up and I was treated as a role model.

Though my parents did not have a high school education, they knew that was the only way for us to have a better life. It was made clear to us at a young age that because of the lack of opportunities in the county, education was the only answer. At that time Indians were still not even being hired to bag groceries in the larger grocery stores. The only jobs for us were as teachers in the Indian schools or the Indian college, or as farmers. A few people ran small grocery stores. For most of us, our highest aspiration was to become a teacher. After all, teachers were rich! They had a decent house and a car, which made them rich in our eyes. So the challenge was to be one of the best in school, go to college, and find a better life as a teacher. It is immensely sad that the only way for young Lumbee people to progress beyond that in life is to leave the area.

Because the whole county was so poor the education we received in the Indian schools was inadequate, though we did have some devoted teachers. I still remember my kindergarten teacher, Liza Wilkins. There was never a time that I didn't want to go to school.

Among the Indian high schools, three were in rural areas and one, the elite Indian school was in the city of Pembroke. To show you how "elite" it was, Home Economics was the *only* elective for girls, agriculture for boys. Lumbee kids who'd grown up in town were prejudiced against the rural Lumbees. Even the teachers, also Lumbees, tended to look down on us. When I went in to town for high school, I knew I could not afford to dress or look the way the town kids did. I could not compete with possessions but I could compete intellectually.

As I mentioned, I was determined to succeed in that school and I actually did, by participating in many school activities and by studying hard. We had an outstanding English teacher who gave us a relatively good command of English. I was accepted in the dominant clique. My aunt was married to a prominent Lumbee man, and their daughter, who was a year older than I was, helped me along the way. But I was the only one of my group from the country to "make it" in that way. Looking back from the perspective of teacher and parent, I see how unnecessarily difficult it was for the other rural kids, and why they didn't all succeed. When we arrived in ninth grade there were thirty of us. Only six graduated.

Ruth Locklear as Miss Pembroke College, 1958-1959

Of those who went on to college, 99% of us went to Pembroke, the local college for Indians. It is now Pembroke State University. But in 1954, it had only 300 students, and until 1963 all of the teachers at the college were local Lumbees. The academics, as a result were very limited; also, it was a teacher's college only. But there were still many advantages. Since we were all Indians, we were the leaders. We were the marshalls, the club presidents, we got the lead roles in the plays. I was very active on campus.

Again, I was fortunate to have a good Freshman English composition teacher and decided to become an English teacher. I got a good background in public speaking, debate and writing, and graduated with honors. Looking back, I wish they had also been able to give us some pride in our heritage, in being Indian, but we did not get that.

Lonnie and Ruth attending a wedding, 1960s

But today, the college is developed and different. Called Pembroke State Universty now, it is only 26% Indian. Most are commuters so it is harder for them to become involved in activities. They do not get the leadership training that we got, and they are not prepared for the outside world as well.

Fortunately, Chancellor Joe Oxendine is a Lumbee who grew up the same way I did. He was away for thirty years, getting a doctorate, serving in the Armed Forces, teaching at Temple University and Boston University, but he came back. He says every Indian has a rubber band at his back that snaps him back home eventually. He cares deeply about the Indian students and is trying to help them to become more involved on campus.

My first teaching job, at the Pembroke Senior High School, was a real honor for me. But at this supposedly elite high school in Pembroke, teachers had to pay fifteen cents for every stencil we cut. There were no teacher manuals, and the textbooks were outdated. There were not even enough books in the school library for everyone to do book reports at the same time. I took it for granted then, but I am very resentful as I look back. The politics of the county were hopelessly entrenched and the schools for Indian children, along with the schools for black children were badly under-funded, to say the least. I look back with great appreciation for the teachers who were dedicated and worked hard under such conditions.

I believe that children are not usually shy if they've had a loving family. They'll have a certain natural self-confidence, and the schools can build on that. But schools can also dismantle a child's self-esteem. Once that self-esteem is shattered, it is very hard to build it up again. When I was teaching I would hear the comments in the teacher's lounge; there was plenty of bias to go around. Some teachers would decide which children were unlikely to succeed and that would be it for those children.

In the three years that I taught the lower levels of tenth-grade language arts I saw so much ability just wasted. I would preach to the students, but they had no self-confidence, no belief that they could achieve anything.

In 1959 Lonnie and I were married; we had our first child a year later. Lonnie was in Special Forces and when he got out of the army, he couldn't get a job in the Pembroke area. We would not have left but for a job opportunity in Charlotte. He started as a salesman and by 1963 was a branch manager. When we left in 1960 for Charlotte, it was the first time I had ever been out of the county.

In those days, Indians who tried to move out would often change their names from the several family names we all shared (such as Oxendine or Locklear), and on job applications they would put "white" in the space for race.

I found a job teaching in Charlotte. I was the first Indian to teach in the Charlotte city schools, and one of the first to venture outside the enclosed Indian world. I was proud of myself that I put "Indian" in that space, and still got the job. That job was pivotal for me because it gave me the beginnings of a positive attitude about moving forth into the larger world. I began to see that not all white people are as prejudiced against Indians as they were in my home area. I began to realize that often in the outside world, our own attitude of "I know I won't get it" has prevented us from trying for new opportunities.

We moved to Greensboro in 1963 and I taught for twelve years at a mainly white high school. During those years of teaching it became clear how very poor had been the quality of our education in Robeson County. All our teachers, high school and college, had been trained at the local Indian college. We were all very insular, never left our environs. My students in Charlotte had to teach me the pronunciation of certain common, everyday words that I had been mispronouncing all my life, along with everyone else in my world.

I had to learn to listen a lot. And work harder and be more competitive than others. I did some extra volunteer work at the school and earned respect and credibility as a result. It meant a great deal to me when the senior class dedicated the yearbook to me one year in the early seventies.

I never thought of myself as a radical, but it was important to me to take a stand on some of the issues I saw before me. I needed to feel comfortable with myself and who I was before I could try to rock the boat. As black students began to arrive in the early days of integration, some teachers were still very biased. Slowly, bit by bit, I began to take a stand. Finally the principal allowed me to add a Black and Indian Literature course to the curriculum. This was years before this material was being offered everywhere. So I had to do extensive research because so little was available at the time.

I offered to take over the Speech and Drama courses, thinking I was equipped to teach because I'd had twelve credit hours in college! I had a lot to learn!

But I soon saw what wonderfully creative work students will do if given an opportunity. We all learned the several meanings of the word "improvise." We had no budget, had to get the Women's Club and others to help. I learned a lot about "resource mobilization and management!" We enlisted support from parents, help from students in drafting, art, music and home economics.

Arts programs in the public schools had so often been for the "cast-off" students, but we encouraged a variety of students to participate, slower students as well as high-achievers.

Together, the students and I developed confidence that we could get things done. And I learned that the arts should not be a separate entity in education, a luxury. They are an integral part, and can also be used to deal with certain problems. Students who are not academically gifted are often talented in the arts; they need to have those gifts honored and developed.

By the time I left the school, Speech and Drama was a full department. While I was teaching, in the sixties and seventies, I was selected Teacher of the Year at both school and county levels. I was also one of fifteen in the state honored for creativity in the classroom. Those honors meant a great deal to me.

I carried over much of what I learned in those years to my work as Executive Director of the Guilford Native American Association. Since I took on that job in 1977 I've needed to know about Federal grants, public relations, non-profit corporations. But having done it before, I knew I could learn on the job.

Coming through all those social, economic and educational disadvantages strengthened my sense of myself as a woman and as an Indian. I learned that part of my strength as a person and as a manager was the need to be constantly promoting, always going beyond the confines of office or classroom. And to promote ideas or programs, I realized it had to be a matter of not just "what we want," but "this is what we have to give."

Eventually, we came in on the coattails of the civil rights movement. We were inspired by the achievements of African-Americans and had the first hope that we could organize local programs to help ourselves. "If they can do it, then perhaps we can too..." The American Indian movement also arose out of those times. You may recall the takeovers of Wounded Knee and the Bureau of Indian Affairs. The publicity was mostly negative, but it did finally call attention to legitimate and long-standing grievances. Until then it had been, and really still is, so difficult to organize anything; Native Americans are such a tiny percentage of the population.

In the late sixties and early seventies the urban Indian centers began to emerge. Lumbees, not being federally recognized, were not eligible for funding via the Federal Bureau of Indian Affairs. We are the largest tribal group east of the Mississippi and have been working for federal recognition for over a hundred years! In 1972 the Bureau of Indian Education was established within the Department of Education and scholarships for our young people finally became available. This was the result of a government report chaired by Senator Ted Kennedy to evaluate opportunities for Indian students across the country. The report described the education of Indians as a "national tragedy."

So we can now access funds through that bureau. Also, because of high unemployment and illiteracy, the Department of Labor set aside funds. In the interest of economic development Health and Human Services will allot funds for projects that will generate income. This made it possible for our local agency to begin our Native American Art Gallery; we could not have begun it otherwise.

Long before the Gallery became a reality it was a major challenge to take a fledgling agency, The Guilford Native American Association, with an $11,000 budget, and make it into a viable force for helping Native American people to become more self-sufficient and independent. I took a large salary cut, after sixteen years of teaching, to come to the agency. We were able to get more funding, but it was a struggle. And then to find other resources, hire staff and develop programs. We are working towards social and economic self-determination for our people. We are trying to train responsible leaders. We have been denied leadership positions for so long that many of us simply do not have the background and experience to become policy-makers.

Voices of the Silent Generation

There are eight Indian organizations in the state. I was the first woman director but now there are five women directors across the state. The Guilford Native American Association has been one of the most productive and progressive Indian organizations. We have good staff, community support and a good board. There is a sense of pride among our people here that we have worked on their behalf, and yet we have also worked well with the city.

I had to work with the board to gain respect for a Lumbee woman. The leadership on the board was mostly Indian men. I was often the only woman at our meetings.

Indian men, like black men, are still struggling to establish themselves, so they tend to be male chauvinists. At one point all the tribal groups in the state came together to form an Indian Council. At an early organizational meeting, one of the men said, "Ruth writes so well, she would make a good secretary." I said, "Absolutely not! Ruth would make a good president!" I have always refused to be the secretary.

It has been a struggle to convince the State Legislature that our organization deserves their respect. I have learned to bring men along when I go to the Legislature, because the legislators tend to respect a man more. My husband Lonnie, by being so active politically, has paved the way for us to gain some political clout.

It is also a challenge to work with Indian people. Since most of us have not participated in decision-making or leadership there is a deep lack of self-confidence as well as lack of confidence in authority. In our Indian world there was little class hierarchy. The idea is "I'm as good as you, who are you to tell me....?" You earn respect through what you actually do, not by what you say or who you are.

The average term of Indian agency leaders is about six months, because all the problems tend to burn people out quickly. We wear many hats; cultural, social, economic and educational. We have units to help with housing problems, employment and a variety of business and personal problems. Sometimes our efforts are not understood and we'll hear: "Who is deciding what the norm is, or what it should be?" or "Do we have to bend to their way of doing things all the time?" People need self-confidence to be able to consider change, to do things differently. Or to gradually learn that perhaps there is a reason for change and growth.

And the young people are a product of their times, some are not willing to sacrifice and work for goals. I try to be a good mentor for the young Lumbee people here, but it is hard to constantly encourage them to keep the faith.

In working with the city government and getting their financial support, you need to consider their expectations and methods too. So it is not easy to live in two worlds and try to bring them together. It can be done, at least some of the time, but it can be a very lonely battle.

I have lasted this long because of the support and encouragement from the city, my family and others, both Indian and non-Indian, who understand our mission.

I am proud of our Guilford Native American Gallery in the city's Cultural Arts Center. I was the first Indian to serve on the State Arts Council—six years with knowledgeable and very well-connected people. Their sophistication made it difficult for me—and then to convince them that Native American art is not purely decorative crafts. We have since demonstrated that it is also more than folk art. Some of the works make strong social and political statements. We are not showing paintings and sculpture only; we give exposure to young artists who work in a variety of media. In events here at the Gallery we try to change attitudes about Indian dance, music and stories as well as visual arts.

Ruth Revels, North Carolina Native American Women of Distinction, 1994 (courtesy Mark Wagoner)

I should say something about my husband's professional life too. During the sixties, Lonnie had done so well as a young salesman and had so many contacts that he decided to go ahead and start his own business. He knew that he would have to work very, very hard in order to make it succeed. But we had no idea of the problems we would face.

Coming from a farm, we simply did not have the know-how that is often passed down from father to son in a business family. So it was difficult. But Revels Printing Company is still in business.

Lonnie has always been active in the community. He has worked with children in scouts and sports. He ran for the House of Representatives. Again, we did not have the money, or the family, or the connections. We did not even have a constituency: at the time, only twenty-five Indians were registered to vote in Guilford County.

But, he felt it was very important to set an example, to be an entrepreneur as well as a community leader. Our young people need to be exposed to the political process, to the work that goes into a campaign. Lonnie led the way to change for Lumbees in this area. He was a founder of the Guilford Native American Association, and is now chairman of the North Carolina Commission on Indians.

We are not as secure financially as we would like to be in our late fifties, early sixties. But we have no regrets. It was always important for us to be advocates for the Lumbees. And because of our relatively small numbers, we have needed to enlist the support of others, whites as well as Indians. We've spent a lot of time on boards and committees, but if we had not been there, no Indian voice would have been heard at all.

I'd like to tell you about our efforts to gain federal recognition for the tribe. In 1887, because we had been denied higher education, the state of North Carolina appropriated five hundred dollars to start a college for Indians. A Lumbee man donated the land for it. That school became Pembroke College.

Until then, the state had an agreement that black people who qualified could go to other states' schools of medicine or law and tuition would be the same as for in-state, which was very low. But no such agreement existed for Indians. With segregation we were not allowed to attend the state schools. If a student did manage to go to law school outside the state, when he came back to North Carolina, he was prevented from passing the bar, and had to practice out of state.

Dr. Martin Brooks was the first Indian medical doctor to finish school out-of-state and be able to come back to practice at home. He returned from Michigan where he attended medical school and started his practice in 1958.

In 1972 Horace Locklear became the first Indian to graduate from a state-supported law school, pass the bar and practice here in the state. And it wasn't until 1977 that Ben Hardin, the first Indian to attend a state-supported medical school, graduated and set up practice in Lumberton where he still lives.

Doors began to open in the seventies. Under the Office of Indian Education, scholarships were made available for us to study law, medicine or business administration. The graduates were then expected to practice only on reservations. The University of North Carolina and North Carolina Central, a traditionally black college, started summer programs, refresher courses, for black and Indian students to help them get into graduate schools.

I try not to dwell on the evils of the past and I'm not one to say, "your ancestors oppressed my ancestors." But it is important for people to understand that the problems Indians have today can be traced back to being denied access to absolutely everything. It's not that we're "lazy" or "backward" or "uncivilized." It's that we had no opportunities whatsoever to progress for many, many years.

Since the doors opened, we almost have an overabundance of doctors and attorneys in Lumberton and Pembroke! One of my brothers is a cardiologist in Raleigh and a first cousin just finished in thoracic surgery at Duke University.

None of this would be possible if we had to work only through the Bureau of Indian Affairs. They focus only on Indian reservations. If Lumbees had federal recognition, we could also find funding for health care, and for our elderly people.

One of the main reasons we have struggled for recognition all these years is to combat the division between Indian groups—the "I'm more Indian than you are," approach. We are all separated as nations and as tribes, so we will probably never have strong national leaders, such as Martin Luther King, Jr. We already have so much division, urban and rural, reservation and non-reservation, West and East, and those west of the Mississippi are considered by some to be "more Indian." So it makes it worse when the government says this group is "federally recognized," and this one isn't.

There are some one hundred and twenty-six items used to define who is an Indian. For some programs the tribal identification number is needed as proof, or you need proof that your grandmother was Indian; it winds up pitting one Indian against another. For anyone administering a program, things get terribly complex.

The Bureau of Indian Affairs is such an awful bureaucracy. They have a few well-paid people at the top, but it seems that precious little trickles down to the individuals. Meanwhile, on some of the reservations, the people are almost without hope. Unemployment can be up to 85%, and the drugs, alcoholism and suicide go right along with that sheer hopelessness.

The reservations that have timber, oil and uranium have brought in white experts and learned from them. But that is the dilemma of the reservations, to still be dependent on a government which is ultimately responsible for the conditions so many Indians must live with today.

Getting back to the need for federal recognition, it's also a matter of posterity, the feeling of pride in who we are and how we have endured as a distinctive group of people. We need to pass that on to our children and their children.

As I mentioned earlier, we have been trying to achieve recognition for over a century and are still denied this basic acknowledgement of our existence. Senator Terry Sanford introduced a bill in the State Legislature for us. It passed in the House and then needed sixty votes before it could go to the Senate for discussion. We had fifty-eight votes and Senator Jesses Helms, instead of being the fifty-ninth, voted against us. Helms had to go into the hospital about that time, and by the time he came out, the whole thing had been stalled. We will have to start all over again in the next session. This is not only terribly discouraging and frustrating to us, but it is also very expensive! There are so many other things we need to be doing with the money.

The irony for us is that here you have a people who have been discriminated against for hundreds of years because of being Indian, and now we have to fight to prove that we are "technically" Indian!

My family has given me my deepest sense of accomplishment. Our son, Bill and daughter, Jennifer, are in their thirties, both are married and each of them has a child. I try to take a moment each day to offer thanks for each of them. I've worked with families and children long enough that I am very grateful that all has gone well for them. I try not to take anything for granted. They have given us so much happiness, and now the joy of grandchildren! In fact, we own land back at home and, with Joe Oxendine's rubber band at our back, had always intended to retire there. But now with grandchildren here, it's a bit more complicated.

Our concept of family is such that we could not have enjoyed our relatively comfortable lives unless everyone else in the family had also done well. Both of my parents are still alive and at my mother's seventy-fifth birthday party, her ten children, their husbands and wives, and all the grandchildren celebrated together. We have been blessed.

Postscript, 2005:

When Lonnie Revels died in July of 2003, he and Ruth had been married forty-four years. Ruth stayed at his side almost continuously for the ten months of his illness, a cancer so rare that less than a thousand cases a year are reported. Lonnie had served in the Army's 82nd Airborne and his veteran's benefits helped with the financial implications of his care. But little in their life together had prepared Ruth for the emotional and physical costs she would bear after Lonnie died. "All the signs were there that he was dying, but I was so sure a miracle would save him," she said months later. "I see now that was pretty unrealistic, but I just kept hoping."

Exhausted and burdened with sadness, Ruth experienced a long period of mourning, and an unfamiliar inability to invest in her many projects. Almost two years later, Ruth misses her husband as much as ever. Son Bill now runs Revels Printing and his family has grown to include two children. The extended family now also includes daughter Jennifer's second child, Ruth's siblings, and their elderly parents, frail but still living on the family farm. Comforted by her family and assisting in the care of her parents, Ruth's energy and capacity for work returned gradually. If her characteristic zest and enthusiasm is somewhat diminished, her drive and commitment remain strong and focused on community needs. Ruth keeps a hand in both Gallery and Center, but has also taken on new responsibilities. "You never really know how you will react until your time comes. Time doesn't heal, at least not yet for me, but it does help you cope," she said recently.

Prior to his illness, Lonnie Revels established the North Carolina Indian Economic Development Initiative to develop management and entrepreneurial skills in members of the eight state tribal groups. The organization includes representatives from businesses throughout the state. With years of varied managerial experience to recommend her, Ruth was recently named chair for the Initiative, and travels frequently to meetings in Fayetteville or Raleigh.

One of Ruth's consolations has been the founding of an institute by faculty members and others at Wake Forest University, her husband's alma mater. To be named the Lonnie Revels Institute for Indian Leadership and Education, it will offer its first programs in summer, 2006. The Winston-Salem campus also hosted the first annual Indian Youth Unity Conference in 2005. These and other efforts confirm that a vibrant spirit still breathes in the cause to which Lonnie and Ruth Revels devoted so much of their lives. Their combined efforts will long be remembered for the comfort, inspiration and hope they offered for many years to those in great need.

GLORIA VAN DUYNE
Introduction

After a harsh winter, the Michigan countryside is at its loveliest in early May. Apple blossoms shade from palest pink to deep rose, redbud stretches its delicate limbs, tulips nod, and woodlands are mantled in yellow-green filigree. Turning into their drive, I found the Van Duyne house and barn backlit by late afternoon sun.

Gloria Van Duyne radiated energy as she greeted me at the door. Rosy-blonde hair framed her face like a fluffy halo. In this mid-western city, Gloria is a legendary figure. Friends, colleagues and clients admire her long, happy marriage to family physician Frederick Van Duyne, six adult children, twenty-four grandchildren (and counting), many years of community service and leadership, and success as a businesswoman in an economically troubled city. People tell "Gloria stories" because they are mystified. How does she do it all? What is her secret?

During our oral history interview, I had the pleasure of spending long hours with the person behind this legend. The reader will discover through Gloria's own words that she would be the last to recognize or accept such a romantic description. Yet I well remember, from my own years in the city, the awe with which Gloria's name was invoked.

A sign in Gloria's kitchen reads: "From those to whom much is given, much is expected." Both Gloria and Erick live by that particular golden rule. Gloria was raised with advantages, but also with limited expectations. Despite the stability, security and protected nature of her life, she has struggled to stretch beyond what was expected. I have known few women raised amidst abundance and comfort who impose as much discipline on themselves, or devote their lives to the service of others as intensely as does Gloria.

During the nineteen-seventies, the six Van Duyne children were on split shifts in the crowded local school system. With young children coming and going throughout the day, their mother found it difficult to leave the house or accomplish very much at home. In an effort to impose some order on her own schedule and to use her natural business skills, Gloria started a small stationery business at home. In time the business outgrew the house. When the children were at last on full-day high school or college schedules, Gloria was able to open two stationery and gift stores, one on each side of the city. They were eventually consolidated into one large store that has stayed solvent and successful throughout more than twenty-five years of economic distress in the city originally made prosperous by General Motors.

Because Gloria requires less sleep than most mortals, her full-time activities at the store imposed no reductions in her numerous commitments to city and state politics, church activities, the local symphony, and several charities for which she does yeoman's work.

Son Alex, and daughters Kim, Jennifer, Bethany, Cindy and Abby, all now married and producing grandchildren, seem to have absorbed the family lessons well. They too, have begun to contribute to their own communities as fully as did their parents to Flint, Michigan, Gloria's birthplace and life-long home. With such genes and family history, who knows what they may accomplish?

Because of her iconic status, I had known of Gloria for many years, but did not truly know her. The closer look afforded by our oral history sessions taught me much about Gloria and her extraordinary commitments to career and community as well as to an ever-growing family. I was surprised to discover the essentially modest and loving nature of a woman as lacking in self-absorption as anyone I have ever met.

Gloria Van Duyne
Flint, Michigan
1990

It does sometimes feel like we're running a tiny General Motors. It's a long way from where I started, selling stationery in my basement!

The great challenge of my life was keeping six children on the right track. We knew people in the sixties, good parents whose bright children went right off the wall in college, ruined their own lives and broke their parents' hearts. So that was our greatest challenge—that we understood and feared the dire possibilities of the sixties. Along with the political turbulence of the times, many parents of adolescents in the sixties were blindsided; they hadn't expected such upheaval and challenge to their authority. The old frames of reference were discarded and even young people who had been given strong values were lost. When we grew up, we never thought to cross our parents. We sought their approval, and behaved...most of the time! But so much changed with the next generation.

It was a real concern that this could happen to your own children. So we learned that from the sixties. Our children were young then and we knew they'd need a strong foundation for their own decisions as they matured. We realized that we'd better be prepared to teach them our own values and beliefs.

We can thank our church for helping the children to develop their faith. We tried to give them the habits, the values we believed in, so that they would eventually understand that some of their own decisions might well have far-reaching effects. I was forever cutting out little bits of wisdom, putting them on the refrigerator, to reinforce what we were trying to teach them, creating that system of moral values. They knew what was important and where we stood. It sounds like such a cliche, but if they care about other people and the world they live in, then I'll feel we've done our job as well as we could.

And of course we had to be willing to put in the sheer amount of time necessary to raise children well. They were on the track and swim team, the hockey team, were involved in plays, the chorale, orchestras, honor society, student council and class presidencies, all of that; a few times we had formal obligations and couldn't go to school events, but 99% of the time one or both of us would be there. And it took two of us. I couldn't have done it without Erick. He has always done more than his share; even today he'll make it to my shows for the store, change his schedule for the children or me, and try to be there when I can't.

starting a business

The other big effort of my life is the business. I didn't go looking for it, but sort of fell into it. Through fundraising work on the alumni board of Kingswood School, I learned about various small stores, including a stationery store. We didn't have such a thing in Flint in the early seventies. The local schools went to half days for a time and I had six children on five different schedules, coming and going all day long. It was impossible for me to leave the house to take part in community activities during that period. So I started a stationery business in my home. I'd always been drawn to certain aspects of the business world. My father started his own construction business so maybe it's in my genes. I enjoyed it all very much. People came to my house to make their selections and place their orders.

Eventually someone was opening a shop and invited me to move into it. I'd never thought of myself as anyone but a mother and a wife, so it was a big decision for me. In fact, for years, I never told anyone that I worked, just that I "owned a business." That was the orientation I'd had. When I heard my children say that I worked to one of their friends, I would bristle! My parents, who were alive then, never liked the idea that I "worked." So I played it down with them tremendously. My father would say, "What are you doing that for?" Sometimes people would say things like, you live in that big house, and you work? They were forgetting that it is a little more expensive to raise six children than two. You know that you shouldn't be bothered by what people say, but I was.

Today, of course, it's the opposite! It's seems normal for mothers to work. In fact, my oldest daughter, who has five children, often has to defend herself because she doesn't work outside the home, but prefers to be with her children. She did work for five years at General Motors before marriage. I have no doubt that eventually she will "do something," but that will be later on. She is perfectly happy staying home to raise her children and her husband is happy to have her at home.

looking back

It is odd, and a sign of those times, that my father opposed my working, because as I was growing up my parents certainly gave me the impression that I could do anything. They are certainly the source of my self-confidence. My mother died when I was born, but I was blessed with a wonderful stepmother. My sister, Elaine, was five years old when our birth mother died, so her loss was infinitely greater than mine. Much in life has been difficult for Elaine. And for me everything was relatively easy.

I went out of my way to be the perfect child and please my parents. I wanted very much to do well, to succeed. I was a normal kid...I liked everybody, did well in school, participated in sports. So my parents more or less assumed that I would do well. My stepmother was a real mother to me. She and I were a lot alike and we got along well always. I loved her dearly.

I spent a lot of my life, even as an adult, trying to gain my father's approval. Dad and I disagreed a lot but I know he respected me. We are a lot alike, both extremely strong-willed. But he never, ever said, "I love you," though he told everyone else what a wonderful child I was. It was important to me that he approve of me, but he never said so. I don't think he has come into my store more than a couple of times in all these years. He loved Erick, but never told me that. Still, he was a wonderful man, with a great sense of humor, rock-solid character and he adored his grandchildren.

Part of it was his generation, and being Scots-Irish. He was one of eight children, and I'm sure his mother never hugged him. He told us they ate standing up because there were never enough chairs at the table. But you should have seen him when our girls grew up and he would take us all out for dinner. He would have five beautiful young women throwing their arms around him and he just loved it! All the other men would say who are you to have all this? It meant the world to him.

My sister lives in Birmingham, not far away, and I give her a lot of credit; she's made a life for herself. We've never been very close and we have somewhat different values. It's extremely painful to me that we haven't been able to manage a better relationship. That's one reason I've tried so hard to see that my children respect one another and get along.

I had a very pleasant childhood growing up in the forties and fifties. But I did not particularly enjoy college. Connecticut College was a very difficult school for me. It was important to do well because no one in my family had gone to a school of that caliber. I felt that I was in over my head the whole time—I was terrified. I majored in chemistry, and it was too late to change majors when I took my first business and economics course and found that I loved them. I was locked into the chemistry major by then.

I'd worked at a hospital during my high school summers and had a genuine interest in medicine. In fact, I met Erick when I went to visit Cornell Medical School. I can picture myself today enjoying hospital administration, the business side of health care. But we didn't have the counseling then to help students find their way.

I'm sure there was also a part of me that had majored in chemistry to prove something. It was not easy for me. In those days, at Connecticut College, if you didn't pass your comprehensives, you didn't graduate. They don't have them today. I was terrified that I wouldn't pass the comps, and that would have been an unbearable humiliation.

I worked like a dog, always in class, in lab. Those comps hung over you like a great black cloud. I had friends who did not pass, did not graduate, so you knew it was real. I can remember as though it were yesterday the day the test results were posted, and the relief.

mentors

I met Erick on a Friday night blind date, talked to my parents on Sunday and told them that I had met my future husband (he didn't know it, but I did). I was twenty-one, would be graduating from Connecticut College the following year. As it happened, we were married the September after commencement.

Erick is the person who has had the major impact on my adult life. He taught me that not everything has to be a crisis, to remember that "this too will pass." He has a wonderful sense of humor, and he needs it because, as a primary care physician in family practice by himself, he has wild days and lots of pressures on him.

Mrs. X comes in because her child has a sore throat, but she really wants to talk about the fact that her husband is mistreating her. Or a very young couple comes in—children themselves, with adult problems and no easy solutions. He does a great deal of counseling. Every day is one crisis after another. But Erick always treated us as if whatever was happening at home was as important as what happened to him. He would come home from work, having left the house at seven in the morning, put his brief case on the table, kiss everyone hello, sit down and instantly feel totally relaxed. He could make that transition lickety-split. I have friends whose husbands had to have a drink and keep the kids away.(Their houses usually weren't nearly as wild as ours, either!)Then one of us always read to the children after dinner and it would be about ten o'clock before we started doing whatever else we had to do.

He feels no need to ever toot his own horn, and has an amazing disposition, always sees the good in people, and is so patient with others. Once when I felt guilty about a cat I'd seen downtown looking for shelter from a pouring rain, Erick got in the car with me at eleven o'clock at night to go down and look for that cat, so we could protect it.

There's nobody I'd rather be with than Erick. It's even hard for me to be in a new situation without him, because I always want to point out all the new things I'm seeing to him. I dearly love Donna, the woman who goes to New York buying shows with me, and we have a wonderful time together. But she has the same kind of marriage as mine and we both admit that, given the choice, we would like to spend the evenings with our husbands.

My other influences are not people whose names you would recognize. I admire people who overcome adversity. We had a babysitter who still helps with my oldest daughter's children. Mrs. Hall looks the same today as she did when she first came to work for us thirty years ago. She is a remarkable woman and I have tremendous respect for her. She raised five children of her own, had tragedies in her family, and yet never let life get her down. She is always productive. I have never seen her without a book, or sewing thread and needle--and a smile.

virtues

The personal qualities that have served me best would probably be plenty of energy, a sense of humor, and, as people who know me would say, a strong will. I have a strong desire to do a good job. Organizational ability and the ability to get along with people would probably be called my talents. And I do like to learn; I'll never live long enough to learn and read about all that interests me. I was determined to learn to use a computer for example, kept procrastinating, but finally did it.

social change

Feminism and the social changes of the sixties made me think more carefully about raising children, especially daughters, for whom the choices are now so complex. Growing up for our generation was so much simpler. We have encouraged our girls to marry and have children and then have a career, and to try to plan their lives along those lines. As a doctor, Erick feels strongly about mothers being at home with the children when they are young.

It bothers me that what the mother misses is never mentioned. I often read about women who realize too late how much of their children's childhood they've missed. I've said to my girls, "You can do whatever you want, but don't tell me you 'have' to work. Just learn to scale down, postpone your wants and desires and realize what you are getting in place of those things that you think you need." One of my daughters said, "Mom, I don't want to miss anything, work or family." We have to remember that with any luck we'll live a long time. You can stay home while your children are young and still work for twenty years or more. You can have your first child at twenty-five or so, have two or three children, and you've still got plenty of productive work years left. I realize that all of this, of course, assumes a kind of ideal scenario of faithful, breadwinner husband. And that doesn't happen for everyone.

There's also the biology of waiting too long to have children. How would you like to cope with your first adolescent in your own fifties? The women who wait until they're well into the thirties to have their first child will be doing just that. And they may be facing the decline of their own parents.

Society is beginning to accommodate women who want or need to work while raising their families. It's far easier now to go back to school part-time. And many jobs allow work to be done at home. I'm all in favor of a career if that's one's choice, but people need to get their priorities straight. Whether you have children at twenty-five or thirty-five, you should plan to spend some time at home with them in the early years. I'm not convinced that you can raise a family, work in a full-time demanding position, and have a happy home. Somebody loses. It may not appear so at the time, but somebody loses. You might both make a lot of money, yet wind up using it not to enjoy, but to accommodate, your style of living. It's the rare person who can manage all that.

Gloria, 1986

children

Having children is one of life's great enrichments. To me, a baby is one of the great miracles of life; they make it complete. Our own lives have revolved around our children and we have both thoroughly enjoyed them. They were easy to raise and we often wish we had gone ahead and had more. The years went by so quickly. And we learned so much as we went along, and were more relaxed with the later children.

The way I related to my parents was the major difference between my childhood and that of our children. We've often joked that if my father said we were leaving for church at ten o'clock in the morning, we did, but as Erick says, with us at ten o'clock the hair driers were going and as we're finally in the car and leaving, someone is running out the door with wet hair. I never thought to question my parents. My father could be a very stern man. I resented my father when he would walk in the room and back up my mother even if he didn't know what the issue was. Erick supported me in disputes, but he usually understood the issue, too.

We tried to instill in our children the ability to cope, to manage your own life. They have had good parents, grandparents, educational opportunities; if they don't do well, who will? The real test for them will be when adversity strikes. That's when real strength is required. I have a lot of faith that there is someone up there helping us. But we do have to be steadfast ourselves.

In raising daughters you need to think about how much importance you will assign to physical appearances and how you'll convey that to them. I get my hair done because I'm not good at fussing with it. But I'll go places, admire the people who look wonderful, and think why didn't I plan what I was going to wear? I grew up being told, "Honey if you're smiling nobody will notice anything else." So of course, I tried to pass that on to our daughters.

But it has come back to bite me. We'll be on the way to church and I'll be fussing that Abby's hair is still wet. And she'll say, "But Mom, you always say those things aren't important!" Now I will say to the girls, "Maybe you should put on some lipstick."

I admire people who are industrious; we tried to convey the importance of work to our children. Not only is it important in a practical sense, but belief in yourself is based to some extent on developing your ability to make a contribution. It feels wonderful to be independent through your own work.

One of the things I admired about my parents was their ability to work and give to others. My mother had an unfortunate home situation, but she managed to graduate from high school. She had natural musical talent, so, to earn money, she played piano in bars when she was twelve and thirteen. Later on, she played background music for the early movies. Meanwhile, her mother took in laundry. They both worked so that she could progress in life. As an adult, my mother was able to be a benefactor of the symphony and music institute here in town. I am not in my mother's league.

And yet people ask me how I can do so much. I think I'm compensating for all my parents' efforts. It's a way of honoring them and all they did for my sister and me.

My father berated me all my life for working too hard. He would tell Erick to make me slow down. But Erick would say, "Mac, she's just like you, you taught her to be that way." I know now I was often looking for his approval.

And it seems I have passed that love of work on to our children. The starting gate is different of course, because we've been able to give our children so many different experiences. They had horses and other animals to care for and plenty of chores. I guess I was a tough mother.

They had no money to spend; it usually leads to trouble. If one of them would ask to go to wandering around the mall, I'd say, "Honey, if that's the best thing you have to do, there are people in the world who could use some help. And I've got a long list myself...."

working after children are grown

I enjoy my store now more than ever. All the years the children were at home I felt some guilt; I was always persuading myself that it was all right. I'm not convinced that a mother can work and not feel some guilt. In the early years, I had guilt and uncertainty. People would ask me why I was doing this and I would feel very uncomfortable.

I have always loved my business. Our children were involved with their horses, music, sports, school work and were active and happy. In the early years I tried not to bring work home, so I had time for the family in the evenings. But I was a little uncomfortable with the work commitment; perhaps more because of what I was missing than what they were missing.

Yet there were enough compensating factors. I enjoy all aspects of managing a business. I've grown, learned a tremendous amount, found it consistently interesting, enjoyed the people and the services we offer to the community.

I'm not foolish enough to think that my little business is anything great. In fact, when I first got into stationery I thought it was just a repeat of all my volunteer work. But in the scheme of my life, that it's all worked without negative effects on the family does give me a sense of accomplishment.

Many women come in to the store and say, "I'll bet this is fun." They have no idea what it takes to run a business, to cover the expenses of what looks like a fun, frivolous little business, full of things that nobody needs but everybody wants. Besides stationery we carry clothing, painted furniture, and a whole array of gift items. It is not a profession, and I'm not running General Motors, but it is complicated. It also involves constant interaction with people, which I enjoy. I've had certain people with me for sixteen years, wonderful people. I feel so fortunate; they are my second family.

We do the invitations for a lot of weddings and people always seem happy with our work for them. We try very hard to treat everyone the same and make something beautiful for them, regardless of their price range.

No, I wouldn't choose a different sequence for my working life. I didn't start work outside our home until my youngest child was in third grade and everyone was happy and busy. I started by working three days a week and I was home at three-thirty every day. Thanks to reliable people working with me, I've had some control over my hours and time.

The blending of personal and professional lives works well mainly because Erick is so understanding and because of the children's situations when I started my work. I'd try to leave the problems behind as I drove home. But the children have said, "We knew when it was a bad day at the store, Mom."

I know people my age still wonder why I'm doing this. But after twenty-five years I still love managing a business. And there is time to do the community work I enjoy.

I don't like it when people ask, "Did you get tired of volunteer work and decide to go into business?" I've always said no, my volunteer work is still important. Our hospitals and non-profit institutions couldn't survive without people who work as volunteers.

I was brought up with a strong sense of community and with the idea that if you've been fortunate in your life you try to contribute to the community. My parents were both very active in the life of the city, particularly at the Institute of Music. They gave money as well as time, long before they had much money to give. So I was brought up with that idea: you always give of your various resources, as much as you possibly can.

Erick was brought up in Connecticut, near New York City. And yet our children have been exposed to much more art and music than he was! Everything is so convenient. You just hop in your car at the last minute and you're there in ten minutes. The Art Institute, the concerts, the wonderful library, the planetarium, the summer theatre. This has been a wonderful place for raising children. The cultural center here is perhaps unique for a city this size and it does enhance life here substantially.

Some people in their thirties, forties and fifties make a good living and put much of it into their travels and their wardrobes. I would like to see our schools offer a course in community responsibility. Our cities, our quality of life cannot survive without commitment from the people.

I do marvel at the people who can just sit back and enjoy life yet still be confident and feel that is a satisfactory way to live. People say to me, "Oh, you can't sit still," or, "You're tense." But I'm not tense and I can sit still. I just don't want to. There is a difference. I don't need a lot of sleep, so I'd rather be accomplishing something. I could go to Florida and catch up on my sleep in one day. I couldn't just walk the beach for two weeks. Fortunately Erick understands that need to do just one more thing. I'd like

Gloria with her daughters and daughter-in-law, 2004

sometimes to have a day just to sit down and read, but there is always something else that needs to be done...

women friends
A few women friends have been very important in my life. I voted against Connecticut College going coed because I'm convinced that one of the greatest advantages of a women's school was the opportunity to develop those strong friendships.

Whenever I did have free time, especially as I got older, I enjoyed spending it with my mother. With six children, there never was much time. I never went to lunch with friends a lot, unless it was related to a community activity.

Also, when you have five daughters, they become your women friends, especially as they get older. But I'm still really very busy and if I do find myself with an occasional bit of free time, I would be more inclined to stay home and enjoy the quiet than to call up a friend and plan something. There may come a time for that. And if I'm left alone, there'll be other people in the same situation and we'll find each other. And I'll still have my daughters, and my very special daughter-in-law, who is truly daughter number six.

looking ahead
I didn't think about turning fifty when it happened. In fact the children

had a surprise party for me and the date had gone right by me! I still had teenagers at home, and that year we also had an exchange student. I just didn't have time to think about it, at least not the way you would if your children were all grown and you were moving into a whole new life. Turning sixty in a few years will be different. Then all of Erick's and my parents will have been gone awhile and our children will all be that much more self-sufficient. And there will probably be more grandchildren! Now there are seven, one boy and six girls. A familiar ratio to us! I now have twelve females to shop for at Christmas, five daughters, one daughter-in-law, and five granddaughters!

I've learned some things about the aging process from our parent's generation. My parents took up skiing at age sixty. My father was never "an old man" until the last year of his life. It struck me only then that he actually was old and here he was ninety! But if I had ever called him old, he'd have hit me with his cane!

I always thought that if my mind was clear I could tolerate old age. Erick's mother had Alzheimer's. Then you see that the patient perhaps doesn't suffer but everyone around her does. I couldn't bear to be a burden for Erick or the children. My father had back surgeries and was increasingly unable to do things. He was mentally sound but very unhappy. That was a combination of not having mother around and not being able to do things, but he didn't like getting old at all. And too, he'd been on his own since eighth grade, done everything for himself his whole life. So he just hated not being able to help himself. They had never had help in the house and he hated having anyone in to help out.

My mother died two years before my dad. They'd had the most wonderful relationship. People who knew them said they were as much in love as when they were young. After Mother had a stroke, they would have dinner together every night. He would help her with her food and put his arm around her and cover her up with his coat. He would chuckle and tease and try to keep her going. Then Mother had to have one leg amputated the week before she died. People said that had Mother lived, my dad would have carried her around on his shoulders.

After Mother died my father was very lonely. He hated being alone. On his eighty-ninth birthday, he went into the hospital for the last time. They were wonderful, brave and gallant people, both of them.

In the years ahead, I'm looking forward to less responsibility and a little more flexibility and freedom. We have been responsible for so many people for so long. Besides our six children, there was Erick's mother, and at the end of their lives, both my parents. In addition, Erick's two maiden aunts had lived with Erick's mother. We brought them here from New Jersey. We visit them frequently and take them to a concert now and then if they are up to it.

Our children really were our whole life, you know. Very often we didn't do social things on weekends because one of the children had an event. And there were endless arrangements of every sort to be made, always. Three years ago Erick and I went to China with the People to People program. With one exception, that was the first time we were away together without the kids in thirty-seven years of marriage.

The one other time was when Erick was a delegate to the 1968 convention. We changed our will the night before we left, and flew in separate planes. But it was not a vacation, just one caucus after another. We never even had a meal together!

If you are in practice alone, when you go away you close the office, pay the staff and no money comes in. So it wasn't the expense of going, but the expense of not being in the office. We felt we couldn't manage trips for us alone, as well as family trips, and we chose family trips. We told the children we would help if they went to graduate school. Three have finished graduate work; now our son is finishing his MBA while working to support his family. One daughter is aiming at medical school. So we still have some years ahead of family responsibility, yet there is more day-to-day freedom now.

rewards

I am most grateful for my parents, husband, and children. And good health. My father used to say all the time, he drilled into us: "If you were born in this country and have good health, then I don't ever want to hear you complain."

And I'm inclined to agree. Raising our family was difficult and stressful at times, but when you think of people whose sons and husbands and fathers went to war or those pioneer woman walking across the plains, or so many other forms of suffering in the world...we were just very fortunate in the time and place in which we were born.

What makes me happiest is that I see our children beginning to be productive, responsible citizens, becoming aware of the world around them, and trying to make it a better place.

I've been in business for a long time, twenty years or so, and I know we have a nice reputation. It does sometimes feel like we're running a tiny General Motors! It's a long way from where I started, selling stationery in my basement!

Voices of the Silent Generation

We try very hard to make people happy with our service. I'm glad to have been able to survive, particularly in the local economy of recent years. I do have a great feeling of satisfaction that I have been able to do this on my own yet not feel that I have deducted anything from my children and husband.

We have been very fortunate in our marriage. But it takes both people and Erick is just the best, such a truly good person. I always think in terms of "we." And I often tell people that if I have been able to accomplish anything in the store, it's because of Erick's encouragement. There are a lot of men of our generation who wouldn't tolerate such a situation, wouldn't even consider it.

Questions I wonder about: I've always been very patriotic and I think anyone given the chance would choose to live in this country. But we are dealing with such enormous and difficult issues today, right on our own streets. All the money in the world cannot solve some of these problems. It's more than money; it's will. How do we teach people to put their families first? How can we teach people to cope with their lives?

Postscript, 2005:
No one in the Van Duyne family has yet retired. Both Erick and Gloria continue their careers with few signs of slowing the pace. The number of grandchildren has reached twenty-four and the Van Duynes continue to give thanks for their abundant blessings.

Van Duyne grandchildren, 2004

VELMA GIBSON WATTS
Introduction

I first encountered Velma Watts at a program given at Bennett College, a small, distinguished school that has served young black women for many years. Velma and her friends, poet Maya Angelou, and scholar Dr. Dollie McPherson, spoke to students about successful black women in twentieth-century America. Each speaker revealed her own unique character and personality through stories of hard lessons learned and wisdom acquired.

The world well knows of Maya Angelou's compelling performances and she gave one that evening, humorous, sagacious, and feisty. Gentle Professor McPherson's quietly eloquent remarks revealed a deep understanding of her audience and were by no means diminished by juxtaposition with those of her celebrated friend. And who was the tall, elegant woman who spoke last, leaving at least one listener wishing for more? It was Velma Watts, who illustrated her points with references and quotations from a broad spectrum of sources--all in polished prose. Her pithy advice, her striking stage presence, and the empathy she so clearly felt with the students suggested an experienced speaker, but also a compassionate woman who had traveled circuitous roads.

Velma was born in a southern state still under full segregation. Protected by a family and community that held strong convictions about education and self-improvement, Velma grew up to be a secure and confident woman. When asked how she coped with racial conditions in a small southern city, she answered, "I learned early on that I had to teach people how to treat me."

Velma's presentation at Bennett piqued my curiosity. How did a woman raised by relatives in the American South during the forties and fifties find her way to a satisfying family life, work she loves, and a PhD from Duke University?

Eager to discover the answers to these and other questions, I managed to be introduced to Velma after the program. She agreed to read the relevant materials on the oral history project and soon thereafter agreed to participate. We met at her office at the Bowman Gray School of Medicine where she was then Director of the Office of Minority Affairs and Assistant Dean for Student Affairs. Part of Velma's work as a medical educator was to raise the retention rates of minority students in medical school. Many need assistance with academic, financial, or psychological problems. She also developed pre-med undergraduate programs to encourage academically talented minority students to consider careers in medicine. And much more.

In addition to her professional work, Velma volunteered over the years to serve a host of Winston-Salem civic and community organizations. Her many awards for leadership and service testify to Velma Watts' contributions to her adopted city.

Velma has been married for over thirty years to Roland Watts, Chairman of the Department of Fine Arts at Winston-Salem State University. Proud of his wife's academic prowess, Roland managed their home and son Brett's early adolescence while Velma lived in Durham to finish her doctorate at Duke.

Prior to our oral history recording session, I had met Velma only briefly at the Bennett College program. One could easily be intimidated by Velma's presence; she is statuesque and dignified. However, the warmth of her personality soon puts visitors at ease. Students would surely feel comfortable taking their problems to Dr. Watts. In describing her work, Velma discussed issues in medicine, race, and education. Later, over lunch in the sunny hospital restaurant, she turned to more personal matters and her own story.

Some of Velma's Gibson ancestors were called free-issue, which meant they had never been in bondage. Velma's father's great-grandfather, Lewis Burton Gibson, was acknowledged by his slave-owner father and given an inheritance. As a landowner of some means he was then able to pass on an inheritance to his own eight children. For generations, the Gibsons have been known in Winston-Salem as people of substance and accomplishment, a legacy not lost on young Velma Gibson.

In her oral history, Velma discusses the family pride her aunts imparted to her throughout her childhood. She tells of her immediate family and its dissolution when she was very young. Years passed before she was able to unravel some of the issues of class and color that shadowed her childhood.

In her middle fifties at the time of her oral history interview, Velma was coming to terms with the complex set of circumstances that led to her life-long separation from her father. It is characteristic of Velma's brave spirit that, after so many years marked by external success and accomplishment, she was willing to embark on a new inner journey.

Velma Gibson Watts
Winston-Salem, North Carolina
1992

I can't think of a time when families didn't reach out to help a person in need, especially one trying to pull herself up. In those days the whole village really did help raise the children.

My parents divorced when I was very young, and my mother died when I was twelve. The sense of loss was overwhelming, as it would be for any young girl. But I was blessed with a strong family. My aunt, Odessa Harris, her husband, Conlous, and other relatives who cared for me after my mother died, did not express love in words, yet there was no doubt I was loved and that they had expectations for me. I believe my family and their expectations are the source of my self-confidence.

looking back

The facts of being black and growing up in the fifties made my guardians impress upon me the need to do well in anything I approached. I was taught the value of learning, and that true confidence comes from competence, and doing well. I absorbed these lessons and saw that teachers could make me feel good, could make me feel worthy. I wanted to be accepted and saw that if I did something well I would be accepted, perhaps not by my peers, but by people who were evaluating me. I learned that very early on.

Also my aunt and grandmother would not permit situations that would be hurtful or insulting to me. I was shielded

Velma Gibson Watts, 1990

from things that other black students had to cope with. Not that my aunt told me that's what they were doing!

But high school was difficult. Having skipped a grade, I was younger than others and paid a price for that. I had not developed physically by ninth grade and, perhaps because of my strict family life, had not developed socially either. I was unhappy the entire four years of high school.

The best teacher I ever had treated me as a mature person and I tried to behave accordingly. She was Dorothy Slade Williams, a no-nonsense woman, an idol for me. She was like my aunt, even looked like her and had the same way of communicating her expectations. I never wanted to disappoint her; all she needed was a certain look.

That teacher is Dr. Williams now. Years after I graduated from college, I went to hear her speak. Afterwards I went up and she didn't even remember me! Yet she'd had such a great impact on me.

My high school and college were segregated; students, teachers and staff were all black. But the choir from a white college would come to visit with us. I was in our choir and could see that these contacts were positive and reinforced the notion that common interests and interaction on the same level could foster communication and respect between the races.

But I did resent that thing out there called Jim Crow. I resented being forced to go to the rear of the bus. Sometimes the resentment welled up in me so much that I sat where I wanted to sit.

On Sundays I would take little outings with friends. We'd get on the bus and ride to the end of the line and back. My aunt had devised this form of sightseeing to let us see the other side of town. The bus would go out past the white neighborhoods and come back to my street. It may be that because the drivers knew me from these excursions, they never told me to move to the back.

The constraints on real travel were substantial. At one point in my childhood, we would go to Ann Arbor for the summer, visiting an aunt who was in a graduate program at the University of Michigan.

We would have a wonderful summer but getting there was made so difficult by the Jim Crow laws. We'd go to Washington, a day's journey, for the train to Detroit. But blacks were not allowed to stay in the nice hotels in Washington, so we couldn't break up the trip with an overnight, and had to just make one very long trip. We also couldn't use the club car on the train so if you ran out of your own food on this long trip, or it spoiled in the heat, well, that was just too bad.

Strong Women Tell Their Stories

I had the good fortune to live near the all-black Agricultural and Technical College, now a large integrated university. The president's wife, Mrs. Bluford, saw to it that all the neighborhood kids attended the Lyceum series. Often, she would bring us all into her home in advance and prepare us for an opera or anything else far beyond our experience.

When Phillipa Schuyler, a twelve-year-old prodigy concert pianist, gave a concert, Mrs. Bluford invited us to meet her. She was the product of a mixed marriage and it puzzled me that she could travel with a white mother. And she was a vegetarian, the first vegetarian I had ever met! Marian Anderson came and I sneaked into the auditorium just to hear her practice. I remember my delight at meeting these wonderful people. My aunt and grandmother made certain that I had many such opportunities for growth.

Ralph Bunche came to speak at the university and was provided with a convertible car so that he could ride down the street and wave to the crowd. Paul Robeson, Mary McCloud Bethune and many others came to our school. I certainly wasn't culturally deprived! Children who are exposed to such people and events develop confidence and pride in being black.

White society may have said that we were "less than," but we could see that was false: they did not know what we knew. How could all these distinguished men and women exist if those negative things were true? They gave me hope and helped define who I could be: studying was not for naught; there were people who could overcome the odds; and there were people who respected others regardless of race.

There was always great respect for learning in my family. My grandmother did not have a formal education, but she insisted on education for her own children. My mother went

Teenaged Velma at the beach, 1953

to college, so I'm the second generation on my mother's side to be university-educated. I am grateful for the unspoken messages. No one ever said, "You've got to go to college," but it was an understanding, just like getting promoted to the next grade.

We also benefited from the strong sense of community. Here are examples from the 1940s: I was walking through the college campus near our home with some friends who were very loud, very boisterous. A dear friend of our family heard us and spoke to us in no uncertain terms about our behavior. I was so embarrassed that I did not resent it. I was just glad she didn't call my home! That incident impressed upon me that the adults around us cared about the children.

Years later when I was a student at that same college, I cut class one day. The professor called my house and said, "I will give you ten minutes to get over here...." I was embarrassed, but appreciated that he was concerned about me.

In later years, I came to understand more fully the meaning of those events, that the whole community was my family. And, indeed, I can't think of a time when families didn't reach out to help someone in need, especially someone who was trying to pull herself up. In those days the whole village really did help raise the children.

As I grew older I wasn't as bitter as I might have been about the situation for black people. I had that strong family/village as a foundation, but in addition, I somehow had faith that things were going to improve. You knew you couldn't dwell on certain things, just move on as best you could.

I knew because of the way I had been trained that I wasn't going to accept certain kinds of behavior. I learned early on that you teach people how to treat you. I learned too that all most people want is respect. One doesn't necessarily want close friendship, but we all need respect.

We faced stone walls, but it was clear we had to keep on going. The civil rights movement certainly helped to vindicate our efforts. The changes the movement brought made it possible for us to live where we wished, travel as we wanted, and, in general, live the life we chose.

Our children attended newly integrated schools. Their attendance at these schools, even in a southern city, was peaceful, probably because they gravitated toward children who had the same values and interests they had. There were incidents however, events our children did not discuss until many years later.

When our daughter started school in 1965, she was the first black child at the kindergarten of a Catholic school. We were interviewed and asked if we thought our daughter would be hurt by being the first and only black child. We said, "No, she has enough self confidence for almost any situation. If we find she can't handle it, we will take her elsewhere." But she was fine, in fact had a wonderful experience that year.

I recall only one incident. Rolonda wanted to be first going up a slide. Another little girl cut ahead of Rolonda and said, "No blacks!" Our daughter looked at her and said, "You don't know your colors. My shoes are black, but I'm brown." That was before the term black was widely used so Rolonda didn't even recognize what the child was saying. The teacher called that afternoon to tell me what happened; they were very sensitive and did not want anything to mar her experience. So the positive things did help to balance the challenges in that situation.

Our daughter attended a private girl's high school, with primarily white students. She went on to Spelman College, and, for the first time, had mostly black friends. She has published an article describing her experiences in the different schools and the problems of transition. It was more difficult for her than we fully understood at the time, but she is stronger for it now.

To some extent, I can control my own environment. So I tried to create for my children that same protected environment that my grandmother and aunt had created for me. But we can't know about all of our children's experiences. And there was enough going on in their school years to leave some deep, negative imprints. Things have changed a lot over the years, though not as much as I'd like. In general though, more people today are willing to accept others for what they can contribute, rather than pre-judge.

Years ago when my husband and I moved into our neighborhood, we were treated for the most part with respect. In fact, one family gave a cocktail party to introduce us. I should mention that this is a neighborhood full of people who were from hospitals and the university. But our next-door neighbor fought our moving in and for the first thirteen years she did everything she could to intimidate us; at some point I had words with her. Finally she stopped and now is polite to us.

As to other social changes of those times, we may not exactly be on the cutting edge of the women's movement! In our family my husband is still the head of the household. I work every day and we combine our resources but he is considered the breadwinner. If he were offered an opportunity to relocate, and wanted it very much, I would not hesitate to join him. I feel respected and valued for my strengths and I'm comfortable with our situation. I like to have doors opened for me; I like being respected and treated like a lady. Black women could not always take it for granted that men of any color would treat them with respect.

heritage and religion

The people on my father's side were ministers and educators from the beginning. My great, great-grandfather, Rev.Lewis Burton Gibson, was a charter trustee of Bennett College. In fact Bennett was founded in his church, St. Matthew's.

Members of that side of the family were never actually slaves. They were free-issue, which meant they were children of the slave-owner, and never really were in bondage. When the owner died, each of the children was given large sums of money, so the Gibsons were once well-to-do.

It was, of course, very unusual for the slave-owner to even acknowledge his children by slave women. I'm just learning about this now; a cousin of mine has found records in the courts and libraries.

My father's great-grandfather, Lewis Burton Gibson, was born in the 1800's in Gibsonville, N.C., the son of a plantation owner named Gibson.

Lewis Gibson became a minister in the Methodist Episcopal Churches of the North Carolina Conference. He owned several properties in and was said to have given each of his children "land with a house on it." He was married twice and had four children by each union.

My great-uncle, Dr. Elmer Pettiford Gibson, was the youngest of these siblings and the only one to follow in his father's path as a minister. Uncle Elmer was an Army chaplain, achieving the rank of Colonel. Upon his retirement from the Army, he became a college president.

My grandfather John, and his brother Michaux, were the Gibsons who visited me during my childhood. I remember my grandfather telling over and over the story of how he had "passed" as white until a colored acquaintance had discovered him. The exact hue of one's skin was of great importance to the Gibsons. I have been told by a Gibson cousin that "color" was the reason my father divorced my mother. She was darker than he. I also have the impression that it had been a difficult divorce. The relatives I lived with did not teach me to dislike my father, nor teach me to love him either. This produced a certain amount of confusion for me. Eventually I will look into all of this.

Uncle Michaux graduated from college and was at one point a school principal. In his later years, he was paralyzed by a stroke and often requested that I write letters for him as he dictated them to me. These letters were always to his brothers or to his sister. In them he would dictate paragraphs about my academic progress and mention that he had paid for my piano lessons. I never asked why none of the letters were ever dictated to my father.

We went to Bethel African Methodist Episcopal each Sunday. If I didn't go to church, I wasn't allowed to do anything else on Sunday. If I pretended to be sick, then I couldn't go for the walk in the afternoon or visit friends or go for the bus ride. The church was such a center of activity; besides Bible School there was an event every Sunday afternoon for the young people. I enjoyed all of it, though the minister's sermon was not fully meaningful to me until I started college nearby. Then I could see that he took relevant issues and brought them into his sermons. That impressed me and I began to pay attention. That's when church became important to me. I loved the fine organ music too.

One of the memories I have of my mother is that she was in charge of the plays and programs we did at the church. She would write and direct and we would perform for different occasions. And I remember the little paper dresses she made for us for those performances.

I don't attend church as often as I once did; religion has become very personal for me. I try to express my Christianity by contributing some of my resources, whether finances or time, to people who haven't been as fortunate as I have.

It seems that my heritage has much to do with the day-to-day living of my life. The older I get the more I respect my upbringing and the way I was taught to deal with challenges. I was taught there might always be obstacles but one doesn't let them stand in the way of achievement. You have to consider the obstacles as a greater incentive.

An example of that occurred when I went to graduate school for my first graduate degree in the late sixties. I felt that I was admitted as a token black. Then when I demonstrated that I had some ability certain professors were not prepared for that. It's important of course to keep in mind that many teachers in those days were prejudiced against women period, never mind a black woman. I earned that degree!

There were other roadblocks, such as not being included in student study groups, while realizing that I needed those groups in order to do well. After they saw my grades, I was "allowed" to join. Then I had to deal within myself with the fact that I finally did join the group despite the way I'd been treated! I convinced myself that it wasn't a personal weakness but just doing what was necessary to get the work done.

Years later I went to Duke for my doctorate. It was an exciting time, but not easy! Roland was willing to be with Brett and keep the household going. I started in the summer of 1978 and lived on campus for the next year and a half. I took fifteen hours each semester and summer and finished the course work plus dissertation in eighteen months. Of course, by the end I was nearly crazy! My advisor had told me that nobody finishes this quickly, and I said well at my age and the cost of Duke, I would have to do it this way. I was fortunate to have been a Rockefeller Fellow.

It seemed to be the right time to do it. Our daughter was in college. Our son was thirteen, at home with his father and that was a challenge for them both! They certainly spent more time together than they'd ever done before. With the kind of studying it took to complete my work in eighteen months, I could not do the usual family things for that period.

I wasn't even able to go to the formal ceremony for the PhD because our daughter was graduating from Spelman at the same time. She finished in three years, so maybe this pace runs in our family.

children

Each of our children was planned and became an important part of our marriage. Having children helps you grow and mature in so many ways. But raising our children was never a simple matter; even with the best of intentions, you make mistakes. As my children grow older, I hope they can look back and see that we did the best we could at the time.

My husband and I lived through difficult times; perhaps that made it all the more important to us that our children have a true sense of values: honesty, a sense of fair play, the importance of developing your talents, contributing to your community. That's been difficult because one doesn't raise one's children alone; the culture around them, other adults, other young people contribute to their growth, and not always in ways you appreciate.

The village isn't there in the way it once was, though I did bring some of the traditions and rituals of my childhood to my family. The simplest, and most important is the family meal, a time when everyone is encouraged to contribute to the conversation.

I communicated more with my children than my family did with me. I verbalized my expectations whereas in my childhood there were many unspoken expectations. Our children knew exactly what we meant. And when they were involved in activities at school, we attended all of them, not just the special events. They were in newly desegregated schools so we had to work harder to help them keep a sense of self. We struggled to help Brett maintain a positive sense of being black.

We've tried to uphold our values and to demonstrate that if we have advantages then we also have obligations to return something to society, to reach out and help others. And we tried to teach them that much of life involves overcoming difficulties in order to progress to a higher level. We never wanted our children to be bitter. We wanted them to examine situations, learn what they could, and go on from there.

For example, we watched the first parts of the television series "Roots" together as a family. I knew that some of what our children (almost adults by then) would see would make them bitter and angry. They are, after all, living in another time. It was important that we watched and discussed it together.

Our children have always been my first priority. Even now, with Rolonda in her early thirties, Brett in his twenties, I am so pleased to be available to them. Wherever they are, they know that almost nothing prevents me from stopping to listen to them and hear what they have to say. Brett called last night to talk about his work in the costume shop. He is excited about being an apprentice with the theatre here. He even has some creative freedom. It makes me so happy to know that he is doing what he wants to do. Then Rolonda called and we talked about a script. She had been asked to write this particular script by Bill Cosby, so she especially wanted to discuss it with us.

The key word there is "hear." At one time they had to do all the listening, but I've grown, through some bruises, to listen and hear *them*. And that's been a difficult thing for me to learn.

I still have a long way to go, but I have evolved from a point of not actually listening to them at all. Can you imagine? Now I do hear them and enjoy being friends with them as young adults, but our friendship had to develop over the course of time.

I went through different stages of being the mother, the teller, the doer, the one who sets an example. I came to recognize that one of those stages was "demander." And that was damaging. I had to learn that I was not always right. I may have been partially right, but my son and daughter needed to have a voice too. I finally had to step back and analyze my behavior, after my bruises became deeper and deeper. I had to engage in extensive self-help work and realize that they were not rejecting me, but rejecting some of my behavior. So I'm glad to have gone through all that and made some progress.

working

My career choices were not originally influenced by social changes of the sixties; I went into teaching after college because it was expected of me. I thought I was a good teacher, but I had a headache every day. So I had to examine that! In college career testing, I had always come out highest in the area of administration.

The changes of the sixties did open up new career possibilities for women and blacks. Until then, opportunities for women as principals or administrators were rare outside the immediate black community.

For the most part, I have always worked. I taught in elementary school during my first pregnancy. The policy then was that one had to leave at the fourth month of a pregnancy. So to use that remaining time, I enrolled in graduate school, and did the same thing again when expecting Brett. I like that part of myself, that I had the initiative to go ahead and do what was important to me. It's also been satisfying to volunteer for agencies that help others.

I've always wanted to work with young black people. I say black in particular because I feel I have a message for them. It bothers me that I meet kids who want to use race as an excuse for not trying. I feel it especially because I came out of a time when everywhere you went there were things to diminish you. Yet, with encouragement, it was still possible to achieve.

In my work now we are trying to encourage and enlighten students, so that they can become a part of the mainstream and still maintain their own identity. We have increased the number of minority students in medical school. Then we try to help them navigate their way through the many potential problems along the way in a medical education: financial, emotional, academic, family, and personal. The administration cooperates with us fully and I appreciate that.

As to what I bring of myself to my work, aside from professional skills or know-how, I do work at extracting the best from others and that is perhaps why I've had some success as an administrator. I set a high standard for people and I believe that they will give their best effort. I try to be very candid. And sometimes it is necessary to have enough conviction to take a stand even when there may be penalties for doing so.

My personal and professional lives have blended well. My husband has always encouraged me in my efforts to develop professionally. Each of us takes time to listen to the other. And the sequence was about right. Each new turn seemed to be supported by what had gone before. If I'd not had children I might have gotten the doctorate sooner, but I did want children and it was important to slow down and take time for them. And we certainly did all the usual things people do for their children. We are a close family.

mentors

I have had many wonderful mentors, people who influenced my adult life. First and most important is my husband, who, as I mentioned, has been so supportive of everything I've done. He doesn't resent my independence and this has certainly contributed to the longevity of our marriage.

My cousin Bobby Bright grew up with me, also raised by our aunt. He is now an administrator for the county schools. He knew that I loved school and learning and always urged me to go back to school for the PhD. I will always be grateful to him for all that prodding.

I've also been blessed with wonderful friends. People who believe in us are so important. We do nothing alone. I have sister friends and we constantly support one another in many ways.

I've been inspired by my grandmother. She had great faith in life and its possibilities. She believed that if you developed your abilities and presented yourself well, the future was open to you. As I've mentioned earlier, she and my aunt both planted those values very firmly.

My children also are a source of inspiration for me: their intelligent way of handling their lives, their courage. Brett says just the right things at difficult moments. On a bumpy plane trip when Brett was very young, it was he who reassured me!

looking ahead

I look forward to continuing with the work that I love. Wouldn't it be wonderful if my job were no longer necessary! After retirement I hope to continue to do volunteer work and perhaps travel a little more.

I've learned a few things about getting older. We should not postpone anything important that we really want to do. It's so basic, but we do need to prepare ourselves financially for growing older. We must also have a circle of friends and family around for the time when we really need them.

My appearance is important to me. My agenda is too full to worry about imperfections, but if wrinkles bother me later, I'll go to a cosmetic surgeon. (Working in a hospital, I have great faith in what they can do!) It's inevitable that how you look conveys a message about how you want to be treated. You prepare yourself with education and experience, but your appearance is a significant part of what you present to the world.

I am most grateful to each of the people who helped to make my life what it is. I've tried to live in a way that expresses my appreciation. I'm both proud and grateful that I was able to follow my hopes and dreams. I would have done some things differently, but nothing major. Life is too beautiful to dwell on things in the past that cannot be changed. I would rather apply my energies to improving today and tomorrow.

Postscript, 2005:

Since retirement from Bowman Gray, Velma continues to participate in Winston-Salem's civic life. She also now has time to investigate her family's history, finding in library archives, old stories and courthouse records some of the hidden wellsprings of her own life.

In the early nineties, Velma's daughter, Rolonda Watts, had her own show, "Rolonda," on network television. Her new show, filmed in Los Angeles, began it's run in 2005. Living now in Florida, Brett continues his career as a writer. Now able to spend more time with Roland at their cherished beach house, Velma at last has time to walk the sandy shores, breathe coastal air, and gaze out to sea.

GAY CHENEY
Introduction

Gay Cheney appears to be a classic free spirit. A dancer and choreographer, her firm body is usually adorned with feathers, beads, and hand-sewn vests. Earrings are, like Gay, often in motion. As an only child, she was encouraged by her parents to do whatever she chose, but to do it well. Her mother enrolled Gay in dance classes at the age of five. Living on the New Jersey shore, she was a child of sun, sand and sea and began her apprenticeship as an artist early, writing and dancing in a world of her own creation. Hers was truly Melville's "Sweet childhood of air and sky."

Woven into a life of art and dance, however, are the activities of a disciplined academic. When we first met to record her oral history, Gay was working on her own choreography and performance while assisting students with their dance projects. She had recently revised for a third edition her book on modern dance, a text widely used in university dance departments. She has also won the Dance Alliance Award for her work.

Gay has an abiding interest in Native American religions and cultures. Her spiritual home is the Southwest, to which she returns often for religious and artistic renewal. After her retirement in 1996, Gay began to design programs on Native American dance that she performs for and with elementary school children. Finding them responsive and eager to learn, she weaves in discussions on conservation and reverence for the natural world. She is also an ardent environmentalist, campaigning continually for more respectful use of land as her city grows.

Gay has lived much of her adult life in a conservative southern city, neither hiding nor advertising two sequential long-term relationships with other women. Her professional and personal lives have required her to be resilient and hardy. An eminently likable individual, Gay has friends from many walks of life. In a medium-sized city, she points out, choreographers work not only as expected with dancers, musicians, costume and set designers, but may well also volunteer at a nature center, or have friends in the sustainable agriculture movement.

I spoke with Gay in her small hexagonal house, perched high above a pond and surrounding woods. Gay's passions are reflected in an artfully designed setting. Sculpture, paintings, drawings, and ceramics offer a colorful greeting; textiles, bleached bones, and driftwood call to be admired from nooks and shelves. Gay seems to have embraced all the shapes, forms, and textures of nature. Nourished by small miracles as well as those of grander scale, she finds inspiration for her art as readily in an intricate shell as in a desert sunrise.

Since the six outer walls of Gay's house are window walls, boundaries blur between indoors and out. The visitor suddenly understands—this is a tree house! And steps into an arboreal mood, a sense of freedom, of floating above mundane ground life. In such a place one gazes lazily through eye-level treetops at a scurrying squirrel. A visitor feels called to sit cross-legged with two friends and a deck of cards.

In her late fifties when she recorded her oral history, Gay continued to seek resolutions to the puzzles and paradoxes encountered in her own life. She looked to the future with some trepidation, but primarily with her customary eagerness and uncommon zest.

Gay Cheney
Greensboro, North Carolina, and Southwestern U.S.
1990

I attribute much of my closeness to nature to my father. He wanted me to be healthy. He would come out on the beach and stretch out his arms and say isn't it marvelous and doesn't it smell beautiful and isn't it glorious to be here!

In my fifties I feel physically as I did at thirty. Psychologically and emotionally, I am weathered and a lot wiser than I was at thirty and relieved not to be that young and green any more. Perhaps seasoned is a better word than weathered. This decade brought many opportunities to risk and grow. And, fortunately, I was able to pursue them. I got loved and admired and clobbered and crazied but I did survive it. There is a reckoning with terrible pain and disappointment which helps one to grow up. And compassion comes from knowing we've been there and, if we haven't yet, we will be soon. My young life was pretty euphoric. In my fifties, I've come to be more real, more of this earth, more of a humane being.

On my fiftieth birthday, I wrote letters to everyone who is dear to me to say how wonderful my life had been and how glad I was to have them in it. My dear friend and colleague, Anne DeLoria, choreographed a dance for two graduate students and me called "Of Songs and Ancient Riverbeds." We performed it in a concert run of three nights, including the night of my birthday. At the end, I was asked to come out on stage, and there were all my friends singing and applauding in the audience. So at fifty, I was deeply appreciative of my good fortune--my life, my friends, my health, my dancing.

In my creative work, I love shaping words and movement. When I am very much moved by something, it is wonderful to be able to shape it in choreography for the stage and theatre. This gives a sense of connection to people, and hope that I can perhaps move others to feel as I do.

Every time you write or choreograph a piece, it's a risk to put it out there. What sort of a response will it create? It means a great deal when people say that my work touched or spoke to them. I have begun to investigate ceremonies of various kinds, especially those used in nurturing and healing. I've been involved in a state program for the care and nurturing of public school teachers in which we use healing movements in ceremony. I am happy to be there and feel what takes place among people.

I don't consider the various things I've done in my career accomplishments as such but just what my work and life were about. I was tenured and promoted to full professor before I came to this university, but that too seemed just part of the natural course of things. I went to California straight out of graduate school, full of energy, built a dance department, developed courses, did workshops, and wrote a book; so to be tenured and promoted on an ongoing basis was just how things evolved.

I rewrote my little modern dance book two years ago and had a wonderful time doing it; it's the kind of writing I love to do, so different from academic writing. It's called *Modern Dance: A Creative Approach*. I rewrote the history of dance with my own coloring and words. I enjoyed the process, and the fact that the book has been successful is almost beside the point. It's nice to have it in a third edition, but what is most satisfying is to have been able to write effectively about dance, to communicate some of what I know and care about.

The close, loving relationships of my adult life have been the areas of greatest difficulty for me. As an only child, it was difficult to come into relationships with people without knowing quite how to manage.

It surprised me that I never married. I was brought up to believe that I would have a husband. Having been an only child, I desperately wanted children, and I used to think I would have eight.

Perhaps the biggest surprise of my adult life is that when I fell in love for the first time at age thirty-two, it was with another woman. Marie and I were together for seventeen years, including one period when we broke up, but came back together again. It was wonderful for a very long time, but we finally realized that for various reasons it was time to separate. It was extremely painful and took me a long time and a lot of therapy to understand what had happened.

I didn't have a strong sense of women as friends until college. Early on, I did have a neighbor who was an ally, like a sister to whom you can complain about your mother. Then there were many friends over the years; the friendships from my California days have been long lasting.

When you love and live with one woman and share your life with her, other women friends become a consideration. But it took awhile for me to separate out all the different strands of relationships, some that had romantic elements, some that did not, and to see how all these different parts of my life fit together. Or didn't fit together.

When Marie and I were together all those years, we had women friends in common and all of us did things together. It seemed simple.

Later with Peggy, it was a matter of learning how to have separate, other friendships and to value them, yet not have them interfere with the love relationship. So that was challenging, not to focus on my love life as the only important source of comfort. Also, at a certain point it became important to me to have men friends, men I felt close to, could hug and laugh with. That seemed to help to get some of this into perspective and has been a good balance.

My own sense of not being successful at loving relationships made me immensely sad and sent me into therapy and much introspection. I've done a lot of looking back at my life and connections with my parents, and thought a lot about humans and our need for love.

I lived for several years with someone who had teenage children. Never having had children or brothers and sisters myself, my relationship to Peggy, along with the children, was a major challenge to me as an adult. I wasn't very successful at it, and there were certain things I had to realize about myself. At fifty-seven I was pretty strongly set in wanting my environment the way I wanted it. I wasn't as flexible as I thought I would be.

She is very close to her children, especially after being divorced from their father. She tried to bring me into that circle and I tried to work my way in. But as you know, the love of a mother for her children is so powerful, ferocious almost, and the children's needs always come first. I got along very well with the children; they are wonderful young people. But it was hard to cope with the fact that every plan, every activity, every conversation can be interrupted for the children. I wasn't prepared for that. As a single person, I have just gone through my life making all my own choices. That's really very selfish, and I wanted to get out of my own solitary mode. But it was hard.

And yet, I need space, my own life. A lot of women are struggling for that now: to have a solid, intimate relationship, yet also have an independent life, friends, work. Men have always had that. Now women are trying to have it as well, and it's a challenge for gay women as well as married women.

My dad had some definite ideas about what women ought to be. I did well in math in high school. My father was an actuary, and he said to me, "Don't even think about becoming a woman actuary. They are cold, heartless people, and women need to be soft and warm. Don't even think about being a mathematician either."

I have a good body sense and, to quote the great choreographer Merce Cunningham, "an appetite for motion." I love dancing and singing, sailing, running on the beach, swimming. I swam a lot, was a lifeguard, and even taught swimming at an early age. When I was fourteen, we had end-of-the-year races and I was thrown in with all the big guy lifeguards and here I was this little fourteen-year-old. I came out of the water not even knowing that I had won the race, and my father grabbed me with tears streaming down his face and hugged me and was laughing and tickled to death, but said, "Don't you ever do that again!" So he was delighted and proud as punch and at the same time saying, "No, no, it doesn't work in the world. You must never beat the men. It's not appropriate."

I was stunned and moved by his reactions, not knowing what to think at the time. So I had some mixed messages. I don't think I ever wanted to become a woman actuary, but I think it has colored my thinking about being a woman: how women are supposed to be soft, and not aggressive, and not pushy, even out in the world. It has been hard for me to figure out how to get what I want in the world and still claim my own femininity, my own softness, and ways of approaching issues as a woman.

I've kept my dance work within the university. I can do academic writing and intellectual writing, but it has been a real challenge to try to get my left and right brains together within this system, to find some way to continue to work and function as an artist and not to get my juices dried up in all the "academese."

When I was the head of the dance department, it was a terrific challenge to figure out how to function within the world of administrators. I can honestly say that I was not trying to get what I wanted but what the dance department needed from the world of academia. That world was essentially men who knew exactly how to operate and what to do to get what they needed and wanted. I didn't know how to do things their way and kept trying to do it my woman's way. But in terms of being efficient and effective as a leader, mine was not the way to go about it.

Even as a child I realized that something was missing. Not that a part of me was missing, but a part of me was unrealized in that I was always being a nice girl, a good girl, sweet girl, and I knew there were other things going on inside. So I felt like a wimp a lot of the time! Discovering I had some unexpressed anger finally allowed me to take stands on issues that I never could before. I was much stronger for understanding that. It took me a long time to get to there though!

As an only child, totally focused on my own world, I was encouraged by my parents to do well, and by the slogan, "You can do anything in this world you want to do." They gave me space and privacy; I wrote and danced in my own self-created world. There was the open door and terrific support from my Mom, though there were some mixed messages, as I mentioned, from my Dad.

I grew up in Millburn, New Jersey, and we lived in a little shore house throughout my childhood. My self-confidence has a lot to do with my "physicality," physical confidence. I ran through the woods and played football and basketball and in summer swam for hours every day. I was strong, accomplished, unafraid, involved with ocean and waves and beach and clouds and sky, feeling very much a part of the natural world. That communion with nature has been a powerful and continuing resource throughout my life, and has inspired much of my work.

I attribute this feeling for nature to my dad. He wanted me to be healthy. He would come

At the Jersey shore, late 1930's.
Gay is dark-haired child, 3rd from left

on the beach and stretch out his arms and say isn't it marvelous and doesn't it smell beautiful and isn't it glorious to be here!

My mother tells a story about my swimming a half-mile out to an island and back with a boy (I was about fourteen and had a crush on the boy). Her heart was in her mouth the whole time, but she never once thought about saying don't do that, or be careful. She just watched and waited for us to get back. So I was raised with feelings of great confidence in myself.

My mother had been a schoolteacher. She had enormous energy and was very bright. She was her "father's daughter," in the sense that he was interested in politics and she was the one he always talked to about issues of the day. My mother taught for a while, but my father didn't encourage that because he wanted her home, taking care of his house. But my mother always had a lot of energy that needed to go somewhere besides bridge parties and house cleaning and making clothes for me.

I somehow got that transfer of her energy and ambition, also the open door. My mother had been a dancer in high school. She'd taken ballroom dancing lessons and hung around the marathon dances of the thirties, was almost a contestant, in fact. All that stopped with her marriage. But my Grandmother Tess always played the piano, and my mother and aunt would sing and dance for the whole family. And then later I got called upon to sing and dance.

I didn't get much sense of the appeal of being a housewife. In fact, I got pushed out of the kitchen, got very little encouragement to cook or clean. My mother kept saying, "Go do your other things, you'll have plenty of time to do this the rest of your life." So I didn't grow up thinking that being a housewife was a very glamorous or important thing to be.

My development had much to do with the times, growing up in the forties and fifties. The war and the death of President Roosevelt made deep impressions on me as a child in the forties. Our lives changed completely during the war. Living on the Jersey shore we felt threatened; we were asked to keep our shades down and to stay off the beach at night. We saw the Coast guard riding up and down the beach on horses because they suspected German submarines were right off the coast.

There was also a sense of deprivation in not having meat or gas, which we knew were necessary for the war. So we felt very patriotic. Every film and song was about the war.

I remember the announcement of peace in Europe: people were so grateful that we all gathered in the storefront church (there were no real church buildings on the beach) and the priest led us in a ceremony. We all gathered, regardless of denominations, people cried, and it was very moving.

Later on though, I was not really involved with issues at all, was somehow unaware of the larger world. Life was so full of possibilities, and I was totally involved in school, various accomplishments, dating, and buying clothes, all the things young girls do.

I had to choose between two schools, one downtown and the other in a wealthy neighborhood. Since we were not wealthy, my mother feared I'd be at the bottom of the pile going to that school. The school downtown was multi-ethnic and multi-racial, and Mother kept saying to me, "I want you to know about and be part of the world." So I went to a class with the only black child in Millburn, as well as Italians, Irish, and Jewish kids. I would never have encountered this variety at the other school. I loved going to their homes, eating all the new foods, hearing the accents.

I was a straight-A student all through high school and graduated in a class of 98 people of which 98% went on to college; it was simply expected that people in that community would do well in school.

I thought I had a call for healing, perhaps from my father's Christian Science background. Also, a lot of us were preparing ourselves to do good work in the world. I went to a school of physical therapy in Boston fully intending to become a physical therapist. But I started taking modern dance classes and was overwhelmed by modern dance ideas. I switched to a degree in dance and went to Connecticut College summer school to meet all the modern dance artists of that time. I planned to do dance therapy. In fact, I have offered dance therapy here, courses in growth or healing through movement.

My first college teaching job was at George Washington University in D.C. There, in the early sixties, I found myself in the middle of international life and people. I attended American University, taught, choreographed, and performed with a group. Some of my students were jailed for participating in marches and demonstrations, and I actually didn't understand what they were doing!

More recently, on Martin Luther King's birthday, there was a big march in D.C. I got on the midnight bus with many people from the black community of Greensboro and a couple of friends. People got up and spoke about their commitments to social justice, and I thought, "It has taken me a long time to get on this bus. Thank God, I'm finally in the world and out of my little artists' pocket." I was very moved to be out there with people, and I felt truly stupid that it had taken me so many years to finally make it.

Strong Women Tell Their Stories

I was right on my little track straight through my job at California State. After seven years there, I was told to think about getting my doctorate. I got a National Defense Act Grant and got my doctorate at USC.

Before I knew it, everything was unfolding before my eyes. I came back to Cal State, was gathering faculty, and doing choreography, and suddenly it was the late sixties: hippies and drugs on the Berkeley campus and rock concerts in San Francisco. Black, Chicano, and other minority students called professors to meetings about who was hired and why. A lot of energy was focused on consciousness-raising. Caesar Chavez, Angela Davis, and others were coming to Cal State to speak; the farm workers were trying to protect Caesar Chavez, and each moment brought a new crisis. We were right in the middle of it.

Gay, 1966

Then came the peace dem-onstrations. Some students wanted to shut down colleges and devote their lives and energies to stopping the war in Vietnam; every issue that could be raised was out there. In 1967-68, it was right in your face everywhere you went. I was being awakened, but it wasn't till years later when I got on that bus that I actually took political action.

My mother was still saying, "These demonstrations are against the United States," and I remember thinking, wait a minute, what is all this about? I had a difficult time sorting through all the issues swirling around us.

I had a terrible nightmare that hippies came over a hill, in through my window, and just kept coming and coming. It was not kin to my spirit to be in the middle of political activity.

I was fascinated by the mix of races everywhere I went. Some good art work was concerned with justice and human equality, Nikki

Voices of the Silent Generation

Giovanni's poetry, for example. A group of singers called "Women on Wheels" was the first to sing women's music, produced and directed by women. Women in their audiences were ecstatic. It was thrilling for me to see artists making statements in their work. I was moved more by the arts than by Germaine Greer or other writers of the time.

I was intrigued by the uninhibited dancing and singing of hippie groups. Looking back, I realize that much of it was drug-induced rather than actually having more personal freedom than I had. But it seemed to me, in my innocence at the time, like a wonderful sort of free-release state.

And it did influence my work. The mood of freedom opened me up creatively. We did some choreography out on the beach, for example. Then, for the first time, my work began to be about social change. We did a multimedia performance to honor the new ideals. I began to be involved in issues of the times, particularly ecological concerns and real estate development. I wrote letters to the newspaper and organized meetings against development in certain areas. In fact, I'm still doing that forty years later!

I wore a pants suit to an opening, not done in those days, and everyone told me how wonderful it was! As a dancer it was liberating to be out of those heels and stockings. How inhibiting those clothes were! I had problems with my feet, and I decided I'm not going to ruin my feet for fashion, or however I'm supposed to look as a woman. I can remember making that decision.

In 1976 I was offered the full professorship in North Carolina, and before I knew it I was driving back East across the country. When I left, the women's movement was sweeping across California, and it hadn't occurred to me that there weren't women's groups everywhere. It was like taking the clock

Gay Cheney, dancer. 1980s

and moving it back. How difficult it was to come back here to the Southeast, to come full circle! But I stayed.

Teachers. I think of Mary Whitehouse, a dance therapist in L.A. when I was doing my doctorate there. She was strong and grounded, with keen psychological insight. Working with her brought many things together for me: that it was all right to deal with the dark side of oneself, to know that we all have those sides. It's the balancing of those aspects of ourselves that we need in order to function in the world and still be ourselves.

As I've mentioned, the sea has been one of my great teachers; all its various moods and the sense of gentleness as well as power, terribly destructive forces, yet it can also be calming and stunningly beautiful. So for a dancer the ocean is a great inspiration.

I've been influenced by many artists; some, like Joachim Netty and Martha Graham, were in their nineties and still choreographing when they died. I learned much about human beings from John Steinbeck. The work of the poet Gerard Manley Hopkins has been important to me.

I aspire toward unselfishness, but the nature of the artist is to spend a lot of time on the self, observing, thinking, and feeling; it's not always a generous life. Mother Teresa gave her whole life to others. I admire that kind of generosity so much; she gave of herself to the whole world, put herself right on the line.

I've been a seeker, a searcher. My father went with his mother to study Christian Science one night a week and brought it all home to me. I was unreceptive at the time. He was giving me religion and all I wanted him to do was hold me in his lap and read to me. He would say, "God loves you, be satisfied with that."

Actually you don't need much more than that; it gave me an optimistic look at life. Eventually I had to

Dancing with Native American children, 1990

reject most of his beliefs and deal with the negative in life as well as positive.

I did find another perspective: I feel in accord with New Age dances and rituals and with Native American ceremonies and celebrations; I have always shared their reverence for the earth and nature and have tried to understand their unique relationship to the natural world. Also, native cultures tend to think of physical movement, whether as used in dance or in ritual, as a powerful healing tool. I have always believed that dance has therapeutic value. Just as scientists have discovered that laughter is good therapy, so too is the exhilaration of movement and dance.

I've done some work in Buddhist meditations with an anthropologist who spent much of her life studying Shamanism and Buddhism. She has tried to find commonalities in eastern and western religions, to weave together those different viewpoints. A lacing together of the hands of the world, you might say. She led me in meditations about compassion, to open the heart to human suffering and feel a part of the world's pain and tragedy, to experience it in one's own heart and soul. She has helped me to be less slapped up in my own happy little framework; I feel more connected to others in my life and work.

The lands of the Hopi and Navaho country were teachers for me. The horizon, the distances, the space, the formations of that land are magnificent. They are so calming and centering. The mountains, vistas and spaces in New Mexico near Santa Fe, and in Lakota country have been powerful lures for me. I love the Red Woods too.

On sabbatical in New Mexico, in Chaco Canyon with my friend Amanda, I did my first Long Dance, a three-day affair with much preparation, sweat lodging, pipe ceremony, cleansing. You give your energy to the dance, and it may be for world peace or the healing of a friend or honoring your children or your lover. Long Dance goes on all night, continuous drumming and dancing for twelve hours from sundown to sun-up. It was a whole new sense of what dance and sending energy can be.

I regret not giving myself to significant causes. I have always volunteered in every neighborhood but haven't really gotten fully out of myself. When I returned from my sabbatical, having lived out of my Jeep among Native Americans, I came back thinking, "I'm going to sell my house and possessions and live in a little cottage in the woods with minimal things and find my way." But I came back, got involved in the university and work, and friends and my life.

Another regret is that I did not have children. I love children, but it was apparently not for me. I felt great sorrow at menopause. A dance therapist in Chapel Hill made me come to grips with the fact that I never had a child. I considered adopting, but the agency said that I would have to spend two solid days a week with the child, and it came down to "Could I do that along with my work at the university?"

Again, it's my lack of ability to give up enough of my life to focus on something else, so the largest part of my regret is about never having had a really meaningful relationship with children. When I was teaching swimming on the beach in New Jersey, I had a trail of kids behind me all the time; they called me the Pied Piper. I loved children, was told I was wonderful with them. But I also knew that I could be with them for two or three hours and then I needed to go home and be by myself. I had grown up with absolute quiet space and still need it.

My father taught me that we grow through suffering. I'd have missed out on much in life if I hadn't come to understand this. In adult life I came to know it from my own experience. I remember watching a friend care for the person she loved and seeing her compassion grow. This contrasted with my own sense of not being fully successful at loving relationships, even though I've gone into therapy, done a great deal of introspection on

Gay at nature center for children, circa 2000

my life, my parents, and the human need for love and understanding.

As I age I fear little because we learn from all of it, the losses, the illnesses, the limitations. I see elders around me learning profound lessons of patience, of acceptance, while being completely powerless and without control of themselves or their lives. They grow in spirit, making peace with the natural processes of aging, life, and death, doing it all gracefully.

I see fulfillment in relationships with all of life, with acknowledging our part in the natural cycle, listening closely for the guidance of the spirit. I see optimism and courage and faith. We may seem to live too long these days, outlive our meaningful, functioning, contributing days. So we need to stay aware along the way of the necessary transition from work, body, entertainment, to meditation and spirit. The late-fifties seems a good stage to start practicing. And older women are often well-equipped to comfort others.

I'm grateful for so much in my life! It's been a very full, rich, and wonderful life. I appreciate the places I've been, the work I've done, the people I've known, my health and strength.

I was so lucky to have had my parents; they gave me the joy of singing, dancing, love of the beach. I was raised in a very sheltering, protective family. I didn't realize how much hurt and pain would be in my life. And yet in addition to protection, they also gave me a lot of faith, a lot of trust. I was raised not to be afraid, to know that I could get through things. I've never gotten completely lost in the pain I had.

I've been lucky in my close friends, my lovers. All the lessons I've had to learn in order to be in those relationships have kept me from getting too stuck. And as painful as some of those lessons were, they have only brought positive, beneficial change. They were often the pokes, pushes needed to move me into other stages of my life.

I do have questions. What is it all about, and what are we meant to be doing here? What are we meant to learn? For me these are still questions without answers. And yet the questions keep spinning out like a spider's web.

Sometimes it all seems to be up for grabs, doesn't it? Who are we meant to be in relation to others, to the earth and to the God-spirit? I hope that we are progressing towards a transformation, a gentleness of being. To evolve toward a better state of being, perhaps that's our end, our purpose.

Postscript, 2005:

Living today in a lakefront house, Gay continues to be active in environmental work and dance programs for children. She also spends much time with her widowed mother at a nearby retirement community. Meanwhile, back surgery one year was followed by a hip replacement the next. Gay's friends took good care of her during two long periods of convalescence. Visitors bearing food, flowers, books and offers of assistance arrived at the lake house in a steady stream. She says today, after long, painful convalescences from the two operations, "I still think of life as an adventure from which we are to learn all we can. Both of my parents gave me that sense of life. I rejoice in my friends and the earth's beauty. I find real joy in life."

DARYL MASLOW HAFTER
Introduction

As we drove south from France into Spain during the summer of 1965, Bill and I were unable to reserve a hotel room in Madrid. Everything was booked. We dug in our luggage for a particular telephone number. One call and presto! A hotel room was ours. Thus began a friendship that has lasted four decades.

We had never met Daryl and Monroe Hafter, who with their two young children were in Madrid for the summer on a research leave. That summer, Daryl was a full-time mother and Monroe a professor of Spanish Literature at the University of Michigan. Friends had given us their Madrid telephone number before we left for Europe that summer.

We dined with Daryl and Monroe the first night and every evening thereafter while in Madrid. Their wit and high spirits ensured good talk and laughter over the sangria and paella. Daryl and Monroe use language with care and precision, yet never with pretension. Both possess a rare combination of fine intellect, modesty, and ready humor.

Still recovering from a village encounter with gazpacho, we noted that all four Hafters cheerfully consumed the local cuisine without difficulty. One of my favorite memories of that week is the sight of Daryl, sitting on a bench in a shady little plaza spooning vegetable stew into the eager little mouth of six-month-old Naomi, who handled it all with ease. Three-year-old Matthew had already developed an international palate.

Expecting my first child and

Daryl, Mathew, and Naomi
in Madrid, 1965

experiencing the usual trepidation, I could not imagine living in a hotel with a baby and active little boy for an entire summer. We were new to academia and had not yet learned that young professors on research leave can be as adventurous as any outback explorer. (Indiana Jones had yet to be born on film.)

We soon discovered that both Hafters were ahead of their time in other ways. Watching this pert, attractive woman chatting in Spanish as she peeled a banana for her baby, one would not have guessed that Daryl had recently earned a PhD in Economic History from Yale University. She had completed the degree while mother to Matthew and pregnant with Naomi, commuting regularly, as work on her dissertation progressed, between Ann Arbor and New Haven.

How had she managed to do this, I wondered? In the early sixties, relatively few women, married or single, earned PhDs. Even fewer young mothers set their sights so high. Daryl's well-trained, eager intellect made the course she had charted seem natural, inevitable. She was quick to add that Monroe's support, extraordinary in a period when few men encouraged their wives to work at all, much less seek advanced degrees, made all the difference.

Many years passed before I would learn of the foundations of Daryl's exuberance, her self-effacing humor, quick mind, essential modesty, and boldness of thought. I discovered that the bubbling spring from which I assumed Daryl had sprung full-grown was a myth of my own making. In fact, she struggled for years to come to terms with her parents' mixed legacy--one that produced significant depression and required much therapy to transcend.

At the time, it seemed quite natural for Daryl to put her hard-won PhD on the shelf for eight years while she raised her children and took the homemaking arts more or less seriously. I recall our joint laughter over Daryl-the-scholar's humble admission that a tome on housekeeping was one of her most useful books and that she had read it from cover to cover. I was introduced to Tona Vitello at Daryl's table and still smile at the two unusual blends: veal with tuna, and a woman with a Yale doctorate who is also a terrific cook. Today we might still register surprise at the former, but take the latter for granted.

With Matthew and Naomi launched in school, Daryl resumed her career as teacher and scholar at Eastern Michigan University, where she is currently a professor of Economic History. She has published articles in scholarly journals, and in 1995, a book on guild women in eighteenth-century France. Daryl has discovered, for example that over five hundred women were guild masters. Her archival work contradicts beliefs of 19th and 20th century historians that women did not work outside the home until the Industrial Revolution in the 19th century. Though Daryl's writing is the product of meticulous scholarly research, much of it done in French archives, the section I read suggests it is also wonderfully readable, and rich with insight into the history of women and work.

The Hafters have returned to Spain many times for Monroe's research and Daryl's work takes her to France for months at a time. But for almost forty years, home has been an airy, pleasant house on a quiet street in Ann Arbor. Daryl and I taped her oral history in a high-ceilinged family room. From the tall windows we could see bright red tulips nodding in the cool breeze of a Michigan spring day. We drank good coffee, digressed from the matter at hand frequently, sometimes productively, laughed often, and finally repaired to the kitchen for homemade vegetable soup and thick slabs of rye bread.

Over lunch, Daryl revealed a new dimension to her life. She has been writing poetry for several years and believes it will nourish her when the rigors of historical research and writing are no longer appealing. And, she confessed modestly, "I have a new idea every day."

I was delighted by that single disarming sentence, though not surprised. As Daryl's life evolved over the next fifteen years, however, the rigors of research not only did not lose appeal, they enriched her life in unexpected ways..

Daryl Maslow Hafter
Ann Arbor, Michigan
1990, 2005

I feel when I'm doing my research, writing, and teaching, that it is religious work, because it seeks the truth. History may appear to have no relationship with religion, but I think that the effort of seeking truth, then saying it as plainly as possible, is a religious endeavor.

looking back

Much of our family lore revolved around a father who thought working too hard was just about right. He used to say to me, "You only got an A, not an A plus? What kind of grade is an A?" It made a big impression on me.

Strong Women Tell Their Stories

My father was talented and won prizes for his student work. He was proud. There's a kind of Jewish, rough way of showing pride--but still it impressed me deeply. I was a shy only child who was eager to please, and if an A+ could be earned then I did all I could to get it.

I should mention my mother too. She was a trained mezzo-soprano and wished to be surrounded by European and American art and music. My parents were both children of immigrants, who just took in this country with great appetite and appreciation for what was here. They rejected their Orthodox Jewish backgrounds completely. They'd grown up in a little community where everyone kept Kosher and couldn't imagine another way of life. So my parents rebelled.

My mother's family was impoverished. Professionals I've spoken to did not seem sympathetic to the impact of early poverty on older people's lives. But many women who were that poor were deeply affected and did not fully recover from those early psychic wounds.

Some therapists seem to have the impression that you can manage your life and choose how to be. That's ironic because they are treating people who need help precisely because they are not the way they want to be, and cannot manage their lives. Standards seem to be different when applied to the earlier generations.

My mother's father ran a little chicken market in downtown Elizabeth, New Jersey, the port where all the immigrants came in. He wasn't a wonderful businessman, but how could he be? He didn't have any money to start. Everybody around him was as poor as he.

They were tough times. Neither of my mother's two brothers went to college although one is very intelligent; I'm sure his life was blighted because he didn't get the education he needed. They went through the Depression, then their mother was injured. My mother raised the younger brothers and, of course, she wanted to protect them from every terrible thing. You could call it a dysfunctional protectiveness. Also I think there's no doubt that she had been so deprived that she couldn't help being jealous of them.

On the one hand, my mother wanted me not to have any hint of difficulty in life, and, on the other, she couldn't help being terribly jealous. She couldn't help protecting me, and she couldn't help being jealous of how protected I was. Life holds such masses of contradictions!

I was the only child of two adults with strong personalities. When I was a child, they seemed enormous to me. I've written poems about this. It was made clear early on that I had to become a professional. And there was a lot of pressure. Since I started out as a bright little kid, this seemed possible. I was reading before I went to school.

My parents had thrown off the yoke of immigrant Judaism, and they were not going to believe, or practice, the rituals. But at the same time my mother never cooked shrimp in her life!

My parents had no idea how to get along with other people. And they never learned. They were very defensive and expressed it by believing that their interests in music and art made them better than those with ordinary tastes.

My mother was a musician. She had managed to attend Juilliard. But it was difficult to give music lessons outside the school system. She would tell me, "You must have a profession, and you must also learn to iron so that you can teach the person you hire how to iron." She suffered disappointments in her profession. But she had other parts to her life: she visited the sick and the poor, and she had wonderful linguistic abilities. She talked with my grandfather in Yiddish.

Because of her early poverty, my mother had a keen sense of being wounded by the external world. Slights were magnified, and, indeed, this was one of the bonds she and my father had. They were about as sensitive as you could get. I used to think that showed how strong they were. It's only as an adult that I have begun to understand their insecurity.

It wasn't just anti-Semitism. I think it was any kind of slight, even among Jews. We knew some wealthy Jews who had mink coats, all kinds of things. My parents ostensibly weren't materialistic--they were "artistes." For them the world of art and culture was the important thing, so, of course, I imitated them.

heritage, religion, education

Part of my heritage is a love of learning and willingness to be a performer. Willingness to take on leadership comes from my Jewish heritage. I was not religious or even curious about Judaism until Monroe and I were married. I had taken great pride in being assimilated. I was glad to learn about Aristotle and Plato, never go to synagogue, and have no religious training whatsoever.

I was irritated by the rabbi at Smith College for inviting me to dinner. How dare he select me, *know* that I'm Jewish! It's mine to choose if I want to! At Smith I heard Will Herberg, the Jewish existentialist philosopher. He was an amazing person, absolutely passionate, who said, "It is your necessity, you must choose, you must *choose* to be a Jew!"

But it didn't seem to be relevant to me in the slightest until I started hearing sermons. We had a wonderful rabbi here in Ann Arbor. He used to end the Holy Day service with something from Abraham Joshua Heschel, a theologian, who, when asked what is a Jew, said, "I know where I'm going; I know from whence I came, and, in effect, I know why."

Because religion played no role in my early life, I didn't like the idea of being bound by anything. But Judaism does have a kind of generalized ethical quality: one owes certain things; one is expected to behave decently to fellow human beings whether you believe in God or not.

I feel that when I'm doing my research, writing, and teaching, it is religious work, because it seeks the truth. History may appear to have no relationship with religion, but I think that the effort of seeking truth, then saying it as plainly as possible, is a religious endeavor.

In talking about the purpose of religion, a former minister I know said, "Religion helps you to get over the little things in life that make you unhappy." In fact, I think it's just the opposite!

It's foolish for a minister to say that, but it was interesting to hear, because the main contact I have with Protestantism is discussing Western civilization and talking about the early Protestant movement and its agony, trouble, and personal anguish. I can understand that. But his teaching about feeling good and that Protestantism is the end to which all other religions were pointed, well, I didn't think so!

It's important to understand that we do not give ourselves what we have. This is hard to convey to anybody younger than we are.

I feel more religious now than I ever did. I have been writing poetry in recent years, and much of what I've written is religious. I seem not to run out of ideas.

I'm busy, and I hardly ever get to sit; services at the synagogue are rare times when one can sit and read and listen and think. I have come to value the ritual and participation in a religious community.

I grew up knowing that I would be a professional, have a career. It wasn't the career that was important but the ability to accomplish something artistic or intellectual and worth accomplishing. Making money was very low on the scale of priorities; we never talked about it. My father primarily encouraged my reading and being a good student.

Sure you were a nerd if you were studying, but that's what I did because it was so supported at home. After all, "only an A?"

My checkered elementary school career made life interesting and difficult. These were the war years. As an architect, my father looked around for defense work.

We were living in Elizabeth when I went to kindergarten. Then I went to first through third grade in Arlington, Virginia, because my father was helping to design the Pentagon. Fourth grade was in Seattle. As the war ended, my father wanted to go back to his design practice. My parents loved Seattle, but my father said, "If you want to be an architect, you have to go where you and your family are known."

So we moved back to New Jersey. I started a new school in the middle of the sixth grade; that's five schools by then. Remember the post-war housing shortage? It was so difficult to find housing that we moved up to Free Acres, a single tax colony.

Henry George was an early social reformer who tried to correct some of the blight of modern industrialized society. He developed a scheme for taxing development of housing rather than land. Land would not be taxed. He was a Utopian who wanted to enhance the life of ordinary people. In 1910, a farm owner who'd been converted to Henry George's ideas donated his farm to become a single tax colony.

It was hard to go through six different schools; I was shy and was constantly being thrust into new experiences. It was painful, lonely. I learned how to be the "new girl," but it was damaging.

And yet, I must have been a feisty little tot. I can remember how I got into kindergarten. During my preschool years we lived above stores on the edge of residential areas. My mother would take me across the street to play with two girls who were a year older. They were drafted for kindergarten but I was only four and wasn't taken in.

The school was on our block, and I would drift around with the other children. I remember playing circle games during the school recess and then must have just washed into the school after recess. They were learning to read, and, since I knew how already, I could participate. I was probably cute because I was sort of pixieish and grinned a lot. Eventually the principal called up my mother and said, "Mrs. Maslow, did you know that your child is attending school?" And, indeed, what was my mother doing while I was spending hours in school? She was typing and working as a secretary for my father.

I began to realize that there was me and there was another layer: parents and other adults. And you had to watch yourself because they didn't always like what you did; you had to be self-protective. You had to figure out how to make a liaison with them, because they were ready to scold and belittle you and put you in the corner.

At the same time, I was able to learn from the kindergarten teacher, and I tell you this not idly because it has been positive. Even at that young age, I had a notion that, yes, you react to people spontaneously, and if they don't like you, or seem unkind, you are sad. But it's useful to be able to turn your emotions off and get what they have to give you. Now, I don't know what that would be called psychologically. Smart? I don't know about that. With teachers, yes; with other people, no.

I remember a wonderful waist-level sand box; there were animals and circles to color. We learned how to cut, and how to tie shoelaces, and how to do buttons. I didn't know how because my mother did all these things for me. I mention this because I think it says something about sense of self.

One day my mother was called because I was being bad in school. So off she went to school, and what was the problem? The problem was that the lesson was how to button buttons. There were carefully created rows of buttons and rows of holes on two strips of ribbon, but the rows were not connected to a jacket or sweater. You were supposed to use these two strips and button them together, and I wouldn't do it. I am reputed to have said, "It's silly. It isn't putting anything together!"

This sense of purpose, a little bit of thumbing your nose at the authorities and saying the emperor has no clothes is at the core of me. I think it comes from my unconventional parents and from what a friend says is the fiesty two-year-old in me. Kindergarten was a wonderful year, even though you couldn't buck that teacher! Many teachers in those days were fine even if they did rap your knuckles.

I think back to age three for the "sense of self" question because I had been so hot-housed as a child. I'm sure my parents never heard of child psychology. At one point, and this is family lore, too, someone asked, "Who are you?" and I said, "I am Daryl Maslow, I am three years old, and I know everything."

That was both good and terrible because, for all the years of my life in school, I thought that I *had* to know everything. In school, I was always supposed to be studying and getting the A+ on the way to knowing everything about the subject. And, of course, you were to know it more profoundly than the teacher did, or else you haven't done the job! I think that this kind of aggrandizement is very damaging for a kid, because, after all, a child is a child. Also, note the emphasis on *know* rather than *learn*.

It's not right to convey all of this to a child; it's not in proportion, and I remain angry at my father especially for giving this unrealistic view of the world to a child. I struggled to put all of this together.

In sixth through eighth grade I couldn't tell time! Also math was overwhelming to me; I couldn't get the times tables. People would explain it again and again, and it was embarrassing because I just couldn't get it.

Except for that, academics were fun and good, so it was the social, emotional, psychological parts of life that were a little harder.

During my adolescent years, we lived in Free Acres, and I went to a regional high school by bus. Living so far from others was fine for studying on the bus but hard to get together with people or date. Learning to get along with others was very difficult.

A major challenge for me was just staying sane for all those years. I did go through a depression in my late forties, and it took a lot of time and therapy to come out of it.

I went to Smith College. The intellectual life was terribly exciting and stimulating, and it never occurred to me that I was not supposed to jump in feet first. I just took off! I still remember the first philosophy class. Since I had been raised to always stick my hand up and show off, it never occurred to me that I should shut up a little bit.

Still, it was the most wonderful experience of my young life. That's why I feel so grateful to the place.

I learned surprising things at some of the Smith reunions. Some of my classmates knitted argyle socks and played bridge (which I never learned how to do) and cut classes because that was being cool. Meanwhile I trotted off to class, because that's just what I did. Now at reunions some of those same people say: "I envy you because academic work is too hard for me now."

History and literature were fun, but novels were a little too elusive for me because they dealt with interpersonal relations that I still didn't understand. I didn't major in literature, though I was sorely tempted to major in French. After college I knew that I wanted to continue with history—there was no doubt in my mind. I never felt that I needed to take time off after commencement.

Gloria Steinem, who was in my class, has written about how sexist Smith was and how debilitating it was to the intellectual development of young women. She was speaking out of her own experience with the English Department. I didn't go to many English classes, but it's hard to believe that they were that different from mine; I never experienced any of what she described.

In fact, at the beginning of our senior year, the Dean of Students gave us a speech—they were famous for little, short pithy speeches—and she said, "This is the beginning of your senior year, and you will be tempted to fling yourself into the arms of a waiting man and let him support you. Don't do it! Don't do it! You are Smith girls, and you can make anything of your life; a Smith woman is independent. You can do anything you want."

I married one year later, but it never occurred to me that I was being shut up or shut down. Everyone around me was busy marrying their "doctor husbands." In the alumni magazines there are a lot of doctor husbands.

But the great thing about Smith was that there really was no snobbery. There were no sororities. You were competing, but everyone was in blue jeans or bermuda shorts. So it never occurred to me that there was any elite social element — putting the teacup on one knee and the cake plate on the other. I didn't have a sense of initiation into an inner circle.

mentors

I had some wonderful professors. Nellie Hoyt, head of history honors, and at graduate school Robert Lopez, in medieval history—a brilliant man and such fun to work with. I realized that they were both Jews, assimilated Jews. They resonated with me and were very influential.

And my husband has been very supportive. He's different from me, and we are opposites in many ways. I am a little wild; I have modern tastes, his are traditional. I went folk dancing and he thought it was horrible. He is a sequential thinker; that's his mental set, and it's taken me years to understand that. Also he's tactile, whereas I'm intuitive and visual, so we approach problems differently.

We're supposed to choose the opposite of our parents, and somehow we wind up with our parents anyway! But Monroe is traditional and very religious. He likes ritual, and he's sentimental. He likes to indulge himself in it, because life is fleeting so we should have rituals and dress up. I came to see that those things are meaningful, and I agreed it was important for our children to have a religious education.

Now and then I like being taken care of, but we do have a fairly egalitarian marriage. It's been interesting to see what happens in our son's home now that he's married. They share childcare, house care, and cooking.

social change

Among the social changes of the sixties and seventies, feminism certainly impressed me. My research now is women's history. I'm doing a long-range research project, writing a book about women's guilds in eighteenth-century France. I've had a number of substantial grants from the National Science Foundation, from my own University, and others that have allowed me to go several times to France for research.

Feminism has stimulated me to be dissatisfied with my lot. Wouldn't it be nice to have a lighter teaching load? But I really don't mind teaching students who need a lot of help. I work hard at making complicated things simple, and I think I'm good at it.

We have a stable marriage, thank God, so I haven't faced the problems many women have today. I'm afraid I'm not a big social action person. During the civil rights movement, I was in the library while others demonstrated. But I'm sure glad to be teaching at a university where more than lip service is given to hiring women and minorities. I would be uncomfortable in a place where this wasn't the case.

children

Having children was one of the profound experiences of my life. Oh, it was wonderful; the involvement takes you out of yourself. It helps you to appreciate your parents. I remember carrying Matthew around when he was cranky, and I thought to myself, "Why should I do this for anyone?" and then the answering wave came: "Why should anyone have done this for you?" Surprises are built into raising children.

Daryl reading a ledger in archives; Rouen, France, 1975

Strong Women Tell Their Stories

In the early years of our marriage, I finished the PhD. at Yale while living here in Michigan. We had Matthew, and I was pregnant with Naomi. I hired babysitters and flew from Michigan to Connecticut, but I can remember being pooped.

I worked part-time for a while the year Naomi was four, and I have regrets about that. Naomi was very young for her age, and my father said, "She's not ready for kindergarten. Why not keep her back a year?" And I said, "Oh, no, you do what you should do, and a child should go to school." I was really thinking that I could have another two hours a day. It was the biggest mistake. If we had kept her back, she wouldn't have been always the youngest in her class. It took her years to catch up. I should have taken his advice. I stayed home with the children for several years after that.

Since my family moved often during my childhood, I wanted our children to have a home and a block with fifty kids. And they did. This neighborhood is so nice and middle class; I love the sidewalks and the bikes and the park. There's something comforting about it to me, and I thought they would appreciate it too. We did, however, spend a lot of time in Spain while they were young so that they did feel a little as I felt as a child. But Naomi is interested in foreign cultures and has been to Israel twice. She is comfortable with European people.

Matthew reads Hebrew, and he has a nice sense of tradition and is courteous and kind to other generations. That is a good foundation.

I didn't push them toward the arts as much as I had been pushed, and I was hoping for them to have a conventional upbringing. Matthew was a clarinetist, shy and a loner. But he managed to have three other good friends; they raised each other and called themselves "the clan."

When people asked what do you want your children to do, I always said I'd like them to have a foreign language and love music, play an instrument. So Naomi has Hebrew, and Matthew plays clarinet.

work

I hope to keep working and not develop a feeling of dèja vu. It's hard to bring the same sort of interest to a thing that you've done over and over. I've never felt that I've fully accomplished what I wanted to. So I'd like to finish my work before I get old and disillusioned. For the first time, I can see that my memory is not what it was. As I go back and forth to France and try to manage both languages, there are times that I am no longer able to put my finger on the right word. I hope I don't get Alzheimer's and will stay relatively healthy and well.

Voices of the Silent Generation

My work has given me great satisfaction; writing and research are always difficult, but you are pushed along by time constraints, the mass of material, and the need to write gracefully.

I have done useful things administratively at the university. I created an oral history program, out of whole cloth. Did it without asking permission; just announced that we were having a committee meeting on Wednesday and got the people together in my department. It has been a wonderful program. I've been helpful to the Women's Studies program, though I can be a pain in the neck!

looking ahead

I thought turning fifty wasn't going to change me a bit. I would just keep going. I have a lot of energy and direction so age would not catch up with me. I was just going to keep on swimming and writing and reading, and I would just become more and more refined in my ability to do things. This is a fairy tale.

Eventually I realized that no matter how I kept going, I was not able to get out of my time. Menopause can make a big difference. It was a real watershed for me. I am a healthy person; I expect to be fine all the time. So to have the body betraying you, it's not fair! And you realize that you too will be swept along in time, and you will be diminished, assaulted, and all of these things that everyone is prey to will happen to you too.

I'm just mortal like everybody else! It has been a tremendous psychological awakening. I had the sense all year that now that I'm fifty-five, even if I write the most brilliant book in the world I will never move from where I am. That was a shock. I don't like to think about time or aging. I don't want to look at boundaries or deadlines or multiplication tables. I like to pretend I can be free of all of that. Another fairy tale!

Suddenly all this came to me, and it was horrible. I had some real downtime. I'm always going to use writing as a way of living. I had a fantasy that I will keep on swimming, that I will always feel alive and strong, and like Descartes' famous "I think, therefore I am," mine would be "I write, therefore I am," and no matter what nursing home I wind up in, it wouldn't matter because I'd be different.

I recognize that thinking because I remember that sense of self even from earliest times, understanding even in kindergarten that you had to guard yourself or you'd get in trouble. So in my fantasy I thought, oh, good, this is something I can use to good stead. But now I realize that just won't do it. I'm not talking about writing history until I drop, but pen, paper, and thinking might still get me through.

Strong Women Tell Their Stories

Ah, aging! I once thought appearance wasn't important, when it wasn't so difficult to keep it up. Now it's important! I like looking young.

My mother aged gracefully, with dark hair, and always looked terrific. She died at seventy-seven and still looked good.

I've learned that it's not good to be angry at the world. My parents would have been a heck of a lot happier in their later years if they had been able to make friends and greet life with a little less anger, more patience. Our generation has been much more fortunate in our choices, our opportunities, our lack of constraints.

I certainly would not like to get depressed again. It's terribly painful. You go through therapy and it's a back-and-forth process, and I remember it as a physically painful thing.

I am extremely grateful for two wonderful children. I am also most grateful to have a husband who puts up with me. Monroe could have been exasperated with me because there were times when I was not in good shape and could get very angry. He really has turned himself inside out: he went to France with me several times and took care of the children when I went alone.

I would like to be remembered as a wife and mother, and a historian who made a worthy contribution, opened paths in history that no one else

Daryl and Monroe, 1980

thought of. I'd like to be remembered as one who wanted to do well in her work, but was also helpful, positive, an enabler of others, and a good friend.

Postscript, 2005:

Daryl's book on 18th century French guild women was published in 1995. (See recommended reading list.) For her scholarship and her creativity, Daryl was honored with the Distinguished Faculty Award in 2000. Her department chairman said at the time, "Her research in France is in many ways revolutionizing the way we think about women in the workplace." Over the last decade Daryl has received other honors for her innovative work, including presidency of the Society for the History of Technology, an international organization of 1500 scholars. Daryl received a fellowship to research and write a second book. Monroe retired in 1995, but continued work on a book published in 2002 to considerable acclaim in Spain. Daughter Naomi is a librarian in Fort Lauderdale, and son Matthew, father of two, is a lawyer in Chicago. Of her grandchildren, Daryl says, "They are spectacular!"

LOUISE KIMBALL AMES
Recalling a Mentor

Louise Kimball Ames was a mentor unawares for me during the late nineteen-sixties. Louise, her husband, physicist Oakes Ames, and their four young children lived for six years in the Three Village area, on the north coast of Long Island. My own just-forming family was there too; my husband and Oakes were both employed by the State University of New York at Stony Brook.

To observe Louise with her three sons (and later, a daughter) was to take lessons in mothering boys. In time I, too, became the mother of three sons and a daughter. Having been raised in a female-dominated household, I needed to learn all I could from watching this strong woman deploy her abundant resources on behalf of the community and her own children. I filed those observations and continued to draw from them for years while raising my own children. Twenty-five years passed before I was able to accurately assess Louise's influence and offer gratitude.

Louise and Oakes are New England aristocrats. Both are superb athletes, fine musicians, and eager students of natural history. Both were born to families of substantial means and grew up accordingly.

During her Stony Brook years, Louise was selective with invitations to her evening musical soirees: all guests were required to perform. But daytime activities for children were open to all. Would you like to put your baby in a backpack and hold your toddler's hand for a walk along the Long Island Sound shoreline, examining sea grasses, shells and fish skeletons along the way? If so, you were welcome. Would you like to walk in the bird-rich woods adjacent to the Ames' beachfront home with Louise as skilled birding guide? Come along. Many of Stony Brook's young mothers were eager to expand their own and their children's interest in the natural world under the tutelage of this knowledgeable woman. Louise was a few years older than most of us, and a generous teacher.

Today, thirty-five years later, the small environmental center that grew from those mother-and-child nature walks has long been officially incorporated. Louise knew how to build a solid organization. The flourishing center maintained ties to university marine science programs long after its founder moved to Connecticut. Parents and children today still make extensive use of the salt marshes, pine barrens, meadows, woods, cliffs, harbors and beaches that we so eagerly explored years ago.

Voices of the Silent Generation

I was just one of the flock of young mothers to Louise. But two characteristics made her a mentor for me. First, a born teacher, who had taught school for six years before starting her own family, Louise was eager to learn, then teach anyone who shared her interests. Possessed of great curiosity, she knew how to ask the right questions about natural phenomena, the arts and sciences. She inspired students to do the same. Children were enthralled, and even city-bred adults were enriched by this happy convergence of fine teacher and coastline wonders. As a new mother, I anticipated spending many hours outdoors with my children. I would teach them to see, to listen, inquire. Which turned out to be much harder to do than it appeared...

It was not insignificant that so many of us had time for exploration of plant and animal life with our children. In that era, young faculty members were typically male, could afford to raise families on one salary, and did so. Today, most faculty wives are working, and the term faculty wife is rarely even used on most campuses.

Second, showiness for its own sake meant nothing to Louise. A home was a place to live and learn, an extension of the schoolroom, as, of course every child's home should be. Oakes and Louise owned a fine house overlooking the Long Island Sound; in spacious rooms large windows framed views of flowers and sky, sand and sea. A collection of small animal skulls next to clay figures made by the children adorned the front hall. Recorders, flutes and a grand piano were played often. Binoculars and field glasses were casually draped on hooks in the front hall, at the ready for bird watching in every season. Books were everywhere. Was there a television set in a closet, to be brought out for a rare viewing? I never saw one. Video games would have been unthinkable.

Home decor meant children's drawings, paintings and a robin's sky-blue eggshell, rescued by a child. The dining room archway supported a children's swing, with ample space to soar out into the wide center hall. (The swing was removed for adult gatherings.)

Many years later, I realized that the Ames' dining room swing had a direct descendant: the ping-pong table that graced the formal Georgian foyer at our family's official campus residence. It, too, was hidden away for social events, though left in place for student gatherings. And our television was once locked away in a cellar closet for an entire year, for "repairs." I laughed aloud as I perceived the connections and was grateful again for all I had learned from Louise about vibrant homes and youthful inhabitants.

After the idyllic Stony Brook years, Louise coped effectively with the constrained life of a college president's wife. For the fourteen years that Oakes led Connecticut College, the Ames family lived in a campus house, and watched their children leave one by one for boarding school and college. At Oakes Ames' last commencement, Louise was awarded an honorary doctoral degree for her own service to the college,

Oakes' next position imposed another adjustment: life in New York City. Meeting with Louise for the first time in twenty-five years, I found her making peace with city life, teaching English-as-second-language classes, walking the city streets for several miles each day, enjoying concerts and museums. At fifty-eight, she was making new friends and delighting in visits from her grown children. I've no doubt she soon formed a natural science group, and sighted scarlet tanagers and pileated woodpeckers the first day out in Central Park.

I had wondered about this gifted woman, who seemed, in the few years of our acquaintance, to be gliding through life on a wave of talent and good fortune. Was the will to share her bountiful resources a form of thanksgiving? Who was Louise, and what had formed her? For various reasons, there had been no opportunity for personal exchanges. My questions remained unanswered until a quarter of a century later when I sought out Louise for this project. The sad story of her own childhood was a powerful reminder that no one glides through life. However, imagination, luck, and ability, combined with love given and received, often prevail over the past, offering hope and transformation.

Louise Ames' complete oral history is not available. However, her vision for childhood and of joint education for parent and child made her a mentor for many, and as such warranted a tribute in this collection. Louise employed six years of teaching experience, her own enthusiasm, and a coastal setting, in the extra-curricular education of a whole community of children. My memories of the enrichment offered to our family are recorded above. Below are excerpts from Louise's own written recollections of those radiant years.

Louise Kimball Ames
New York City and Martha's Vineyard
1990, 2005

My child-raising practices were as different as possible from the way I was raised. The boys and I peered at ants in the sandbox, then carried home an armful of books on insects from the library. Our scholarly neighbor, Dr. Robert Cushman Murphy, whistled chickadees to his finger. How to connect boys, birds and Murphy? A friend persuaded me to organize bird walks for children with Dr. Murphy billed as star and leader. Two years later two large moon snails were painted on the door of the barn whose hayloft and stalls were transformed into office/classrooms/museum of the Setauket Science Center Inc. The May bird walks had developed into year round, "hands on" programs on beach, pond and pine barren. Mothers with babes on backs, fathers, kids all learned together.

We asked and tried to encourage such questions as, " Why? Why not? What if? Is it fair? If not now, perhaps later?"

Our shoreline house was the site for mini-Olympics and pirate birthday parties. Numbers made us move our Sunday multi-family soccer and baseball games from back lawn to a school field.

In our music/playroom as many as sixty people celebrated Christmas, all ages performing. With two other sets of Stony Brook parents we produced an annual play on Christmas Eve. Each child created costumes and scenery. Each designed, sewed and stuffed an animal.

One reason for squeezing in my flute practice and Oakes's piano before our very serious adult "salons" was to set an example for children learning piano, violin and recorder.

While I tossed leftovers into the soup, my children and their friends built block towers on the kitchen floor, played with their cat, chattered and sketched at the kitchen table. Their drawings of mountains and dragons, their poem fragments hung from all four walls. Mantis eggs hatched on the window-sill next to sea-washed skulls of voles and gulls.

Often I was offered a found gift—a flight feather, a handful of buttercups, years later a pebble from the Loire. In a more recent version, one son and his girl friend showed up last week for four days, carrying their own black bean soup and two pots of chrysanthemums.

Having children meant everything to me while they were growing up in our home. A constant challenge and delight. Now that they are adults, creating their own circles and branching paths, my view is more distant, and properly so. But if the phone or doorbell rings, or a letter arrives, my response is deep and immediate. I cherish each as a very special friend.

Conclusion

At the dawn of the turbulent sixties, many married middle-class American women who had come of age in the nineteen-fifties were at home caring for children. Time-honored mores so dictated; jobs for their husbands were plentiful and young families could manage on one income. But not all. African-American feminist historian Paula Giddings and others note that most black mothers in the fifties had children and jobs. So too, did a growing percentage of married white women, even as a "woman's place" was still believed to be the home.

Feminist activists worked vigorously to cast off the constraints with which women lived for centuries. Thanks in large part to their efforts, American women today have opportunities undreamed of in earlier times. To some young women who now take their freedom for granted, their elders' past predicament seems almost quaint.

Still, new generations serve themselves best by noting the successes and failures of those who came before. The transfer of information, however, is not automatic. Historian Gerda Lerner emphasizes that women's progress was impeded for centuries because each generation's hard-won insights were not passed on to the next. Only in the twentieth century did women begin to learn of earlier efforts on their behalf and pass on what they knew.

It may again be time to listen to older voices. Much can be learned from the life stories of women who came of age at a relatively inhospitable time yet still created productive and satisfying lives.

What can we extract from their experience? Certainly, the stories suggest the notion of "sequencing," or managing one's adult life in sections—the first focused on family, the next on career. A number of recent books and articles discuss the idea of sequencing, but it seems fair to say the silent generation introduced the pattern. Statistics and much anecdotal evidence suggest as much. Most of the stories collected here describe sequenced lives.

Other messages may lie in the personal qualities and experiences these women had in common. Foremost is the shared heritage of having been born during the Depression. As discussed earlier, men and women born between 1930 and 1940 tend to share several characteristics, not least of which is the strong work ethic inherited from their beleaguered Depression-era parents. For them, little was simple or easy, but working hard seemed almost instinctive, and is one of the few virtues of the silent generation later applauded by historians. The high value attached to productive effort runs through all the oral histories and the decade as a major theme.

Reverence for education was the norm. Most were encouraged as children to pursue their studies, the labor of youth. All possessed the intelligence, energy and health to be good students. Study habits thus formed translated into lifelong patterns of disciplined effort. Several also worked in other capacities during childhood. Gloria Lewis devoted much of her childhood to serious study of the violin. As farm children, Shirley Frye, Ruth Revels and Marilyn Lockwood worked with their parents. To support her sick father and younger brother, Sato Hashizum, age fourteen, combined school with work as a domestic. Upon arrival in the United States, Shelly Weiner became translator and guide for her parents until they learned English.

Although not all grew up with intact families, most were blessed with either loving parents or mentors who were important sources of strength; relatives, teachers, co-workers, and husbands supplied encouragement at critical moments. Marie McKeever's father taught her to love poetry. A loving, extended family provided Velma Watts with a rich and full childhood, despite Jim Crow laws and segregated schools. Vivian Shapiro's mentor recognized and deployed her gifts; and a school principal helped new teacher Shirley Frye cope with travel and life in the segregated South.

Half the women attended women's colleges and attributed some of their self-confidence to the encouragement and leadership opportunities offered at such schools. Brookings Institute scholar Diane Ravitch and others cite abundant evidence that women's colleges have long produced a disproportionate percentage of high-achieving women. Such schools account for less than five percent of all female graduates, but have produced almost half the women in Congress. Women's college graduates are more than twice as likely as their peers in co-educational schools to earn doctorates in any discipline.

Perseverance was the chief virtue cited by virtually every woman. In their fifties when the oral histories were recorded, they still followed patterns of steadfastness established as children. Although resiliency per se was not frequently cited as a central value, it was repeatedly demonstrated in the fortuitous choices made throughout life. Each evidenced the courage to cope with hardship, extract lessons from experience, and press on. Eva Weiner set an example of unimaginable perseverance, resilience and courage, by keeping her daughter Shelly alive during the Holocaust, then emigrating to a new country where their family could flourish.

Most of the women came from families with firm religious commitments, and credited family and faith for their strong moral sense. They still practice the religion of youth, though the nature and intensity of their religious practices vary widely today. Additionally, most had lived in relatively stable communities during their formative years.

The oral histories seem to suggest a connection between a solid foundation established early in life and the ability to find a suitable mate and stay in a viable marriage. Most of the women interviewed are still married to their first husbands. Several appear to be extremely happy marriages; in other cases, years of diligent joint effort held couples, hence families, together. Long-married actress Ruby Dee once said, "Don't marry for better or worse, marry for good." But not everyone is so fortunate. Indeed, some husbands of the silent generation left their wives, just as men do today. That experience is not chronicled here because most of the divorced women I sought chose from the beginning not to speak about the end of their marriages for publication. Others withdrew from the project at a later date. Their childhoods, remember, did not encourage ready self-disclosure. Understandably, women who chose to end their own marriages were more comfortable discussing the subject.

A majority of the women noted a positive relationship with their fathers as a significant source of their self-confidence and emotional stability. Though it was not a message heard by most young girls at the time, several women offered variations of, "My father told me I could do anything I set my heart on." They felt protected, but also free.

The opposite experience, growing up poorly-fathered, has particular significance for today. In recent years, the public has become acutely aware of the deleterious effects of fatherlessness on young boys. Meanwhile, it is less often noted that young girls also sustain considerable losses when a father is missing or ineffective. Sponsored by Dartmouth Medical School, a report from the Commission for Children at Risk notes that young girls growing up with unrelated males in their homes are, by a large margin, more likely to experience early puberty than girls who live with their fathers. Studies in other countries have reached the same conclusions. David Blankenhorn reports in his book *Fatherless America* that a fifteen-year-old girl who has lived only with her mother is more than twice as likely to become pregnant during adolescence as one who has lived with both parents.

Additional research reveals a pattern of fatherless girls in their early teens being impregnated by young men in their twenties. Young girls have always needed good fathers, but only recently has public discourse noted the pivotal role of a father's nurture and *protection* in the lives of daughters as well as sons.

Uniformly evident among the seventeen women was a willingness to adjust personal goals for the well-being of family. In many cases, the goals were not so much sacrificed as postponed. Not having been promised at an early age that they could "have it all," most, nonetheless, had marriage, children and careers, but in the aforementioned sequence, rather than simultaneously. The majority of those who were mothers remained at home well into the children's school years. Less pushed by the economic pressures confronting young parents today, they returned to work gradually, according to individual timetables. Not all lives worked out perfectly, or exactly according to plan, but from the vantage of their mid-fifties, and later, their late sixties, the group had few regrets.

Daryl Hafter finished her PhD in Economic History at Yale just as her second child was born. Daryl had the determination to finish Yale's doctoral program, but was also a woman of her times, and as such, remained at home until her children were in school before resuming her career as scholar and teacher. Attending to her three children until the youngest entered first grade, Doris Betts then turned to full-time writing and teaching. Gloria Van Duyne founded a business after her children were in school.

Having raised children while in their own twenties, some of the women who remained at home paid permanent career penalties. Others were able to re-enter the work force in their thirties or forties and compensate for some of the time lost. Throughout their forties and fifties they enjoyed free and unfettered commitment to careers. Ruth Revels' years of unstinting work on behalf of Lumbee Indians produced a variety of social services and a thriving Native American Art Gallery. Vivian Shapiro achieved a long-postponed goal, an advanced degree, in her fifties. I heard versions of the following comment frequently: " I enjoy my job, and my life! Now I look forward to time for family, friends, grandchildren. And just a little less work."

These women, as the silent generation in general, had more children, on the average, than today's young couples. Larger families heightened the need to stay at home. Some women possess the requisite energy and drive to voluntarily perform two full-time jobs simultaneously. Others simply do not. Of the twenty-five mothers initially interviewed, seven had four or more children, fifteen had three or more. But ten of that fifteen went on to found a business, earn a doctorate, or otherwise establish themselves professionally.

The women with the largest families, Gloria Van Duyne and Sidney Callahan, with six and seven children respectively, had sufficient health, talent and will, as well as encouragement from their husbands, to begin careers at home. Gloria, eager to apply her talent for business, was exhilarated by her work from the beginning. Sidney Callahan possessed a rare ability to shift gears rapidly: she could break up a fight, dry tears, tend a bloody knee, and return serenely to her writing while her six sons continued their strenuous activities in the next room.

The single women found rewarding careers early in adult life. Personal lives developed in ways consistent with their own natures. Long active professionally, by their late fifties most anticipated a future less controlled by work. Sato Hashizume in retirement volunteers her professional skills but cherishes her leisure and new activities. For Sister Barbara Philippart, pastoring a village in the High Andes, running a radio station and keeping guerrillas at bay were all interwoven into a seamless whole, with retirement no more than a change in locale for her work. Gay Cheney works on behalf of a cleaner environment and volunteers at a nature center for children. Virginia Seipt can at last weave a lighter producing schedule into enjoyment of New York City's myriad offerings.

Surely these seventeen women are among the people Daphne Merkin had in mind when, writing in *The New Yorker,* she offered a wise response to Freud's question about women's wishes, "Ask them one at a time!"

Their current support of the women's movement ranges from mild to ardent. Looking back, most of the women report their careers were not particularly limited by gender discrimination. Yet feminist writers and theorists have collected hundreds of stories of bias and harassment in workplaces of the nineteen-fifties.

Corporate women and female lawyers are not readily found in this age group, though they do exist. Supreme Court Justice Ruth Bader Ginsberg, a member of the first class at Harvard Law School to include women, has described the near-impossibility of finding work as a lawyer after her graduation in the late 1950s. The legal profession did not welcome women forty years ago, and these capable women were consistently turned away from the positions they sought. Only half of their law school class made careers as lawyers; others eventually chose teaching or jobs related to law.

Voices of the Silent Generation

Why did so few of the women interviewed describe such problems? They typically cited several reasons for their own lack of discriminatory experiences: first, bias against women was so deeply entrenched in language and culture that it was widely accepted as a permanent condition of life and history. Early in their careers many may not have consciously recognized discrimination; nor were all actively looking for thresholds to cross. Consciousness-raising groups would not appear until the sixties and seventies.

Too, as women coming of age in the fifties, many accepted the premise that teaching, nursing or social work was the most suitable occupation for a woman. The arts were acceptable and often connected to teaching. A born entrepreneur speaks of difficulty in discussing such interests with her father, a successful industrialist who wondered why on earth his daughter would wish to start a business of her own. For those who did pursue careers in education or health-care, the doors had long been open. Of the women profiled here, eleven taught school at some point in their lives, though nine went on to develop other careers. The five who started as musician, dancer or writer were teachers at some point, but still pursue their crafts. Seven are connected with social work or medicine.

Finally, most middle-class married women were at home raising children when the first wave of contemporary feminists took to the barricades. Later, when the homemakers did enter the work force, major battles had already been won. Additionally, many women who entered graduate school or the work force in their thirties or early forties had already survived the crucibles of marriage, home management and the raising of children. A few were initially unsure of themselves in the working world, but, recovering their confidence quickly, brought a high level of maturity and judgment to their work. (One is reminded of post WW II managers choosing to employ experienced and mature women.) Some feel that such assets may have protected them from gender-based discrimination. And again, they were often seeking employment in traditional women's arenas.

These conditions certainly did not prevent cases of gender discrimination across the country, but it is reasonable to assume that this particular group's lack of difficulty is at least in part related to the way they presented themselves. African-American Velma Watts said, "I learned early in life that I had to teach people how to treat me." And she taught them well.

Strong Women Tell Their Stories

As I finished collecting these stories it became clear that they form a composite portrait of the woman who has found a measure of equilibrium in her adult life. By equilibrium I mean that most of the great life struggles of career, marriage, and raising children have been resolved reasonably well. I learned much about what characterized such a woman and how she had arrived in her middle fifties relatively at peace.

Indeed, the apparent predictors of a satisfying life found among these women are substantiated by social science research such as *The Rimm Report* and *Hardwired to Connect,* the report by the Commission on Children at Risk. In 2004 the Commission clearly acknowledged the impact of faith, family and community on the health and well-being of the young. None of these conclusions is surprising, but we live in times that often resist common-sense notions.

These women's lives are by no means free of anxiety or challenge. Compromises and trade-offs were accepted from the beginning, whether consciously or not. For most of these women, now in their sixties and early seventies, life has yielded a message somewhat alien to current sensibilities: it is not necessary to be happy in order to persevere. Instead, happiness sometimes arrives as fortuitous by-product of intense effort.

All remain engaged with the world through their own work and volunteer activities. They are coping with late mid-life issues: health problems, adjustment to retirement, grown children and grandchildren, aging parents, retired husbands or single-person uncertainties, financial and otherwise. Life is not simple; decisions will hound them to the end. They are successful in that they navigated many years of adult responsibility, ineffable heartache, and social change. Along the way their efforts improved their own lives and the lives of those they love. Every woman brought something new into the world and a tale no one else could tell.

Clearly, the choices we make in each decade, from adolescence on, have profound implications for the decade that follows. As our forties edge into our fifties, the spectrum of infinite options we thought we owned in youth has already narrowed. There isn't much time; it slips away silently and we are often unaware that life patterns have been established, perhaps irrevocably.

During a quarter century on college campuses I talked with countless young people who sought answers in frightening times. Unmoored from traditional standards, many were unsure how to live, how to cope, which paths to follow and why. They hunger for stories of resolution.

Voices of the Silent Generation

    Women of the silent generation, older than the mothers of those young seekers, have traveled long and winding roads into a new century. The choices made in youth and the middle years served them well. Now they seem knowing and wise, and perhaps, indeed they are.

Appendix

During the years of collecting and editing the oral histories for publication I was invited to read excerpts to college and church classes, discussion groups and women's organizations. Certain questions recurred: What were your criteria for selecting participants? How did you find them? How did you gain their trust? How did you choose which questions to ask?

I had no particular ideology for selecting the women, no points to prove. However, several questions had long piqued my curiosity. The women's movement, begun in the sixties, but with its roots much earlier, is believed to have released women from their traditionally subservient roles. But what of those women who seemed able to manage their lives unusually well before the arrival of feminism? From whence came their courage, their determination and ability to overcome obstacles? What constitutes a successful life from the vantage point of the fifth and sixth decades of women's lives? These questions took hold and I began to seek women described as strong individuals. They are articulate and have made choices that led to both satisfying personal lives and rewarding work.

Women born during the Depression are members of the last birth cohort to begin their adult lives without the benefit of modern feminism or the civil rights movement. I sought strong women of that era who also represented a wide spectrum of background and experience. The collection of stories does not attempt to define or describe the typical American woman in her fifties, though I invested substantial effort in finding a cross-section of middle-class women who, aided by varying measures of good fortune, had managed their lives admirably. They had come of age in the nineteen-fifties, and were in their own fifties as we began the interviews. The project was begun in 1989; thus most of the women are now well into their sixties or early seventies. All were born during the nineteen-thirties; I did not think it important to offer individual dates of birth.

Participants were located in a variety of ways. I tapped into a wide range of acquaintances and followed many recommendations. I had access to several nationally known women but chose not to pursue those leads. Our media assures us of an ample and continuing stream of information about the famous and infamous. I preferred to hear from women with whom readers could connect more personally. Of the forty women approached, thirty agreed to tell their stories. They represent all the major regions of the country and, as mentioned above, a range of racial, religious, ethnic and socio-economic backgrounds.

Another book could be filled with stories of finding thirty women across the country and the pleasure of traveling to each city, meeting a new woman and recording her oral history. Editing and transcribing the tapes, then winnowing the group down to seventeen, was taxing, but always stimulating. It has been a great privilege to be invited into the lives of such admirable individuals.

The seventeen women offer a spectrum of life experiences. Most faced serious adversity at some point in their lives. Surely most dramatic were the wartime experiences of Sato Hashizume and Shelley Weiner, each confined for years in childhood, and each making an impressive, though protracted and difficult, recovery. Gloria Kitto Lewis's life is a story of loss and redemption: death of a much-loved husband to illness, followed by the demise of one of her three young sons. Gloria struggled to absorb and transcend great sorrow, while raising two sons and pursuing her profession.

Almost all of the women have jobs, careers, or productive volunteer work. While only three of the final seventeen made careers in education, a substantial percentage taught school at one time or another. In the late nineteen-fifties, teaching or nursing were still the primary occupations available to educated women. Since then, of course, opportunities have expanded considerably.

The range of career choices among the original thirty women also includes psychologist, television producer, flute soloist, violinist, social worker, social agency administrator, librarian, businesswoman, store owner, painter, professor, legislative lobbyist, literary agent, medical educator, city planner, novelist, poet, university president's wife, television actress and journalist.

Having identified people with the help of friends, acquaintances, newspapers and alumni offices, I sent out invitations to participate, along with several pages describing the project and the nature of the commitment. I remain deeply grateful to each woman for taking time from a full schedule to consider my questions and welcome me into her life.

"How did you gain their trust?" It was clear from preliminary conversations that most of the women were hesitant to have their life stories published. I could offer them nothing in return but assurances that their personal stories would be valuable to others. Most were persuaded by the possibility that their struggles might influence and inspire current and future generations.

Delving into one's childhood memories, recollecting stories of adolescence and early adult life involves personal revelation. It was not unusual for a woman to weep as she uncovered painful events; reliving those moments with her, I shed tears as well. There was much laughter and good womantalk too.

I struck a bargain. Participants agreed to answer the questions as fully and candidly as possible. In turn, I promised to send the transcripts of their own oral histories for editing. Few women deleted material from their transcripts; in fact, some added to their original answers.

For many, the recollection process itself was a compensation for participating in the project. Most of us love to hear stories, yet we rarely consider benefits to the teller. Because time to prepare was built into the project, most of the women reviewed their lives in ways they had not previously done, then later thanked me for imposing such self-examination on them. One was inspired to find a long-lost brother, another to begin a journal.

"How were the questions selected?" The original list of questions was written out long before the project had fully developed in my mind. I imagined myself interviewing women of my generation: what would I ask? Since many issues were of long-standing interest to me, the questions came quickly

After much reading and planning, I sent the questions and a project prospectus to several social scientists. Each made minor suggestions but basically approved the list as appropriate for the project. Several writers and historians were also consultants.

Hoping for thoughtful commentaries, I sent the questions well in advance of the oral history interviews. Each participant was encouraged to supplement the questions as she chose. I received more than I could have wished for.

No personality can be readily distilled, or easily compressed, into fifteen or twenty pages. Thus, the portraits are inevitably partial and incomplete. However, the women were so generous with their time and their reflections that I have little doubt readers will be richly rewarded.

The final edition of questions is included in these pages. I invite the reader to use the list and offer it to friends for reflection and discussion.

Oral History Questions for Voices of the Silent Generation

Looking back

What have been the major challenges of your life?

Can you reminisce a little about growing up in the forties and fifties? What left the deepest impressions?

What in your life has given you the deepest sense of pride and accomplishment? What made it possible?

Can you describe the most significant contributions of your ethnic, racial or religious heritage to your life?

What are your primary sources of self-confidence, your sense of who you are?

Who had the deepest impact on your childhood? On your adult life?

Were you inspired by any heroes or heroines?

Have certain books influenced you?

How did the social changes of the sixties and seventies affect you and/or your thinking?

What has been the role of religion in your life?

Traditional religious belief teaches that we grow through suffering. Has this been true for you?

Living, coping

What risks have you taken that have been worth taking?

Do you have major regrets; would you do anything differently a second time around?

Which personal virtues have taken you through your life?

Do you have particular talent or ability? If so, has it given focus to your life?

What have been the big surprises of your adult life? Positive, negative?

Have you ever experienced a sense of community where you lived?

Which aspects of your physical surroundings are most important to you?

Do you experience guilt over the material comforts in your life? If so, how do you handle it?

Do you have favorite sources of relaxation or recreation? Or an avocation with special significance to you?

How important have women friends been to you over the years? Are they more or less so now?

Children
What has it meant to you to have children?

Which aspects of your childhood and adolescence are most unlike the experiences of your own children?

Were your child-raising practices very different from those of your own parents?

Were there virtues or qualities you have tried especially hard to instill in your children?

Working
Were your career choices influenced by the social changes of the sixties and seventies?

Would you describe your personal and professional lives as blending successfully? If so, what explains that success?

Would you change the sequence or time-table used to pursue your working life?

What have been the major satisfactions and/or accomplishments of your work?

Looking ahead
How has turning fifty changed you, if indeed it has?

How old do you feel psychologically and emotionally?

What are you looking forward to in the next twenty-five years?

Do you have specific goals for that period? Or expectations?
What have you learned about the aging process from observing your mother's generation?

How important would you say your appearance is to you?
Are you willing to go to great lengths to enhance, preserve and protect your appearance?

What do you fear most for yourself in the next few decades?
Are there any unusual, or important aspects of your life that have not been touched on here?

Postlude
For what in your life are you most grateful?

Which, for you, are the great unanswered questions?

Acknowledgements

The project that became "Voices of the Silent Generation" spanned many years. I crisscrossed the nation several times and relied on help and encouragement from many people.

My family of origin has earned my heartfelt gratitude. My mother, Eleanor Gendron Baillet, was the first strong woman I knew. Born half a century too early, she possessed the drive and energy to lead a battalion, and to instill timeless values in her willful children. My father, Theodore Roosevelt Baillet, a high-school teacher, exemplified the virtues he taught his students. He too, was ahead of his time in many ways, not the least of which were his daily contributions to family life and household work.

Richard Baillet is as loyal a brother as one could ask for. Rich and his wife Carole create merry occasions from ordinary days. My sister and lifelong friend Diane Baillet Meakem has always inspired me with her courage and generosity. Her husband Jack Meakem regularly provides sympathy and havens of rest and recreation.

Friends provided invaluable assistance: Kathryn Beam Troxler and Mary Jellicorse are superb editors of content and copy who devoted hours to the manuscript. Steve and Catherine Popell are lifelong friends and unsparing, but loving critics. Patricia and Loren Schweninger provided counsel and comfort throughout. Literary agent Jane Gelfman offered indispensable advice and encouragement.

Each of my literary mentors inspired me with her writing, and, with her friendship stirred me to extend my reach. For their loving guidance, I am much indebted to the late poets Elizabeth Sewell and Evalyn Gill; and to the brilliant and imaginative Brenda Schleunes.

I am grateful to Mark Moore for the many hours he devoted to the arduous task of transcribing the oral history tapes. Jim Dunn gave unforgettable lessons in the art of the tenth draft, used daily. Barry Blose shed light on the long process of shaping the history section of the manuscript. Amid an ocean of information, what to omit, what to keep? He kept me on track. Martin Hester offered assistance in many aspects of manuscript preparation, not the least of which was his advice on selection and design of photographs. Bill Foster's gracefully-designed book jacket and title page invite readers into the book. His elegant graphics were an unexpected bonus for the project.

Voices of the Silent Generation

The work of several photographers illuminates the text beautifully. I deeply appreciate Susan Mullally's gift of several fine portraits. Also much appreciated are the contributions of Otis Hairston, Chris English, Robert Cavin, Mark Wagoner, Barry Edmunds, Patrick Adams and Abby Santamaria. Carlos Photographers and Moffitt Studios also provided portraits. Archivists Betty Carter and Beth Carmichael of the Women Veterans Historical Collection were most helpful, as was Dan Smith who prepared images from large World War II posters for inclusion in the book. Thanks also to Joan Williams, archivist at Bennett College. Several project participants did not have ready access to family photograph collections. Those who were able to provide images, many taken half a century ago, have enriched the book immeasurably .

In the early design phases of the project, helpful suggestions and moral support were supplied by Christina Green and Barbara Harris of the Department of Women's Studies at Duke University, and Jacquelyn Dowd Hall, Director of the Southern Oral History Program at the Center for the Study of the American South, University of North Carolina, Chapel Hill.

Vivian Bussey is housekeeper for the chancellor's residence at the University of North Carolina, Greensboro. During the early years of the project, Vivian's efficiency and good cheer guaranteed me a few quiet, protected hours a day.

I welcomed the encouragement offered by the Wachovia Competition fiction award, and an Emerging Artists Grant from the United Arts Council. Special thanks to Hope Cammareri, Bronson Cooper, Linda Gangloff, Tim Moore, Harrell and Ivory Roberts, Marilyn Rickard, Rene and Wayne Lasher, Robert and Marianne Rosthal, Michael Cauthen, Pat Bowden, Laurie White, and a group called Sanity Salad, for their continuing interest and confidence in the project. I learned much from writer Abby Santamaria who, long before I thought to, recorded a fine oral history of Shelly Weiner's experiences as a child in Poland/Ukraine.

I am indebted to the thirty women who took time from full lives to spend hours delving into their memories on behalf of a new and untested project. Beyond the final seventeen, another group of accomplished and articulate women who told their stories includes: Sally Vasse, Margaret Golembiewski, Elizabeth Fuchs, Karen Hogarth, Ramona Craniotes, Saniya Hamady, Lia Poorvu, and Peg Wagner. We were unable to record Louise Ames' complete oral history, but as she is a remarkable woman who was a mentor for me and many others, I have chosen to close the section with a tribute to Louise. I deeply regret that all the life stories could not be included in the final manuscript.

The potential length of a book of thirty oral histories imposed the necessity of selecting a smaller number of women who would nonetheless provide a wide variety of experience and background. I offer heartfelt gratitude to the final group of seventeen who so generously allowed me into their lives, took the personal risks involved in a prolonged oral history project, and remained loyal and patient as it evolved over the years.

I have been sustained by my husband and children. Our sons Chris, Colin, Kevin Moran and his wife Hope, our daughter Kathryn Moran Silberman and her husband Geoff taught me more about courage and perseverance than I dreamed was there to learn. They brought new purpose and joy to our lives. Grandchildren Ryder Moran, Claire and Sebastian Silberman, sacred gifts to the family, have provided much happy respite from solitary work.

My deepest gratitude is reserved for my husband, Bill Moran, who repeatedly assured me that I could do this when I was certain I could not. A merciless editor, he sent me back for frequent rewrites. His invitations to take long walks no doubt prevented computer-induced atrophy of brain and body. Bill's reassurance, unfailing support and endless patience made it possible to complete this long labor of love.

Barbara Baillet Moran
2005

Endnotes
The Fifties and Its Silent Generation

1. In first paragraph, the reference to "sifting through landfills" and ways of ordering the past into ten year sections is from Paul Johnson, *The Renaissance* (New York: Random House, 2000), 3. Louis Menand, "The Seventies Show," p.128 (The New Yorker, New York, May 28, 2001). Douglas Dreishpoon, Exhibit: "The Tumultous 50's: A View from the New York Times Photo Archives." Preface to catalog for the exhibit. New York Historical Society.
2. Marty Jezer, *The Dark Age: Life in the United States, 1945-1960* (Boston: South End Press, 1982), 232. Jezer offers sharp criticism of the era, his book title revealing his convictions. See also Douglas T. Miller and Marion Novack, *The Fifties: The Way We Never Really Were* (Garden City: Doubleday, 1975). William O'Neill, in *American High, The Years of Confidence, 1956-1960* (New York: The Free Press, 1986), 289-91, offers a contrasting view, arguing the nation needed time to repair itself from war and depression before it could tackle social and economic injustices.

I. WHAT IS THE SILENT GENERATION?

3. *American Women*, U. S. Government Printing Office, (Washington, DC) 1963. US birthrate sank to under 20 per 1000 in 1935, compared to a high of 33 per 1000 in 1900. See also, David M. Kennedy, *Freedom from Fear, The American People in Depression and War, 1929-1945* (New York: Oxford University Press, 1999), 857
4. Newsweek, "U.S. Campus Kids of 1953: Unkiddable and Unbeatable," Vol.42, 2 November 1953: 52-53. Ronald J. Oakley. *God's Country: America in the Fifties* (New York: Red Dembner Enterprises Corporation, 1986), 288. Norman Podhoretz, interview on C-Span, January 7, 2001
5. Robert D. Putnam, *Bowling Alone: The Collapse and Revival of American Community* (New York: Simon and Schuster, 2000), 254-255 Putnam describes a larger "civic generation,"people born between 1910 and 1940. These are men and women who participated in church, civic and social organizations at rates which began to fall precipitously starting about 1960. See also Diane Ravitch and Joseph P. Viteritti, ed., *Making Good Citizens: Education and Civil Society* (New Haven: Yale University Press, 2000)

II. GROWING UP WITH PLENTY AND PARADOX

6. Joseph C. Goulden, *The Best Years: 1945-1960* (New York: Athenaeum, 1976), 81
7. James T. Patterson, *Grand Expectations: The United States, 1945-1974* (New York: Oxford University Press, 1996), 77-81. Patterson provides a complex set of reasons for the elevated postwar birth rate, one being the varied ages of new mothers. Not just young veteran's wives, but older women who had postponed childbearing during the war, began to have children immediately after the war. He dismisses as "glib and conspiratorial" the

Strong Women Tell Their Stories

idea offered by some historians that behind the baby boom was a national effort to force women back to their homes. On the other hand, a review of some of the women's magazines suggests that motherhood to the exclusion of all else was unduly glorified by the press and popular culture.

1. innovations and daily life

8. "American Women," U. S. Government Printing Office, (Washington, DC) 1963. The percentage of (all) working married women rose from 21.6% in 1950 to 30% in 1960. Figures on women working are varied and are often used without the necessary qualifiers. Do the figures refer to women with or without children? If the women have children, are they infants or school-aged? Are the women working full-time or part-time? If part-time, is it 2 hours a week or 22? During the first half of the 20th century far more poor and working-class married women were likely to hold jobs than those in the middle-class. Thus, when the *average* woman is cited in this text, all classes are included. All of these variables should be acknowledged when statistics are quoted. Figures in the government document refer to all women and James Patterson, *Grand Expectations*, 34 refer to all working married women. Both are helpful, with their sweeping scope, as an index of acceptance for the idea of married women working at all.

9. One federal act alone generated enormous economic activity, and put people on the road. In 1956, President Eisenhower signed the Federal-Aid Highway Act; authorizing the construction of 43,000 miles of highways over the next 30 years.

2. social climate.

10. Urie Bronfenbrenner and Peter McClelland, Elaine Wethington, Phyllis Moen and Stephen J. Ceci with Helene Hembrooke, Pamela A. Morris and Tara L.White. *The State of Americans: This Generation and the Next.* (New York: Free Press, 1997), 162-184

11. All italicized anecdotes and stories are the author's reminiscences from the 1940s and 1950s

12. Joan Didion, *The White Album* (New York, Simon and Schuster,1979), 206-207

13. Interviews with Ivory Roberts, Vivian Bussey, Shirley Frye, Greensboro, NC, 1995. Interview with Mary Rhodes, Philadelphia, 1992. Interview with Velma Watts, Winston-Salem, NC, 1991. Ramona Taylor Craniotes, New York City, 1991. See also: Parker Lee Nash, "Teaching From Memory: Ida Jenkins's Life," Greensboro News and Record, 25 February, 2001: Sect. D,1. Also Lynne Olson, *Freedom's Daughters: The Unsung Heroines of the Civil Rights Movement from 1830 to 1970* (New York: Scribner, 2001)

3. stabilizing influences

14. Several books and films however, offer another view: as early as 1951 Norman Mailer's book, *The Naked and the Dead* would offer a far less heroic vision of war, as did the film *From Here to Eternity* in 1953. By 1959 European films such as *Ballad of a Soldier* and *Die Brucke* would emphasize the dread, pain and waste of war.

15. O'Neill. *American High, The Years of Confidence, 1956-1960,* 36

4. learning wariness

16. Joseph Goulden, *The Best Years, 1945-1950* (New York: Athenaeum, 1976), 264

Voices of the Silent Generation

5. a climate of intimidation

17. Joseph Goulden, *the Best Years*, 340
18. Allen Weinstein and Alexander Vassiliev, *The Haunted Wood* (New York: Random House, 1999), xxi-xxiv. The authors provide the names, along with individual Russian code names, of 57 American citizens who served as espionage agents for Russia's KGB during the Cold War. The list was found in Russian intelligence files, made available to Weinstein and Vassiliev from 1994-1996 by the former Soviet Union's Foreign Intelligence Service, now called SVR.

6. art, not action

19. The abstract expressionist movement developed in New York during the fifties, with artists such as Hans Hoffman, Mark Rothko, Barnett Newman, Robert Motherwell, Karel Appel, Franz Kline, Willem De Kooning. Sculptors Jacob Epstien and Lippold, architects Eero Saarinen and le Corbusier, Oscar Niemeyer all did some of their best work in the fifties, and Jackson Pollock introduced his unique style with "Number 12."
20. The 1920's Harlem Renaissance had earlier given wings to selected black artists and writers. Ellison and Richard Wright's *Native Son*, were widely read in the fifties, as was the poetry of Langston Hughes. Painters Jacob Lawrence, Romare Bearden and Lois Maillol Jones achieved national recognition. Lorraine Hansberry's 1958 play *Raisin in the Sun*, is still produced today on college campuses and community theatres. James Baldwin published *Nobody Knows My Name* in 1960 and went on to a distinguished career as writer and critic.
21. Mark Gavreau Judge, *If it Ain't Got That Swing:The Rebirth of Adult Culture* (Dallas: Spence Publishing, 2000). See also Dan Wakefield and Betsy Blankenbaker, "New York in the 50's," documentary film based on Wakefield's book of the same name.(New York, Avatar Films,2001). Jonathan Yardley, William O' Neill, Dan Wakefield, Tom Wolfe, Carolyn Graglia, Russell Baker, Nat Hentoff, Calvin Trillin, Lynn Sharon Schwartz, William F.Buckley, Joan Didion, Nan Talese and others have commented on the high caliber of cultural offerings during the fifties.

7."Problems have been solved."

22. Marty Jezer, *The Dark Age*, 293- 295
23. William Chafe, *Unfinished Journey*, 141. The comment was made by Seymour Martin Lipset.

8. student activism: absent and present

24. William O'Neill, *American High*, 38
25. David Brooks, "The Next Ruling Class: The Organization Kid," (The Atlantic Monthly, April, 2001: 35 Nor were they, in regard to social activism, very different from 1999 elite collegians, except that the later group is more likely to serve local communities. Journalist David Brooks interviewed Princeton students in 1999 and found characteristics virtually identical to students fifty years earlier. Among serious and ambitious students, Brooks found that commitment to studies, social service activities and career plans left little time for political activism.

26. Fred Seigel, *Troubled Journey, From Pearl Harbor to Ronald Reagan* (New York: 1984), 120. Also Patterson, 407

III. INHERITED VIRTUES

27. Paul B. Firstenberg, "A Child of the Fifties: Encountering Conflicts between Expectations and Reality," Princeton Alumni News, 5 May 1980: 29
28. Benita Eisler, *Private Lives* (New York: Franklin Watts, 1986), 78

1. stoicism, self-reliance and reserve

29. Studs Terkel, *Hard Times: An Oral History of the Great Depression* (New York: Pantheon Books, 1970), 80
30. Benita Eisler, *Private Lives*, 78
31. Ibid., 78-79
32. Norman Podhoretz, interview on C-Span, January 7, 2001
33. Eugene O'Neill's *Long Days' Journey into Night* won the Pulitzer Prize in 1957. Arthur Miller's *Death of a Salesman* was a Broadway theatre success, followed by a film in 1951, and later televised versions. Considered classics, both are still produced occasionally, and at this writing, an English cast is performing *Death of a Salesman* in Frankfurt, Germany, starring Jennifer Jellicorse.
34. John Podhoretz, "Elvis to McDonald's, a Decade Catalogued," Wall Street Journal, June 23, 2003

2. religious belief

35. Newsweek, "Religion on Campuses", Vol. 42. 2 November 1953. 53-55
36. Joan Didion, *The White Album* (New York: Simon and Schuster,1979), 206-207

3. frugality and consumerism

37. Vivian Bussey, Conversation with the Chancellor's housekeeper, University of North Carolina, Greensboro, 1990
38. Josephine Hoyt Wilson, *7ll West Main Street* (privately published, undated), 2
39. Doris Kearns Goodwin, *Wait Till Next Year* (New York: Simon & Schuster, 1997) 76-77
40. Sally Helgeson, *Everyday Revolutionaries: Working Women and the Transformation of American Life* (New York: Doubleday, 1998) 34,183

4. trusting everyone over thirty…

41. Benita Eisler, *Private Lives*, 76
42. Leonard Pitts, Lecture at Guilford College, Greensboro, N.C., September 6, 2000
43. Judith Shulevitz, "Holden Reconsidered and All," New York Times Book Review, 29 July, 2001: 23. See also George Will, "The Pouting Holden Caulfield," Washington Post, 2 July 2001. *Catcher in the Rye* was reevaluated in 2001 by a variety of critics. Will and Shulevitz, John Updike, Joan Didion and others agreed with the Cornell students, challenging Holden's position as fictional avatar of a new age for youth. Kip Kotzen and Thomas Beller, editors of *With Love and Squalor:14 Writers Respond to the Work of J. D.*

Voices of the Silent Generation

Salinger, and other readers over the years have seen Holden as a beacon of sanity in a crumbling world.

44. Jonathan Yardley, "When Best Sellers Weren't the Same," Washington Post and Greensboro News and Record, 5 December, 2001: Sect. A, 17. In a single day, Feb.2, 2002, The New York Times featured the following: a full page article on the enduring qualities of *To Kill a Mockingbird*, advertisements for a new production of *The Crucible*, and for concerts by Joan Baez and the great cabaret singer Barbara Cook, an obituary of Harold Russell, the star of "The Best Year's of Our Lives," references to Patsy Cline and to Dylan Thomas's 1952 recording of "A Child's Christmas in Wales." All were cultural products of the fifties, still in the news in 2002. The city of Chicago in 2002 chose *Mockingbird* for its all-city read, and a revival of Rodgers and Hammerstein's *Oklahoma* opened in New York in 2002.

45. Joseph Pearce, "True Myth: The Catholicism of The Lord of the Rings," Vol.11, no.11, Catholic World Report, December 2001: 34. Pearce cites a poll of England's 50,000 member Folio Society, and other polls by booksellers and readers, in which Tolkien's book is not only selected as the favorite book of the century but Tolkien himself as the greatest writer. Auden quotation is from Julia Keller, Chicago Tribune and Greensboro News and Record, 12 Dec. 2001: Sec.D, 2. Many critics such as Edmund Wilson, Harold Jacobson and Griff Rhys Jones reviled the trilogy as mere fantasy. By 2002 larger numbers of academic critics began to agree with Auden.

46. Ralph Ellison, *Invisible Man*, (New York, Random House, 1952) 237,153

5...or not

47. Published in 1950, *The Lonely Crowd:A Study of the Changing American Character*, was the rare scholarly book that found wide readership. The book was written with Reueal Denney and Nathan Glazer but Reisman's name alone is usually associated with it. Vance Packard is best known for two popular books for lay readers: *The Status Seekers* and *Hidden Persuaders*.

48. Fred Chappell, "Jack Kerouac's Moonshine and Cocktails," Raleigh News and Observer, 16 April,1995: Sect.B, 5

49. Julie Salomon, "Setting the Stage for the 60's," New York Times, 31 May, 2000: sect. B, 3

5. sexual mores: inherited but changing

50. Enid Haupt, The *Seventeen Book of Young Living* (New York:David McKay,1957), 155-56

51. Brett Harvey, *The Fifties: A Women's Oral History* (New York: HarperCollins, 1993). Also, Elaine Tyler May, *Pushing the Limits: American Women 1940-1961. (New York: Oxford University Press,1994,) 135*. May refers to "devastating sexual mores" of the fifties in her book for high school students, implying that current mores represent improvement. Wini Breines, Germaine Greer, and the majority of other feminist writers and historians consider the postwar era and the fifties to be a period of unhealthy sexual repression. Emerging in the 90s, however, a new group of young feminist writers such as Rene Denfield, Wendy Shalit, and Danielle Crittenden disagree with feminists of the 70s and 80s. As they assess high divorce and illegitimacy rates, increased child abuse and abandonment and higher rates of sexual activity and STDs among pre-teens, these and other writers urge a rethinking of current sexual mores.

Strong Women Tell Their Stories

52. Paul B. Firstenberg, *A Child of the Fifties: Encountering Conflicts between Expectations and Reality,* Princeton Alumni News, 5 May 1980: 26 Anecdotal evidence and reports from a variety of memoirs support Firstenberg's story. Literature of the time, however, is filled with protagonists who ignored such rules. Films, being censored at the time, were highly circumspect about sexual matters.

53. Jonathan Gathorne-Hardy, *Sex the Measure of all Things: A Life of Alfred C. Kinsey* (Bloomington: Indiana University Press, 2000) and James Jones, *Alfred C. Kinsey: A Public/Private Life,* 1997. The two biographies offer contradictory views of Kinsey's work. Kinsey's *Sexual Behavior in the Human Male* (Philadelphia and London, 1948) and *Sexual Behavior in the Human Female* (1953) were pioneering efforts to report on the sexual practices of American men and women. Both reports surprised the public with statistics suggesting a huge gap between social façade and actual practices, that more pre-marital and extra-marital activity took place than previously acknowledged. The latter book suggested a higher intensity to female sexual experience than understood before.

Jones' book repudiates Kinsey's work, and reveals serious problems with Kinsey's sampling methods. For example, Kinsey reported that "homosexuality was most common among men who do not go beyond high school, and least common among college graduates."(Kinsey p. 610) But it was later discovered that Kinsey found most of the gay men he interviewed in prisons or bars. Jones also reports that professional statisticians had warned early on that Kinsey's methods in general were not representative of the population.

Gathorne-Hardy gives Kinsey high marks for his original work on a hitherto unreported subject, and suggests the charges of selection bias were excessive. Regardless of criticism, the Kinsey Reports have long been credited with opening the gates to the sexual revolution that followed. Margaret Mead's now-discredited report on adolescent sexuality, *Coming of Age in Samoa,(1928)* is another building block of the sexual revolution revealed in later years to be unreliable.

54. Urie Bronfenbrenner, Peter McClelland, Elaine Wethington, Phyllis Moen, Stephen J. Ceci with Helene Hembrooke, Pamela A. Morris and Tara L.White. *The State of Americans: This Generation and the Next.* (New York: Free Press, 1997), 91-121

55. Dr. John Rock. I was privileged to have several private conversations with Dr. Rock throughout the spring of 1963. Boston, Mass.

56. Barbara DaFoe Whitehead, *Modern Sex:Liberation and Its Discontents,* ed. Myron Magnet, (New York, Ivan R. Dee, 2001) see also Whitehead,"Dan Quayle was Right,"(The Atlantic Monthly, 1993:47-84. The article is widely credited for changing the national conversation about unmarried motherhood, and its effects on children. See also Canadian writer Meghan Cox Gurdon,"Modern Sex,The Legacy of the Sexual Revolution," Wall Street Journal, 25 October 2001: sect. A,18

IV. MUSIC FOR A NEW ERA

1. rock n' roll

57. The same disconnect from the adult world made a strong anti-war movement possible. As the nation became more deeply entangled in the disastrous war in Vietnam, the social and political distance between young and old gradually became a separate disaster in its own right. That large subject takes us out of the fifties and will not be covered here.

58. Played in the rural South, New Orleans, St. Louis, Harlem, Detroit, Chicago and dozens of other towns across the country, these strains by the late 40s and early 50s had

Voices of the Silent Generation

fused into race music. Major record companies released white versions (called covers) of songs originated by black artists. In l951 Freed's enthusiastic white audiences were the first to hear Freed call race music "rock and roll,"a phrase already used by black musicians.
59. Ronald J. Oakley. *God's Country: America in the Fifties* (New York: Red Dembner Enterprises Corporation, 1986), 271-272. Promptly named the Nabob of Sob, Ray stirred near riots among frenzied young females. Not since the reign of Frank Sinatra in the forties had a singer needed police protection from fans.
60. Teenagers in American and European movie theatres jumped up and danced in the aisles when "Rock Around the Clock" was heard in the film. Riots broke out and property was damaged; parents, teachers and town officials held anxious meetings Younger singers such as Fabian, Rick Nelson, Bobby Rydell, Frankie Avalon, Bobbie Darin became teen idols who were themselves teenagers. With few exceptions, women had not yet been welcomed to rock music.
61. Presley's initial hits included "Heartbreak Hotel," "Don't Be Cruel," "Love Me Tender," "Blue Suede Shoes." While critics and parents reviled Presley for his bumps and grinds, teenagers propelled his career. They gave him fourteen consecutive million-seller records between l956 and l958. He made 38 gold records, thirty movies and built a multi-million dollar souvenir business. No entertainer had ever exploited his talents in so many directions at once. Life Magazine complained that Presley incited young girls to hysteria and tears.

2. but not for all…

62. Kathryn Beam Troxler, unpublished memoir, 2002
63. John Cohen, "There is No Eye", an exhibit and CD-Rom of photographs taken by Cohen, founder of the New Lost City Ramblers, starting in l948 and continuing throughout the years that he collected music in Kentucky, Harlem and Peru. The exhibit toured the country in 2002. John Cohen created the term "high, lonesome sound," to describe the astonishing music he heard in unexpected places during the late 40s. Roots music gained recent nation-wide popularity when the soundtrack of the 2001 film "O, Brother Where Art Thou" introduced it to a new audience, more than fifty years after Cohen began collecting.

V. RACE, ETHNICITY AND CIVIL RIGHTS

1. postwar ethnic issues

64. Two other films of the 40's, "Valley of Decision", and "Kitty Foyle," for which Ginger Rogers won the 1940 Academy Award, depict additional ethnic prejudices. Both films portray heroines of working-class Irish descent whose marriages to upper-class men were unthinkable. The country had progressed beyond "No Irish Need Apply" signs in store windows, but intermarriage across class and ethnic boundaries was not yet acceptable.
65. Mei T. Nakano, *Japanese American Women: Three Generations 1890-1990* (Berkeley and Sebastopol: Mina Press Publishing, and San Francisco: National Japanese American Historical Society, 1990). Also interview with Sato Hashizume, (San Fransisco, 1991)
66. Richard Rodriguez, *Days of Obligation: An Argument with My Mexican Father(*New York: Penguin Books, 1992). The New York-Puerto Rican hybrid literature known as Nuyorican thrives in New York City. The 2001 film, "Pinera," celebrates the movement's

Strong Women Tell Their Stories

founder. Actors Hector Elizondo, Jimmy Smits, Jennifer Lopez, John Leguizamo, James Edward Olmos and others are nationally known, as are a host of musicians. Linda Chavez was considered for a national cabinet post and numerous others with Hispanic surnames are now active in politics. Poets Mark Smith-Soto and Pepe Sanchez-Boudy are widely published and respected.

2. black members of the silent generation: civil rights vanguard

67. William O'Neill, *American High*, 18-23.Well beyond the first half of the century, segregation of all public facilities was legally sanctioned throughout the South. Jim Crow laws and their enforcers provided daily humiliation to black citizens. Fair trials were unlikely and persons of color had virtually no voice in politics. Racial prejudice, restricted jobs and housing were also endemic for blacks across the nation. By 1950 median family income among whites had risen to $6405; for blacks the figure was $3449.The forties and fifties saw almost three million blacks migrate from the South looking for better jobs in industrialized cities such as Chicago, Detroit and New York, cities ill-equipped to house them or educate their children

68. William O'Neill *American High*, 246.

69. Virgil T. Blossom, *It Has Happened Here* (New York: Harper and Row, 1959) see also, Benjamin Muse, *Ten Years of Prelude: The story of Integration Since the Supreme Court's 1954 Decision* (New York, Viking Press, 1964), See also Ronald J. Oakley. *God's Country: America in the Fifties* , 200

70. Lynne Olson, *Freedom's Daughters, the Unsung Heroines of the Civil Rights Movement from 1830 to 1970* (New York: Scribner, 2001). JoAnn Robinson, a professor at Alabama State College, had written to the mayor in 1954 threatening a boycott. As president of the Women's Political Council, an organization for black professional women, she was ready for this moment. Robinson and a few helpers spent the night in the mimeograph room of her college printing, folding and bundling 35,000 fliers. "We urge the women of Montgomery to support a one-day boycott of all city buses on Monday, December 5, 1955." That morning aided by Council members, Robinson supervised distribution of the fliers throughout the black community. If Martin Luther King's words later inspired his audience, it was Professor Robinson's foot soldiers who earned support from the women who would walk to work for over a year. Ms. Robinson was relieved that Monday morning to watch one empty bus after another roll by. The bus boycott had begun.

71. The six women and three men who endured national scrutiny and local harassment all went on to lead successful lives. They created the Little Rock Nine Foundation to help young black students today. The group was interviewed on NBC television's "Today Show" on February 2, 2002. While all agree they are grateful for the opportunity they had to serve, their comments about that year in Little Rock High School were revealing. Minnejean Brown: "It was pure hell the entire year," Jefferson Thomas: "I came from a home where I was loved. It was terrifying to feel hated." Ironically, one of the three men, Dr Terence Roberts, now a desegregation consultant for the Little Rock Public Schools, confirms that the task is not finished yet. The other participants were: Thelma Mothershed, Elizabeth Eckford, Melba Patillo, Ernest Green and Carlotta Walls.

72. Personal conversations with Joanne Smart Drane of Raleigh, North Carolina. Discussions with Ms. Drane took place between 1989-1995 in the Alumni House of The University of North Carolina at Greensboro.Their portraits are included in a campus mural and in 1992 a parlor of their dormitory was named for Ms. Drane and the late Bettye Ann Davis Tillman. Ms. Drane, a state government official, spoke at the dedication ceremony.

Voices of the Silent Generation

73. Miles Wolff, *How it All Began: The Greensboro Sit-ins*, (New York: Stein and Day,1970) 167, 176. Originally published as *"Lunch at the 5 and 10"*
74. Hal Seiber, "The 1960 Sit-In Victory: Why Here?" The Greensboro News and Record, 30 Jan.2000: sect.H,3. Among the leaders negotiating with the city for an end to the "sit-down" and segregated eating facilities were Chancellor Louis Dowdy, Dr Hobart Jarrett, activist Ed Zane. Ralph Johns never received the credit he deserved. Through friendship and editorials in a black newspaper, the *Champion*, he encouraged young black men to take action.
75. Teresa Annas, "Taking Her Seat," Greensboro News and Record, 5 Feb. 2001: Sect.B, 2. Life-sized bronze sculptures of the four men were unveiled in February, 2002 on the campus of North Carolina Agricultural and Technical University at Greensboro, N. C.
76. Miles Wolff, "*How it All Began: The Greensboro Sit-ins*," 167
77. It is not accidental that the Civil Rights Movement ignited and captured national attention at exactly the time that television producers perceived that the "the seductive urgency" of television made riveting news stories. Martin Luther King grasped early on the usefulness of television for his cause and soon began planning his announcements and actions in time to make the evening news.

VI. "WE NEVER KNEW WE WERE A GENERATION"

78. Jessica Less and Kathy Keily, "New Senate, House Feature Record Number of Women," USA Today, 19 December, 2000: Sect. A, 6. Also Rena Pederson, "Historic Moment for Nation," Greensboro News and Record, 5 February, 2002: Sect.A,7. Of approximately 12,000 members of Congress in U.S. history, 209 have been women. Of the 435 House members 62 are women, up from 19 in 1980. In the same interval the number of women in the 100 member Senate has risen from 2 to 13.
79. Wade Green, "Fiftysomething, and in Charge," New York Times, 2 January 1990: Sect.A, 2

Historians and Sociologists

The following were consulted for information and insight into the fifties. For books in which a single subject was investigated, that subject has been noted.

William O'Neill, in *American High, The Years of Confidence, 1956-1960* (New York: The Free Press, 1986)
Marty Jezer, *The Dark Age: Life in the United States, 1945-1960* (Boston: South End Press,1982)
Douglas T. Miller and Marion Novack, *The Fifties: The Way We Never Really Were* (Garden City: Doubleday, 1975).
Ronald J. Oakley. *God's Country: America in the Fifties* (New York: Red Dembner Enterprises Corporation, 1986)
Robert D. Putnam, *Bowling Alone: The Collapse and Revival of American Community* (New York: Simon and Schuster,2000) On social capital.
Joseph C. Goulden, *The Best Years: 1945-1960 (*New York: Athenaeum, 1976)
James T. Patterson, *Grand Expectations: The United States, 1945-1974* (New York: Oxford University Press, 1996)
Brett Harvey, *The Fifties: A Women's Oral History* (New York: HarperCollins, 1993). also Elaine Tyler May, *Pushing the Limits: American Women 1940-1961 (New York: Oxford University Press,1994)* On changing conditions for women.

Strong Women Tell Their Stories

Lynne Olson, *Freedom's Daughters, the Unsung Heroines of the Civil Rights Movement from 1830 to 1970* (New York: Scribner, 2001) On women and civil rights.
Virgil T. Blossom, *It Has Happened Here* (New York: Harper and Row, 1959). Also Benjamin Muse, *Ten Years of Prelude: The story of Integration Since the Supreme Court's 1954 Decision* (New York, Viking Press, 1964). Also Miles Wolff, *How it All Began: The Greensboro Sit-ins* (New York: Stein and Day,1970) On the civil rights movement.

Other writers consulted for this introduction may be found in the recommended reading list.

VII. WOMEN OF THE SILENT GENERATION

80. Eugenia Kaledin, *Mothers and More: American Women in the 1950s* (Boston, Twayne Publishers, 1984), 1 (Preface). Kaledin offers a positive interpretation of women's lives in the fifties. The majority of contemporary historians primarily assess negative aspects of those lives, citing numerous examples of institutional prejudice against women, the low-paying jobs women held after the war, the declining numbers of women doctors and lawyers and the 5 percent quotas on female admissions imposed by medical schools. Additionally, almost 3/4 of all hospitals refused to accept women interns.
81. Alexis de Toqueville, *Democracy in America,* translated by George Lawrence, edited by J. P. Mayer (New York: Harper & Row, 1966) 603, 592-4
82. American Women (Washington, D. C.:U.S. Government Printing Office, 1963) William O'Neill in *American High*, 43 and William Chafe, *The Unfinished Journey, 126* and other historians give approximately the same figures.
83. Robert Putnam, *Bowling Alone: The Collapse and Revival of American Community* (New York: Simon and Schuster,2001). See also: Mary Jo Festle, "We Deserve to Know Women's Stories," Greensboro News and Record, 4 March, 2001: Sect. H,1. Festle describes a new phase of women's history in which women's whole lives are studied, rather than just oppressive conditions. Also, journalist Brett Harvey, in her book, *The Fifties: A Women's Oral History (*New York, HarperCollins, 1993) was surprised by the strength she found in the women she interviewed and admired their strategies for coping with discrimination. Numerous other books echo the same themes.
84. National Manpower Commission Reports, funded by a grant from the Ford Foundation. (Columbia University, 1957). See also, Eugenia Kaledin, *Mothers and More: American Women in the 1950s*, (Boston, Twayne Publishers, 1984), 2 (Preface and Ch. I).
85. Mary McCarthy, "The Vassar Girl," in *On the Contrary*: *Articles of Belief 46-61* (New York; Farrar, Straus & Cudahy, 1962), 210; first published in Holiday Magazine, 1946-1961. McCarthy was describing her ideal educated woman.

1. American women, work and World War II

86. Charity Adams Earley, *One Woman's Army (*San Antonio: Texas A&M Press, 1989*)* see also, Richard Goldstein, "Charity Adams Earley, Black Pioneer Dies at 83" New York Times, 22 January, 2002: Sect. A,1. See also, Gail Buckley, *American Patriots* (New York: 2001)
87. Newsweek, 21 May, 1951:23. Newsweek's cover story was on Col. Hallaran.
88. Kristine Lacy and Colin Gray, Prospectus for documentary film, "The Women of Willow Run," produced by Gray and Lacey of Wolo Entertainment, Hollywood, Calif. Registered WGA West, March 10,2000. See also Stephen E. Ambrose, *The Wild Blue: The*

Voices of the Silent Generation

Men and Boys Who Flew the B-24s Over Germany (Simon & Schuster, New York, 2001) See also "Fly Girls," documentary film, shown on Public Television, Fall, 2001. "Fly Girls" celebrates the female pilots who flew fighter planes from factories to the front in Europe. Also, Julie I.Englund, "Why Won't Arlington Honor Female Pilots?" Washington Post, 19 May, 2002: Sect. H,4

2. postwar years

89. A hangar the old Willow Run factory now houses the Yankee Air Museum. B-24 bombers are maintained by WWII veterans and are flown for exhibitions several times a year.
90. Cynthia Harrison, *On Account of Sex: The Politics of Women's Issues, 1945-1968* (Berkeley, 1988), 4-5.
91. William Chafe, *The American Woman: Her Changing Social, Economic and Political Roles, 1920-1970* (New York: Oxford University Press, 1972) 218
92. Claudia Goldin, *Understanding the Gender Gap: An Economic History of American Women* (New York: Oxford University Press, 1990). Goldin offers statistics on working women beginning in 1900 and continuing through most of the century.

3. stirrings in the 1950s

93. Life Magazine, 16 June, 1947: 107-115
94. Simone de Beauvoir, *The Second Sex* (New York, Alfred A Knopf, 1952),vii.
95. Not all young women accepted conventions of the time. A host of popular writers and feminist scholars offer eloquent testimony to the dissatisfaction felt by many women of the fifties, especially intellectually gifted, middle-class white women. Among the carefully-documented books are: Wini Breines,*Young White and Miserable: Growing Up Female in the Fifties* (Boston: Beacon Press, 1992).Stephanie Coontz, *The Way We Never Were: American Families and the Nostalgia Trap*(New York: Basic Books,1992).Betty Friedan, *The Feminine Mystique (New York, Dell Publishing Co.,1963)* Among the many books on the same subject by journalists: Benita Eisler, *Private Lives: Men and Women of the Fifties* (New York, Franklin Watts, 1986). Also Brett Harvey, *The Fifties: A Women's Oral History* (New York, HarperCollins, 1993) While lamenting the condition of women, Harvey also admired the resilience and purposefulness of the women she interviewed.
96. Robert Coughlan, *"Changing Roles in Modern Marriage"* Life Magazine, Dec.24, 1956:109, Coughlan's article is subtitled "Studying Causes of Our Disturbing Divorce Rate, Psychiatrists Note Wives Who Are Not Feminine Enough and Husbands Not Truly Male." Coughlan went on to say, "The emerging American woman tends to be assertive and exploitative. The emerging American male tends to be passive and irresponsible." Others, such as Ferdinand Lundberg and Marynia Farnham wrote similarly a decade earlier in their widely-read book, *Modern Women: The Lost Sex* (New York, 1947) and reiterated ideas of female unsuitability to the world beyond home.
97. *Life* Magazine, Dec. 24, 1956. The entire issue was devoted to the subject.
98. Gwendolyn Wright, Building the Dream" A Social History of Housing in America (New York: Pantheon Books, 1981), 256

4. welcome to the sixties...

99. Betty Friedan, *The Feminine Mystique* (New York:W.W.Norton & Co.)1963

Strong Women Tell Their Stories

100. Lucy Freeman, Review of *The Feminine Mystique*, New York Times, 7 April, 1963
Alan Wolfe, "The Mystique of Betty Friedan," Atlantic Monthly, September, 1999:102-109

Interviews
(1) Marcy Gray, Ann Arbor, Michigan, telephone interview, September 19, 2000. Letters, October, 2000.
(2) Mary Rhodes, Interview, Philadelphia, Pennsylvania, May, 1991
(3) Vivian Bussey, Interview, Greensboro, North Carolina, April, 1989

Historians and Sociologists
Writers consulted for this section include:
Eugenia Kaledin, *Mothers and More: American Women in the 1950s* (Boston, Twayne Publishers,1984). Kaledin offers a comprehensive view of women of the fifties, citing particularly their ability to find useful work within the restrictions of the time. Kaledin also provides brief sketches of women who distinguished themselves in science and medicine, social work and education, academia, the military, journalism and photography and the arts.

Simone de Beauvoir, *The Second Sex* (New York, Alfred A Knopf, 1952)p.vii. Mlle. De Beauvoir's central thesis is that women's subjugation does not spring from inherently 'feminine characteristics' but is imposed by men wielding power over educational and social traditions.

Sheila Tobias, *The Faces of Feminism: An Activist's Reflections on the Women's Movement* (Boulder: Westview Press, 1997) provides a thorough assessment of the feminist movement from its earliest days in the sixties, when she was herself an ardent participant, through its many stages to the present.

Marty Jezer, *The Dark Ages, Life in the U. S. 1945-1960* (Boston: South End Press,1982) Jezer provides a sympathetic review of the early stages of family fragmentation during the fifties, and a generally bleak view of the decade.

William Chafe, *Women and Equality: Changing Patterns in American Culture* (New York: Oxford University Press, 1977). Also by Chafe:*The Unfinished Journey: America Since World War II* (New York: Oxford University Press, 1984) and *The Paradox of Change: American Women in the 20th Century* (New York: Oxford University Press,1991) In each book Chafe provides extensive information on working women as well as particularly sensitive interpretations of the evolution of women's roles in American life after WWII.

Jean Bethke Elshtain, *Power Trips and other Journeys: Essays in Feminism and Civil Discourse* (Madison:University of Wisconsin Press, 1990) In this and other books, ethicist Elshtain provides a humane, collaborative approach to the polarizing elements in civic life. She also notes the need for society to acknowledge the family as essential to a functioning democracy.

Phyllis Moen, *Women's Two Roles: A Contemporary Dilemma* (Westport,Auburn House, 1991) Moen discusses the need for society to support mothers in the work force, and the dilemma faced by families as women work without such support.

William O'Neill, *American High: the Years of Confidence, 1945-1960* (New York: Free Press, 1987) O'Neill's thesis, that the challenge of wartime recovery caused the nation to postpone addressing women's subjugation until the late fifties is at odds with Jezer's dark age view.

James Patterson, *Grand Expectations,The United States, 1945-1974*. (New York:

Voices of the Silent Generation

Oxford University Press, 1996) Patterson's superb history provides an insightful treatment of women's work during the war and its aftermath.

Elaine Tyler May, *Homeward Bound: American Families in the Cold War Era* (New York: Basic Books, 1988) May describes the pressure during the fifties for women to remain within the confines of home and family. She sees parallels between the insecurities of the Cold War and pressures on women to mold themselves to fit an ideology she finds reprehensible.

Gerda Lerner, *The Creation of the Feminist Consciousness,* (New York: Oxford University Press, 1993) Lerner delves into ancient cultures and religions in a comprehensive investigation of man's domination of women, and the unique responses to patriarchy by women in many societies. She emphasizes the need for women to learn the history of past feminist efforts in order to progress in their own times.

Lynne Olson, *Freedom's Daughters: The Unsung Heroines of the Civil Rights Movement from 1830 to 1970* (New York: Scribner's, 2001) Olson traces efforts by black women, and a few white women, from the time of enslavement on, to improve conditions for themselves and others.

Paula Giddings *When and Where I Enter: The Impact of Black Women on Race and Sex in America* (New York: Bantam Books, 1984) Giddings offers a piercing analysis of the sharp differences between white and black women in America, with particular emphasis on black women's struggle against the twin tyrannies of racism and sexism.

Robert Putnam, *Bowling Alone: The Collapse and Revival of American Community*, (New York: Simon and Schuster,2001) Putnam describes the social bonds that connected people to one another and their communities in the fifties and earlier, (he calls those born from 1920 to 1940 the "civic generation") and compares those bonds to the seriously frayed social capital of the late 20th century. He sees reason to hope for improvement in the 21st century, however.

Ann Dally, *Inventing Motherhood: The Consequences of an Ideal* (New York: Schocken Books). British psychiatrist Dally emphasizes the importance of careful reflection as women make choices regarding home, family and work, and sees few simple solutions to these now-familiar dilemmas.

Other writers whose work was helpful in preparing this material can be found on the recommended reading list.

Recommended Reading List

Memoir, Biography and Oral History

Baker, Russell. *Growing Up.* New York: St. Martin's Press, 1982
Bateson, Mary Catherine. *Composing a Life.* New York: A Plume Book, 1990
Boxer, Senator Barbara with Nicole Boxer. *Stranger in the Senate: Politics and the New Revolution of Women in America.* Washington, DC: National Press Books, 1994
Brokaw, Tom. *The Greatest Generation.* New York: Random House, Inc., 1998
Buckley, William F. *Miles Gone By: A Literary Autobiography.* Washington: Regnery Publishing, Inc., 2004
Carter, Rosalyn. *First Lady from Plains.* Boston: Houghton Mifflin, 1984
Cary, Lorene. *Black Ice.* New York: Alfred A. Knopf, Inc., 1991
Cleage, Paula. *Mad at Miles: A Black Woman's Guide to Truth.* Southfield, Michigan: The Cleage Group, Inc., 1993
Coles, Robert. *The Call of Stories.* Boston: Houghton Mifflin, 1989
____ and Jane Hallowell Coles. *Women of Crisis: Lives of Struggle and Hope.* Reading: Addison-Wesley Publishing Company, Inc., 1978
Conway, Jill Ker. *True North.* New York: Alfred A. Knopf, Inc., 1994
____. *When Memory Speaks: Reflections on Autobiography.* New York: Alfred A. Knopf, 1998
____. *The Road from Coorain.* New York: Vantage Books, A Division of Random House, 1990
____. *Written by Herself: Autobiographies of American Women: An Anthology.* New York: Vintage Books, A Division of Random House, Inc., 1992
Day, Dorothy. *The Long Loneliness: The Autobiography of Dorothy Day.* San Francisco: Harper & Row Publishers, 1952
Delaney, Sarah and A. Elizabeth Delaney with Amy Hill Hearth. *Having our Say.* New York: Dell Publishing, A Division of Bantam Doubleday Dell Publishing Group, Inc., 1993
D'Este, Carlo. Eisenhower, *A Soldier's Life.* New York: Henry Holt & Co., 2002
Dillard, Annie. *An American Childhood.* New York: Harper & Row Publishers, 1987
Dinnerstein, Myra. *Women Between Two Worlds: Midlife Reflections on Work and Family.* Philadelphia: Temple University Press, 1992
Disher, Sharon Hanley. *First Class Women Join the Ranks at the Naval Academy.* Annapolis, Maryland: Naval Institute Press, 1998

Dudley, Joseph Iron Eye. *Choteau Creek, A Sioux Remembrance.* Lincoln: University of Nebraska Press, 1992

Gates, Jr., Henry Louis. *Colored People: A Memoir.* New York: Alfred A. Knopf, Inc., 1994.

Goodwin, Doris Kearns. *Wait Till Next Year.* New York: Simon & Schuster, 1997

Graham, Katherine. *Personal History.* New York: Vintage Books, A Division of Random House, Inc., 1998

Haizlip, Shirlee Taylor. *The Sweeter the Juice: A Family Memoir in Black and White.* New York: Simon & Schuster, 1994

Heilbrun, Carolyn J. *Writing a Woman's Life.* New York: Ballantine Books, 1988

Hoopes, James. *Oral History.* Chapel Hill: The University of North Carolina Press, 1979, 1987

Horn, Miriam. *Rebels in White Gloves: Coming of Age With Hillary's Class—Wellesley '69.* New York: Times Books/Random House, 1999

Howard, Susan, Carol Anderson and Sonia Dimidjian. *Flying Solo: Single Women in Midlife.* New York: W. W. Norton & Co., 1994

Ives, Edward D. *The Tape-Recorded Interview: A Manual for Field Workers in Folklore and Oral History.* Knoxville: The University of Tennessee Press, 1974,

Kenneally, James J. *The History of American Catholic Women.* New York: Crossroad, 1990

Kirkpatrick, Jeanne. *Political Women.* New York: Basic Books, 1974

Koppelman, Susan. *Two Friends, And Other Nineteenth-Century Lesbian Stories by American Women Writers.* New York: Penguin, 1994

Lamott, Anne. *Bird by Bird: Essays on Writing and Life.* New York: Pantheon Books, A Division of Random House, 1994

L'Engle, Madeleine. *The Summer of the Great-Grandmother.* New York: United States Journal, 1974, Penguin, 1994

____. *Two Part Invention, The Story of a Marriage.* NewYork: Farrar, Straus & Giroux, 1988

____. *A Circle of Quiet.* New York: Farrar, Straus & Giroux, 1972

Lorde, Audre. *Zamio: A New Spelling of my Name.* Freedom, California: The Crossings Press, 1982

Loudon, Mary. *Unveiled: Nuns Talking.* London: Vintage, 1992

Markham, Beryl. *West With the Night.* New York: Farrar, Straus & Giroux, 1942

McCullough, David Willis. *American Childhoods: An Anthology.* Boston: Little Brown & Co., 1987

____. *Truman.* New York: Simon & Schuster, 1992

McGrayre, Sharon Bertsch. *Nobel Prize Women in Science.* New York: Carol Publishers, 1993

Milletti, Mario A. *Voices of Experience: 1500 Retired People Talk About Retirement.* New York: Teachers Insurance and Annuity Association College Retirement Equities Fund, 1984

Nixon, Julie. *Pat Nixon: The Untold Story.* New York: Simon & Schuster, 1986

Painter, Charlotte. *Gifts of Age: Portraits and Essays of 32 Remarkable Women.*

Strong Women Tell Their Stories

San Francisco: Chronicle Books, 1985
Petrement, Simone. *Simone Weil: A Life (1909-1943).* New York: Pantheon Books, 1976
Rappaport, Doreen. *American Women: Their Lives in Their Work.* New York: Thomas Y. Crowell, 1990
Reagan, Nancy. *My Turn: The Memories of Nancy Reagan.* New York: Dell, 1990
Roberts, Cokie. *We Are Our Mother's Daughters.* New York: William Morrow & Co., 1998
Rosengarten, Theodore. *All God's Dangers: The Life of Nate Shaw.* New York: Alfred A. Knopf, Inc. 1974
Rountree, Cathleen. *On Women Turning 50: Celebrating Mid-Life Discoveries.* San Francisco: Harper San Francisco, A Division of HarperCollins Publishers, 1993
Schlesinger, Arthur M. *A Life in the 20th Century.* Boston: Houghton Mifflin, 2000
Sherman, Janeann. *No Place For a Woman: A Life of Senator Margaret Chase Smith.* New Brunswick: Rutgers University Press, 2000
Spence, Linda. *Legacy: A Guide to Writing Personal History.* Athens, Ohio: Swallow Press/Ohio University Press, 1997
Steinem, Gloria. *Outrageous Acts and Everyday Rebellions.* New York: Holt, Rinehart & Winston,1983
Stratton, Joanna L. *Pioneer Women: Voices from the Kansas Frontier.* New York: Simon & Schuster, 1981
Thompson, Paul. *The Voice of the Past: Oral History.* New York: Oxford University Press, 1988
Troester, Rosalie Riege. *Voices from the Catholic Worker: Oral History.* Philadelphia: Temple University Press, 1993
Welty, Eudora. *One Writer's Beginnings.* Cambridge: Harvard University Press, 1984
Wilson, Emily Herring and Susan Mullally Clark. *Hope and Dignity: Older Black Women of the South.* Philadelphia: Temple University Press, 1983

Social and Political Change

Allen, Frederick Lewis. *The Big Change: America Transforms Itself 1900-1950.* New York: Harper & Brothers, Publishers, 1952
Baumgardner, Jennifer and Amy Richards. *Manifesta: Young Women, Feminism and the Future.* New York: Farrar, Straus & Giroux, 2000
Bellah, Robert N. and Richard Madsden, William M. Sullivan, Ann Swidler and Steven M. Tipton. *Habits of the Heart:Individualism and Commitment in American Life.* Berkeley: University of California Press, Ltd., 1985
Berry, Thomas. *The Dream of the Earth.* San Francisco: Sierra Club Books, 1988
____. *The Great Work: Our Way Into the Future.* New York: Bell Tower, 1999
Bronfenbrenner,Urie and Peter McClelland, Elaine Wethington, Phyllis Moen and

Voices of the Silent Generation

Stephen J. Ceci with Helene Hembrooke, Pamela A. Morris and Tara L. White. *The State of Americans: This Generation and the Next. New York:* Free Press, Division of Simon & Schuster, 1997

Buckley, William F., Jr. *God and Man At Yale. Fiftieth Anniversary Edition,* Washington, DC: *Regnery Gateway, 2002*

Crittendon, Danielle. *What Our Mothers Didn't Tell Us: Why Happiness Eludes the Modern Woman.* New York: Simon & Schuster Publishers, 1999

Didion, Joan. *Slouching Towards Bethlehem.* New York: Pocket Books, Washington Square Press, 1961

Elshtain, Jean Bethke. *Real Politics: At the Center of Everyday Life.* Baltimore: Johns Hopkins University Press, 1997

____. *Democracy on Trial. New York:* Basic Books, A Division of HarperCollins Publishers, 1995

Galbraith, John Kenneth. *The Affluent Society.* Boston: Houghton Mifflin Co., 1958

Gerson, Mark. *A Choice of Heroes: The Changing Face of AmericanManhood.* New York: Houghton Mifflin Co., 1982

Harrington, Michael. *The Other America: Poverty in the United States.* New York: MacMillan Co., 1963

Henry, William A. , *In Defense of Elitism,* New York: Doubleday Publishing,1994

Kunstler, James Howard. *Home from Nowhere: Remaking our Everyday World for the 21st Century.* New York: Simon & Schuster, 1996

Magnet, Myron. *The Dream and the Nightmare: The Sixties Legacy to the Underclass.* New York: Morrow, 1993

Orenstein, Peggy. *Women on Sex, Love and Life in a Half-Changed World.* New York: Doubleday, 2000

Schlesinger, Jr., Arthur M. *The Disuniting of America.* Knoxville,Tenn.: Whittle Direct Books, 1991

Tocqueville, Alexis de. *Democracy in America, ed. J. P. Mayer and Max Lerner, pt. 2.* New York: Harper & Row, 1966

Whyte, Jr., William H. *The Organization Man.* New York: Simon & Schuster, 1956

Young, Cathy. *Ceasefire! Why Women and Men Must Join Forces to Achieve True Equality.* New York: The Free Press, 1999

Family Life

Barras, Jonetta Rose. *Whatever Happened to Daddy's Little Girl? The Impact of Fatherlessness on Black Women.* New York: Ballantine, 2000

Blankenhorn, David. *Fatherless America: Confronting Our Most Urgent Social Problem.* New York: HarperPerennial, A Division of HarperCollins Publishers, 1995

Coles, Robert. *The Moral Life of Children.* Boston: Houghton Mifflin Co., 1986

Crittenden, Ann. *The Price of Motherhood: Why the Most Important Job in the*

Strong Women Tell Their Stories

World is Still the Least Valued. New York: Metropolitan Books, Henry Holt and Co., 2001
Curran, Delores. *Traits of a Healthy Family. New York:* Ballantine Books, 1983
Fraiberg, Selma. *Every Child's Birthright.* New York: Basic Books, 1977
Gerstel, Naomi and Harriet Engel Gross. *Families and Work.* Philadelphia: Temple University Press, 1987
Harrington, Mona. *Care and Equality: Inventing a New Family Politics.* New York: Alfred A. Knopf, 1999
Hersch, Patricia. *A Tribe Apart: A Journey Into the Heart of American Adolescence.* New York: Ballantine Books, 1998
Hewlett, Sylvia Ann. *When the Bough Breaks: The Cost of Neglecting our Children.* New York: Basic Books, 1991
Hochschild, Arlie and Anne Machung. *The Second Shift.* New York: Avon Books, 1989
Krasnow, Iris. *Surrendering to Motherhood: Losing Your Mind, Finding Your Soul.* New York: Hyperion, 1997
Lerner, Harriet Goldhor. *The Dance of Anger,* New York: Harper & Row Publishers, 1985
Mack, Dana. *The Assault on Parenthood: How Our Culture Undermines the Family.* New York: Simon & Schuster, 1997
May, Elaine Tyler. *Homeward Bound: American Families in the Cold War Era.* New York: Basic Books, Perseus Books Group, 1988
McCullough, David. *A Bully Father: Theodore Roosevelt's Letters to His Children.* New York: Random House, Inc. 1919
Ostar, Roberta H. *The Partnership Model: A Family Perspective on College Presidency.* Washington, DC: American Association of State Colleges and Universities, 1986
Popenoe, David. *Life Without Father: Compelling New Evidence That Fatherhood and Marriage are Indispensable for the Good of Children and Society.* New York: Martin Kessler Books/Free Press, 1996
Roiphe, Anne. *Fruitful: A Real Mother in the Modern World. Boston,* New York: Houghton Mifflin Company, 1996
Secunda, Victoria. *Women and Their Fathers: The Sexual and Romantic Impact of the First Man in Your Life.* New York: Delacorte Press, 1992
Skolnick, Arlene S. *Embattled Paradise: The American Family in an Age of Uncertainty.* New York: Basic Books, 1991
Thurer, Shari L. *The Myths of Motherhood: How Culture Reinvents the Good Mother.* New York: Houghton Mifflin, 1994
Walsh, Elsa. *Divided Lives.* New York: Simon & Schuster, 1995
Whitehead, Barbara Dafoe. *The Divorce Culture.* New York: Alfred A. Knopf, Inc.1996
Wrigley, Julia. *Other People's Children.* New York: Basic Books, 1995

Voices of the Silent Generation

Religion and Spiritual Growth

Anderson, Sherry Ruth and Patricia Hopkins. *The Feminine Face of God: The Unfolding of the Sacred in Women.* New York: Bantam Books, 1992

Bloom, Harold. *The American Religion: The Emergence of the Post-Christian Nation.* New York: Simon & Schuster, 1992

Brewi, Janice and Anne Brennan. *Mid-life:Psychological and Spiritual Perspectives.* New York: Crossroad, 198

Buckley, William F., *Nearer My God,* New York: Harcourt Brace,1997

Cahill, Susan. *Wise Women: Over Two Thousand Years of Spiritual Writing by Women.* New York and London: W. W. Norton & Company, 1996

Ellwood, Robert S. *The Fifties Spiritual Marketplace: American Religion in a Decade of Conflict.* New Brunswick, NJ: Rutgers University Press, 1977

Finch, Ann. *Journey to the Light: Spirituality as we Mature.* New Rochelle, New York: New City Press, 1993

Frankl, Viktor E. *Man's Search for Meaning.* New York: PocketBooks, 1959

Gray, Elizabeth Dodson. *Sacred Dimensions of Women's Experience.* Wellesley, Massachusetts: Roundtable Press, 1988

____. Green Paradise Lost. Wellesley, Massachusetts: Roundtable Press, 1981

Hudson, Winthrop S. *Religion in America: An Historical Account of the Development of American Religious Life.* New York and London: MacMillan Publishing Company and Collier MacMillan Publishers, 1987

L'Engle, Madeleine. *Walking on Water: Reflections on Faith & Art.* New York: Bantam Books, 1960

Lindbergh, Anne Morrow. *Gift From The Sea.* New York: Pantheon Books, 1955

Luke, Helen M., *Old Age. New York:* Parabola Books, 1987

____. *The Way of Women: Awakening the Perennial Feminine.* New York: Doubleday, 1997

____. *Woman: Earth and Spirit: The Feminine in Symbol and Myth.* New York: Crossroad, 1987

Occhiogrosso, Peter. *Once A Catholic: Prominent Catholics and Ex-Catholics Reveal the Influence of the Church on Their Lives and Work.* New York: Ballantine Books, 1987

Peck, M. Scott. *The Road Less Traveled.* New York: Touchstone Books, 1988

Stearns, Ann Kaiser. *Living Through Personal Crisis. Chicago, Illinois:* The Thomas More Press, 1984

Ethnic and Racial Issues

Chafe, William H. *Civilities and Civil Rights: Greensboro, North Carolina and the Black Struggle for Freedom.* New York: Oxford University Press, 1980

Chapman, Abraham. *Black Voices: An Anthology of Afro-American Literature.* New York: A Mentor Book, 1968

Cone, James H., *Martin & Malcolm & America: A Dream or a Nightmare.*

Strong Women Tell Their Stories

Maryknoll, New York: Orbis Books, 1991

Edelman, Marian Wright. *The Measure of Our Success: A Letter to My Children and Yours.* New York: HarperPerennial, A Division of HarperCollins Publishers, 1992

Ellison, Ralph. *Invisible Man.* New York: Vantage Books, A Division of Random House, 1947

Franklin, John Hope. *Race and History: Selected Essays 1938-1988.* Baton Rouge: Louisiana State University Press, 1989

Funderburg, Lise. *Black, White, Other: Bi-Racial Americans Talk About Race and Identity.* New York: William Morrow and Company, Inc., 1994

Giddings, Paula. *When and Where I Enter: The Impact of Black Women on Race and Sex in America.* New York: Bantam Books, 1984

Haley, Alex. *The Autobiography of Malcolm X.* New York: Ballantine Books, 1964

Hooks, Bell. *Sisters of the Yam: Black Women and Self-Recovery.* Boston: South End Press, 1993

Jones, Jacqueline. *Labor of Love, Labor of Sorrow; Black Women, Work and the Family from Slavery to the Present.* New York: Basic Books, 1985

Kotlowitz, Alex. *There Are No Children Here.* New York: Nan A.Talese/ Doubleday, 1991

Kozol, Jonathon. *Death at an Early Age.* New York: Houghton Mifflin Co., 1967

Kunjufu, Jawanza. *Countering the Conspiracy to Destroy Black Boys.* Chicago: Jawanza Kunjufu Publishing, 1985

McBride, James. *The Color of Water: A Black Man's Tribute to His White Mother. New York:* Berkley Publishing Group, 1996

Meister, Richard J. *The Black Ghetto: Promised Land or Colony?* Lexington, Massachusetts: D. C. Heath and Company, 1972

Monroe, Sylvester and Peter Goldman with Vern E. Smith, Terry E. Johnson, Monroe Anderson and Jacques Chenet, *Brothers: Black and Poor—A True Story of Courage and Survival.* New York: Ballantine Books, 1988

Nakano, Mei T. *Japanese American Women: Three Generations 1890-1990.* Berkeley and Sebastopol: Mina Press Publishing, and San Francisco: National Japanese American Historical Society, 1990

Olson, Lynne, *Freedom's Daughters: The Unsung Heroines of the Civil Rights Movement from 1830 to 1970.* New York: Scribner, 2001

Patterson, Orlando. *Freedom in the Making of Western Culture.* New York: Basic Books, A Division of HarperCollins Publishers, 1991

Pogrebin, Letty Cottin. *Deborah, Golda and Me: Being Female and Jewish in America.* New York: Crown Publishers, 1991

Rodriguez, Richard. *Days of Obligation: An Argument with My Mexican Father.* New York: Penguin Books, 1992

Smith, Jane I. *Islam in America.* New York: Columbia University Press, 2000

Sowell, Thomas. *Race and Culture: A World View.* New York: Basic Books, A Division of HarperCollins Publishers, 1994

Voices of the Silent Generation

Stack, Carol. *All Our Kin: Strategies for Survival in a Black Community.* New York: Harper & Row, 1974
Steele, Shelby. *The Content of our Character: A New Vision of Race in America.* New York: St. Martin's Press, 1990
West, Cornel. *Race Matters.* Boston: Beacon Press, 1993

Women's History

Allgor, Catherine. *Parlor Politics: In Which the Ladies of Washington Help Build a City and a Government.* Charlottesville: University Press of Virginia, 2000
Apter, Terri. *Secret Paths: Women in the New Midlife.* New York: W. W. Norton & Company, 1995
Belenky, Mary Field and Blythe McVicker Clinchy, Nancy Rule Goldberger and Jill Mattuck Tarule. *Women's Ways of Knowing: The Development of Self, Voice and Mind.* New York: Basic Books, Inc. 1986
Bequaert, Lucia. *Single Women: Alone and Together.* Boston: Beacon Press, 1976
Breines, Wini. *Young, White, and Miserable: Growing Up Female in the Fifties.* Boston: Beacon Press, 1992
____. *Not June Cleaver: Women & Gender in Post-War America 1945-1960.* Philadelphia: Temple University Press, 1994
Brownmiller, Susan. *In Our Time, Memoir of a Revolution.* New York: A Delta Book, Dell Publishing Co., A Division of Random House, 1999
____. *Feminity.* New York: Fawcett Columbine, 1984
Clodius, Joan E. and Diane Skomars Magrath. *The President's Spouse: Volunteer or Volunteered.* Washington, DC: National Association of State Universities and Land-Grant Colleges, 1984
Clowse, Barbara Barksdale. *Women, Decision Making, and the Future.* Atlanta: John Knox Press, 1985
Coontz, Stephanie. *The Way We Never Were: American Families and the Nostalgia Trap.* New York: Basic Books, 1992
Corbally, Marguerite Walker. *The Partners: Sharing the Life of a College President.* Danville, Illinois: The Interstate Printers & Publishers, Inc., 1977
de Beauvoir, Simone. *The Second Sex.* New York: Alfred A. Knopf, Inc., 1953
Denfield, Rene. *The New Victorians: A Young Woman's Challenge to the Old Feminist Order.* New York: Warner Books, 1995
De Pauw, Linda and Conover Hunt with Miriam Schneir. *Remember the Ladies: Women in America 1750-1815.* New York: Viking Press, 1976
Dworkin, Andrea. *Letters From a War Zone.* New York: E. P.Dutton, 1989
Eisler, Riane. *The Chalice and the Blade: Our History, Our Future.* San Francisco: Harper & Row, 1987
Fisher, Helen. *The First Sex: The Natural Talents of Women and How They Are Changing the World.* New York: Random House, 1999
Friedan, Betty. *The Feminine Mystique.* New York: A Laurel Book, Dell Publishing Co., 1963

Gerson, Kathleen. *Hard Choices: How Women Decide About Work, Career and Motherhood.* University of California Press, 1985
Gill, Evalyn P., ed. *Women of the Piedmont Triad.* Greensboro, NC: Trans Verse Press, 1989
Gilligan, Carol. *In A Different Voice: Psychological Theory and Women's Development.* Cambridge, Massachusetts: Harvard University Press, 1982
Graglia, F. Carolyn. *Domestic Tranquility: A Brief Against Feminism.* Dallas: Spence Publishing Company, 1998
Helgeson, Sally. *Everyday Revolutionaries: Working Women and the Transformation of American Life.* New York: Doubleday, 1998
Hewlett, Sylvia. *A Lesser Life: The Myth of Women's Liberation in America.* New York: Warner Books, 1986
Higginbotham, Evelyn Brooks. *Righteous Discontent: The Women's Movement in the Black Baptist Church, 1880-1920.* Cambridge, Massachusetts: Harvard University Press, 1993
Horowitz, Daniel. *Betty Friedan and the Making of The Feminine Mystique: The American Left, The Cold War, And Modern Feminism.* Amherst: University of Massachusetts Press, 1998
Jamieson, Kathleen Hall. *Beyond the Double Bind: Women and Leadership.* New York: Oxford University Press, 1995
Jones, Jacqueline. *Labor of Love, Labor of Sorrow: Black Women, Work and the Family from Slavery to the Present.* New York: Basic Books, 1985
Kaledin, Eugenia. *Mothers and More: American Women in the 1950s.* Boston: Twayne Publishers, 1984
Kaminer, Wendy. *Women Volunteering: The Pleasure, Pain and Politics of Unpaid Work from 1830 to the Present.* New York: Anchor Press, 1984
Kinsey, Alfred C. *Sexual Behavior in the Human Female.* Philadelphia: Indiana University, 1953
Lerner, Gerda. *The Creation of Feminist Consciousness.* New York: Oxford University Press, 1993
____. *Black Women in White America: A Documentary History.* New York: Pantheon Books, 1972
____. *The Creation of Patriarchy.* New York: Oxford University Press, 1986
May, Elaine Tyler. *Pushing the Limits: American Women 1940-1961.* New York: Oxford University Press, 1994
____. *Homeward Bound: American Families in the Cold War Era.* New York: Basic Books, 1988
McLaughlin, Steven D. and Barbara D. Melber, John O. G. Billy, Denise M. Zimmerle, Linda D. Winges and Terry R. Johnson. *The Changing Lives of American Women.* Chapel Hill: The University of North Carolina Press, 1988
Mervin, Sabrina and Carol Prunhuber. *Women Around the World and Through the Ages.* Wilmington, Delaware: Atomium Books, Inc., 1990
Millett, Kate. *Sexual Politics.* New York: Doubleday, 1970

Moen, Phyllis. *Women's Two Roles: A Contemporary Dilemma.* New York: Auburn House, 1992

Morgan, Robin. *Sisterhood is Powerful: An Anthology of Writings From the Women's Liberation Movement.* New York: Vintage Books, a Division of Random House, 1970

Muntz, Steven and Susan Kellogg. *Domestic Revolutions: A Social History of American Family Life.* New York: Free Press, 1988

Ogden, Annegret S. *The Great American Housewife: From Helpmate to Wage Earner, 1776-1986.* Westport, Connecticut: Greenwood Press, 1986

O'Keefe, Deborah. *Good Girl Messages: How Young Women Were Misled by Their Favorite Books.* New York and London: The Continuum International Publishing Group, Inc., 2000

Rhodes, Carolyn H., Mary Louise Briscoe and Ernest L. Rhodes. *First Person Female American: A Selected and Annotated Bibliography of the Autobiographies of American Women Living After 1950.* Troy, New York: Whitson Publishing Co., 1980

Rimm, Dr. Sylvia and Dr. Ilonna Rimm. *See Jane Win: The Rimm Report on How 1000 Girls Became Successful Women.* New York: Crown Publishers, Random House, 1999

Roosevelt, Eleanor and Lorene Hichock. *Ladies of Courage.* New York: Putnam Books, 1954

Schiner, Miriam. *Feminism in Our Time: The Essential Writings of World War II to the Present.* New York: Vintage Books, A Division of Random House, 1994

Sommers, Christina Hoff. *Who Stole Feminism?* New York: Simon & Schuster, 1999

Tobias, Sheila. *Faces of Feminism: An Activist's Reflections on the Women's Movement.* Boulder: Westview Press, 1997

Tsuchider, Nobuya. *Asian and Pacific American Experience: The Women's Perspectives.* Minneapolis: University of Minnesota Press, 1982

Welty, Eudora. *The Eye of the Story: Selected Essays and Reviews.* New York: Vintage Books, A Division of Random House, 1942

White, Jr., Lynn. *Educating our Daughters.* New York: Harper Brothers, 1950

Woolf, Virginia. *A Room of One's Own.* San Diego: Harcourt Brace, 1991

Post World War II History

Branch, Taylor. *Parting the Waters: America in the King Years 1954-63.* New York: Simon & Schuster, 1988

Chafe, William. *The Unfinished Journey: America Since World War II.* New York: Oxford University Press, 1985

--------------. *Women and Equality: Changing Patterns in American Culture.* New York: *Oxford University Press, 1977*

--------------. *The Paradox of Change: American Women in the 20th Century.* New York: Oxford University Press, 1991

Strong Women Tell Their Stories

Conquest, Robert. *Reflections on a Ravaged Century*. New York: W. W. Norton, 1999

Craters of the Moon Natural History Association. Numerous titles on the Japanese-American internment camp experience. Available through Minidoka National Monument website.

Divine, Robert A. *Eisenhower and the Cold War*. New York: Oxford University Press, 1981

Douglas, George H. *Postwar America: 1948 and the Incubation of Our Times*. Malabar: Krieger Publishing Co., 1998

Eisler, Benita. *Private Lives: Men and Women of the Fifties*. New York: Franklin Watts, 1986

Goodman, Paul. *Growing Up Absurd*. New York: Random House, 1960

Goodwin, Doris Kearns. *No Ordinary Time: Franklin and EleanorRoosevelt: The Home Front in World War II*. New York: Simon & Schuster, 1994

Goulden, Joseph C. *The Best Years, 1945-1960*. New York: Atheneum, 1976

Halberstam, David. *The Fifties*. New York: Fawcett Columbine, 1993

Hersey, John. *Hiroshima*. New York: Alfred A. Knopf, Inc., 1946

Jackson, Kenneth T. *Crabgrass Frontier: The Suburbanization of the United States*. New York: Oxford University Press, 1985

Jezer, Marty. *The Dark Ages: Life in the United States, 1945-1960*. Boston: South End Press,1982

Kennedy, David M. *Freedom From Fear: The American People in Depression and War*. New York: Oxford University Press, 1999

Lewis, Peter. *The Fifties*. New York: Lippincott, 1979

Miller, Douglas T. and Marion Nowak. *The Fifties: The Way We Really Were*. New York: Doubleday, 1977

Oakley, J. Ronald. *God's Country: America in the Fifties*. New York: Red Dembner Enterprises Corp., 1986

O'Neill, William L. *American High: The Years of Confidence,*1945-1960. New York: Free Press, 1987

Patterson, James T. *Grand Expectations: The United States 1945-1974*. New York: Oxford University Press, 1996

Time-Life Books, Editors. *This Fabulous Century,* 7 Vols. New York: Time-Life Books, 1970, Vol. 6: 1950-1960

Weinstein, Allen and Alexander Vassiliev. *The Haunted Wood: Soviet Espionage in America—The Stalin Era*. New York: Random House, 1999

Websites

American Women's History: A Research Guide Link and resources assembled by librarians at Middle Tennessee State University
www.mtsu.edu/kmiddlet/history/women.html

Women's Sport's Foundation

Voices of the Silent Generation

Information on women's sports history and Title IX
www.Womenssportfoundation.org

National Women's History Project
Insights and information about women throughout history
www.nwhp.org

Japanese American Relocation Digital Archive

http:/suddenlysenior.com/silentgeneration.html

http://www.us,edu/dept/gero/research/4gen/norella.hym

Books by Doris Betts
Short Story Collections:
The Gentle Insurrection, New York: G.P.Putnam, 1954
The Astronomer and Other Stories, New York: Harper and Row, 1966
Beasts of the Southern Wild and Other Stories, New York: Harper and Row, 1973

Novels:
Tall Houses in Winter, New York: G.P.Putnam, 1957
The Scarlet Thread, New York: Harper and Row, 1964
The River to Pickle Beach, New York: Harper and Row, 1972
Heading West, New York: Alfred A. Knopf, 1981
Souls Raised from the Dead, New York: Alfred A. Knopf, 1994
The Sharp Teeth of Love, New York: Simon and Schuster, 1998

Books by Sidney Callahan
The Illusion of Eve: Modern Woman's Search for Identity, New York: Sheed and Ward, 1965
Christian Family Planning and Sex Education, Ave Maria Press, 1969.
Beyond Birth Control: The Christian Experience of Sex, New York: Sheed and Ward, 1968, paperback edition: Exiled to Eden, 1970.
The Working Mother, Warner Paperback, 1972.
Parenting: Principles and Politics of Parenthood, New York: Doubleday, 1974.
The Magnificat: The Prayer of Mary, New York: Seabury Press, 1975
Abortion: Understanding Differences, co-edited with Daniel Callahan, New York: Plenum Press 1984.
With All Our Heart and Mind: The Spiritual Works of Mercy in a Psychological Age, New York: Crossroads/Continuum, 1988. Winner of Christopher Award, 1988.
In Good Conscience: Reason and Emotion in Moral Decision-making, New York: HarperCollins, 1991.

Strong Women Tell Their Stories

Parents Forever, You and Your Adult Children, New York: Crossroads, 1992.

By Gay Cheney
Modern Dance: A Creative Approach. Princeton: Princeton Books, 1996. Third edition, 1975

By Vivian Shapiro
Complex Adoption and Assisted Reproductive Technology: A Developmental Approach to Clinical Practice. With Janet R Shapiro and Isabel Paret. New York: Guilford Press, 2001
Bridging the Losses in Biographical Discontinuity through Narrative Reconstruction. Smith College School for Social Work, 1994

By Daryl Hafter
European Women and Pre-Industrial Craft. Bloomington, Illinois: Indiana University Press, 1995
Equality Through Privilege: Guild Women and Industrial Workers of 18th Century France, (forthcoming.)